Where the Popsicles Are

A Memoir by Bob Kallberg

All the Best
Bob Kallberg

Where the Popsicles Are
Copyright © 2017 Bob Kallberg

Publisher: Rush Candle Books
Digital distribution | 2017
Paperback | 2017
Photo Credits, Copyright 2017 Bob Kallberg
For information address:
Rush Candle Books
1821 N. 11th St. #1805
Bismarck, ND 58501

ISBN: 978-0-9993900-0-9
Library of Congress Control Number: 2017914372

To Joanie's two families:
Bud and Phylliss Wigen,
who taught her about courage, and
her second family, her sister Virginia and Ed Stringer
and
her Aunt Del Piper, who saw the person she had
become and embraced her.

To all of Joanie's friends who supported
her and witnessed
the light she brought with her
even during the darkest times.

CONTENTS

Foreword.. vi

Introduction.. x

Section One.. 1

Section Two... 55

Section Three.. 172

Section Four.. 183

Section Five... 232

Section Six.. 336

Section Seven.. 400

Epilogue.. 459

Acknowledgements.. 461

Addendum.. 466

ABOUT THE AUTHOR

I am a writer living in Bismarck, North Dakota. I have spent most of my working days as a reporter covering government and politics in North Dakota and west-central Minnesota. Over the years I have written for television and radio news, newspapers, a wire service, and have done freelance writing projects.

I didn't start out to write a book but about halfway through this twelve-year battle, Joanie suggested that I write some columns about what I had learned being a caregiver to someone who was faced by a serious disease. That was the beginning, but I soon realized that I couldn't just write about the lessons learned without telling how I came to learn them, and over time it became Joanie's story, *Where the Popsicles Are*.

In the telling of Joanie's story I made an effort to show that while there some very dark times, there were many times that were filled with light and joy, and Joanie was the source of that light.

She handled it all—the good times, the dark times, the ups and the downs of those twelve years with such great class and dignity, and I never once heard her say, "Why me?" I'm in awe of it to this day. This is her story.

FOREWORD

Joanie

I can tell you what she was wearing.

I walked into the Town House bar on Friday, November 7, 1980, about five o'clock, not knowing I would meet someone who would end up changing my life. The Town House Motor Inn was the premier political bar in Bismarck during the 1970s through the mid-80s, and if you were in town, you at least stopped by to see who else might be there.

The lounge was packed. It was the end of a long week, and there were many of the political types engaged in post mortems on Tuesday's election results. I had spent the campaign working for the two-term attorney general, Al Olson, who had run for governor against Democrat Art Link. Al won, and I was looking to celebrate with some of the Olson campaign folks.

I didn't know Joan Wigen in 1980. In fact, I didn't even know she existed. I knew her father, J. O. "Bud" Wigen, and her mother Phyllis, but knew little about their family. I had been a reporter covering politics and I had first met Bud. He had served two terms as state insurance commissioner, but in 1976, he lost his bid for reelection to little-known Democrat, Byron Knutson, and in 1980, he ran again and this time he won.

As I entered the bar, immediately on the right against the wall were long tables filled with Wigen supporters, celebrating his win, and feeling vindicated after his loss of 1976. I knew a lot of the people at their table, not all, but most. Bud and Phyllis waved me over. We had become good friends during the campaign, spending a lot of time at the same county fairs, district meetings, and campaign rallies. But I didn't know the attractive brunette sitting against the wall. Bud called to her and she came out from behind the table to stand next to her dad while he introduced her to me. Her name was Joan. She was tall, and she had shoulder-length, wavy, raven-black hair that framed her fair-skinned face, and bright, blue eyes, that shone even in the dim light of the lounge.

We shook hands and spoke briefly about how good it was that Bud had won his election. I told her how nice it was to meet her and that her folks had become good friends during the campaign. She smiled, thanked me, and I turned toward the bar to get a scotch, and she rejoined her table.

I stood at the bar for a while, visiting with friends and well-wishers, and after about an hour, Joanie came up to the bar next to me and we began to visit a little more. It was then I began to use what I had learned as a reporter, a brief stint in graduate school, and work at a mental health center, and that was to listen carefully to what the other person was saying.

It wasn't long before I learned she was working at Bismarck Junior College (later renamed Bismarck State College) with student activities, a job she seemed to relish. She had graduated from BJC, and then went on to North Dakota State University where she got her degree in physical education. She said she had also worked for a time in sales at the Town House. I was surprised I'd never seen her before, since any time I was in Bismarck, I stayed there.

We talked more, and as I listened, I found out she was an active Republican, and, because she grew up in Bismarck, she seemed to know everybody. My boss, Al Olson, the newly elected governor, and his wife Barb were good friends of hers. In fact, she told me Barb had gotten her hired for her first job in Bismarck after she graduated from NDSU. That job was at the YMCA.

I discovered she was living with two other women in a rented house, was an avid skier, and had a Siamese cat named "Snowball." I also figured out she wasn't involved with anyone at the time, and that fact stuck with me as the evening was coming to a close. We parted company, but I knew before long, I would call her to see if she'd like to go out to a movie with me.

As the years went by, I watched her grow from her job at BJC to the United Way, and then on to work for Ed Schafer's political committee, after he became governor, and then on to John Hoeven's gubernatorial campaign in 2000 and his political committee until 2008. Even as she was engaged in politics, she was also heavily involved at the Trinity Lutheran Church, and building activities there, not knowing that was where we were to be married in 1989. Testimony to the respect people had for her was the fact that three of the pallbearers at her funeral were governors or former governors, John Hoeven (now a U.S. senator), Jack Dalrymple, lieutenant governor at the time and a former govenor and Allen Olson also a former governor, along with three of our closest friends.

Her father Bud introduced me to her, but none of us that night could have predicted what that introduction would lead to, or how it would change our lives. I still remember vividly what she was wearing that night. She wore a blue blazer over a white turtleneck and red sweater vest, khaki slacks, penny loafers, and white socks. For me it was her signature look. Classic and classy, just like she was her whole life.

INTRODUCTION

The CA: A Cancer Journal for Clinicians estimated that in 1996 there were just over 1.3 million new cases of cancer diagnosed in the United States. Of that number, there were approximately 764,300 males and 594,850 females affected. Joan Wigen was one of those women.

When they called me into Joanie's gynecologist's office on that day in 1996, I had a bad feeling. Joanie Wigen was my wife. We were married in 1989, after being together since the early 80s. When I saw she had been crying, I knew the news was not good. Dr. Bury said her tests showed cervical cancer, and our lives changed forever.

Joanie, in the intervening years, underwent numerous surgeries, major and minor; weeks of radiation; many episodes of chemotherapy; trips to the Emergency Room; stays in the Intensive Care Unit; lengthy hospital stays, and did it all with a tremendous courage and strength of spirit.

That day, May 7, 1996, marked the beginning of a roller coaster ride that ended that quiet April night in 2008. I have been encouraged to write about what I have learned about patient advocacy, the complexities of the medical system today, and the role of caregivers by people who are familiar with what went on with the woman I loved during those twelve years. Most importantly, Joanie encouraged me to put it all down on paper, so I began taking notes, writing down observations, doing research, and keeping track of the progress of this enemy: cancer.

I struggled with the idea for some time. It wasn't until I realized that I couldn't separate what I have learned from also telling of Joanie's remarkable fight that I was able to begin to write and share this story. I began several times, only to put the project aside because I found it too painful to relive her struggle and my loss. It is only now that I feel ready to do what I set out to do years ago.

So began the incredible journey that day in May. The first of my lessons came the first evening at home when some of Joanie's dear friends stopped by to see her and wish her well. She was on the couch, visiting with them, and she said, "I might have cancer." I quietly corrected her by just saying, "Joanie, it is not a question of might; you do have cancer. The only question right now is what stage it is."

From that point on I knew that her defenses were up and working well, and that the news she had heard earlier that day was so overwhelming that it was going to take a while for her to come to grips with it. This all seemed perfectly natural to me; however, it also made clear to me that every time she was going to be see any doctor in the future I would have to be there so I would know what exactly was being said and what was being planned, and I was. Lesson One: Never let the patient see the doctor alone.

I invite you to travel with me on our incredible journey so that you may learn what I did, and hear a story of Joanie's battle—one she waged with a courage, strength, and dignity that I'm still in awe of years later. It is my hope that you will learn something valuable, and in the retelling, I will learn something more myself.

The years of Joanie's fight against cancer were a learning experience for both of us. For me, if I were to provide the kind of support she needed to deal with this disease, I needed to find out as much as I could, as a layperson, about this disease, its treatments, its outcomes, its effect on her, the things she wouldn't, or couldn't, talk about, and where the popsicles are.

SECTION ONE
1996-1997

How It All Began

Dr. Bury's dictation from May 7, 1996, read, "IMPRESSION: 1. Probable invasive cervical carcinoma." All we heard that morning was "cancer."

Joanie and I left her gynecologist's office late that Tuesday morning stunned and shocked. As we were walking to the car in the clinic lot, no words were spoken, both of us trying to get our heads around the word cancer and what it meant for her. I had never felt so helpless in my life.

I was thinking about my sister Judy who died in 1984 when she was forty-two, a short three and half years after she had been diagnosed with the same thing that Joanie was now facing, along with the uncertain future that comes with that news. Joanie had only known Judy a short while and we didn't talk about her that day, as if we both felt to do so would be bad luck, and we never did.

Joanie was silent as we drove away, and I suggested we get lunch. We went to one of our favorite haunts, ordered a glass of wine each, which under the circumstances seemed okay, and took a deep breath. The news was so overwhelming for Joanie; it was then I learned to just shut up and listen and let her lead me where she wanted to go rather than trying to drag anything out of her. It was a lesson that served me well in the days and years ahead.

After the wine was served and we ordered lunch, she looked at me and asked, "What do we do now?" We were both thinking the same thing. My answer was, "I don't know right now."

We began to talk a bit about it, and one of the first things I cautioned her about was borrowing trouble based on what little we knew then. We talked about the fact we didn't know what stage the cancer was, how large any tumor might be or how serious it was, and that wasn't information we would know until the results of the biopsies were in tomorrow. Her doctor had put a rush on the lab work and we were to return to her office the next day. I told her that for either one of us to begin imagining things that may or may not happen was fruitless and would only serve to make us crazy. I told her that we needed to avoid what Fritz Perls, the Gestalt therapist, called "mind fucking." She seemed to agree with me, but I knew that was easier said than done, especially when it comes to the word cancer.

Then Joanie wondered aloud about whom she should call and what she should say and what to do next. I just told her that she should go ahead and do whatever she wanted, but as far as what to do next, we'd deal with that tomorrow when we met at Dr. Bury's office. As we left lunch, I said that knowing was better than not knowing, even if the news was bad, for then, at least, we could put a name on what we were dealing with, and we could make a plan to take care of it. She seemed to agree, but I also knew she was still in shock and scared to death.

A cancer diagnosis gives you a ticket to a ride on an emotional roller coaster that you really don't want to take, but when you get the ticket, you will find you have no choice. To prepare for the ride you will have to learn a whole new vocabulary.

2

Initially you will find the beginning of the trip so intense, and the emotions associated with it so overwhelming, you will pay little attention to the words the doctor is using. As a caregiver, and as a layperson, however, you owe it to your patient to learn the words associated with the disease, and by doing so you can be a calming influence during difficult times. The patient, and this is the only categorical statement I will make regarding this disease, never hears exactly what the doctor is saying, and it is left to you, the caregiver, to do so. It is very important they know you are there and hearing what they don't. Always.

After a quiet Tuesday night, we met with Dr. Bury the next morning, and began learning the new words that are associated with this particular disease and its treatment. She told us that the results of the biopsies taken yesterday were back and, as we expected, it was "most likely an invasive large cell squamous carcinoma of the cervix." Cervical cancer, as we were told yesterday. Still trying to process what we'd experienced yesterday, all we could ask her now was the same question that Joanie had asked me at lunch yesterday, "What do we do now?"

Dr. Bury told us that she wanted Joanie to be admitted to the hospital the next day for examination under anesthesia and the possibility of performing a cone biopsy as part of what they call a staging process. "Staging" the cancer that gives them an idea of what type of treatment will be pursued. That was the first of many terms we became familiar with over the coming years.

The term, cone biopsy, as we learned, was a procedure whereby a cone-shaped wedge of tissue is removed from the cervical canal and then examined under a microscope. It can determine the exact location and size of the cancerous tissue. Depending on how large or small the amount of cancerous

3

tissue is, it might be possible to remove some healthy tissue around it so there would be a cancer-free margin afterwards. Should that be the case, it might be there would be no need for further treatments. In short, a cone biopsy could take care of the problem, assuming we were dealing with something that had been caught soon enough and cancerous tissue hadn't moved off the cervix. At least those were the words we heard, and with them came the thought, "Could she be so lucky?" We would have to wait and see. The doctor cautioned us that any involvement of the upper vagina would change the game plan.

Suddenly, Joanie's attitude about her situation began to emerge. For the first time I heard her say she was going to do whatever was necessary to beat this, and she was praying tomorrow would the first step towards putting this behind her. It was an attitude that only grew stronger as the years went by.

We appeared at the hospital the next morning, Thursday, May 9, the day before her birthday. Joanie was admitted for the procedure, which marked the first time Joanie was to be put under anesthesia, but it would not be the last. The roller coaster took off from the platform, and all I could do was wait, something caregivers in these instances do a lot of. Everything is out of your hands at this point, no matter how much you care. I was told to go the surgery waiting room where the doctor would find me when her work was done.

As a caregiver, you will find that in the waiting room, time slows down. Seconds become minutes, minutes become hours, the magazines are all six months old and the coffee is bitter, and it is all because you feel so helpless at the time when the person you love needs you the most. It was a feeling I was to experience many times, both in Bismarck and Minneapolis, in the years ahead.

The "procedure," as they called it, was uneventful to use their word, but we were to be disappointed when we heard there was some involvement of her upper vagina, and a cone biopsy would not be the answer and solution we had hoped for. However, more tissue was taken for further biopsies and staging, the results of which we would not know until the next Monday. We might get a definitive answer about what comes next then, but we also were to learn that definitive answers regarding this disease are not always easy to come by.

So, we spent the weekend of her forty-sixth birthday with friends, trying to think good thoughts and not dwell on the situation Joanie was facing. Considering that this was the most serious health issue of her life, she exhibited a remarkable ability to put it aside, regardless of what she was feeling. It was as if she knew that openly worrying accomplished nothing, and was wasted energy that was better directed in a positive direction when we had more answers. She didn't have a background in psychology or counseling, but she knew.

That weekend, I began to use my background as a reporter. Knowing how to do research, I sat down at our computer and started to search. I had always known my way around a library, but the internet made this research much easier. It was in that process of searching I began to learn more than I ever thought I'd know about this particular women's health issue. I became, as a nonprofessional, more familiar with the vocabulary of this particular form of cancer.

Out of this beginning came the realization that this process was more complicated than I had ever imagined. These factors were all part of the mix: the individual characteristics of the disease; the female patient's age, health, and her family health history; the location of cancerous tissue and degree of invasion; whether it was a slow-moving cancer or an aggressive type; the staging of the cancer, and whether or not the cancer had entered the lymph system. This list doesn't begin to cover all the information needed as the doctors try to figure out how to treat it.

I had always figured that when it came to cancer, you had to know three things: where the tumor was, how big it was, and had it spread from the point of origin. Then, with these answers, the next question was, "how do we get rid of it?" That was the depth and breadth of my knowledge at that time. I was quickly being disabused of my simple assumptions. It became obvious to me that while every cancer is different, every individual is different, and cervical cancer, or any cancer, for that matter, in one individual won't be the same in one person as it is when it manifests itself in another. All of which makes the process of treatment more complicated.

So, we waited until Monday to see where the roller coaster would take us next.

How we got to where we were on that day in May.

I'll be the first to admit that as a man, I was totally ignorant of women's health issues at the time Joanie was diagnosed, even though my younger sister Judy had died from cervical cancer in 1984 and my mother Marie died from uterine cancer in 1987.

Like most men, I either didn't know, or didn't want to know, and chose to let that kind of information remain the province of a woman and her doctor. Little did I know what effect the shockwave that came from those two words on that May morning would have on my ignorance. Little did I know what I would learn from research, experience and dealing with doctors, nurses and helping someone who has a life-threatening disease. Little did I know that, as a reporter, someday I might be writing this story.

Now then, the beginning. In mid-April of 1996, when Joanie began to experience some vaginal bleeding, I asked her what was going on, figuring she certainly might know. She told me it was nothing, just something associated with her menstrual cycle, and it would be fine. I thought okay, naively assuming that if she didn't think it was abnormal, how was I to know. My mistake was in thinking that she knew more than I did. In fact, this was not the first time she had experienced the bleeding and wouldn't be the last. She just hadn't told me about the other times. It happened again, then it happened again, and I began to realize there was something going on more than just a "minor problem" with her menstrual cycle.

I began to insist that she make an appointment with her gynecologist. Then I found out she didn't have a regular gynecologist, and, in fact, hadn't seen a doctor for anything at all in the sixteen years I had known her. I was only to learn when we met with her doctor that she hadn't had a Pap smear since 1976, and that was the only one she had ever had. That was something that I think weighed on her, and it revealed itself with a telltale sign when she was sitting in our living room with some of her supportive women friends, and as she tried to put a good face on her situation, reminded them to be sure and get their own Pap tests.

Joanie always told me how she hated going to doctors, and I assumed that was because she was in excellent health, which she was, up to that point. Looking back later, I realized that she had a better idea of what was going on than she was willing to share with me, and she had put off going to a doctor because she was afraid of what she might learn. I realized later that she didn't want to know. Upon reflection, I don't think she was unique in that respect from most of us. She avoided calling, even after my repeated questions of when she had an appointment and the urging of some of her close friends who were concerned as well.

In late April, she came home from her office over the noon hour because of another bleeding incident. Before she went back to her office, I handed her the phone and insisted she make an appointment right then. The appointment was to be for some time mid-May, but she made no effort to be seen any earlier, or explain why she needed to be seen at all. I relaxed somewhat, however, knowing that at least she was going to see a doctor, and we'd know what was going on.

Things seemed to be going along fine until May 4 when we were in Fargo for my niece's wedding. While we were at the motel changing clothes, she began bleeding, and it seemed to be more than ever before. She was visibly upset, and I began to realize that she was suffering from something far more serious than even I had thought. My reaction was to go the emergency room, and failing that, if the bleeding stopped, to get back in the car and return to Bismarck. The bleeding did stop, but she would have none of either going to the emergency room or returning home. The rest of the evening and the next day were uneventful. Joanie had a good time at the wedding reception that evening, and it was as if the episode that afternoon had never happened. On the way back to Bismarck the next day, she said nothing about it.

Come Monday, I was no longer willing to wait for her appointment in mid-May, and called her doctor's office. Talking to the doctor's nurse that morning, I told her about the bleeding and impressed on her the need for someone to see Joanie as soon as possible. The nurse told me to bring her in the next day.

I called Joanie and told her the appointment had been moved. She didn't object and somehow seemed a bit relieved, now that the issue had been forced. What I learned by calling her doctor's nurse that day was that there are times when you must act because the patient, for whatever reason, cannot or will not. It was to be an important lesson.

So with that Tuesday, just three days shy of her forty-sixth birthday, we began an incredible journey with cancer as our constant traveling companion for the next twelve years.

When we find out what we do now.

In trying to find the answer to the question of what we do now, we found there are no easy answers. For every answer, there are considerations and ramifications that are not easily seen from the beginning, and clarity can turn out to be nothing more than an illusion. But you go on.

Dr. Bury had told us that Joanie needed to see a gynecologist-oncologist, which meant a physician who specialized in gynecologic cancers. There were gynecologists in Bismarck; there were oncologists in Bismarck; but there were no gynecologist-oncologists in Bismarck. In fact, she told us there were none in North Dakota, at least at that time. She said that Denver was a possibility, as was Kansas City, where she had done her residency, and of course Rochester at the Mayo Clinic. There was also the possibility of the University of Minnesota Hospital and Clinic, now the University of Minnesota Medical Center-Fairview.

Over the last few days of talking with friends, we had met with a woman from Bismarck who had the same diagnosis Joanie was now facing, and had been treated successfully at the U of M. It was then I decided to some research of my own on finding a place for treatment. As Joanie and I talked it over on the weekend, we ruled Denver out immediately. It was too far away, and we didn't know anyone there. Kansas City was ruled out for the same reasons. Rochester was an option, but it was a bit further than Minneapolis, and we didn't know anyone there either. We had decided that we would go there if that were the only option, but preferred Minneapolis-St. Paul because we had friends there and Joanie had a sister in St. Paul. We also knew the Twin Cities well so we wouldn't have the added stress of being in a strange city, and it was only a six-hour drive from Bismarck, if you were in a hurry, maybe six and a half if you weren't.

Since we were dealing with unknowns as far as how long and how often we'd have to be gone, as well as the expense of being away from home, we figured the closer we were to Bismarck the better. However, our primary concern was getting Joanie good treatment and putting this behind us, and if that meant going somewhere besides Minneapolis, we'd find a way.

I made a couple of calls to friends in Minneapolis who were quite familiar with the medical community there at the time. One was former Governor Al Olson, whom I worked for, and the other was Tom Forsythe, whom I worked with in the North Dakota governor's office, in the early 1980s. I outlined the issue Joanie was facing, and the options, which we had boiled down to U of M or Mayo. A day or two later they both called and told me for what Joanie was dealing with the Women's Cancer Center at the U of M was the place to go. We decided on the U of M and that was the decision we were prepared to take to Dr. Bury. At least we were able to provide an answer ourselves to the question of what do we do now in terms of treatment. It was a decision we never regretted.

Monday morning, May 13, we got to Dr. Bury's office, and we were informed that all of the results of the biopsies and examinations were in, and they were calling it Stage II-A cervical cancer. Bury explained that meant the cancer had spread to the upper part of the vagina, even though there was minimal involvement, but the lower third was unaffected.

Then, came the same question again, "What do we do now?" Bury told us she had consulted with a doctor in Kansas City where she had done her residency as to whether or not at Stage II-A, Joanie would be a good candidate for a radical hysterectomy, and the consensus was she would be. Bury also explained to us other options would be radiation or possibly a combination of radiation and chemotherapy.

It didn't take Joanie long to make up her mind, and I think just the thought of radiation and the possibility of chemo did it for her. She would take her chances on the radical surgery with the hope that it would take care of the cancer once and for all. Joanie told Dr. Bury to go ahead and arrange for a referral to the Women's Cancer Center at the University of Minnesota, now the Gynecologic Cancer Clinic. She said she would call when an appointment had been made.

The learning curve steepens.

Within three days, Dr. Bury's office called to say that Joanie had an appointment at the Women's Cancer Center at the University of Minnesota Hospital in Minneapolis for Tuesday, May 21, 1996. We were to meet with Dr. Linda Carson, a physician whom we would come to know quite well over the next twelve years. I began to understand what I had to learn about helping Joanie as we prepared to make the trip in about five days' time.

First, we needed to inform our employers about the need to take time off, and we didn't know how much. Joanie was the executive director of the Schafer Volunteer Committee, the political office of then North Dakota Governor Ed Schafer, and I was doing news at a Bismarck radio station. Joanie was told to go and not to worry about anything. My boss told me, "Go and get her the help she needs and don't worry."

I took charge of getting reservations for a place to stay and found the Radisson on the campus of the university just a couple of short blocks from the clinic and hospital. They also had a medical rate, which is something I checked on in any motel we stayed at over the years near the clinic. Over time, it

12

did save us a considerable amount, and it was convenient. We could just walk to the clinic from the hotel and not worry about parking.

Then, all that was left to do before we left on Monday was for her to decide what she wanted to pack for the trip, and to arrange for the care of Muffin and Peaches, the two Siamese female cats who owned us at that time. Joanie was really attached to them, especially Muffin, and I think the prospect of leaving them alone was harder on her than knowing what she was facing at the end of this trip in Minneapolis.

It was in preparing for this trip that Joanie established a ritual when it came to leaving her kitties. We had arrangements with her sister Ann to stop in and tend to their needs. When the car was finally loaded and she knew it was time to go, she would look around the house, and before we walked out the door, she would shout out, "Treats," and the kitties would come running, for they knew what that word meant. She would say goodbye to them and we would be out the door and down the road toward Minneapolis, with uncertainty as an unwelcome traveling companion.

Perhaps the most important thing I learned about helping Joanie during periods like this was to observe her demeanor, and react accordingly. As the day of departure neared, little things set her off: she wasn't as talkative, and spent a lot of time on the couch with Muffin on her lap, the TV on and a book at hand. When the tension was building I determined to try to ensure there were no surprises and to let her know by just being there that she wasn't alone. I handled the details, and that's the way she liked it.

On the day of our departure, everything slowed down. It was as if Joanie knew we had to leave, but if by slowing the process down, she could somehow, magically, make it go away. She dallied over early morning coffee, take a longer

13

shower than usual, and spend more time packing and agonizing over what to take, and that was okay with me. I just told her, "Take your time, we don't have an appointment today, and we have all day to get there." She would.

In 1996, according to **CA: A Cancer Journal for Clinicians,** *there were an estimated ten cases of cervical cancer in North Dakota.*

Joanie just happened to be one of those, and since her issue could not be resolved by a cone biopsy, we were now on our way to the University of Minnesota Hospital. Today, Dr. Carson is the chair and professor of the Department of Obstetrics, Gynecology, and Women's Health at the University of Minnesota. Minneapolis is about 420 miles, give or take a few, from our driveway in Bismarck, but on this day it seemed like it was twice that far. I think that even if the clinic we were going to were across town it would have seemed twice that far on the Monday morning we left the house.

I learned during Joanie's battle was that the stress of the situation, often exaggerated time by slowing it down, or in other cases making it fly by at warp speed. Today, on this trip stress was slowing us down.

Joanie didn't talk much on the car trip. As we pulled out on I-94 headed east, she made a couple of calls back to the office to check on some detail or other about what business she thought she needed to attend to. This was a routine that repeated itself every time we left town. Her boss, Ed Schafer, was running for reelection as governor, and she didn't want to miss out on anything. Outside of that, she either dozed or read, and I was sure she was preoccupied with what was going on and what lay in store for her. Joanie was a voracious

14

reader of romance novels and always had a supply for our road trips, or we'd have to stop at Target and get a few new ones for the ride.

Joanie and I had made many trips to Minneapolis dating back to the early 1980s, and the Twin Cities was one of our favorite places. This trip, however, was different, but we kept our routine about the same, as if to deny that. Our practice was to leave Bismarck, drive as far as Fergus Falls, and stop at the restaurant Mabel Murphy's for a break in the drive. The stop there put us about two and a half hours out of Minneapolis, and it made the trip seem shorter. The stop at Mabel's was one we made well over a hundred times, without fail, over the next years, as if to not do so would bring some kind of bad luck.

As we approached the Twin Cities, she began to talk a little bit about what was in store. As I had learned before, I let her guide the discussion to give her the opportunity to give a voice to her fears, rather than trying to drag them out of her. I think it served us both well over the years, and by doing so I was able to get a better picture of what she was thinking and feeling.

We talked about the coming appointment with Dr. Carson, whom we'd never met, and the surgery that she was about to endure. We both put a positive spin on the prospect of the radical hysterectomy putting the cancer to rest. In the meantime, I told her that we were going to check into the Radisson, clean up a bit, and enjoy the evening.

A new doctor, a new city, a new clinic, a new problem.

As a caregiver to someone who is faced with a life-threatening disease, there are three things you need to have with you anytime you meet with a doctor. I always had a portfolio with

15

a legal tablet in it, and two pens. I always carried two in case one ran out of ink at the time when I needed it most. I think that was from my experience working as a reporter.

One of the things you will learn that medical issues are rarely as simple as they seem, and there are no straight lines. For a nonprofessional like me, that was brought home with Joanie's case. We had come to Minneapolis on the heels of the disappointment that a cone biopsy couldn't take care of the problem, and now she faced a radical hysterectomy that again we hoped would. Dr. Bury had sent all of her films of the CT scan and other tests they had done, as well as her medical records and the pathology slides from the biopsies, so we figured she'd have the surgery on Thursday, be in the hospital for two or three days, and we'd turn around and go home.

So, there we were, on the ground floor of the Phillips-Wangensteen building, where the clinic was located, on the campus of the University of Minnesota for our first meeting with Dr. Carson. The first floor, by the way, is three floors below street level and I found out early on that our cell phones would not work so far down, at least not in 1996.

Joanie checked in, and we sat down in the waiting room so she could fill out the pages of the intake document. That done, we were soon ushered down the hall by Dr. Carson's nurse to a small examining room. Before we met her, however, the nurse went through the questions from the intake sheet and made notes. As we waited, the nurse mentioned that we might also be visited by a resident physician who would go over much of the same information as the nurse did. Later, it dawned on me that this was a teaching and research hospital, and it was all part of the process.

After the nurse completed her questioning, and recorded Joanie's blood pressure, pulse, and weight, she smiled, closed the file folder, and told us the doctor would be in shortly. This

16

is when you begin to learn that the word "shortly" has a different meaning in a clinic than it does in the outside world.

So my job now, as we waited in the examining room, was to amuse Joanie until the doctor made an appearance. I did so by reading anatomy charts on the wall and pointing out important parts, fiddling with instruments that were lying about and, in general, playing the fool, all in an attempt to ease the tension of the hour. I'm not sure if it ever really worked, but I would occasionally get a smile out of her. I knew she sometimes was afraid that I might embarrass her, and I did push that envelope occasionally, but I also knew that humor, even in dark times, can be a powerful tool. In some ways, it may have helped me more than it helped her.

I was doing an impression of a tour guide, giving Joanie a trip through the various parts of the anatomy, including the "naughty bits," on a poster on the wall, using a small flashlight doctors use to look into ears and eyes as a microphone and my pen as a pointer, when there came a light rap on the door and in came the doctors.

I cut short my improvised lecture, and we were introduced to Dr. Carson and Dr. Jonathan Cosin. Dr. Cosin was a Fellow at the clinic and was also a gynecologist-oncologist, and we would be getting to know him since he would be involved in Joanie's treatment as well.

Our first understanding that things would not be as simple as we hoped was at this initial appointment with Dr. Carson. After they spent some time talking to Joanie, and getting to know each other a little bit, Dr. Carson got down to business.

She told us that they were going to perform exploratory surgery and possibly continue with the radical hysterectomy. I was to learn later it was called an "exploratory extraperitoneal laparotomy," and that was the clinical term for what I referred to as "opening her up and taking a look." We were also told

17

that while Joanie was anesthetized, they would also be taking a number of lymph nodes to check on any possibility of the cancer having spread.

The mood in the examining room changed with the news and the possibility that, depending on what they found, they might not do the hysterectomy. Joanie just sat there quietly as she heard the words Dr. Carson was saying, but I wasn't sure if they were registering. The announcement about the lymph nodes made both Joanie and me realize that there was something else to be concerned with, and it produced another cloud.

After meeting with the doctors, we stopped by the lab, which was next to the Women's Cancer Center, so they could draw some blood for the necessary lab tests. While we waited for Joanie to be called, I asked her what thought about our appointment with the two doctors. She told me she was comfortable with both the doctors and was feeling a little better about doing the surgery, though she admitted that she hadn't thought about the lymph node business and was a little nervous about what that would show.

Another disappointment and more uncertainty.

The day of the surgery arrived, Joanie was admitted, and we were escorted to the pre-op room, the last stop before the operating room. I accompanied her into the pre-op as I would every time she was faced with surgery in the coming years. I didn't know what to expect when we went in, my only idea of a surgical prep room coming from episodes of one hospital show or another on TV, and as you might imagine, it didn't look the same. The one thing similar was that it was all white and stainless steel, with nurses and doctors in light blue or light green scrubs, going about the business of preparing patients for their trip to the operating rooms. I don't know how many ORs they have there, but judging from the level of activity and number of patients in the pre-op, I knew it was several.

There, in that cool, sterile, brightly lit, noisy place, we were taken to a curtained area where Joanie changed into a gown and got into bed. A nurse brought her a warm blanket as a defense against the cold, took her blood pressure, and began the process of hooking her up to an IV, all the while making small talk to put Joanie at ease. You could tell she had done this before.

We met her anesthesiologist who explained what he would be doing; we met her nurse anesthetist who explained what her role would be; and then Dr. Carson came in to describe what was about to happen. She basically went over what she had told us in her office, and she also told us there would be three other doctors involved in some way in the procedure. Dr. Cosin was one of them, but we didn't recognize the other names, and I'm not sure it mattered anyway.

Joanie didn't seem anxious. She seemed to like and trust Dr. Carson, and she appeared to be comfortable with her. That made me comfortable too. Even as a person with no medical training, I felt the comfort level between a patient and doctor was critical, and never more so than when the patient is dealing with a deadly disease.

They told us the time was near, and then came the favorite nurse in the pre-op, the one with the Versed. That is the drug that makes you forget you were even there, and it does work. The nurse gave Joanie the shot of Versed, I squeezed her hand, gave her a kiss, and as her eyes began to glaze over and a relaxed look came to her face they wheeled her bed off to the OR. I went to check into the surgery waiting room and then go out for a smoke. It was going to be a long few hours.

19

I was joined in the waiting room by Joanie's sister, Ginny Stringer, who lived with her husband Ed in St. Paul. How we found her is a story for another time. Joanie had grown up with her adoptive parents, Bud and Phyllis Wigen and her siblings. She had never known her natural mother, and, as it turned out, when she found out about her, she discovered she had a sister. Ginny was that sister, and she was to become an important part of this story in the coming years.

We knew about how long this procedure should take, assuming they did the radical hysterectomy. Should Dr. Carson make an appearance after a shorter period, I knew they probably did not do it. We were hoping that they would take the time they needed.

As I look back on it now, I don't know how much time went by but I knew it was not enough time to perform the complete procedure, plus taking lymph nodes for biopsies. Dr. Carson came out, and we went to an anteroom off the waiting room and she told us that Joanie was in recovery, she had tolerated the procedure well, and they had removed twenty-six lymph nodes to send to pathology for examination to see if any cancer had spread. She told us they couldn't do the radical hysterectomy because the tumor had moved off the cervix, and though it had not reached the pelvic wall, there was not enough of a margin to do the hysterectomy. I assumed that to mean a cancer-free margin, but I did not know what exactly what it meant. I only knew for certain that Joanie was going to be faced with another disappointment, something we had hoped we could avoid.

We were to learn at this point that treatment for cervical cancer, as I imagine it is for any type of cancer, is determined at this stage by centimeters and millimeters. It was hard to imagine how something so small could cause so much damage, fear, and anguish, but it does. Dr. Carson said Joanie

20

would be brought up to 7C, the Women's Cancer Center floor at the hospital after her time in recovery. I went out to have smoke, make a few calls back to Bismarck, and begin to process what I had heard and try to anticipate how Joanie was going to take it, and what I would say to her. I didn't have a clue.

When they brought Joanie up to her room, I went in, and she began to cry, knowing that they hadn't done the hysterectomy. The scene reminded me of the one in Dr. Bury's office in Bismarck just a short sixteen days before. I remember feeling how cruel this was, and so sorry for her, because I knew how much she had her heart set on getting this over and done with. It was not the last time I had that helpless feeling, knowing there was nothing I could do but help her get through this.

Joanie was still in pain from the surgery at this point, so we didn't talk a lot about what had happened or didn't happen. Since she was to remain in the hospital for another three days or so, there would be time enough for that. This was the first hospital stay in her life. My job now was to keep her company, keep her spirits up, and in between her naps go for walks on the floor with her.

The questions on our minds again were, "What happens next, and what do we do?" The answer to those questions would have to wait until we found out what the biopsies of the lymph nodes would show, and we wouldn't know that until the next day.

The attack dog, cancer.

The insidious thing about cancer, besides the obvious damage it inflicts on the body and the threat to life, is the mental aspect that accompanies its diagnosis. Cancer, it seems to me,

21

is the attack dog of major diseases. Once it sinks its teeth into you it doesn't want to let go, and it messes with your mind, whether you are the patient or caregiver—the patient because of the threat to her life, and the caregiver because of the feeling of helplessness.

There have been major advances in diagnosis and treatment of most kinds of cancer, and with early detection many are able to be contained and eradicated. Timing is critical in being able to call off the dog. Joanie knew this, though we never really discussed it. She knew that if she had been having regular Pap smears, she might not be in the situation she found herself in. She never spoke about what should have been done, or what could have been done. Neither did I. She knew the futility of that without ever having talked about it with me. When she was faced with the diagnosis, she knew that what went before didn't matter, and the important thing was what we do now to call off the dog.

The good news and not-so-good news, and with it again the question. The good news resulting from Joanie's surgery was this: all of the lymph nodes were found to be negative for cancer. That was the good news. The cancer hadn't spread. The not-so-good news was that the cancer was still there and had to be dealt with.

They staged her cancer at II-B. We had come down to Minneapolis thinking that they had staged her cancer as II-A, and she could have the radical hysterectomy and go home okay. The attack dog had other ideas. Now she was a candidate for radiation treatment, or a combination of radiation and chemotherapy.

We met with Dr. Carson, and she outlined the options for treatment for us to consider. On one hand, Joanie could do the six weeks of radiation treatment at the U of M, or; if Joanie was comfortable, she had the option of having it done in Bismarck.

Our next meeting was with Dr. Kathryn Dusenbery, head of the radiation-oncology department at the U of M Medical Center. She would be the doctor in charge of Joanie's radiation treatment should she decide to have it done there. Joanie was immediately comfortable with Dr. Dusenbery. She had also been involved in Joanie's surgery. This was another one of those times when it was really important that the patient feel comfortable with her doctor.

Dr. Dusenbery outlined what would be a six-week long regimen of external beam radiation along with two radiation implants, which required a two-to-three-day hospital stay. The implants demanded a certain amount of precision as the tubes that received the cesium beads would be inserted under a general anesthetic and then x-rayed to ensure they were in the proper and optimal place. If they weren't, they would be adjusted before the rest of the procedure was completed. She would then be brought up to her room on 7C and they would insert the beads, where they would remain for the specified time. The external beam treatments would be daily, five times a week for the duration. These would be done on an outpatient basis, and wouldn't take much time at all.

Like Dr. Carson, Dr. Dusenbery gave us the option to have this done in Bismarck, and if we wanted to consider that she would send the records to a radiologist there. Joanie and I talked it over, and since it was going to be an extended program, Joanie told her to go ahead and send the records and we would make a decision on where she would have it done after we had met with the radiologist in Bismarck.

The problem with doing it in Minneapolis was food, lodging, and transportation for six weeks, something that involved an expense that would severely strain our budget.

This is when I learned that hospitals have a social work department whose job is to help patients who are facing an extended treatment program that requires them to be far from home. Most hospitals have a list of nearby lodgings where patients can stay at a reduced cost while they are receiving treatment. Should you find yourself in a city where you know no one, or do not have family, this is an option that is worth looking into. It can save you money, and at least lower the stress level in that area.

For us, the lodging issue was taken care of when Ginny invited Joanie to stay with her and Ed while she was getting treatment. That generous offer was something we thought about while deciding between Bismarck and Minneapolis. We had little time to ponder it because Dr. Dusenbery wanted to begin treatment on June 3. Joanie wasn't discharged from the hospital until May 27, and we would have arrangements to make if the treatments were to be done in Minneapolis.

The ride back to Bismarck was another long one. Joanie, I could tell was having a difficult time with the prospect of being gone from work, home, and her kitties for six weeks, but at the same time she had become very comfortable with both Dr. Carson and Dr. Dusenbery. I had as well. I just told her we would go to the appointment with the radiologist in Bismarck on the twenty-ninth, and any decision could wait until after that meeting. I had the feeling, which I left unsaid, that she was going to opt for Minneapolis even if it meant being gone for so long.

In the meantime, there were arrangements to be made in case she decided on the U of M. Governor Schafer told her not to worry about being gone from her job and that her salary would continue to be paid. My boss told me to take what time I needed, even though I wouldn't be gone for the whole time. Those assurances, along with the knowledge that Joanie could stay at Ginny and Ed's home, were in the back of our minds as we were meeting with the radiologist in Bismarck and trying to decide what to do next.

In the short span of twenty days, we had gone from hope, to disappointment, to hope and to another disappointment, and now we were pinning our hopes on our next option. The attack dog, cancer, has a way of doing that to you. Just as you feel like it might let go, even a little bit, it grabs on tighter, as if to let you know you are in real fight.

Decisions, decisions.

The American Cancer Society estimates there will be 1,660,290 new cases of cancer in the United States in 2013 affecting both males and females; in North Dakota the estimate is 3,510 new cases. Among those affected will be wives, husbands, partners, parents, sons, daughters, employers, colleagues, doctors from different disciplines, and close friends of the cancer patient. Many of them will play a part in the decision-making process regarding treatment, but the patient needs to choose the kind of treatment he or she will undergo and where that treatment is administered. That control gives something back to patients who feel as if cancer is taking away their autonomy.

Making any decision on health care or treatment of any serious disease is never easy, and you will find that every time you make one decision, it is followed by the demand that you make another one. At this point the question demanding an answer was where Joanie would have the radiation therapy. There would be other questions, depending on how that one was decided.

We had a good idea of what was in store with the radiation therapy Dr. Dusenbery had proposed. Joanie and I understood there was the risk of possible damage to her bowel, bladder, vagina, and ovaries with the radiation, but that was about the only option at this point. This was one of the times when the disease dictates the decision and the course of action that you must take. The doctor had been very clear and thorough about what the radiation would entail. We also knew that the procedure would be much the same if she did it in Bismarck.

The decision was now in Joanie's hands. We went to the appointment with the radiologist in Bismarck, and it was obvious they were prepared and familiar with Joanie's case from the records they had received from Dr. Dusenbery and Dr. Carson.

If we decided on Minneapolis, we would have to leave on Sunday. I knew the uncertainty about this question was placing undue stress on Joanie, and it had to be settled. I didn't try to dictate where I thought it should be, even though I had an opinion on that question. I told her it was her decision, and whatever it was, we would make it work. She, after all, was the one who needed to be comfortable with the decision, not me. It was her body and her life at stake. My job was just to be there and see that she got what she wanted and needed.

At the meeting with the radiologist, he explained the procedure in much the same terms we had heard from Dusenbery, and while Joanie didn't make a decision while we were in the office, I knew before we left the room what it was likely going to be. The statement, "They do more of these down there than we do," caught our attention, and while those words were not the determining factor, and were not taken by either of us to mean they couldn't do the job, and do it right, it was something we did talk about afterward. That statement, along with the fact there was also a slight variation in the procedure from what was described by Dr. Dusenbery, did not do much to contribute to our comfort level.

There was no doubt in my mind they could have done the therapy in Bismarck, but it all had to do with her comfort level. I remember thinking when I heard the statement about how many more of these therapies the U of M did than they did in Bismarck, that they would be doing another one. You can see where my comfort level was.

We left the office, and before we got to our car in the parking lot she had made up her mind. As I had suspected, she decided to take her treatment with Dr. Dusenbery. Katie, as we soon came to call her, it seemed to me, had instilled a feeling of confidence in Joanie that was really important. When she had outlined the procedure for the external beam radiation, and the precision demanded in doing the implants, it had given me confidence as well. Dr. Carson, now her primary doctor, was also in Minneapolis, and she knew both of them were intimately familiar with her case, especially after the surgery where they were both involved.

We went for lunch, and I could see in her face and demeanor that she was relieved to have made a decision. While the disease may have dictated what the therapy should be, at least she felt she had some control over where it would be done. Having some sense of control with the treatment of the disease that had invaded her body made her feel less like a victim. I think it was something she needed to feel, and it's a feeling that every caregiver needs to reinforce for the benefit of the patient.

We ordered lunch and a glass of wine, and began to talk about getting things in order before we left on Sunday. She said she would call both Dr. Carson and Dr. Dusenbery and tell them we would be back in Minneapolis on Monday. She would also call Ginny to let her know when we'd be coming down. Ginny's generous offer to have Joanie stay at her home in St. Paul while she was having radiation made the decision for her to have the treatment in Minneapolis easier, but Joanie was still a bit concerned about being an imposition on her sister and husband, especially for six weeks. Ginny and Ed were wonderful in making her feel otherwise. Without their graciousness and hospitality, it would have been difficult for us financially since insurance doesn't pay for food, lodging, or transportation.

We solved the transportation problem by driving the Volkswagen down on Sunday, and after she had her first session of radiation on Tuesday, I would fly back to Bismarck, leaving the car with her. When I would come down to see her after that, I would use our other car.

For the first time in almost a month, she seemed relaxed, and though she wasn't looking forward to what lay ahead, wasn't looking forward to being gone for six weeks and wasn't looking forward to the two hospital stays, she was ready to take it on, and take it on in her terms. With that we raised our glasses and toasted to a positive outcome that would put this unpleasant situation behind us.

Statistics are only part of the story of disease.

I'm interrupting the narrative on the lessons I learned from helping Joanie deal with cancer all of those years to consider something that helped me better understand the process that comes along with a diagnosis of cancer. I include statistics on occasion for one reason, and that is to show the pervasiveness of a disease like cancer, which is no surprise to millions of people across this country.

Statistics can show trends in certain kinds of cancer and if the incidence is going up or down. Statistics can show trends relative to long-term survival rates of certain types of cancer, and statistics can show trends that reflect progress gained or loss in the battles being fought every day in the treatment and prevention of cancer. I also have included statistics to make the point that figures don't tell you everything that's important. I also include this to show you that if I could figure this out anyone can.

Statistics don't tell you that, if you're a patient, when you hear the word cancer it can totally overwhelm you for a time. Statistics don't tell you how the people you love and love you can also be overwhelmed for a time. Statistics don't tell you about the helpless feeling that accompanies that word, even if it has been caught early enough to be treated and brought under control, and statistics don't tell you about the cloud that will travel with you for years, knowing that it could come back.

Statistics can't give the patient or family answers the first question that comes to mind, "My god, what is happening?" Statistics can't provide an answer to the question, "Why is this happening to me?" Statistics can't tell you anything about the anxiety and uncertainty that both patient and caregiver experience when facing a deadly disease.

Having said that, I can also say that statistics give you an idea of survivability of cancer for any type or stage at diagnosis, and we all know cancer survivors; not everyone who gets diagnosed with this disease will die because of it, even though that is the fear that comes with the word in the first instance.

I found, that when weighing treatment options, statistics became important, and I did find those resources on the internet, and I did use them for my own education. These numbers are not important in and of themselves, but taken together with your doctor's opinion, the particular kind of cancer you or your loved one may be dealing with, and the type of treatment being considered help provide a complete picture.

All of that emphasizes how important it is that your patient is comfortable with his or her doctor, and that you are all on the same page regarding treatment options, and the statistics surrounding the treatment. That consideration would come into play for Joanie and me in 1998.

The music of the road.

I loved our Sunday mornings together. They were a quiet time in both our lives that began with my going to pick up the paper, mainly because Joanie wanted the ad inserts, especially the Target ad, then having coffee, bagels, cream cheese, and bacon for a late breakfast. Joanie would then spend her time going through the advertising inserts from the paper, followed by a nap with Muffin on her lap.

This day, however was different. I picked up the paper for her to read on the way down, but we skipped the bagels and fixings, and we waited to pick up coffee on our way out of town.

She was quiet, showered longer than usual, fussed with her hair more than usual, fretted about what she would wear for the trip more than usual and went about the morning as if she delayed long enough she wouldn't have to leave.

We had packed the suitcases with most of the clothes she would need for the next six weeks. All that remained was what she would wear on Sunday, and her books and notebooks. The car was gassed up and ready to go.

"Treats," she shouted, as she rattled the bag of cat treats, and Muffin and Peaches came running. Misty-eyed, Joanie reached down to give each one of her furry friends a fanny scratch, rub their heads, and pet them. She was going to miss them, especially Muffin, who was her constant lap cat.

She had left a note for Ann about the cats and their food. She gathered up her purse and bag of books and looked around at the house she was leaving, a sad look on her face, then she looked at me with those incredible blue eyes that seemed to have lost their sparkle, and it hurt to see. It was time to go.

We pulled out of the driveway, picked up some coffee for me and diet coke for her and headed for the interstate. It would be a long drive today, and tomorrow was going to be the start of a longer, more intense summer.

It was almost noon when we pulled out onto I-94 heading east. There were no phone calls and no conversation as she stared out the side window at the green, seemingly endless prairie, seeing it but not seeing it, lost in thought about what lay in store for her at the end of this trip.

We had made this drive many times since the early '80s, and as usual, the soothing sounds of Chuck Mangione's "Bellavia" poured out of the speakers. It was one of Joanie's favorite songs, but I'm not sure she heard it today. She seemed lost in thought about what was happening in her body. Lost in thought about leaving home for six weeks and about whether this treatment was going to work or not. I didn't want to break the spell and was quiet as the miles rolled by.

The view through the windshield and the miles of road ahead gives time to think about the uncertainty she faced. The questions that run through your mind are all centered on one thing, the result of the treatment. Will it work? What will the effect be on the course of the disease? How will Joanie tolerate the radiation? Will there be any permanent side effects? And, most importantly what will be the emotional toll on her?

I knew how much being away from home and a long-term guest in someone else's home was bothering her. I told her it was only about six hours for me to get to her if she needed me. I would also be down on some weekends, and would be there for the hospital stays when she had the radiation implants. I don't think it really helped, but she nodded in agreement.

Even the sound of "Bellavia" wasn't making it any easier.

There was a dog named Piper, a wonderful golden retriever
with the spirit of a mustang and the heart of a friendly bear.
He was Ginny's dog and he only had three legs.

32

He was Joanie's friend.

We stopped at Mabel Murphy's in Fergus Falls again on our trip. It was time we took a breath, have a little sustenance, and talk face to face about where we were headed.

Joanie was worried. The radiation treatment was one thing and being concerned about intruding on Ginny and Ed's life for the next six weeks was another. The actual radiation treatments would only take about a half-hour, at the most, each day. The implants would take about three days each in the hospital. Joanie was a sensitive person, and she understood the difference between being a houseguest for two or three days, but when it stretched for up to forty-two days, she didn't want to be a problem.

As an adoptee, Joanie had spent much emotional capital in trying to find out about her natural mother and family in recent years. She had even gone to court to open records but to no avail. She had been supported in those efforts by her adoptive parents, Bud and Phyllis Wigen, as well as her brother and sister. So when Joanie found Virginia, or Ginny as she was called, it was a special time in her life. No matter how gracious the invitation, she was afraid of straining their relationship. Her stay did not.

Sitting at a heavy wooden table in the cool, dark, pub-like surroundings of Mabel's, we quietly talked. A beer for me and a glass of wine for her; we ordered some nachos. We didn't talk about the radiation; we had done that much of the weekend. I did my best to reassure her that Ginny's offer was heartfelt, and their generosity and hospitality were genuine. They had always made us both feel at home, and it was something we could never thank them enough for.

Attempting to lighten things up a bit, I reminded her that she'd have Piper to help her make it through the day. Piper

33

was Ginny's dog who had greeted us the first time we parked the car in front of Ginny and Ed's house in St. Paul. They lived in the Grand Avenue neighborhood, on a secluded, narrow, tree-lined, one-way street. He met us at the edge of the lawn, this beautiful golden retriever, tail wagging and jumping around like you see happy dogs do, and then we saw it. He only had three legs. It didn't take long for Joanie to fall in love with Piper, and they became real friends.

Piper had been hit by a car and lost his right rear leg in the process, but it had done nothing to dampen his spirit. It always seemed to me, in watching him, that he felt having three legs instead of four was perfectly normal, and that dogs with four legs just had one as a spare. A few times I accompanied Ed on Piper's evening walks around the neighborhood. He wore no leash, and it was a joy to see him romp around the block, with Ed having to call after him from time to time so we could keep up.

I reminded Joanie that Piper would now have somebody to play with during the day for the next six weeks, and she would too. I promised I wouldn't tell Muffin or Peaches that she was consorting with a dog, let along having feelings for him. She smiled, with that look that told me she knew what I was trying to do, so she let me get away with thinking I'm succeeding. I think she wanted to buy it, but I'm not sure she did. What I did know was that Piper would be good for her during this stressful time.

We finished up at Mabel's and got back on the road, and she seemed more relaxed now. It may have been the wine, or it may have just been that she was tired. As we walked up the driveway at Ginny's in the early evening, Piper came running.

He headed for Joanie, tail wagging and jumping around, glad to see his new friend. Joanie rubbed and scratched him, showing her affection right back. I thought to myself, "This dog with three legs and this woman with cancer are gonna' get along fine."

They did.

"Nothing in life is to be feared, it is only to be understood more, so that we may fear it less." –Marie Curie

Marie Curie, who wrote those words, is credited with being responsible for the use of radiation therapy in medicine for over the last one hundred years and more. Joanie and millions of other cancer patients have been treated with it without knowing who they could thank for the procedure that was being used to help them fight their disease.

In June 1996, on the eve of the beginning of Joanie's radiation therapy, we didn't know Curie's words, but when Joanie and I talked about what was going on with her when this all started, my words to her were, "Knowing is better than not knowing, even if the news is bad. If we know what we're facing, we can make a plan to deal with it." In Curie's words, "...so that we may fear it less."

As I reflect on it now, Joanie knew what I was talking about. She had lived with the abnormal bleeding for far longer than she admitted, and the not knowing must have weighed heavily on her mind, but she had said nothing to me. Instead she had wandered alone in the fog of fear that comes from not knowing or understanding what is happening. Now we knew, and while the fear was still there, it was lessened.

Joanie's attitude underwent a transformation as she got settled at Ginny's home. She had gone from feeling helpless to hopeful. She had gone from being fearful to being optimistic, and she had made it known to me that she was going to fight this thing, and she was not going to lose.

My job as a caregiver now was to make her life as easy as I could, even if I couldn't be there with her every day during the treatments. While the fear may not have been as great now, it was still there, and it was for me to see that the routine of her life with the radiation treatment held no surprises for her.

On Monday, so she would know how she was to get where she needed to be every day, we made the fifteen-minute trip from Ginny's in St. Paul to the U of M campus in Minneapolis, and then, so she could see an alternative to the freeway, I showed her another way of getting to the hospital she could use if she chose to. She had a car, she had a cell phone, she knew where to park, and she knew how to get to Katie's office for the treatment. She also knew some good places for lunch on the campus, or on Grand Avenue near Ginny's, and she knew where the Target store was. I think the latter item was as important as anything.

On Tuesday, we met with Dr. Carson for her post-operative examination, and Carson was pleased with how well Joanie had recovered from the surgery. We then went to see Dr. Dusenbery for the first of the external beam radiation treatments. Treatment time, we were to find, from the time she got to the department until the time she walked out the door wouldn't take more than fifteen to twenty minutes.

As we left the hospital for the parking ramp, I asked her how she was feeling now that the first one was over. She said she felt okay about it, and now that she had been through one and understood the process better she was less apprehensive, or as Madame Curie would have said, "she feared it less." Then she said, "Only twenty-five more to go." She was already looking forward to the end.

After we left the campus, we headed for the airport, where she reluctantly dropped me off, and I reluctantly went to catch

36

my flight to Bismarck. She knew I would be back on the weekend, and that seemed to make her a bit more comfortable about saying good bye, plus, by the time I came back, there would only be twenty-two left to go.

Things began to settle down, as we adjusted to living with cancer in our midst. Up to now, things had been very intense, stressful, and disappointing as we began to find our way on the path from diagnosis to treatment. Now, with Joanie entering a treatment regimen, even though it was in the Minneapolis, we were both feeling that something positive was happening, even though we didn't know what the outcome would be.

Joanie and I talked every day. I was in Bismarck, back at work and taking care of Muffin and Peaches. She was getting her radiation every day, but it took less than an hour for the treatment and the travel time to and from the hospital. I could tell she had time on her hands when we talked. Her voice had a wistful quality at times that told me she was lonely, even though Ginny and Ed were there to help her make it through the evenings, and Piper, her three-legged friend, was there to help her make it through the day.

I know she talked to the campaign headquarters often, and was missing her daily involvement in Gov. Ed Schafer's reelection campaign. I know she missed being there because she told me so. Time weighed heavily on her, but she had gotten into a daily routine in just a few short days, that she seemed comfortable with. She had also come to terms with the idea that this process wasn't going to go as swiftly as she would like, but she believed it was going to be the answer.

I drove down to St. Paul to spend that first weekend with her, and when Sunday afternoon rolled around, she didn't want me to leave. I stayed as long as I could, and then about six o'clock I told her that if I was going to be home by midnight, I'd better get going. She knew that, but it didn't stop the tears as we hugged, and I walked to the car, and headed for the interstate and the long road back to Bismarck. Both of us felt the pangs of regret that she wasn't able to come with me. We shared a sense of loneliness, and the silence that greeted me when I arrived home was palpable, even though I knew it was temporary.

In the back of our minds that weekend was the first of the radiation implants, in just over two weeks. We didn't really know what to expect, except she would have to be in the hospital for three days. We agreed that I would come down one more weekend, and then I would be there for the implant and hospital stay.

The uncertainty and fear of the first few weeks was giving way to resignation, and acceptance of the changing circumstances of our lives. Now, it was the goal of finishing the twenty-six sessions of radiation and the implants that was forefront in our minds, but lacking was the intensity that had been present before. You find your mind has a way of protecting you from a period of protracted stress by introducing resignation and acceptance. Otherwise, unprotected, you might go mad.

Your mind also has a way of changing your focus from what happened, which is of no use, to what's going on now, which is more productive, and makes dealing with the current situation, scary as it is, easier. It becomes your job as a caregiver to help your patient keep that same focus.

The way we looked at it then was that, while our lives were being disrupted by the threat of this cancer, it would be another five weeks before it would return to anything resembling normal, and we could deal with that. We were confident it would, and no one was more confident than Joanie.

"A library is a hospital for the mind." –Anonymous

Conversely, "A hospital was a library for my mind," as the learning curve about cancer and treatment began to steepen, and Joanie entered the hospital for the first of her two radiation implants.

Since my two weekend visits to spend time with her in St. Paul, life had been uneventful for us. Joanie had made all of her daily radiation treatments, and so far was not experiencing any side effects that we had been told might accompany the radiation. At home, besides my work and the cats, I was spending time on the computer getting a crash course in the language of cancer, and the subtleties and variations of treatment. It seemed to me that every time I stumbled on something that I thought was a positive, something we could latch onto, I would run across something else that would dampen that initial enthusiasm. That was true from the beginning. We found that there was something you could do if the cancer was Stage IIA, but couldn't do if it was Stage IIB, with the difference being measured in centimeters and millimeters.

On June 27, we found ourselves back up in a room on 7C, the women's cancer wing at the University of Minnesota Hospital. We had an idea of what was involved in this procedure, but I don't think we understood all of it at the time, even though Dr. Dusenbery was there to go over it once again. What we did know was that she would be put under anesthesia, and they would place tubes in her uterine cavity near the offending cancer cells on her cervix, and then they would take her down to x-ray to determine that the tubes,

39

called ovoids, were precisely in the place where they would do the most damage to the cancer cells, without doing too much damage to normal tissue nearby. Were they not exactly where they wanted them, they would take her back and adjust them and repeat the x-ray process.

Once completed, they would bring her back up to her room on 7C, where radiation oncology physicists, would place the appropriate dose of cesium beads in the ovoids and wheel in a lead shield that measured about 6 x 4 feet, and place it beside the bed. This shield was used to protect nurses and doctors who would be stopping in to take care of her. They would all wear badges that measured any exposure, something that gave me pause even though I figured they knew what they were doing. Then they would put up a sign by the door indicating that radiation was present in the room. During all of this, I was left standing in the hall outside of her room, and would not be able to enter it for the three days until the implant was removed.

Something we had not fully understood was that Joanie would have to lie still for the better part of three days, not moving lest the ovoids be jostled out of position. That meant they had to put in a catheter to drain her bladder and bowels. I didn't get a chance to talk to her ahead of time about this immobilization, but I knew she wasn't happy about it. If it were me I wouldn't have been either. You can imagine how slowly time must have passed for her having to lay still for that long. It was long enough for me, and I wasn't the patient.

Another thing that made this first implant difficult was that I couldn't be in the room with her because of the radiation. Her room was one of the smaller ones, and there was the lead shield beside the bed. What they did so I could talk to her when the door was open was to place a full-length mirror near the foot of her bed, so she could see me as I stood in the doorway, and I could see her. Not the most ideal situation if you are trying to be supportive and help someone get through an unpleasant situation.

Consequently, our conversations were short, though frequent, and she spent a good deal of the time sleeping. I spent my time, when not talking to Joanie, at the end of the hall reading old magazines, doing crosswords, or outside having a smoke. I was learning something else from this experience, and that was how important it was to get know the nurses on the floor. Some of them had remembered me from Joanie's surgery in May, and they were very helpful if I had a question, and one of them even brought me a chair one day so I could sit in the doorway instead of standing. What a curious sight that must have been for someone coming on the floor to see me sitting on a chair in the hall, amidst the hustle and bustle of 7C, talking to a mirror. When I think about it now, I can't help but smile.

She had been admitted on Thursday and on Saturday we happily checked her out. She was stiff and a bit sore, but really glad to be done with it. She knew there were only nine more daily sessions left, and one unpleasant implant session. The light at the end of the tunnel was in sight, and she felt better about it. Besides, she would be home over the Fourth of July weekend, and was looking forward to being home with Muffin and Peaches and seeing her friends.

The hospital was becoming a library for my mind, and I was learning a lot, but I wasn't the only one when I think about it. The University of Minnesota is a teaching hospital, and for med students, student nurses, interns and residents, a hospital is the library, and the patients are the books from which they learn some of what they must to become like the doctor they accompany on rounds in the evening as he visits patients and talks about their different problems and treatments. For me,

41

Joanie was my book in this library, and there was so much more to learn.

Hope and numbers.

"There is no medicine like hope, no incentive so great, and no tonic so powerful as expectation of something better tomorrow" –Owen Swett Marden

When it came to Joanie's attitude about cancer, and what she was going through, it was absolute. Her faith and hope were going to see her through this, and that's just the way it was. She never wavered, and if she ever had any doubts, she never voiced them to me.

After her first implant, and a few more daily sessions, she flew back to Bismarck for the Fourth of July weekend. Our plan was that I would drive her back and stay for the second of the implants on Monday the eighth. Her friends who saw her that weekend could see in her demeanor, she didn't come home a cancer victim, she came home as someone who had a disease she was going to beat. Of course, Muffin and Peaches couldn't see that, they were just happy to have her home.

All she wanted to do that weekend was to hang out at home, have coffee with her good friends, celebrate the Fourth with more of our friends, catch up on the campaign news, and not think about having to go back. So, that's what we did.

I too, had hope, not only because the woman I loved was so strong, but because of the numbers I was becoming familiar with. While she was in St. Paul and I was in Bismarck on the computer, I began looking at the numbers. Statistics for me were always abstract numbers, but when cancer involves someone you love, the numbers surrounding it become more real. Now, Joanie didn't give a damn about the numbers surrounding her disease, and I never talked with her about what I had found, and she never asked. As far as she was concerned there was a 100 percent chance she would survive.

As I noted earlier, I found statistics to be helpful some of the time. Statistics can show you a small part of the total picture of a particular kind of cancer, but they cannot show you anything of the emotional ebb and flow that accompanies the onset of this disease. Neither can they quantify hope. If they could, Joanie's attitude would have skewed the results.

In Joanie's case, the five-year survival rate for women diagnosed with cervical cancer in 1996 was 74 percent, according to the National Cancer Institute. While it wasn't 100 percent, I thought it was a pretty good number, and one that provided reason for hope. The other number that gave me hope, was from the American Cancer Society. Those numbers showed that for women with Stage IIB cervical cancer who received external beam radiation, like Joanie was getting at the University of Minnesota Hospital, had a five-year survival rate of 65 to 80 per cent. Again, not 100 percent, but still a pretty good number to give hope. What those numbers meant to me was that if you were alive five years after you were diagnosed with cancer and were treated, you were considered a cancer survivor.

Joanie didn't care about the numbers, and I doubt that she ever sat around at coffee with her friends telling them she had a 74 percent chance of surviving this disease. Her hope was what kept her going, not the numbers. Her hope was what kept her spirits up when she had to lie flat on her back, not moving for almost three days, not the numbers. Hope was what kept a smile on her face for everyone who was worried about her, not the numbers. The only number she really cared about right now was the number of days left till she would be done with radiation and could come home.

On the Sunday we left for the drive to St. Paul, her ritual before leaving was much the same but she didn't seem as reluctant to get going as she had the other two times, even though she would have her second radiation implant the next day. The end of this was in sight, and she would be back home in about ten days and this would be all behind her. So, she gave treats to Muffin and Peaches, we stopped to pick up coffee for the road and headed for the interstate toward St. Paul. She was relaxed, and this time our traveling companions were hope and a number.

"Drugs are not always necessary. Belief in recovery always is." ~Norman Cousins

Norman Cousins, the author of *Anatomy of an Illness*, details in his book a unique partnership between him and his doctor, a partnership that helped him overcome a crippling disease. Cousins was the editor of *Saturday Review*, one of my favorite magazines in the '50s and '60s. He was editor of the literature and arts magazine until 1972.

Joanie had never heard of Norman Cousins, nor had she read his book or the *Saturday Review*, but she knew instinctively the truth of his statement, especially the last five words. She knew it without ever having verbalized it, at least to me.

Her partnerships were now with Dr. Linda Carson and Dr. Katie Dusenbery at the University of Minnesota Hospital, and she was going to do her part as patient to see that these partnerships worked. My job was to help her do her part, and do the worrying for both of us, but keep the latter to myself.

Come Monday morning, we were back in Minneapolis at the hospital. We met with Katie, and they took Joanie down to get her ready for her second radiation implant and another

44

three days in the hospital. She wasn't looking forward to it, but now that the end of treatment was in sight, she wanted to get it over with. The procedure was the same as for the first one, and when the brought her up to her room on 7C, they brought up the lead shield as well. The physicists came and got her situated, and the clock started on the implant. Dosage and time were all factored into the treatment.

This time, however, I found that I wouldn't have to sit in the hall to talk to a mirror while she lay flat on her back, not moving for three days. Now, I would be allowed in her room for brief periods during the day. One of the nurses would give me the badge they wore to measure exposure to radiation and a record would be made as to time spent. I was told I could sit in a chair and not get to close to her during my brief visits, but at least it was an improvement over the first time.

Joanie appreciated being able to look at me face to face rather than talking to my reflection, and I think it reduced her stress level too. She was also able to take phone calls, and hearing from friends from time to time helped as well. She never really complained, until it got close to the time when they would remove the ovoids and catheters and she would be released from the hospital. Of course, she only complained to me, not the nurses or doctors. That was another part of my job. I was the one she could vent to without fearing she would offend anyone.

Joanie made it through the last day of the implant, and when we left the hospital she was feeling so good she suggested we go to Sally's for a celebratory glass of wine. Sally's was a restaurant near campus where we went a lot, just two short blocks from the hospital parking ramp. There, I could see on her face the release of tension now that she had made it through the toughest part of treatment, and there were only five more daily sessions to go. She ordered another celebratory glass, and it was obvious to me that her belief in her recovery was stronger than ever.

We began to make a plan, since those five treatments would take us into the following week, and right then, we had two cars down there. We agreed I would leave the following day, and would fly down the day of her last treatment to drive her back home. She was now getting excited about being done and being able to get back home to her kitties, her job, and her friends.Joanie picked me up at the airport on the last day of her treatment. When she was finished, she made an appointment with both Dr. Carson and Dr. Dusenbery for follow-up exams in a month and a half. We went to pick up her stuff and say good bye to Ginny, Ed, and Piper. She was not going to stay another night. She wanted to get on the road home, and she wanted to do it right now.

That's what we did, and this time the trip back home didn't seem so long. She was just excited to be headed west, and I don't think she stopped smiling for the next several hours. It had been a long time since May 7 when all of this started, and she was ready for the pressure to be off for a while.

The thing about cancer is that it plays with your mind. You find it, then you treat it, and it lets you think you've won. At least for a while. But here's the rub, it hangs around in the background of your consciousness, moving into the foreground and then receding again and then when you are approaching your follow-up appointments with your doctors, it moves into the foreground again, and with it comes the dark clouds of uncertainty and fear. Those clouds only being dispersed by the magic words from your doctor, "No evidence of persistent cancer following treatment," followed by cancer, once again, receding into the background.

So, here we were. Joanie's treatment was completed with surprisingly few side effects, and she was happily back home, back at her job, and we were trying to restore a degree of normalcy to our lives.

For Joanie, cancer was in the background now. She returned to the Schafer Volunteer Committee and got involved in the campaign again with all of the enthusiasm she had before the forced hiatus of the past two months. Getting Ed reelected governor had once again become her focus, and she went at it with gusto.

We had resumed the tradition of our long Saturday lunches where we would go the Ground Round in Bismarck for wine and appetizers while we would "talk of many things," including our dreams, and where we were going. Those lazy Saturday afternoons were some of the best days for us, and it was good to have them back. It was just the two of us, and as I think about those days, even now, it makes me smile and realize how wonderful those afternoons were, and how much they meant to both of us.

We also resumed our quiet Sunday mornings with the paper and the Target ad for Joanie, along with bagels, bacon, and cream cheese and early afternoon naps. After a week or two, it was as if nothing had happened. She was not one to wear her disease on her sleeve, and anyone meeting her for the first time would never know what she'd been through or what she was dealing with.

Joanie, then, was one of the most centered people I knew, and I don't think she even knew that she was. For her today was important, and she never dwelled on yesterday, which for her meant not thinking about cancer. As far as she was concerned, that was behind her. If there was any worrying to be done about it, that was left to me. I don't know what she would tell her friends at work, or at coffee, but we never talked about "what if?"

Her follow-up appointments with Dr. Carson and Dr. Dusenbery were scheduled for August 30, about six weeks from the end of her radiation treatment. While cancer had been in the background of her consciousness for the better part of that time, about three days before we were scheduled to leave for Minneapolis, her demeanor changed, at least at home with me. She became more subdued, and the closer we came to the day of leaving, more short with me about little things. Her Irish temper could be set off at something insignificant, but it subsided in a moment as well. I learned to just listen and watch, and not to try and persuade her to feel something different from that which she was feeling. What she was doing was dealing with the cancer that had forced itself into the foreground of her life again.

We left for Minneapolis the day before her appointments, and the ritual was the same as before. Joanie would delay departure by a slow and deliberate morning of a long shower, a long decision on what to pack, fussing about what else she would take, and finally shaking the bag of kitty treats, which brought Muffin and Peaches running. Then it was out the door and heading east on I-94 toward the next day's meetings with her doctors.

Friday arrived and we went to see her doctors who both did exams. Both exams were positive, and Dr. Carson said, "There is no evidence of persistent invasive squamous cell carcinoma of the cervix." The tension of the past few days vanished in an instant with those words. We stopped at the lab next to Carson's office so they could take some blood for a lab workup, and headed directly for Sally's.

The walk to Sally's was an easy one. Joanie and I were smiling and happy, and bordering on positively giddy that this follow-up had given us reason for celebration, and something positive she could share with her family. We ordered wine, took a deep breath, and toasted the day. She made a couple of calls to her sister and brother, and then we went to Ginny and Ed's for the evening. She had a chance to see her three-legged buddy Piper, who had helped her make it through the six weeks of radiation, and it was a grand evening.

We left for Bismarck the next day, and after a stop in St. Cloud at my sister Joni's home to tell her of the good news, we sailed the rest of the way to our house with nothing but the road and a future ahead of us. Cancer was once again receding to the background. It was a good trip.

Eggs Benedict, Champagne, and Strawberries.

The news we got at the August follow-up to the radiation was enough for both of us to feel good about the future, and life did return to normal. Joanie went back to work with a new enthusiasm, and we started to believe that this thing was going to fade into the past.

Another follow-up, in November gave us hope again, since every time a clinic appointment was pending, there was still a little uncertainty about what they would find, and that weighed on her, despite what she might have said to anyone else. I knew it did. She met with both Dr. Carson and Dr. Dusenbery, and Katie's notes said, "Ms. Wigen returns today approximately five months after completing her radiation therapy. She is doing very well. Her candidate won the campaign and this obviously good news for her. She has been working 12 hour days. She does have some fatigue which is quite understandable." She went on to say, "A CT scan of the abdomen and pelvis today was unremarkable without any evidence of disease."

The tumor marker was normal, and in Dr. Carson's words after her exam, there was "no evidence of persistent cancer following radiotherapy." Then it was off to Sally's. That was another good trip to the Cities, and it set the stage for a happy Thanksgiving. The bonus for Joanie was that she didn't have to come back for three months.

The holiday season of 1996 was one that she pursued with gusto. We both enjoyed the Christmas holidays, but this year was something special. Our house was always decorated from stem to stern inside, and that year she pulled out all the stops. The tree secured— we were still doing live trees then—it was my job to put on lights, and for her there were never enough. She would then spend time placing the hundreds of decorations she had accrued over her life, some dating back to her grandmother, on the tree, and we lit fires in the fireplace when the holidays were in full swing, or anytime we just wanted to have one. Things were good, and as we looked ahead to the new year, we did so with confidence.

On Christmas morning that year, we talked about what a year it had been for her, and for the first time she admitted to me how scared she had been that day in May in Dr. Bury's office, but after what she had been through in the following months, even given the disappointments, she was less afraid now. All seemed normal to me, and quite healthy. I had always told her she was a lot stronger than she thought she was, and the last seven months had proved that, if not to her, to me.

A new year was upon us before we knew it, and with it came a schedule of appointments with her doctors in Minneapolis. Each one was accompanied with the same kind of uncertainty. The first one was in February, both Dr. Carson and Dr. Dusenbery gave her the same news, "no evidence of disease," followed by us going to Sally's for our celebratory wine. She was scheduled to return in three months.

After we returned to Bismarck, however, we were notified that the blood work showed an elevation in the tumor marker, and Carson wanted to see her again in early March for a CT scan and physical exam. This news was unwelcome, but the doctor said it was not unusual for this number to rise and fall, but they wanted to keep a close eye on her. This put us back on the emotional roller coaster that comes with cancer and its treatment, and as we prepared to leave Bismarck for the March appointment, her routine of slowing everything down resurfaced.

Though she never said anything to me, I knew she was worried about this trip. It hadn't been a year yet, and now uncertainty had reared its ugly head again. Once at the clinic, she had yet another abdominal CT scan and a pelvic scan. The good news now was there was no evidence of disease, and she didn't have to come back for three months. The tumor marker had also returned to just a point over what they called "normal." So, it was off to Sally's once again, breathing great sighs of relief that the roller coaster had slowed down, at least for the moment.

Easter Sunday that year was March 30, and in celebration of the day, we started a tradition of eggs benedict, champagne, and strawberries. It was a way of not only noting Easter, but of remembering the good news from her appointment earlier in the month. It was something we did every year after that, and something I still do today, minus the champagne.

On May 13, three days after her forty-seventh birthday, and just over a year since she had been diagnosed, the clinic appointment at the U of M was nothing but good news. Carson's assessment was, once again, "No evidence of recurrent cancer," and Katie's assessment was, "She is doing well with no evidence of recurrent disease 10 months following completion of radiation therapy." By now you know we went straight to Sally's. This time we had two glasses of wine, one for each of the doctors.

For me, knowing the statistics surrounding her disease, I figured it was one year down and four to go before she would be called a survivor. Joanie and I never talked about those numbers, as far as she was concerned, she already was. I think she also thought it would be bad luck to keep track of the time like that.

Her next appointment came in September, and Carson's assessment was the same: "No evidence of recurrent cancer." Again we felt good about it, and the roller coaster slowed down. We went to Sally's and toasted the day's news, knowing that she didn't have to come back for another three months.

We were in the middle of the December holiday season for her next appointment. While the news was good, this time they didn't schedule for three months out. Instead, an appointment was made for January 20 for a CT scan and physical exam. This put something of a damper on the holiday season, since it interrupted the routine we had begun to count on.

The uncertainty that comes from not knowing became our companion once again, and the roller coaster started back up.

All of this after we had considered 1997 to be a pretty good year. We now had no idea what the new year would bring.

"In these matters the only certainty is that nothing is certain." –Pliny the Elder

While I don't think old Pliny was talking about medicine when he wrote that, but he just as well could have been. The truth of that statement became evident to me when we got the call from Dr. Carson's office that we needed to come back in January, instead of the usual three-month interval that would have put us into late March or early April.

That news changed the atmosphere of our home for the Christmas of 1997. Not altogether, but at times it would manifest itself when I would see Joanie lying on the couch, staring at the TV, knowing that she wasn't really watching what was on, but with a look in her eyes that told me she was somewhere else, somewhere I couldn't yet go, and so I would let her be in her reverie. While it hurt to see her like that, I had learned to wait for her to invite me in instead of trying to barge into her very private place. Those moments were some of the times when I felt closest to her.

What concerned us now was why they wanted to see her so soon. From what we knew, her squamous cell cancer antigen, the tumor marker, was in the normal range when they checked it at the December appointment, but there was something else they were concerned with, and it was something they didn't mention to us. I had learned over the first year of going through this with Joanie that things were not always what they seemed, and doctors, at times are not sure exactly what is going on either, so they tell you just what they know, and leave you wondering. They, of course, were also wondering, and that was why we were going back down in January. I began to have a bad feeling, but it was one I kept to myself.

While the thought of cancer was an unwelcome guest in our house the Christmas of 1997, it was a guest that was kept out of sight as best we could. We went about the usual tree trimming, house decorating, party going and living through the holidays as if life at 1205 N. Mandan St. was as normal as ever could be.

It had become my job to make her candy, which at Christmas had become a tradition. At first I just helped her out, then it became my job alone. It was a candy she made from almond bark, chocolate chips, peanut butter, and lightly salted, dry-roasted peanuts. It was a labor-intensive process, and since her list of people who would get a box of her candy had grown over the years, and every year more were added, it was time-consuming as well. I didn't mind since I loved the stuff and would make extra that I kept in the refrigerator to handle my own chocolate cravings. Surprisingly, Joanie didn't eat them very often. Her main sweet treat was always a package of Twizzlers nearby, not chocolate.

SECTION TWO
1998

"The Big One"

After the holidays were over, Joanie went back to work, and we did our best not to let cancer be the focus of our lives. Then as we prepared to leave for her appointment on the twentieth, as before, things slowed down. Facing the uncertainty of another appointment, especially one that was coming so soon after her last one, it made the pressure more evident. On the nineteenth, she moved slowly, as if by stalling as long as she could, somehow, magically she wouldn't have to go. I told her, as I did many times before, we didn't have any appointments that day, and she could take her time. We would get there when we got there.

Finally ready, she would call for Peaches and Muffin and give them treats and pats on their heads before saying goodbye and we would be down the road. After a stop at Mabel Murphy's in Fergus Falls, it was on to Minneapolis and dinner with Ginny and Ed.

We went to Dr. Carson's office the next day, and after a physical exam, she ordered an abdominal pelvic CT scan. Back in her office later, Carson told us the scan revealed a low density mass to the left of her cervix. As alarming as this was to us, she told us they weren't sure if it was something caused by the radiation, or if it was cancer that had come back. She told us they wanted to do an examination under anesthesia and take some biopsies of the tissue in question. It would be outpatient surgery. That bad feeling I had earlier came back. If Joanie felt the same way, she kept it to herself.

The next day we showed up at the hospital at the appointed time, and after the admittance process was done we were taken to the pre-op. It was the same place we had been when she had the surgery in May of 1996. This time, however, the procedure would not take near as long, and after it was over we could leave the hospital, which made Joanie very happy, considering how nervous she felt.

The procedure in the pre-op was much the same as it had been before. It wasn't long before she was prepped, had her shot of Versed through an IV, and was wheeled off to the operating room. Sitting in a surgery waiting room with other worried people is something I never got used to. I waited, doing a crossword, and every time the door opened, my head, like all others there would look up to see if it was the doctor who was taking care of their loved one coming out to give them news.

It wasn't long before the door opened, and Dr. Carson came out to talk to me. We went to an anteroom off the main area, and she told me it appeared the cancer had come back. She could see the effect the news had on me. I asked her what stage the cancer was, and she said that once it comes back, they don't call a stage, it is just called recurrent cancer. She then said something that I totally missed upon reflection later, and it had to do with cleaning out her pelvis. I took that to mean they were going to do a hysterectomy and didn't pursue it any further.

I went to see Joanie after she got out of recovery, and she knew the news was bad. We both just looked at each other and didn't say a word. Neither one of us could believe this was happening. This news was the biggest disappointment in a string of them over the last nineteen months.

56

Carson told us to come back to the clinic on the third of February and we would go over the options Joanie faced now. Joanie got dressed, and we left the hospital and took a slow walk over to Sally's. We had no celebratory glass of wine this time, just a glass to sip on while we took a deep breath, looked at each other, and asked the same question we had asked on May 7, 1996, a day that seemed so long ago now, and that was what do we do now?

We didn't know. Again the feeling of helplessness. We had absolutely no idea of what was in store for her. The only thing we knew for sure, was that the cancer was back, and that wasn't a good thing.

Since we both agreed there was nothing we could do about it right then, she smiled at me and suggested we have another glass of wine. We did. At that moment, as I sat across the table from her, I knew why I loved her more than ever.

"You gain strength, courage, and confidence by every experience in which you really stop to look fear in the face. You must do the thing which you think you cannot do."
–Eleanor Roosevelt

The trip back to Bismarck was typical, even if the news we carried with us was not. We stopped in St. Cloud to see my sister Joni and again in Fargo to visit my other sister Jane to bring them up to speed. These were stops we would make with frequency over the coming years. It broke up the trip for us, and it gave us a chance to vent. It made the trip a bit longer than we could have made it, but that really didn't matter.

On the drive back, Joanie and I didn't talk much about what we had learned, nor did we speculate on what the where the next step in this journey was going to take us. We long ago

57

had agreed that speculation was futile, and it was especially so since we had no idea of what she would be presented with when we next appeared at the Women's Health Center on February 3.

Back in Bismarck, while Joanie went about her life at work and with friends and kept a positive outlook, I went back to the computer and back to research, wanting to find out as much as I could about what Dr. Carson was now calling recurrent cervical cancer. What I found gave me some pause, and I realized that she was facing a difficult fight. I chose not to share some of my concerns with her, seeing no reason to worry her any more than she already was. It was my job to find out as much as I could so that I could help her understand what was going on if she had any questions. If she didn't ask, I didn't offer anything.

The twelve days we had at home flew by, and before we knew it, it was time to hit the road again. It was going to be a short trip, just overnight on Monday, meet with Carson on Tuesday morning at 9:00, and depending on anything she might want to have done, head back to Bismarck afterwards. We stayed at the Radisson on campus, to be close to the clinic since it was an early morning appointment. After we checked in, we met Ginny and Ed for dinner at the Lexington on Grand Avenue in St. Paul. Despite the uncertainty surrounding this visit, we had a great evening. They always did their best to make her feel okay.

Tuesday morning dawned, and though we were up early enough, she dawdled much as she would do on the mornings when we were preparing to leave Bismarck for a clinic appointment. I didn't care, since the clinic was so close, and if we were a bit late it would not be a big deal. Chances are whenever we got there we would have to wait anyway, so I was in league with her on this day's dawdling.

We descended the three floors down to the clinic, and while I went for coffee for me and orange juice for her, she checked in at the desk, and then we waited. The waiting room there had become familiar grounds for us by this time, and we would see familiar nurses from time to time as well. This was not the kind of familiarity we had ever thought we would be comfortable with, but there it was.

One of Carson's nurses came to the door and called Joanie's name, and down the hall we went to the examining room and the meeting we were dreading. This time the nurse just checked her weight, took her blood pressure, and left us, saying, as they always do, "The doctor will be in shortly." This was my cue to try once again to amuse her to release some of the tension, but it was evident today that I would get no smile from her.

There came a rap on the door and in walked Dr. Carson and Dr. Jonathon Cosin. I sat down, and after a little small talk, Carson got down to business. She went over what they had discovered from the January biopsies, and CT scan, and then began to explain what the options were for further treatment. While the cancer was still limited to the cervix, had not spread, and there was no apparent lymph node involvement, she told us that further radiation was not an option because that area had been heavily radiated before. She also told us she didn't think chemotherapy was appropriate at this time either. Joanie welcomed that statement.

Carson then brought up what they said appeared to be a viable option for treatment—a total pelvic exenteration. She could have been speaking a foreign language because neither Joanie nor I had any idea of what that term meant. We were about to find out. What the doctors said next stunned us into silence. While we were barely able to grasp what they were explaining to us, they described in great detail what this major surgery would involve. It would last up to fourteen hours and would involve the removal of her bladder, vagina, rectum, uterus, cervix, and ovaries. They would also take her appendix while they were in there. The next step would be the creation of what they called a continent urinary diversion, also known as a "Miami pouch." The surgeons would also create an ileostomy that could be taken down at a later date when her bowel would be hooked up again. They would also use part of the colon to create a neovagina.

Carson went on to say that this procedure is one that is not done that often, but they did more of them than most hospitals in the country. It is meant to be curative. That word is one we hung onto and would only later find out that is also a relative term. The Miami pouch was an internal device that would act as her new bladder, and she would have to use a catheter to empty it three to six times a day for the rest of her life. The ileostomy hopefully would be temporary, and that after a sufficient healing time, they would take it down, reconnect her bowel, and she would have a normal function in that area. By now, it had dawned on me what Carson had alluded to that day in January when she mentioned something about cleaning out her pelvis.

Joanie's face flushed. She asked Carson when they wanted to do the surgery, if she agreed to do it. Carson told her they would temporarily schedule it for February twelfth, just eight days away. Joanie said, "So soon?"

Carson and Cosin ask us if there were any questions, and Joanie asked if they were sure this was the only viable option. They said given her current situation, the answer was yes. Joanie told them she would need some time to think about it, and with that we left the clinic, walked back to the Radisson, checked out, and headed back for Bismarck.

What we heard that day was so overwhelming that it was hard to get our heads around it. It was by far more overwhelming than the day in May 1996 when she had been diagnosed in the first place. It was incomprehensible, frightening, and I felt so sorry for her that it hurt.

"I don't think I can do this."

The drive back to Bismarck was quiet. The only thing you could hear in the car was the music of Chuck Mangione's "Chase the Clouds Away." Joanie spent most of the ride with a Kleenex in her hands, occasionally picking up another one after she had shredded the previous one. We both concentrated on the interstate highway before us, not seeing anything of the scenery passing by the windows, lost in the thoughts of what we had just learned from her doctors. We didn't talk about it. She had a book in her lap that she picked up once in a while, looked at a page or two, not really reading, and put it back down in her lap. The only thing I heard from her for a good part of the trip was an occasional sigh. As before, I didn't press her; she would tell me when she was ready.

I had plenty on my mind as well. It was frankly overwhelming when I thought about the prospect of her having to endure such a violent and traumatic surgery. She was facing the fact that she could lose control over two vital bodily functions, and that it could be for the rest of her life, even though they had told us if everything went right, they could hook up her bowel and that function would return to normal. I know it scared the hell out of her, as it did me. I was also thinking about what would happen if she decided not to go through with the surgery and what would happen if she did.

I remembered my mother, Marie, on that road back. In the fall of 1986, just a short time after my father Wes's funeral, mom had surgery for uterine cancer, something that none of us kids even knew she was scheduled for. I hadn't even been aware of the diagnosis. I drove her down to Fargo for the surgery and remained there for the week. The surgery went off without a hitch on Monday of that week, and on Friday when she was being discharged I went with her to meet with her doctor. Her doctor told her that the operation to remove the grapefruit-size tumor from her uterus was a successful one, but then he dropped the next news on her, and that was that he wanted to see her back after she had healed up from the surgery to begin talking about chemotherapy. He explained in plain language to her that while the surgery removed the mass, chemotherapy would be used to attack any systemic issues.

When she heard that, I could see her jaws tighten. She told the doctor she'd have to think about it. He told her, of course, that was okay, but again told her the reasons they wanted to do it, and asked her to give herself some time to heal, and not to rule it out. I sat there watching her as she clenched her jaw and knew what she was thinking. She was thinking about my sister and her daughter, Judy, and how she had watched her die from cervical cancer, and how much she had suffered from chemo and other treatment options she had endured.

I remembered that drive back to Carrington that day, and the similarity was striking. Mom didn't say much on the ride back, except after we had been on the road for about forty-five minutes she said to me, "I don't think I can do this." I waited a moment or two wondering how I was going to respond, then I said, "I know this is difficult, and I know it is your decision to make, but I want you to remember you have kids that love you, grandkids that love you and

62

they all want to see you around for a while. Just don't make a final decision right now." She nodded her head, as if in agreement, but I found out later she would make a decision and it wasn't the one we wanted. She died about nine months later, and I wept.

It was getting dark now as we passed Jamestown and as the miles clicked by, all we had were the headlights, music, and the noise of the road. We had said only a few words by the time we crested the hill just east of Bismarck when the lights of the city lay out before us, and we knew we would be home in a few minutes. She said, "I'm so glad to be home to see my kitties."

When we pulled up in the driveway, she could see Muffin in the window of the kitchen, and she smiled. I told her to go in, and I would get the bags. Once inside, she was greeted by her two Siamese friends, and went straight to the bathroom. I brought the bags in, dropped them on the floor, sat down at the kitchen table, and took a deep breath, also glad to be back home.

About that time, the phone rang. It was her uncle Dick from Birmingham checking in to see how things were going. I handed phone to her, and after just a few minutes of small talk she looked at me with an unforgettably, sad look on her face, and said, "Here you talk to him." She couldn't talk about it with him, and so she left it to me to bring Dick the bad news. It was a role I was to fill for many years. I talked to him and told him what I understood the situation to be, and that we would keep in touch with him as we knew more.

Ordinarily when we would return from one of these trips, the first thing Joanie would do after getting home would be go to the bathroom, put on her sweats, turn on the TV, and head for the couch for some lap time with Muffin. This night was different.

She was clearly nervous and agitated and was pacing around our small kitchen/living area, all the time shredding a Kleenex in her hands. Muffin, her favorite kitty, sat off to the side, seeming to sense that something was wrong, and was just staring at her. I sat at the table and scratched Peaches as Joanie quickly went through the mail, not really paying any attention to what she was looking at, and continued to pace and shred Kleenex for a few more minutes. Then she stopped and looked at me, her cheeks red, and with tears streaming down her face, she shrugged her shoulders and said, barely audibly, with a cry in her voice, "I don't think I can do this." I felt my heart break as I stood up, put my arms around her and hugged her close, feeling so sorry for her, now that the anger, fear, and confusion that had consumed her since the doctors broke the news was erupting to the surface.

I held her there for a bit, and then with my hands on her shoulders, I looked into her teary eyes and said, as softly as I could, "Joanie, you know this is your decision to make, and I know it is a difficult one, and whatever that decision is, know I'm here to help you with it and I'm not going away."

I added, "But, please remember you have some people who love you and want you to hang around for a while, and that includes Dick and Ann, Ginny and Ed, your good friends, Muffin and Peaches, and me." She wiped away some tears, blew her nose lightly and smiling slightly, she looked at me and said wistfully, "I know."

I told her she didn't have to make a decision right then and now, and that she had time to think about it. She nodded at that, took a deep breath as if she had gotten something off her chest, and told me she was going to get into her sweats now and relax. I went out for a smoke, thinking to myself, "I know what she's going to do, and I can wait, I don't need to press."

When I came back in she was on the couch, but hadn't turned the TV on. Instead she had put some of our favorite Harry Chapin and James Taylor CDs on the player. Looking at me, now much more relaxed, she asked me if she could have some wine. Somewhat surprised, but happy to see her that way, I said, "Indeed," and grabbed a bottle of her favorite Chardonnay from the rack and a couple of glasses and joined her on the couch. We spent the next hour or so, with the tension of the day slipping away, sipping wine, listening to the songs and stories from Chapin and Taylor we both loved, and feeling more in love with each other as the night wore on. We were forgetting for the moment, and it was right.

That night after we got into bed, we held each other closer.

"There is in every true woman's heart, a spark of heavenly fire, which lies dormant in the broad daylight of prosperity, but which kindles up and beams and blazes in the dark hour of adversity."—Washington Irving

Wednesday morning, the fourth of February, dawned, and I don't remember if the sun was shining or not. What I knew that morning was that Joanie looked different to me than she had the night before. She came into the kitchen after showering and dressing to get the coffee I had waiting for her, and she looked at me with shining eyes and said, "I can do this."

I knew that in the dark of night, before she fell asleep, alone with her thoughts and prayers, she had made a very important decision. She told me that she was scared, but she was not going to give up, and that she was going to beat this thing. I had never been more proud of her and the courage she was showing than at that moment. I gave her a kiss and hugged her and told her we were going to do this together, and she would win.

That morning I realized how important that decision was to her. The cathartic experience from the night before had given her back control of her life. The decision had put her in charge. She was the one now, not the doctors, who would determine the course of her life. It was, for her, a liberating moment. She knew, without knowing, that when faced with a sea of confusion and doubt, a decision gives you control, and with that control comes the bridesmaid hope. What I saw and heard from her that morning gave me reason to believe. Four words, that said, "I can do this," gave flight to that rare bird courage.

I loved her for that.

"We've got a lot to do."

She seemed less vulnerable the morning she told me she was going to do it, stronger and more resolute. I could hear it in her voice, and I could see it in her face and demeanor. Now it was time to get down to business, and she said to me that morning, "We've got a lot to do to get ready." It was Wednesday, and we would be leaving for Minneapolis the following Monday.

There were people to talk to about what was going on, employers to talk to, and arrangements to made for the care of Muffin and Peaches. We would be gone a minimum of two weeks, and the care of her kitties was foremost in her mind. I think she was more concerned about them being alone for such a long time with both of us being gone than she was about why we were going to be gone.

I was told it was my job to call Dr. Carson and tell her Joanie had made a decision to go ahead, and confirm that the surgery was for the twelfth. Joanie was to check in at the University of Minnesota Hospital at 3:00 p.m. on Tuesday afternoon to begin preparation for the operation of a lifetime.

She told me she would talk to her friends and others who needed to know about what was about to happen, and the first one she called was her boss, Governor Ed Schafer. Joanie was director of the Schafer Volunteer Committee, the governor's political and fundraising office. Ed told her, as he had in June of 1996, she could take whatever time she needed, and her job and pay would continue on. That was something that took a load off of her shoulders, because she had wondered how we were going to get through this financially. We had good health insurance, but that wouldn't cover other expenses.

I talked with my employer and told him I might need to be gone for at least two to three weeks, and he told me just to do what I had to do to see Joanie was taken care of and getting what she needed. When I think of it now, I wonder if had we'd been living somewhere else we would have had the kind of support and understanding from our employers that we had. I'm not so sure we would have. The news she broke to her close friends about the surgery she was facing, was, I think, as incomprehensible to most of them as it was to her, but the way in which she approached it gave them reason to believe she would be okay. Joanie never presented herself as someone whom they should feel sorry for, and even now, given what she was facing, no one could say she was looking for anything like that. The decision she had made gave her the strength she would need, and I think people recognized that,

67

and they felt a little less uncomfortable talking with her about it.

As for me, for the next couple of days, my job was simply to make sure that everything was in order for our departure on Monday, and to make sure there were no surprises. I did call my friend, Wayne Tanous, to sit down with him and go over what was about to happen to his friend Joanie. Wayne and his wife Karen were our good friends, and Wayne is one of the closest friends I've ever had. He had been a corpsman in the navy and could understand some of the medical stuff surrounding Joanie's treatment. He would be the friend I would rely on to keep people in Bismarck who would want information on Joanie, or her condition, informed while we were in Minneapolis. It made it easier for me to be able to call him, and he could talk about it to whomever wanted to hear the latest news.

I found, over the years, it was also a good way to help keep inaccurate rumors about her condition to a minimum. I learned during this time, while Joanie needed someone close to talk to besides me, it would be important for me as her caregiver to have someone to vent to as well, and for me that person was Wayne. I knew I could call him anytime, and he would be there. For any caregiver, I think it is important to get away from the constant tension surrounding a serious situation, and have someone, like Wayne to let off steam with, even for a little while, for the sake of one's own mental health.

All the details were handled, and by Saturday, everything was pretty much done that needed to be in preparation for the trip. Knowing that, Joanie and I went for one of our long lunch Saturday afternoons and spent a couple of hours nibbling on appetizers, drinking wine, and talking about what was to come. It was a bittersweet time, since we both knew it would be a long time until we would be able to do it again, and when we did, her life would have changed.

The evening was spent at a dinner party with two other couples, and Joanie was the center of attention, as you might imagine. She did her best to put everyone at ease, and after a little wine she was even able to make light of her situation. She continued to surprise me, and it would not be the last time she would do so. We stayed too long, probably had too much wine, but we didn't care. She needed a night like that, and I was not going to deny her. We went home that night feeling good. The evening had been another example of how life with this disease wasn't dark all the time, and there were good times to be had in between the ups and downs, that made us appreciate them even more.

The countdown begins.

Sunday morning came, and we got settled in for one of our favorite times. I was dispatched to get the *Sunday Tribune*, and pick up some fresh bagels, bacon, and cream cheese. We had once tried lox, which is traditional with bagels and cream cheese, but found our love of bacon too much to resist, and it turned out to be an excellent replacement. Joanie had decided we would have that to munch on for our usual late morning lunch. I fixed coffee, and we turned on *CBS Sunday Morning*, that low-key, gentle-on-the-mind look at the arts, music, nature, and human interest. For us it was the perfect way to start a leisurely Sunday morning.

The one thing that was different about this Sunday morning, however, was that it was the start of an incredibly difficult week, and the thought of that was not far from either of our minds. I could see it in Joanie's demeanor that morning, as she went through the paper, pausing every so often, putting it down and looking out the window for a moment before taking another sip of coffee and picking it up again. We didn't talk about what was coming, having done enough of that over the past few days, but we both knew the clock was ticking, and tomorrow morning we would be leaving.

I spent most of the time drinking coffee, looking at parts of the paper she was through with, and wondering to myself if I had taken care of all the details that needed attending to. At this point, I didn't want any surprises that would put any more stress on Joanie than there already was. Near as I could figure, they were. The only thing left for us to do later today, was do the preliminary packing.

With the packing for this trip came a role reversal. For the first time on a trip, I would be packing more clothes than Joanie. We had talked about what she would need this trip, and decided that she needed something to wear for the trip down, something to wear to dinner with Ginny and Ed on Monday night, and something to wear on Tuesday before we checked her in to the hospital. Going home afterwards, she could wear the same. In the end, I just told her she could take whatever she wanted, and as much she wanted. She did.

Joanie was a tall woman and always fussed about how she looked, which accounted for her often packing more than she would need. Her clothes leaned toward classic looks: blue blazers, white turtlenecks, gray slacks or skirts, sweaters, etc. Like many people she worried about her weight, and she carried a lot of it on her hips and waist. Consequently, she tried to wear clothes that drew attention away from that area. Every so often, I would get the question every husband dreads, when she would ask, "Does this make me look fat?" I never gave a wrong answer.

When it came to what I wore, she had some definite ideas of what was right and what was not, and from time to time, I would hear the words many husbands hear, when she would ask, "You're not going to wear that, are you?" She would look at me in disbelief as I said I had planned on it, and asked her why I shouldn't. Her reply was always the same, "I don't want you to look like a doofuss," and as always, I would change. It became a joke over the years when I would ask her before we were going out, if I was looking doofussy or not.

Anyway, we would get to the packing later on that Sunday. The first order of business after we had our late lunch was nap time. Joanie would stretch out on the couch with Muffin on her lap, and I would go downstairs to the couch in the basement to be joined for a while by Peaches. It gave us both some alone time to consider the unspoken thoughts about what was coming, and I remember feeling really angry about Joanie's upcoming surgery. I kept those feelings to myself.

Late afternoon, as Muffin and Peaches jumped in and out of the suitcases on the bed, as if wondering what in the world was going on, we packed everything but what we'd be wearing in the morning, including more clothes than she could wear. Getting all of that out of the way eliminated one more thing we'd have to do on what would be a stressful morning.

With the suitcases packed, Joanie suggested that I get some French bread, and we would bring out the olive oil we had for dipping, open a bottle of wine, light a few candles and relax as best we could. While I don't think our efforts were entirely successful, some of the tension let go with the bread and the wine, and it was a good night in spite of the fact we knew the clock was ticking.

"We must travel in the direction of our fears."
–John Berryman

I got up early on Monday morning, not having slept well at all. When I came up from downstairs after my shower, Joanie was sitting on the couch in her sweats, Muffin on her lap, watching one of the morning shows on TV. Without looking up at me she said, "Good morning," and nothing more. I knew it was going to be a hard morning for her. She asked for a cup of coffee. I had started the coffee going before I went downstairs to shower, and brought her some. It was only 8:00 in the morning. She hadn't slept that well either. After a while, when she did get up from the couch to take her shower, she stopped at the kitchen table where I sat, looked at me and, half smiling, said. "Do you think we can put this off?" Taking her hand, and smiling myself, I said, "We can do anything you want to do, darlin', but if we do, I'll have to unpack those suitcases."

She laughed half-heartedly, and said quietly, "Okay, I know, I know." I told her we could stay home another night, but we'd have to leave very early on Tuesday morning, because she was due to be admitted to the hospital at 3:00 that afternoon, and then we wouldn't be able to stop at Mabel Murphy's. She smiled again, knowing that we were going to dinner that night with Ginny and Ed, and she would have some time for shopping on Tuesday morning, and she wasn't going to miss that.

With that Joanie headed for the bathroom, followed by Muffin, who always waited outside the bathroom door while she took a shower, and when she was done, and the door would be open, even a crack, she would join her in there. It was a routine that never varied. That morning, she took one of the longest showers she ever had, and after I heard the water shut off, and she finished brushing her teeth, I heard her ask loudly, "What time is it?" I said, "Don't worry about it, we've got plenty of time, as long as we're in Minneapolis by six, we're okay, so take your time." She did.

She didn't want to leave that morning, and, quite frankly, neither did I. She fussed around, with details, and soon we had the last things that needed to be included packed. I took the bags out to the car. Joanie then went about setting the timers she had for the lights in the house, lights that would give any would be intruder an indication that there was activity in the house. I had already alerted, at her request, a couple of our neighbors to the fact that we were going to be gone for an extended period, and told them that the only car they should see in our driveway was her sister Ann's, who was going to look after the cats.

Finally, around ten, she had her coat on, purse on her shoulder, had left the usual note for Ann regarding the care of her kitties, and had grabbed the treats for them. When she rattled the bag, and they came running, and as she knelt down to pet them and dole out the treats, Joanie started to cry. I almost melted, but knew I couldn't. My job was to let her do so, and not make it any harder on her than by losing it myself. She never looked more vulnerable than she did the moment she was saying goodbye to her kitties, and I don't think I ever loved her more than at that moment.

We got in the car, stopped to pick up some coffee for me and a Diet Coke for her and headed in the direction of our fears. Joanie had taken a tranquilizer before we left, and as we pulled onto the interstate, she made a couple of calls, one to her office, and the other to Ann. The latter call was basically to repeat what she had said in the note she had left for her and really to just connect. After that she found a book in her bag, put it on her lap, not reading it, and in a while, she dozed off. As we approached Fergus Falls, I asked her if we should stop at Mabel Murphy's. She told me we'd never made a trip to

73

Minneapolis without doing so, and it would be bad luck to start now, so we did. We stopped into the familiar surroundings of Mabel's, and it seemed like the tension of leaving home melted away. Now, we weren't that far from the Cities, and she began to look forward to seeing Ginny and Ed for dinner that night.

We stayed a little longer at Mabel's than usual, but we made it to the Radisson by six o'clock that evening. We had time enough to check in, change clothes, and wait for Ginny and Ed to pick us up for dinner at Ruth's Chris Steak House. Under the circumstances, the evening with Ginny and Ed was a wonderful prelude to what was to be an incredible time of her life. They had an ability to make her feel special, and the evening of food and wine was just what she needed. Their consideration and care for her that evening is something I will never forget.

We talked, drank, ate, laughed and for that night, at least, we had a moment when we were able to forget why we were there, and the fears we all shared about what Joanie was facing beginning tomorrow.

Ginny and Ed dropped us off at the Radisson with words of encouragement. Ginny told Joanie she would be stopping by at the hospital when things got settled before the surgery. After we walked into the hotel, Joanie looked at me and said, "Let's have a Baileys for a nightcap." That was a tradition we'd carried on for years on our trips to Minneapolis and she thought we should do it again on this night. I told her, I thought that was a great idea since it would be a few weeks before she could have one again.

She smiled and we headed for the bar, somehow less afraid of what we didn't know than we had been.

Tuesday's Unwelcome Surprises

I think anyone who tells you they sleep well in a hotel is either lying or has a good supply of Ambien with them. Neither Joanie nor I slept well, and were both up early on this very important day. We skipped making a pot of the notoriously bad, in-room coffee, and instead, showered, dressed and walked a couple of blocks to Bruegger's Bagels for better coffee and a great bagel.

Joanie was relaxed and pensive, as one might expect, but did not appear the least bit anxious that morning. Our conversation over breakfast was low key, dealing mainly with her outlining what shopping she wanted to do that morning, and wondering how Muffin and Peaches were doing. Choosing to ignore the elephant in the room, neither one of us said a word about what was coming later in the day. We dallied over coffee, like two people who had all the time in the world, both getting a second cup, and I remember thinking I wanted the moment to last for the whole day, and then we could go home. She broke the spell abruptly when she said, "We should get going." We walked back to the hotel and drove across the Mississippi to downtown Minneapolis, finding a spot in the parking lot on 1st Avenue across the street from the Loon Cafe, one of our favorite spots, and where we might have lunch later.

Walking a couple of blocks to the Nicollet Mall, our first stop was Neiman-Marcus. Lest you think we shopped at a store like that on a regular basis, we didn't, but I had found, over the years they always have any number of items in the price range we could afford, which means $25-$50, and they had these great gift boxes and bags. Joanie found an angel pin she wanted, and had she wanted a dozen of them, as far as I was concerned, she could've had them. Our next stop was

Dayton's where she picked up a pair of sweatpants and she found a pair of shoes. I wasn't sure why she picked that time to buy a new pair of shoes, but said nothing, and again if she wanted two more, she could've had them. I didn't care.

We dropped of the purchases in the car and walked across the street to have lunch. Dr. Carson had told Joanie that she could eat a good lunch, could eat as much as she wanted, and if she wanted to have wine with it that was fine. We didn't know it then, but it would be the last solid food she would have for about three weeks. We stopped at Champps, just down the block from the Loon, ordered a big chicken salad to share and a glass of wine. As the food and wine came, the mood changed, as the elephant in the room cleared its throat and got our attention. We started to talk a little bit about what was to come, where I was going to stay, and how we were going to handle things. I told her I would be leaving the Radisson on Saturday and would be staying with a friend of ours, Tom Sand, who had called me and offered a place to stay. Joanie and I had stayed with him on other occasions. He had a place a few blocks north of the state capitol building in St. Paul. It would be an easy drive from there to the hospital. She seemed a bit relieved one expense item was taken care of.

It was obvious that neither one of us was very hungry, as we just picked at the salad, and barely sipped at the wine. It wasn't long before Joanie said she wanted to go back to the hotel. It was around two o'clock now, with just barely an hour left before she was to check into the hospital.

Back at the hotel, we got to the room, she went to the bathroom, and when she came out, she sat down in one of the chairs and let go a heavy sigh. She looked at me and smiled weakly, and it was like the air being let out of a balloon. She seemed deflated totally. We sat there, silently for a few minutes, until she said, "Well, I suppose we should go."

Joanie never liked to be late for anything, even this appointment, as if doing so might offend someone. For me, I didn't care if we were a little late, I knew it wouldn't make any difference, but right then I was going to do anything she wanted me to do.

We slowly walked the few short blocks to the hospital, and as we went to the admitting office, the trouble started. When we approached the fellow behind the desk to check in, she told him who she was, and he started going down a list of names he had in front of him, and then he went through it another time, and then he looked at another list, and finally said, "I'm sorry, but I don't see your name here. Who's your doctor?" I could see her face, and it told me she was on the verge of losing it. I stepped in and told him she was Dr. Linda Carson's patient, and she was scheduled for surgery on Thursday, and we had been told to check in today to begin preparation for the surgery. He again apologized, but said her name wasn't on the list.

I was livid. I was pissed at myself for not double-checking on Monday that everything was in order. This was one of the surprises it was my job to prevent. I was also pissed at the bureaucracy because someone who was supposed to set this up hadn't. Joanie knew I was mad, and I really had to control myself because she would get upset herself if she knew I was upset, and besides that she was, unlike me, conflict averse.

I went outside, got on the cell phone to Carson's office, and asked them what the hell was going on. I did so out of range of Joanie's hearing, and I expressed my displeasure to the voice on the other end, and I was promised it would be taken care immediately. Which in hospital parlance means, "Who knows when," especially since three o'clock was the time when you had shift changes going on. In the meantime, Joanie sat in the waiting room, looking sadder and smaller than I had ever seen her. It hurt to see her that way, and it pissed me off even more. This wasn't supposed to be the way this whole thing was to start. What she was facing was hard enough for her without throwing in a paperwork screw up.

Finally, after close to an hour, the admitting paperwork was done, and we headed for the elevator for the ride up to 7C, where another unwanted surprise awaited. We walked down the long hallway to the Women's Cancer Center floor, and approached the nurses' station to announce her arrival. By this time they had been alerted and were expecting us. Unfortunately, there was no private room available, and Joanie burst into tears standing there in the open. It caused quite a stir among the nurses until Barb, one of the nurses we would get to know well in the coming weeks, put her arms around her and tried to comfort her. She settled down, and while she dried her eyes and blew her nose, Barb told us they would arrange soon for the private room. I kept my cool, but I was seething inside. This thing was turning into a nightmare for Joanie, and I was really helpless to do anything about it. I felt like I had let her down again by not double checking that things were ready for her.

They got her settled in a room, but as you know, semiprivate rooms in hospitals are anything but spacious, or private, and considering what Joanie was there for, I didn't like this at all. She changed into the hospital gown, and we waited for the next surprise.

We didn't have to wait long, before we were introduced to Dr. Kris Ghosh, a gynecologist-oncologist that we'd not met before, and he told us they would be putting in a line below the right side of her neck for the IVs she would be receiving from now on. Then another surprise came. Every time Dr. Ghosh would try to find the vein to begin hooking up the line, something strange would happen. It was like there was no vein there. He tried several more times, and each time he failed. Now, Joanie was getting nervous, and so was I. In all fairness, no one could have foreseen what was happening when he tried to set the line. Finally, the took Joanie down to radiology, and, using a dye, they found what they were looking for, and Ghosh explained that the difficulty was that each time he stuck her trying to set the line, the vein would collapse.

They got the line set, and now Joanie, back in the room a little more relaxed, began another part of the preparation she hated, GoLytely. Anyone who has had any kind of abdominal surgery, or a colonoscopy knows what that stuff is. As she began that regimen, she began to be visited by nurses, who would be fiddling with her IV, taking her blood pressure, and hooking up various things, and trying to put her at ease. They weren't succeeding to any degree, and as the bowel prep began to do its work, it was even harder. Finally, about six hours after we were supposed to have checked Joanie in, Marcia, one of the older nurses on the floor came in and said this was unacceptable, and they began to get her ready to move to a private room. Marcia was this diminutive, grey-haired, Irish woman, and one you just knew was a veteran on 7C. She was also one who somehow figured out right away that Joanie was Irish, and she took a liking to her and would be one of her main nurses throughout her stay on 7C.

While they moved her, I went outside to have a smoke. When I came back up, she was in the private room and seemed more relaxed. She was getting more comfortable with the nurses, and every so often Barb or Marcia would pop in to see how she was doing. I began to feel better myself, and had all but forgotten my anger from earlier in the afternoon.

I stayed with her until about eleven o'clock, when she looked at me and told me I should go. I asked her if she was

79

okay with that, and she just smiled at me, told me she loved me, and said she'd do fine. I kissed her, told her I loved her, and said I'd see her in the morning.

Hospitals are big buildings built to accommodate a lot of people and a lot of drama, but at eleven o'clock at night, when they are empty and quiet and lonely places, they have a different feel. As I walked through the main area on the ground floor the only person I saw was a hospital security guard. He said good night to me, and I to him and walked back to the Radisson.

Back at the hotel, I stopped at the bar, picked up a beer and headed for my room. Once inside, I sat down at the table by the window from where I could see the top floor of the hospital, lit up a smoke, and thought about what Joanie had been through since we first tried to check her in and how it affected her. It had been one helluva day, and I was tired.

"So, you're here for the big one."

When I got back to the hospital Wednesday morning, Joanie was awake, had taken a shower, and seemed to be in pretty good spirits. I had stopped in the hospital lobby area where they had a coffee cart and picked up a mocha, and she chided me in a good-natured manner about why I hadn't brought one for her. She grinned at me, knowing the answer, and told me she didn't mind.

She had been more comfortable after she had been moved to the private room but hadn't slept well. I don't think anyone sleeps any better in a hospital than they do in a hotel, except that you don't usually have as much noise or as many interruptions in a hotel as you do with the nursing staff checking up on you at all hours.

On this morning, we met another nurse named Barb. You could see by the way she dealt with Joanie that she was a veteran on this floor, and Joanie took a liking to her as she had to Marcia, the little Irish nurse the night before. They were cheerful, no-nonsense professionals, and exuded an air of confidence and warmth that put both Joanie and me at ease.

It was from Barb that we first heard the phrase "So, you're here for the big one," meaning a total pelvic exenteration. She said it more as a matter-of-fact declaration than a question, and she told Joanie she was in the right place for that kind of surgery. Both Barb and Marcia had cared for women who had undergone the procedure, and they assured Joanie they were going to take good care of her. Joanie asked Marcia why the called it, "the big one," she said it was a more difficult surgery than a heart/lung transplant because of what was involved. We didn't know if that was true or not, but it answered Joanie's question.

Joanie was still facing the unpleasant task of the bowel prep. She hated it, and I knew it, so I said we'll play a game. I asked one of the nurses if there was a deck of cards around that we could use, and after she found one for me, I told Joanie we were going to play blackjack, and every time she lost a hand, she would have to take a big drink. She reluctantly agreed, and the game was on. I didn't cheat, but I did win more times than she did, and it really didn't take that long to dispense with the GoLyetly. The problem now was that she couldn't get too far from the bathroom. To her credit, she did it all with a good bit of humor as well. It didn't take long for things to settle down, and while Joanie took a nap, I went for lunch.

Mid-afternoon, Ginny came up to spend some time with Joanie, and I left to find a battery for the cell phone, because I knew I would be needing an extra one. Mission accomplished, I got back to the hospital, and about five o'clock, Dr. Cosin came in to go over the details of what was to come in a little over fourteen hours. Joanie liked him, and he had been familiar with her case from the beginning.

With Ginny and me standing by, he began to lay what was in store for her in great detail, and it became obvious shortly after he started this was a hard discussion for Joanie. She had a Kleenex at the ready, and before long was wiping her eyes, and trying not to lose it completely. Cosin did his best to present the details of the procedure in as non-threatening manner as possible, but the fact remained this was an incredibly difficult and traumatic surgery, and her life would change forever when it was over. Joanie was not successful in her efforts to keep from losing it, and broke down several times before he was finished. After about forty-five minutes, he was done, and before he left us, he told Joanie the surgery was scheduled for seven o'clock in the morning, and they would bring her to the pre-op about six to get everything ready.

I wondered what Ginny thought having heard, for the first time, the magnitude of the surgery. She told me later she was "stunned." At dinner together the night before, Joanie had talked some about it but did not go into the kind of detail Dr. Cosin did. I told Ginny that Joanie rarely dealt with the details when she talked with people about her medical treatments. Ginny said, "I was stunned at the extent of what was going to be done to this woman's body, and I was struck by the courage Joanie exhibited in going through with it."

For the rest of the evening, Joanie and I spent a good deal of time watching TV, but we were not really watching, when nurse Marcia came in to the room and unrolled a six-foot poster to put on the wall next to Joanie's bed. It was an Irish-themed poster complete with leprechauns, a rainbow with a pot of gold at the end, gold stars, and an Irish blessing in large letters. Joanie's face lit up. I liked this Marcia even more.

About ten-thirty that night, Joanie told me it was okay for me to go. She said, "If I have to be awake at five-thirty in the morning, so do you, and I will expect to see you here." I kissed her and told her I wouldn't miss it for the world, and she laughed.

The night before.

I like the nighttime. Something happens when the darkness slowly creeps in and quietly wraps its arms around you, your hopes and fears, and holds on tight. The lights you see then are warmer and brighter, holding the promise of illumination into the darker corners of your life. Ideas and thoughts become more clear and focused, promising illumination into the darker corners of your mind. It is the kind of focus that is difficult in the harsh, unforgiving light of day and the cacophony of noise that comes with it.

Back at the Radisson, alone, my first thoughts were about her, alone, lying on a bed on 7C, and wondering what she was thinking now, on the eve of the day when her life would change. When you are married to someone, you often say, "Well, I know her." But really, what you are saying is you know some concrete things about her. The rest of your knowledge is based on the shifting sands of the assumption that you know more than you do, or can. Tonight there were a few things I assumed I knew. I assumed I knew she was dreading it more than she let on to any of us. I assumed she was afraid, and I assumed she was praying. I was to find out later these assumptions turned out to be true, but I only found out they were after she told me they were. I knew that.

83

I thought about what Ginny had said about Joanie's courage in the face of this surgery. I had always told Joanie she was stronger than she thought she was, and she was proving it to all of us now. I wondered then if I was faced with a similar circumstance I would have been as strong. One of the things about Joanie's character that was clearer than ever was the determination she was showing in the face of adversity. Once she had made a decision to do this, in spite of her fears, she would devote every fiber of her being to seeing it through and because of that, the bird courage took flight. Ginny said it might be a family trait. She said, "It might be in her genes." All I knew that night, was I was proud of her.

As I sat there staring out the window looking toward the hospital, I began to go over the surgery again, in my mind, as I understood it from a layman's point of view. Both of us had heard Dr. Carson's explanation in January, and we both heard Dr. Cosin's briefing today. From what I understood, this is what was going to happen when she entered the operating room on Thursday morning. I think, for me, going over it again would help me make it through the next day.

There were to be three teams of doctors, and the surgery was to take from twelve to fourteen hours. The first phase I hadn't focused on before was to be exploratory. They were going to open her up, take lymph node samples, tissue samples, look at all the sidewalls and organs in her pelvic area for any signs of cancer that might have spread, in an effort to insure that there would be a cancer-free margin after the surgery. I hadn't focused on the fact that were they to find something that would make that impossible, they would not go ahead with the surgery. That would be bad news. I never told Joanie until long after she had healed up, but I began to understand Carson's words better now when she told us "not everyone is a candidate for this procedure." So, the first hour

84

and a half of this surgery was going to be the key to Joanie's long-term survival.

Assuming they had their margins, what they call the exenteration phase would start. They would begin to remove her ovaries, fallopian tubes, uterus, cervix, part of her vagina, appendix, and bladder. Part of her lower intestine is also involved which accounted for her facing an ileostomy until she had sufficiently healed at which time they would hook it back up and take down the ileostomy.

Next would come the reconstruction phase. They would use part of her colon to create what they call a continent urinary pouch. The nickname they used for that was "Miami pouch." She would then use catheters to drain the pouch through her belly button. They would construct a neovagina using part of her stomach muscles to graft to the part of the vagina that was not involved in the cancer. The ileostomy would be created, and they would sew her back up and take her to recovery.

It was getting late, but I wasn't tired, and I think my nighttime reverie had made it so. I looked at the clock, and decided to call Joanie. I was surprised she answered after just two rings, so I knew I hadn't woken her. She said she hadn't been able to sleep yet either. She asked me what I wanted, and I just said, "I wanted to say good night again, and tell you that I love you." She paused, and told me she loved me too, and then said, "Good night and now go to bed, I'll see you in the morning." Her tone of voice told me she was going to be okay, and after I set the alarm, I did as I was told.

A large city at five o'clock in the morning is a quite different place than it will be in just two more hours. The city is just beginning to stir in the dark light before dawn, and the only sounds one hears are those of distant trucks off on their early morning rounds, and the occasional footsteps echoing through

85

the canyon-like walls of buildings. There is a melancholy quality to the sound of this early morning city that greets any early riser, a quality that will slowly diminish as the sun clears the horizon, and human activity shifts into high gear for the day.

I woke before the alarm I had set for 4:30 A.M on Thursday morning, turned on the in-room coffeepot, lit a cigarette and started to organize my thoughts for the day. I hadn't slept well, and I suspected Joanie hadn't either. As I sipped the coffee, I took note of the time, and knew I had time for another smoke and a half a cup of coffee to at the hospital at five-thirty as I had promised her. As I got ready to leave, I checked the Land's End bag that had been with me for years, and made sure I had my notebooks, portfolio with legal pad, extra cigarettes and pens, lists of important phone numbers, and the extra battery for the phone. That bag had traveled far and wide with me, and I never ceased to be amazed how much stuff I could cram into it. It was about to be tested again, this was going to be a long day. I left the hotel for the short walk down Harvard Street toward the hospital. It was cold and still dark and I was the only one on the street.

I got to Joanie's room before five-thirty and found her wide awake. My suspicion that she hadn't slept well was confirmed, but she seemed to be in good spirits. There was some activity as nurses came and went from her room checking to see last-minute details were being attended to, and Joanie met each of them with a cheerful smile. The mood changed somewhat when a nurse brought in the papers she had to sign acknowledging she was aware of the surgery that was about to be performed, and knew the risks associated with it. It was standard stuff, and we had seen it before when she had surgery, but this day, it was harder one for her to sign.

Ginny came by, and so we had a chance to visit with her, and then we were joined by the hospital chaplain who was making his morning rounds of surgery patients. He talked briefly with Joanie and asked her if she wanted to pray. She said she did, so he read one a nondenominational prayer, said, "Amen," wished her well, and was on his way.

So far this morning, Joanie was holding it all together quite well. It was shortly after six when the word came it was time to head for the pre-op. One of the nurses brought in wheelchair for the trip, and Joanie smiled and said goodbye to Ginny and thanked her for coming this morning. Ginny was leaving that day for meetings out of town, and I told her I would call her when I had news after the surgery was done.

The pre-op area of the hospital was the same one we had been in before. It was this cold, brightly lit, noisy place, and this morning seemed busier than it had been the last time we were there. It was obvious this Thursday was a big surgery day at the hospital. They showed Joanie a bed, and began the process of hooking up the IV, and checking her blood pressure and pulse. They brought her some blankets that had been heated to ward off the chill in the room, then a nurse came with her file and asked questions regarding her medicines, the last time she ate, any allergies, and the same kind of questions she had answered many times. They were nothing if not thorough in their preparation. I did my best to keep her amused, but I didn't do a very good job, for she had a Kleenex at the ready, and more than once was forced to use it. I began to feel the weight of what was about to happen even more, as I sat there with her. I couldn't imagine what was going through her mind right then, and she never did tell me, even long after it was over.

Next we were visited by the anesthesiologist, a cheerful fellow, one we hadn't met before. He explained to Joanie what

87

his role was going to be during her surgery, and assured her they were going to take very good care of her. Ever the one to want to please, she smiled, thanked him, and he was gone. He was followed shortly by the nurse anesthetist. She explained that she would be helping the anesthesiologist in taking care of Joanie during her surgery, and went to great lengths to reassure Joanie that she was in good hands.

It wasn't too long before Dr. Carson appeared. She was wearing her scrubs, looking every bit the part of the doctor in charge of Joanie's surgery. Joanie liked and trusted her completely, and they talked about what was going to happen next, and she did her best to reassure Joanie that she was in good hands with the doctors who would be participating in the operation. She told Joanie her excellent physical condition boded well for a good outcome, and then she told us it was time to go. The nurse with the Versed came over, but before they gave Joanie the drug that would make her forget where she was, I took her hand, told her I loved her, and kissed her. She said she loved me too, and then the Versed took effect in moments, and as I walked with them while they wheeled the bed toward the OR, I could see it in her eyes. I said goodbye and that I would see her later, though I don't think she heard it. They turned right toward the OR, and I turned left for the surgery waiting room. It was shortly after seven o'clock in the morning. Now there would be nothing left for me to do but wait and worry, especially for the first hour and a half. Assuming the exploratory phase went the way they hoped, I could breathe a little easier, but the worrying would not be over.

I signed in at the surgery waiting room. They wanted the name of the patient I was waiting for and the doctor's name. They also wanted to know where I could be reached in case the doctor needed to talk to me, and told the volunteer at the desk, an elderly older woman, I was going outside for a smoke. I don't think she approved, but I didn't care, it was going to be a long day.

> **"Hope smiles from the threshold of the year to come,**
> **Whispering 'it will be happier'..."**
> **—Alfred Tennyson**

The thing about surgery waiting rooms during the busy times is that you are not alone, but you are. The ones I've been in are generally not very large, and they can seem crowded at times, filled with anxious people, like me, who are waiting for the doctor to come out to see them after the operation on their loved one is over, and rarely, if ever, talking to one another. Isolation in a crowd.

After checking in at the waiting room, I went outside for a smoke and ended up having more than one, not wanting the waiting to begin, even though it already had. I think I was trying to trick my mind into believing that the clock wouldn't start until I took up residence in the waiting room for the day. I picked up the *Star Tribune*, a copy of the *Pioneer Press*, a free copy of *The Onion*, stopped at the coffee cart in the lobby of the hospital for a large cup of coffee and went back up the two floors to begin the waiting.

The place had filled up by now. Looking around it wasn't hard to see the dynamics at play in this room where hope had also taken a seat. I first noticed a group of seven or eight people who were obviously from the same family. Looking around the rest of the room you could also see a couple here, a couple there, and several lone individuals like me. Except for the couples and the family group, you didn't hear much conversation going on, but I noticed one thing they seemed to have in common was the vacant, kindred look of people who were both hopeful and afraid of what they might hear when the doctor comes out to see them. I wondered if I looked the same to them as they did to me. I found a place to sit, drink my coffee and opened one of the newspapers.

It was shortly after eight when I got a surprise. My son Ryan showed up to spend some time with me. He was a student at the University of Minnesota, and it turned out he was there to spend the day with me. It did give me a lift, and we went back outside to talk and so I could have a smoke. I told the volunteer where I was going, and we were only gone about twenty minutes. When we got back to the waiting room she told me that Dr. Carson had been out to see me. My heart stopped. Then she told me the message she got from Carson was that the first phase of the surgery went fine, the margins were good, and they were going ahead with the exenteration. I breathed a sigh of relief, and Ryan and I found a place to sit where I could wait and worry in earnest. The next time we would see Dr. Carson that day would be when the surgery was done.

Anyone who has gone through the waiting and the hoping when a loved one is in surgery, knows that something happens to time. The clock never seems to move, no matter what you try to do to pass the time. For me, reading the newspapers, doing the crossword puzzles and drinking coffee usually would help speed things up. Today, it didn't work.

Ryan and I spent much of the time talking. I got brought up to date on his life at the university, and I updated him on what was going on with Joanie. The time still didn't seem to move. Little by little, in the waiting room, there were fewer and fewer people, as doctors came and went, and family members and couples who had been there in the morning had left after receiving news on the results of whatever surgery had been done on their loved one.

By late afternoon, there were only a few people left, and it wasn't long before Ryan and I were the only ones remaining. These last few hours were going to be the longest ones. I suggested we play some gin, and we found a deck of cards lying about. However, after we checked, we found there were two cards missing from the deck, both jacks, so we had to play the cards we had. We just adjusted how we played around them.

We were still playing at six that evening when Ryan's friend Kim came to join us. I didn't know it then, but they would be married one day. As we talked, and the clocked moved ever so slowly toward the hour of seven, I felt more nervous. I couldn't leave now, in case the surgery was done earlier than they said it would be. Finally, at seven-fifteen that evening the door opened and Dr. Carson came walking in.

Her first words were that Joanie was fine. She told us they were finishing up the surgery, and everything looked good. They would take her to the recovery room where she would remain for about two hours or so, then she would be taken up to the Intensive Care Unit, most likely for two days so they could keep a very close eye on her for any complications that might arise.

She told me the good news about the procedure last, and that was it appeared they would be able to take the ileostomy down after Joanie had time to heal, and hook up her bowel again, so the only thing Joanie would be left with would be the Miami pouch. That was the news I had been waiting to hear, and I know it is the news that Joanie would want to hear. Facing a colostomy for the rest of her life is something she had been dreading.

I felt like a heavy weight had been lifted, and Ryan, Kim, and I headed back to the hotel so I could make calls I needed to her family, Ginny and others. I was so excited to hear the news about being able to take down the ileostomy, I was almost giddy on the walk back. I called her brother Richard in San Francisco and her sister Ann in Bismarck, Ginny and several other people I was supposed to call with news of the surgery. Dick told me he would be flying in the next day to spend a day or two with Joanie. I opened a beer and felt the tension of a day spent wondering, worrying and hoping melt away. Then I walked back to the hospital. I told Ryan and Kim I would meet them later at Stub and Herb's for something to eat, and I headed for the Intensive Care Unit, having no idea of what I would find when I got there.

Joanie hadn't been brought up yet when I arrived, so I just stood around watching what appeared to me to be a chaotic, noisy place with nurses and doctors running about doing nurse and doctor things. It was not what I expected to see.

I walked around for about fifteen or twenty minutes when I saw nurses wheeling a bed toward the ICU, and what I saw almost brought me to my knees. It was Joanie on the bed, but I had to look twice to be sure. What I saw was Joanie, with tubes coming out seemingly from everywhere. They had put in another line on the other side of her neck, and there were IV's connected to both of them. There was the NG tube in her nose that was draining her stomach, and there were bags hanging from both sides of the bed draining her bladder and bowel and I didn't know what else. They had her on a ventilator, so she could hardly talk, and her wrists were tethered to the rails of the bed to keep her from pulling out anything. She was frantic, I could see it, and I was shocked into silence, and felt paralyzed. As a reporter, I had seen some troubling sights in my life, but nothing prepared me for this.

I stood there dumbly wondering what I should do. I stood at the side of her bed, with her looking at me, awake, agitated, frantic and trying to talk, but barely able to be understood. I

92

knew she wanted the ventilator out of her mouth, but the nurse told me that would have to wait. As I stood there helpless, I wanted to cry, but I couldn't. I had never seen anything like this in my life, and I wondered, "What the hell has happened?" All of the clinical talk we had heard before the surgery couldn't have prepared us for what was going on right then. I've never fainted in my life, but that night, I almost did.

I asked one of the nurses if they were going to give her something to settle her down, and she told me they were doing everything they were supposed to be doing, and for me not to worry. I thought, "For Chrissakes, she's telling me not to worry. How am I supposed to do that?"

I admit that I was absolutely as close to losing it as I have ever been, and all I could do was to stand there by her bed, hold her hand, and try not to think about the suffering she was going through and me not being able to do anything about it. It hurt so bad. After being there about an hour after they brought Joanie up, and after they gave her something to sedate her, I left. I couldn't stay any longer, and the image of her lying there stayed with me for a long time.

Walking out the hospital, I was feeling as empty and sad as I ever had in my life. It was different from when, just a few hours earlier, we had walked out feeling so good at the news about the surgery. I got Stub and Herb's and met Ryan and Kim, and they asked me how things were. All I could say was, "I've never seen anything like that in my life." I nibbled on some appetizer we ordered, drank a beer and went to the hotel. Back in my room, I checked the clock, and it was midnight, I sat down at the table by the window, lit a cigarette, and looked out toward the place where Joanie lay, and thought, "I'm really tired."

The morning after, some good signs.

I woke early on Friday morning, and, after shaking the cobwebs out of my brain, and half hoping the nightmare scene I had witnessed the night before, was just that, got busy getting ready for another day at the hospital. Of course, I knew it wasn't, but I could still wish that it was.

Back at the hospital before eight, I went directly to the Intensive Care Unit. I found Joanie sleeping, and the ventilator gone. I took that as a good sign. I asked the nurse how she was doing, and was told she was doing well, and they might be able to move her out of ICU later in the day. I took that as another good sign. Initially they had expected her to be in ICU for two to three days.

The ICU didn't seem to me to be as chaotic as it had been the night before, and I think that was partly because I had settled down myself, and partly because it truly was not. My focus was back on what we do next, and what part I might play in helping her through this recovery.

She had obviously been in much pain the night before, and still was this morning. In her hand was the morphine pump, the device that is connected to an IV bag that contained the relief giving drug. I was to observe later, that she would pump it even when nothing would come out. I don't think she knew right away that it was programmed to only release a prescribed dose over a specified period of time, no matter how many times you press the button, and when you're in pain it doesn't make any difference, you push it anyway.

I hadn't been there too long when she opened her eyes and looked at me. It was a much different look than I had seen the night before. It was obvious she was heavily medicated, and our conversation was short. I think it was enough for her to know that I was there and would be close by, and she drifted off to sleep again. I went for coffee and a smoke, and began thinking about her recovery, and how long that was going to take. I couldn't help but think it was going to take longer than the optimistic estimate of two weeks we had been given. I would turn out to be right.

As I have been in the process of constructing this narrative, I thought a couple of other points of view would help in understanding what I had seen that night when they brought Joanie up to ICU from the recovery room. So, I contacted two people who saw her the next day, and asked them to recall what they saw when they came to visit Joanie. About mid-morning, Barb Olson, a longtime friend from Bismarck came to the hospital. Barb was the former First Lady of North Dakota when her husband Al was governor. Barb had known Joanie much longer than I had and was a close friend. I met her in the lobby and tried to prepare her for what she might see when we went up to the ICU. I warned her this would not be Joanie as she was used to seeing, and it might be that she wouldn't remember seeing her.

When we got to Joanie's bed, she opened her eyes, and recognizing Barb, she made an attempt to smile, but it was a weak one. We weren't there very long when she closed her eyes again, and Barb and I left. Barb was stunned at what she had seen, and recently I asked if she remembered what she thought after that visit to the ICU. This is what Barb told me: "I know I was nervous when you said I should go in to see her even though she was deeply sedated. I didn't know what to expect after hearing how radical her surgery was and also how long it took. I remember that she had tubes coming out of everywhere. She was so swollen and so still. I think I just told her I loved her and was so glad she was so sedated because I couldn't imagine how painful her body must be after all they did. My other recollection was your positive outlook. It was going to be curative and so now it was just getting Joanie through the recovery of this surgery. The worst was over."

Later that day, another friend from Bismarck, Cathy Rydell, one of Joanie's closest friends who was in town for a meeting came up to see her. This is what Cathy had to say about that day in ICU: "What I remember most is her face. Joanie had always had the face of an angel. Bright eyes, expressive smile, cheerful glow...it was a face full of sunshine. There was no smile like a Joanie smile. I walked into the room and the woman in the bed was unrecognizable to me. Her face was gray and unexpressive. Her eyes were blank and her body looked so frail. My heart sank. I knew she had been through hell with such a radical surgery but I wasn't prepared for what I saw (even though Bob had tried to prepare me). I held her hand and told her I loved her. She attempted a smile and said a few words. I left the room, broke down, and started praying that the Joanie I knew and loved would be back soon. After seeing her Bob sat with me in the lobby and told me about the surgery, the anticipated recovery and the challenges ahead. I think I heard about 10 percent of what he said. I do remember that I was amazed at his knowledge and his determination to find out all he could about her illness."

I remember thinking that after seeing Joanie in ICU, they had an idea of the magnitude of the surgery she had gone through, and how slow the recovery might be.

Her brother Dick arrived from San Francisco and had a chance to see her. I think it gave her a lift to see that he was there, but she was still groggy and in and out of being awake and not able to talk much. Dick and I went for a bite to eat, and I filled him in as best I could on what had transpired. Then, back at the hospital, about seven, they brought Joanie back up to her room on 7C. She had been in ICU for fewer than twenty-four hours. I took that to be a good sign.

The healing begins.

It always seemed to me that the aim of surgery was to make the person whole again. In Joanie's case, it was different. While the surgery she underwent, was meant to be "curative," it wasn't going to make her whole again; instead, it was meant to create something different in order to prolong her life. The recovery from that surgery meant it would take an exceptional effort on her part to make it a reality. Starting on the Friday night she was wheeled back up to her room on 7C from the Intensive Care Unit, it all began.

Back in her room on 7C, Joanie still had multiple tubes coming out of her body, several drainage bags hanging on the sides of the bed, and IV poles holding bags of fluid and pain killers being fed through the line in the side of her neck. It didn't seem as dramatic as it had the night when I saw her come up to the Intensive Care Unit from the recovery room, and now the focus had shifted to healing.

Having Dick with us seemed to help her, but it was hard to tell. She was still groggy from the drugs and the morphine that were dripping into her veins, and would drift off regularly. Talking to her days later, as one might expect, she remembered Dick being there, but not a lot else about that first day post-surgery.

On Saturday morning, when I got to the hospital, I could see a difference already. While still groggy, she was more alert than she had been the night before when Dick and I had left her. As we were talking that morning, a nurse came in and informed Joanie it was time to get up and try to go for a walk. She seemed a little uneasy about that, but as a patient who wanted to please the nurses and doctors, she said okay.

Getting ready for that first walk post-surgery took some doing. The first thing they had to do was remove the pneumatic leggings, the ones used to stimulate blood flow to her legs while being bedridden. Then, once she was sitting up, they adjusted the IV lines, and hooked the bags to the IV pole so she could begin her walk. Her first steps were tentative, and I knew she was nervous. Holding on to my arm, she walked about ten feet, which took her to the door of her room, and then walked the ten feet back to the bed. That, she informed me was enough for her first time. Later that afternoon, we would do it again, and this time she made it 60 feet out and 60 feet back. I figured it was a remarkably good start.

Earlier that day, after her first walk, I told her I was going to go and check out of the Radisson and move my stuff over to Tom Sand's place. Dick was there, so that was okay. My son Ryan came to the hospital, and he helped me move to Tom's, where I would crash for the duration.

The remainder of Saturday with Dick and me there was spent in and out of the hospital room. It was then I first learned about sponge on a stick. Joanie couldn't have anything by mouth until the NG tube was either clamped or removed, and that meant anything. The pink sponge on a stick was just that, a small bit of sponge on a stick like you would find when you got a Tootsie Pop. It was something she could use to wet her lips with some cold water when she was thirsty, but nothing more. It would be one of my jobs to see the water the sponge was dipped in was ice cold. The fact she couldn't drink anything, did nothing to help her disposition, but at this point, it was all she could do.

Considering it was only day two since she had surgery and she was still dealing with a good deal of pain, Saturday turned out to be a pretty good day. We still had a long way to go, but the healing process had begun, and so we said good night to Joanie and I gave Dick a ride to where he was staying and headed for St. Paul. There would be more work to be done tomorrow.

Progress is measured in steps, and those damn numbers.

Sunday morning, the third day after her surgery, I found Joanie still very much in pain, but it was under control. She had the morphine pump close at hand but wasn't pressing it as often as she had yesterday. The pain by itself was not surprising since her body was trying to retain equilibrium after Thursday's assault. I began to see the process more clearly now, and what my role was going to be for the immediate future.

One of the first things I learned was, besides being Joanie's support in the hospital, I was going to be the nurses' friend. While I had just one to worry about, the nurses on the floor each had four or five patients, at any given time, under their care. That meant it was my job to keep an eye on Joanie when they weren't around and to call things to their attention that I thought they needed to know. Once they realized I was going to be around all of the time, and wasn't being overly demanding, but was interested in helping them help Joanie, I got along fine with all of them. I was struck at the time by the professionalism and compassion every one of the nurses on the floor exhibited in their dealing with patients who were in the worst possible place in their lives. My respect for them remains to this day.

This morning, Joanie was not as groggy as she had been the day before, and her energy level was better. After some small talk, the nurse who was her charge for the day, came in and told her it was time for walk. Again it took some arranging to get her ready, and once she was standing, and the bags were hooked onto the IV pole, she took my arm and we headed out of her room. It was quite a sight, Joanie in her hospital gown, bags hanging from the pole, which was on wheels, lines going into her neck, and holding on to my arm and trying to smile. She was more relaxed today and with my encouragement she walked further. On Saturday, she had walked 120 feet in the afternoon. Today, she made it 320 feet. Later that afternoon, the scene was repeated and she walked with her brother Dick for a total of 400 feet. Progress, I was to find, was measured in steps. She was proud, but not as proud as I was.

Dr. Carson stopped by in the afternoon to check on Joanie while her brother Dick and I were there, and then I heard something I wasn't prepared for when Carson said something about there being a 60 percent chance of long-term survivability, i.e., the magic five-year number, from this procedure. I don't think Joanie heard it, and if she did, I don't think it registered. I waited until she was done with Joanie and followed her out into the hall, and asked her about the number, since that surgery was supposed to be "curative." She said it was the statistical number based on the number of patients who had undergone the procedure and had been followed. The number didn't, or couldn't, include the number of patients who for one reason or another weren't followed, or who had died from some other cause. At the time, I was dismayed by having another uncertainty factor introduced, but when I checked out the literature later on the computer, I found the doctor, not surprisingly, to be correct. Joanie and I wouldn't talk about that number until a couple of years down the road. But, for me, the statistical five-year clock had begun ticking again.

Since her brother was still here and would be leaving on Monday afternoon, I took the opportunity to meet friends of ours, John and Deb Milne, for dinner at Monte Carlo, one of our favorite restaurants in Minneapolis. Joanie told me it was okay, and instructed me to greet them for her. I did as I was told.

It was good to get out of the hospital, knowing that Dick was there. The chance to spend time with friends was a pleasant respite, as I knew Monday was going to be a stressful day. With radiation treatment entering the picture and Dick leaving it, I was expecting a difficult time for Joanie.

"I hate to take time away from somebody who is really sick." — Joanie

It was Monday, February 16, and we had only been gone from Bismarck for a week, but it seemed like a month already. Joanie was awake when I got to the hospital in the morning, and Dick showed up not long afterwards. They got her up for a walk, and to her credit, she made it further than she had on Sunday. She was, however not looking forward to what was coming next radiation.

During the exenteration surgery, they had placed nylon catheters in the area of her pelvis they considered a "higher risk for local recurrence" of the cancer. Today they would load iridium seeds, and they would remain there for five to six days. She tolerated this part of her recovery better than I had anticipated, remaining alert most of the time despite the drugs and being so tired. On Tuesday, we were told they would take her down to radiology on Wednesday, and increase the dosage so they could take the catheters out sooner. Later that afternoon, Dr. Cosin stopped in to see Joanie and told her she was doing well, and they may be able to clamp the NG tube, the one that drains her stomach, when the radiation ends, and then, if she doesn't get nauseous, they will take it out. This would be a major step in the progress of her recovery.

Another bit of good news that day was that she was beginning to pass some gas. It was probably the first time in her life she wasn't embarrassed about doing so. It was especially good news, because she still can't take anything by mouth until they're sure her bowel is working. It had been a week now since we checked her into the hospital, and that was the last time she had any solid food.

On Wednesday, I talked with Dr. Dusenbery, and she brought us up to speed on what the plan. She said they would come up to Joanie's room, unload the seeds that were in there now, take her down to radiology and put in a stronger dosage so they could take it out a day early, which would mean Friday. Joanie was doing well that morning, and was alert and joking with the radiologists who were taking her down to the therapeutic radiology department to put in the stronger dosage of seeds.

The next morning, however, wasn't the same. When I got to the hospital, I found her to be uncomfortable and slightly agitated. She told me she had a bad night. They hadn't been in her room yet this morning to clean her up and change clothes, and it was hot in the room. She told me she didn't know if she could go through another week like this one, but then hastened to add, "I won't have to because the radiation will be gone." In some ways I felt I had let her down, since my job was to be there and see that she got what she needed.

I went looking for Barb, Joanie's nurse for the day shift, and told her that Joanie was uncomfortable and agitated, and wondered how to turn down the heat in her room. When I got back to the room, Joanie said, "I hate to take time away from somebody who is really sick." I couldn't believe I heard what she said, but then I realized who I was hearing say those words.

When Barb got to the room, Joanie almost apologized, and said to her what she had said to me a few minutes earlier. Barb told her she had gone far above and beyond the call of duty. Joanie said others had had this surgery, but Barb told her that not all have had radiation during their immediate recovery period like she was having.

Barb got her cleaned up, and clothes changed, and the room began to cool down. The activity tired Joanie out, and she drifted off to sleep. As I sat and looked around her room then, I continued to be amazed at this whole thing. She lay there with about half-dozen tubes draining out of her into bags hanging on the side of her bed, five in her mid-section and one from her nose. Then she had another half-dozen bags hanging from the IV pole, including the one with the morphine, all dripping stuff into her through the IV line on the right side of her neck.

All of that, and she hates "to take time away from somebody who is really sick." I couldn't have loved her more at that moment than I did.

Joanie has many friends.

It hadn't been a week since Joanie's surgery, but her hospital room was taking on the look of a greenhouse. There were flowers that had been being delivered since the first day, and almost every day since, and they took up every open space in the room except for her bedside table and the chair in which I sat.

Nurses who would deliver the gifts, both cut flowers and plants each day, marveled at the sight in her room. Even my chair might have been used, but it was too unstable for a vase of flowers, or I think they might have put flowers or a plant there too, and I would be forced to stand or squat on my haunches providing an interesting sight to anyone passing by the door to her room. You never really know how many friends you have until you are in a difficult situation. Joanie was in a difficult situation, and the outpouring from friends, co-workers, acquaintances, and others was something that astounded her. The flowers, the cards, the phone calls, and the visits amazed me as well. I knew she had a lot of friends, but had not expected anything like I was seeing, as every day brought a new batch of cards and gifts. Joanie couldn't believe it either, and even though in the early days after the surgery she was tired and under the influence of the heavy duty painkiller, morphine, she would shake her head in disbelief at each card or gift I would open for her.

I had become her social secretary, as well as the indoor gardener, for the duration of her hospital stay, and per her instructions, I recorded every card she received, on the date she received it. I also kept track of every phone call we received or made during the time she was in the hospital, and I did the same with gifts and flowers, and had a complete record by the time we were ready to get her out of the hospital and back home to Bismarck and her kitties.

The office of Governor Ed Schafer sent a box of gifts from the staff with the instructions that she was to open only one per day until the box was empty. We never varied from those instructions, and I recorded each and every one. Some days, I wasn't sure she knew what it was, or remembered who it was from, but she had the record to look at when she got home.

Cathy Rydell, one of her best friends who had seen her in ICU the day after "the big one," called me about a week after surgery and told me she wanted me to check with Joanie and see if it was okay with her that Cathy could start a fundraising effort, called "The Friends of Joan Wigen," to help us defray the costs associated with the medical problems she was facing and help with costs that weren't covered by insurance. I ran it by Joanie, and she shook her head, not believing anyone would do that, but she said okay. One thing she didn't want to know was who the contributors were, and I relayed that to Cathy. Cathy would be in charge of any funds raised and would disburse them based on bills and receipts presented. She told me her aim was to raise five to ten thousand dollars. When I told Joanie about that, she couldn't believe it. We never did see a list of those contributors, but, jumping ahead to December 1998, Joanie wrote a letter for Cathy to send out to the donors, thanking them for their support.

This is what she wrote:

December 17, 1998

Dear Friends,

I would like to have personalized this letter, but since Cathy hasn't shown me a list I don't know who I should be addressing it to. This greeting, however, is personal as are the words that follow. This year, as you know, has not been one of the easiest that I've experienced in my life, and since you will be receiving this you are among those who have an idea of what has taken place since February.

I thought that this letter, which is basically an update on the state of my health, both physical and mental, is in order this holiday season. It seems to me that this is a good time for reflection and thanks that I'm doing well, and to thank those of you who were so generous in your support for us during the difficult period earlier this year.

First of all, I'm doing well. I'm feeling fine, and feel stronger every day. I'm back to work almost full-time following surgery in September, and I'm adjusting to my new situation with what the doctors call my "appliance" as best I can.

As you know, I had what was supposed to be a temporary ileostomy following that unpleasant surgery in February, and had been looking forward to them being able to reverse that process. Unfortunately, there had been too much tissue damage from radiation in 1996, and February of this year, and they were unable to do that. That was a disappointment, because it meant a permanent colostomy. However, the good news is that cancer is nowhere to be found, and my doctors say I should be around for a long, long, time now. Long enough I suppose to turn every last hair on Bob's head completely white.

Bob, by the way, has been my rock through all of this. His quiet confidence and unflappable nature has helped me through the darkest hours of this medical ordeal and I'm not sure what I would have done without him, though he tells me I would have done just fine.

So, that's the update, and now on to the real purpose of this letter. I want each and every one of you to know how much your generosity was appreciated, and how much it helped ease the financial strain connected with my illness. Your friendship is a valued thing, and in some ways, a simple thank you doesn't seem enough. What you and others did for Bob and me this year is something that will never be forgotten. I want you all to know that, and this Christmas, especially, we will be thinking of you, even though we don't know the names on the list.

Again our thanks, and have a great Christmas. Joanie

This wasn't the only show of support and generosity she would experience over the ensuing years and it would not be the last, but it was indicative of just how many real friends Joanie had, and what they would do for her when she was sick.

"Home by the first."

One of the gifts Joanie got was a Walkman and a tape of the highlights of *Les Miserables*. She wasn't going to use it for a while, so I opened it today and while I listened to it, I was reminded that while one is surrounded by pain, disease, and suffering there are beautiful things like great music. It was easy to forget that when you are in the middle of helping someone get through a major life-threatening situation.

I got the hospital around nine Friday morning, February 20, the eighth day after Joanie's surgery. When I got there I saw that what we called the "nose tube" was gone. The technical name was the NG tube, and it was the one that drained her stomach to keep her from getting nauseous. They were also giving her a unit of blood because her hemoglobin had dropped, something they attributed to the fact that there was so much fluid being fed on the IVs her hemoglobin tended to drop over time, Not a serious matter. The first thing she asked me after I had been there but a few minutes, if I checked the plants and flowers for water. I did so, and added water where it was needed as she watched to be sure I didn't miss any. She did this every day, and I didn't mind. It was my job.

The nose tube coming out was a major deal in our minds, since it signaled some real progress in the healing process. It would still be some time before she would be able to resume clear liquids. They were being very cautious in this process, and she had to be passing gas well before she'll be able to consume any quantity of anything.

Another positive today was the end of radiation, and the removal around five o'clock, of both the iridium seeds as well the vaginal mold they had made when they constructed her neovagina during surgery, using part of her stomach muscle. Taken together, all of this made for a good Friday for us. She

107

was now able to sit comfortably and feel like progress is being made despite still being tethered to the IV pole and with all of the drains yet to come out.

I had gone out for a smoke around three that afternoon, and as I was watching the transition from a weekday to weekend, it occurred to me that hospitals are like a lot of businesses. Friday afternoon signals the arrival of the weekend and the weekend staff. In a building that is built to accommodate a lot of human activity and a lot of people, it is really noticeable when the weekend rolls around. All of sudden, say three-thirty in the afternoon at the U of M Hospital, that meant the shift change had taken place, and when I walked back in to the lobby, I could feel the change. It was quieter, and there were fewer people milling about. The lobby coffee cart was gone. The piano in the corner was silent, and as I rode the elevator up to 7C, I was the lone occupant, something that happened rarely on weekdays, but was normal on the weekend.

When I got to Joanie's room, she was sleeping, with morphine pump in hand. She looked relaxed, as if the tension of the week of radiation had melted away. On 7C, you could feel the change as well. It seemed less frantic than it had earlier in the day, and from Joanie's room, when the door was open, you could hear the muffled chatter and laughter of the nurses and interns who had drawn the weekend duty. I knew most of them by now, and they knew me, and occasionally I would stand and chat with them at the station when Joanie was sleeping and things were slow on the floor. They were also the ones who validated my parking ticket and would often ask me before I left if it had been stamped. They remembered I had once walked to the ramp before I realized my mistake, and had to make the trek back to 7C to get the stamp. I thought of their kindness as caregivers taking care of another caregiver.

Later, when Joanie awoke, she was feeling better, and we began talking about how much longer she might have to be in the hospital. For her, it had already been too long, and she was ready to go home, though she knew that wasn't possible right now. We got a visit from Dr. Cosin that changed everything that night. While we had been told that the recovery time from the surgery would be about two weeks, after I saw her after surgery I didn't believe it. Tonight, Cosin told us barring anything unforeseen, she would "be home by the first"!

Her smile lit up the room, and it almost made a believer out of me, for that would be seventeen days after the surgery. For her sake, I hoped she wouldn't be disappointed. We talked more about this news, and both agreed to keep our fingers crossed. Around ten o'clock that night I kissed her goodnight and headed for Tom's. As I got off the elevator on the main floor and walked through the darkened lobby, the night security guy, whom I gotten to know by now, asked my how she was doing. I told him she was doing better than ever, and we could be getting her out of here by the first. He smiled at me and said, "Good for her."

As I walked to the parking ramp, I thought to myself, "Yeah, good for her."

"Hope is the thing with feathers, that perches in the soul, and sings the tune without words, and never stops at all."
—Emily Dickinson

Saturday morning arrived, and when I got to the hospital that morning, Joanie and I walked. This time she walked all the way around the nurse's station on 7C, which meant down one long hall, around the corner and down another long hall and back by the nurse's station and to her room. It was a major walk, the longest she had taken in the nine days since her surgery.

I think the energy came from hearing Dr. Cosin tell her yesterday she should start thinking about going home by the first of March. That hope, along with the take down of the NG tube seemed to have given her more life than I'd seen since before the surgery. She had a shower and then for the first time a shampoo of that thick, black, wavy head of hair she wore so well, and then she decided she would nap for a while. I went out for a smoke and to make a couple of calls. It was a little chilly that day, but I hardly noticed.

Ginny and Ed stopped by in the morning to see her, and she was glad to be able to tell them all about the possibility of going home in just over a week. I learned something from Ed that day about hospital visiting protocol. They had been in Joanie's room over five minutes or so, when Ed told Ginny they should go since they were over the five-minute rule. I asked Ed what that was about, and he told me in his family the rule when you came to visit someone in the hospital was you never stayed any longer than five minutes. Since visitors can tire a patient out, and five minutes is plenty of time to let the patient know you are thinking of them and long enough for the visitor to get an idea of how the patient is doing. I thought of what Ed had told me on a couple of occasions when I invoked the rule without telling people I was doing so.

Two people who didn't need to be told about the rule were my sisters: Jane, from Fargo, and Joni, from St. Cloud. They came down today to, as Joni said, "To lay my eyes on my friend." Both Jane and Joni knew a thing or two about hospitals, so after they spent some time visiting with Joanie and heard our news, they suggested we go get some lunch and give her a chance to rest.

We headed for the Loon Cafe, and it was a welcome chance to spend some time with them, and as always, when we would be together, laughter reigned supreme. I learned during this stretch, that as a caregiver, you need timeouts. They help keep you on an even keel.

When I got back to the hospital after lunch, they were preparing to change Joanie's IV, and being unhooked from the IV and morphine for the first time caused her some anxiety. Anxiety because they couldn't hook her back up until after they had taken her down for an X-ray and had a look at it, and that would take a couple of hours. They didn't tell either one of us what they were hoping to see, but I assumed they knew what they were doing.

The anxiety seemed normal enough to me under the circumstances, especially since she had become dependent on the morphine during these last nine days to keep her pain under control. They knew that, too, and assured her it wouldn't be very long, and they were right. When they hooked her back up, she relaxed and once everything was back in its place, she drifted off to sleep and I went for a smoke. On the elevator down, I thought, "I wonder if they give frequent rider miles?" I had already made so many trips up and down, I couldn't begin to count, and thought they should be worth something.

When I got back to her room, more good news. The first drain tube came out! For us, this was an event. It meant maybe Cosin was right. Couple that with her having her first drink of anything, when she had some Sprite, and Saturday was shaping up to be one of the best days yet.

Around 5:30 or so, I walked over to Sally's for a beer and a little dinner. I was feeling better about how things were going than I had since the beginning, and I called her siblings, Dick and Ann, to let them know how positive things were looking today.

When I got back to the hospital, the rest of the evening seemed to fly by. We went for another long walk and watched some TV, and about 9:30 she looked at me and said, "You should go now." When I asked if she was sure, she just smiled and said, "Go."

As I left the room she was relaxed and smiling. As I walked through the lobby, I saw my friend the night security guy, and as he did every night, he asked me how she was doing. I just gave him a thumbs up, he nodded and smiled, and I headed for the parking ramp and the drive to Tom's in St. Paul feeling really good. It had been a good day, and hopes were high.

"Her Baxter is beeping."

Sunday morning, and my drive to the hospital was a quick one. Traffic was very light, and I was looking forward to getting there and perhaps getting some more good news. For the first time since Joanie's surgery, I began to feel that Dr. Carson's prediction of a two-week recovery rate could become a reality. I hadn't feel that way initially. When I saw her in ICU that night after surgery, I doubted we'd be out of here in a month.

My drives from our friend Tom's place were usually accompanied by some apprehension, with me never knowing what I might find when I got to Joanie's room. I assumed that because I had not received a phone call that things were okay, but I still traveled those few short miles not knowing. Today was different, and I was optimistic about what I would find when I got there, and it also could be the first day of her last week in the hospital.

It was Sunday, and so the lobby coffee cart wasn't open, much to my disappointment. While it wasn't Starbucks, they did have it all; freshly ground coffee, lattes, mochas, espressos, and some killer pastry. When it was open, especially in the morning, there was always a line. You would find nurses and doctors in scrubs, patients, and visitors like me waiting patiently to purchase the magic elixir that would help them make it through the day. On Sunday, however, I was forced to go to the cafeteria on the eighth floor for a cup of the stuff you would expect to find in a cafeteria. If you have spent any amount of time in a hospital, you know what I'm talking about.

Joanie, like me, was a coffee drinker, and at first I felt a little guilty about arriving in her room with a cup of coffee that she couldn't enjoy as well. I once asked her if it bothered her and told her I wouldn't bring it with me if it did. She just told me it was okay, and besides, she couldn't have had any if she wanted to.

When I got to her room, I saw that there was one less IV hanging on the pole, and one of the Baxters was gone. Baxter was the brand name of the machines that the IV tubes were threaded through and then they could be programmed to deliver a prescribed amount of fluid over a specified period of time. I would learn later they were called "infusion" pumps, and at one time Joanie had three of them hanging from the IV pole by her bed. One of the things I noticed early on, was that the Baxter would beep from time to time, and the first time it happened while I was in her room, it concerned me. I wasn't sure what it meant, the only thing I knew was that it was beeping, and I assumed it wasn't supposed to be, and if it were, something must be wrong. So, in connection with my job of helping the nurses take care of Joanie, I would go and stand in the doorway of her room hoping to catch the eye of her nurse for the day and tell her, "Her Baxter is beeping." If her nurse was busy with another patient, and the Baxter was still beeping, I would go to the nurse's station and just quietly tell the nurse there, "Her Baxter is beeping," They knew me, and they knew who I was talking about, and seeming not the least bit alarmed, the nurse would tell me someone would be by soon to take care of it, and it was nothing to worry about.

She was, of course, right. When Joanie's nurse came in, she just calmly pressed a button, the beeping stopped, and she told me this time it just meant they had to change IV bags. She also told me that sometimes the plastic tubing that was used to deliver the fluid to the line in her neck would get kinked, and that would cause the Baxter to beep. She told me all I had to do next time, was press the nurse call button, and someone would be in to take care of it. So, the beeping Baxter being taken care of, we got her ready for a morning walk. Today it would be different. They unhooked her from the IV, and for the first time, we went for a long walk without the IV pole. There were still drain bags hanging from belt around her waist, but to be out and about without the IV was a major step from our perspective. I could tell it in her demeanor, and her spirits were good as well. They were so good that we walked on several occasions that afternoon and evening.

Later that day, more good news came when another of the drain tubes came out, and they began to give her pain control by pill to get her off the morphine. She didn't seem to mind at all when she lost the morphine pump. I was glad to see it gone myself. She was drinking water and sipping on some Sprite during the day, and though she could have tried eating a bit of solid food, she wasn't comfortable enough yet for that. All in all, it had been a very good weekend, and we both felt that real progress toward the goal of getting out of here by the first had been made.

There was still a long way to go. She had to be able to handle solid food, there were a few more drain tubes to come out, and then there was the business of self-catheterizing of the Miami pouch to be dealt with, along with the learning curve surrounding the changing and care the ileostomy. While both Joanie and I were aware of what needed to be done yet, that knowledge did nothing to dampen the optimism that came with the positive developments that had taken place over the last two days.

When I left her that night, her eyes were bright, her Baxter was quiet, and she was as relaxed as I've seen her since they brought her back to her room ten days ago.

Where the Popsicles Are

Post-surgical thirst leaves
Dry lips and mouth.
Small ice chips soothe
As do the cool wet sponge swabs.
But someone needs to know
Where the popsicles are.
With their promise of
Cherry crystals and icy, cold relief,
Comes a sweet, wet cold that washes over your lips
And rolls around in your mouth.
A cold, as you swallow, that says things are better,
And you will be okay.
But someone needs to know
Where the popsicles are.

Joanie had already had a shower and a change of clothes by the time I go there on Monday morning, and it had tired her out. She told me she hadn't slept that well last night either.

115

For her, showering was not a simple exercise, so we put off walking for later and I let her sleep for a while. I went out to pick up a mocha from the lobby cart and my two daily papers so I could get going on the crosswords for the day. Besides a book or two I carried with me at all times, they helped me pass the time when she was sleeping.

We walked that afternoon, and the rest of the day was made up of her drifting off, me going out for a smoke, and going for a walk again. What wasn't routine was after our last walk she notice one of the tubes leaking, and it turned out to be one from her kidney. The nurse didn't seem alarmed, improvised a solution and as far as we knew all was well. It had shaken Joanie just a bit, but the professionalism of the nurse and the way she handled the situation put her at ease.

One of the things I had learned early in this process was to find out where the ice cubes were so I could keep the pitcher on her bedside table filled with cold water. Even when she couldn't drink anything, we would dip the little pink sponges in the ice water to cool her tongue and lips. If you've ever been really thirsty, you know there's nothing like that icy liquid to cool off the inside of your mouth. Now that the nose tube was gone and she could take in liquid, it was more important than ever that I keep the pitcher cold at all times. Plus, every time she asked me if I had checked the plants and flowers, I would be ready.

The nurses who showed me where to find the ice and cups and what I needed were happy to do so. They knew I was there to help them, so when Joanie was ready to try other liquids, one of them showed me something special. She showed me the freezer where they kept the popsicles. She told me I was free to come and get one for Joanie anytime she wanted one. After that, I went to the room and asked Joanie if she'd like to try a popsicle. They had several flavors, and she

116

was both surprised and happy to opt for cherry, so I hurried off to get her one. They were not singles, but the old familiar popsicles with two sticks that you separated. We shared the popsicle, since I knew she wouldn't have more than one, and we both enjoyed the cold sensation that comes with that frozen treat more than we ever had. Anytime she wanted one, I could tell her, "I know where the popsicles are."

Around seven o'clock that night, they brought her the first solid food she had even seen since the Tuesday we had lunch before she was admitted. The menu included turkey, dressing, gravy, pineapple chunks, a roll, chocolate chip cookie, and skim milk. She ate, not that much, but she ate. She had a bite of the roll, about seven bites of turkey, (and yes, I counted them) and a little of the milk.

About 8:30 that night, Dr. Cosin came by to see her, and told her in all of the exent cases he had been involved in, "No one has ever eaten solid food so soon after surgery as you have." He then went on to say they would be taking down the IVs tomorrow, and she should start thinking about going home this weekend. He said, "You're a star!" Even though Joanie had a somewhat uncomfortable day, this brought a smile to her face, and she forgot everything that had happened earlier.

Taking charge.

Today marked the seventeenth day we'd been gone from Bismarck, and the fourteenth since her surgery. It seemed like we'd been gone a month.

What I came to understand about time going through this process was that when you are involved in an intense situation, and your focus is on only one thing, the days just run together, and it was only when I would look at the calendar or my notebook would I think about the actual

117

number of days we'd been gone. This was the longest we'd ever been away from home, and for some reason today, out of the blue, she said, "I wonder how my kitties are doing." Then she dozed off, and I left for lunch with a friend or ours, Tom Forsythe. As I was leaving, I ran into Dr. Cosin in the hall, and he asked me how she was doing. I told him she was sound asleep, and he said she needed to catch up. By Thursday morning, it became obvious Joanie would not be discharged this weekend, and now, it appeared we might get her out by midweek, assuming there were no more problems cropping up.

When I got to her room that morning, she was sleeping, and the NG tube was in place. After she woke up, she told me the nurses must have heeded Dr. Cosin's order not to disturb her, and no one had bothered her until about six o'clock in the morning, when they gave her another shot of Ativan. She was tired, and told me she didn't want to talk to anyone today, so we kept the phone turned off all day. The rest of that day was quiet, with her sleeping through most of it. Around five I went to Stub and Herb's for a beer and some munchies. When I got back, she was awake, and waiting for them to take her down for another stomach X-ray. I don't know how many times they took pictures of her, but it seemed like they were doing it every day. We weren't even sure what they were looking for, and they didn't tell us.

Around eight o'clock they gave her another shot of Ativan, and shortly she was out. I left around eight-thirty, the earliest I had left since we got here.

Friday morning came, and when I got to Joanie's room, I saw that the NG tube was gone again. Seems they had been trying to adjust it, when it came out, and they had some trouble trying to reinsert it. The doctor on duty told them as long as she was doing okay to leave it out for now. The rest of the day was spent sleeping, walking, and for me, watering the plants, doing the crosswords, and riding the elevator going out for smokes. Ginny and Ed had stopped by for a while, and the quiet of another Friday washed over the hospital around mid-afternoon as another weekend was upon us and time slowed down again.

On Saturday morning I could see that Joanie had improved somewhat. As usual, the process of taking a shower and changing clothes tired her out, but she seemed to be doing better in spite of it. One of the nurses suggested I take her for a ride outside in a wheelchair, and it sounded like a good idea. She hadn't been outside in a long time, and had nothing to breathe but hospital air.

While it was late February, the weather hadn't been too bad, and this morning, I thought we might be able to get her out for a few minutes. Well, as luck would have it, that afternoon, it started to snow, not much, just a few flakes, but it was enough to put off the ride outside. Instead of that we walked around the halls of 7C a few times.

They took the surgical staples out today, another good sign, and I went to the convenience store and picked up some 7-UP for her. She had had enough of Sprite for the time being. That evening she was out of sorts, and I mentioned it to Barb. She came in and gave her something to relax, and it wasn't long before she went to sleep. Sunday morning and it was March 1. It was hard to believe that February was gone and Joanie was still in the hospital.

When I got to the hospital, she said she didn't have a bad night, and after taking a couple of sips of the real 7-UP, she told me she didn't want to go walking until later and was going to take a nap. I went for the Sunday paper and some coffee.

It was a quiet day, with the only visitors today, Ginny and Ed, who came by shortly before noon. For the rest of the day it was just Joanie and me, and we went for a short walk, she took a nap, and I went for a smoke, a routine we repeated several times that day. That evening, she was feeling pretty alert, and I thought it would be a good time for us to have a talk about how we were going to handle this change in her life after the hospital. We talked about the reality of the ileostomy, which we hoped would be temporary, and the catheterization of her Miami pouch. Just these two changes alone are enough to put stress on anybody. The other thing we had to live with was the fact that she wouldn't be considered "cancer free" until five years from now.

I suggested to her that we had two options to choose from. The first was that we could let this disease dictate the course of our lives from now on outside of the demands of the ileostomy and the Miami pouch that would have to be dealt with. The other option was that we could take charge of this disease and its effect on our lives from now on, and outside of the clinic appointments and keeping an eye on everything, we could go about living as if this whole thing were something of an inconvenience, something that could be handled without making it a big deal.

Joanie looked at me while I laid out what I saw were the two options, and she told me as far as she was concerned, there was only one option, and that she was going to get on with her life when she got out of here, and nothing was going to get in her way. She was going to survive, there was no question. She let me know that she was going to take charge, and that was it.

I never doubted her, and I was to see evidence of it later this week.

Things begin to move.

Monday morning it had been three weeks since we left Bismarck. Today, Dr. Chen told us he wanted Joanie out of her before Dr. Carson got back. She was out of town for a week or so. That meant out of here by the weekend. That pronouncement from Chen seemed to give her some energy. She did have a little bit of toast in the morning, and the rest of the day we spent walking and sleeping. The phone was back on, and things were starting to look up.

On Tuesday morning, she had some orange juice, but didn't eat anything. She was still a little gun shy of eating too much. She was fearful of getting sick like she did last week, and she didn't want that to get in the way of getting out of here by the weekend. She lost one more IV bag in the morning and had taken a couple of pills and kept them down.

Most of the rest of the day, she was uncomfortable with what they figured were gas pains. We would walk, and she would sit up, but nothing seemed to help. Then, later that evening while nurse Nan and I were in the room, she threw up. After we got her cleaned up, she said she felt better than she had all day. There wasn't any reason as near as we could determine, but the important thing was that she was feeling better.

They were scheduled to take a look at the stents tomorrow with the idea of taking them out, and that would be another important step in getting out. Joanie was beginning to make plans. On Wednesday morning when I got there, Barb and a student in the room were working on Joanie. Seems her stents had come out while she was taking a shower, and Barb told me she didn't think it was anything to be concerned about. She had been scheduled for an X-ray for today to see if they could take them out. Now, the X-ray was just to see if things

121

were okay. Barb told me her Miami pouch was putting out a "ton of urine" which was a sign that things were working the way they were supposed to.

She had a surprise visitor today. Nancy Jones Schafer, North Dakota's First Lady, came by to see her and spend a little time with her. Nancy's visit gave her a lift, and Joanie told her she would be home and back to work soon. The last of the drains was also removed today, and that was another hopeful development. Nurse Nan told her she could eat again, but it would be a low residue diet for the first few days. They wanted to be sure she could keep solid food down before they would let her go.

By now, Joanie was determined more than ever that she was going to get out of the hospital. All of the drains were gone. The stents were gone, all but one of the IV bags were gone, she was eating, albeit not that much, and everything was looking good for the weekend.

Joanie was a Taurus. I used to say to her, "You're strong, like bull." What she had been through these past three weeks bore that out. I don't think she believed me when I used to tell her how strong she was, but her attitude and how she endured what she'd been through since this whole thing started told me I was right.

There was still some work to do, but by now there was no doubt that nothing was going to keep her here any longer than something major. She wouldn't allow that to happen.

Reality comes calling.

Today, Thursday, March 5, marked three weeks since Joanie's surgery, and I had learned a lot in my time at the hospital. I knew not to get excited when the Baxter beeped. I got to know all of the nurses who cared for Joanie. I learned not to get excited when she threw up, but just go about matter-of-factly cleaning her up. I knew where the ice cubes were. I knew where the popsicles were, and I had learned that things don't always go as planned, and not to get excited when that happens. I had also learned not to be afraid to ask questions of either nurses, or doctors. I learned that the nurses on 7C were as knowledgeable about Joanie's situation as anyone who wasn't a doctor could be, and there was a comfort that came with that knowledge. I had learned where every joint where I could go for a burger and a beer on the campus was, and there was some comfort there as well.

What we had focused on during the past twenty-one days was just getting her healed up so she could go home. We really hadn't dealt with the reality of the change the surgery had brought with it. That was about to change.

When I got to the hospital Joanie was doing well, but then I discovered they were treating her for a fungal infection, something I had been unaware of. Seems like even when you think you've been paying attention, things get by you. I was told it was something that would not hold up her discharge. The discharge nurse came by and said she would notify home health care in Bismarck that Joanie would be home shortly, and would be clearing any help we might need when we got home with the insurance company.

Now we got down to the business of what Joanie would be facing for the rest of her life. The first thing was learning about dealing with the Miami pouch, her new bladder. The change meant that unlike it was before the surgery, when she could feel the pressure telling her that she needed to relieve herself, now there would be no pressure. Her kidneys would just drain into the Miami pouch, and she would have to empty it at least four times a day, or more depending on her intake.

Today we were getting our first good lesson in the mechanics of emptying the pouch. Up to now, there had been a Foley catheter that drained it into a bag on the side of the bed, doing the work on a full-time basis. One of the nurses, Lori, guided Joanie through the process. The first thing we were told was that she would insert the catheter, called a #14 Red Robinson that had small holes in the end of it through her navel. She would have to put just a small dab of Surgilube on the end of it to help get it past the flap that was built in to keep urine from leaking out. The next step, one that didn't have to be done every time, was irrigating. Because of the nature of the pouch, mucus would have a tendency to build up, and it could plug the Robinson. We were given what looked like big plastic syringes, and a bottle of saline solution. There was a plunger in the tube, and we were told to fill the syringe with the saline, and then slowly push the fluid into the pouch through the Robinson. The catheter had a larger opening at the top to facilitate irrigation and drainage. When all of the solution was in the pouch, we were to reverse the process and pull on the plunger to begin drawing fluid out of the pouch, and let it run a receptacle until it stops. Think of it as priming the pump.

We would find out, over the course of years, irrigating the pouch was not always necessary, but we never went anywhere out of Bismarck without a bottle of the solution, at least two of the syringes, a tube of Surgilube and a supply of #14 Red Robinsons. I had made up a special bag that was ready to go anytime.

Joanie handled the lesson well, irrigating the pouch by herself, under Lori's guidance, but that was probably the last time she did it by herself, usually leaving that job to me. Lori also cautioned her about going too long between emptying, since a buildup of urine in the pouch could make it difficult to

124

get the catheter into the pouch because of pressure on the flap. This would then present a bit of a problem that could require some medical attention.

When they finished the lesson, they hooked the Foley catheter back up to the pouch so she wouldn't have to worry about again until tomorrow.

The reality of what this surgery meant in terms of changing her life, was no longer an intellectual idea, but an emotional reality. As I said, up until now we had just been focused on getting her healed up so we could go home. Tomorrow, would come another lesson, dealing with the handling of the ileostomy, something Joanie wasn't looking forward to, but the thought of it being temporary made it a little easier for her to adjust to it. Around five o'clock or so, Dr. Chen came in and informed us that Joanie was "out of here on Saturday."

That news made both of us happy, if not just a little apprehensive. So the rest of the evening, until I went back to Tom's place, we walked a couple of times, and talked about the new reality of her life. She seemed ready to meet it head on, and there was no doubt in my mind, as difficult as this situation was, she would.

The last full day.

Friday, March 6, dawned with the sun out for the first time in weeks. I took it as a good sign. That morning I loaded up the car with my bags and Joanie's bag and left Tom's place in St. Paul, where I had stayed since a couple of days after her surgery, and headed for the hospital. I would check into the Radisson sometime in the afternoon. We were getting close to going home.

When I go to the hospital that morning, I found that Joanie had thrown up around six, but they weren't concerned, and there was nothing to indicate a delay in her discharge. We went for a walk around the halls of 7C, and she was doing quite well, I thought. She didn't look that good, but her determination was evident. She was going to go home, and nothing was going to stop her.

They took her down for another X-ray of her abdomen for a last look to be sure there weren't any problems. As of late that afternoon, we hadn't heard anything, so we assumed there were not.

The second reality check.

Then it came time for the session on the ileostomy. We were going to learn how it works, how to change it, and how to avoid any problems with it. This was the one change Joanie had dreaded, but now that it was here, she accepted the fact we had to deal with it.

The ileostomy is formed by making an incision creating a hole about the size of a quarter, called a stoma, and bringing the small intestine up to the surface of the skin and then suturing it in place. This means basically that waste goes directly from the small intestine into the "appliance," as they call it. I never could figure out why they called it an appliance. When I thought of an appliance, I thought of a toaster, stove, washer, or dryer. They were appliances, but I thought of this as being more like a medium-sized sandwich bag with an opening that covered the stoma.

The ET nurse who gave us the lesson started out with the basics. There were the bags, or pouches, which had a hole in the back on the side that was attached to the skin. There was a tube of stoma adhesive, which you would use to squeeze out a bead around the stoma before applying the bag. There was adhesive removal, to be used when the bag was changed, and it would remove any residue from the previous change and help to insure a good seal.

The back side of the bag, the side with a hole in it, also had a larger, adhesive-based flange, that when pressed over the stoma made a seal between the skin and the bag. A good seal was important, mainly because Joanie would have no control whatsoever on what came out of her body into the pouch. We were also told it would help the seal if Joanie would hold her hands over the pouch for a few minutes after it was applied, as the heat from her hands would help the bonding.

We were also shown how to prepare the pouch. The ones they were using didn't have a hole in the back, just a small opening that would have to be enlarged using a sharp scissors to cut out the hole and make it the right size to fit over the stoma and not interfere. Later, after we were back in Bismarck, we were able to get custom-made pouches with the right size hole already cut. The bottom of the pouch was narrower than the top, and it was folded over and held in place by a clip that would be removed to facilitate emptying it.

I began to see the problem we were going to have right away. First off, since the stoma was located on her right side, Joanie couldn't look directly at it to either clean it, put on the adhesive or place the "appliance" over the stoma and insure there was a good seal. One suggestion the nurse made was to lay the bead of adhesive around the hole in the flange of the bag before applying it over the stoma. I saw where that could work, but I knew the business of changing, at least at first, was where I was to come in, and I got quite good at changing it over time. Besides that, I too was planning on this being temporary, and when she was sufficiently healed in a few months, they could take down the ileostomy and restore the normal function of her bowel. At least that what we were hoping for.

The lesson, and the reality had tired Joanie out. I was a little worn out myself. She slept and I went over to Sally's for a beer and to consider all that had gone down the last two days, and how things were going to go when we got home. I had a good idea of how to handle everything by now, but it was the unknown that I was sure would pop up, as it always does that left me uneasy.

Back at Joanie's room, we went for a walk, and talked about tomorrow. Before I left for the night, she asked me to get her a popsicle. I did, and I think I enjoyed it as much as she did. When we were done, I kissed her good night and headed for the elevator.

The lobby was quiet, as it was every night around ten o'clock, and my friend the night security guy asked me how things were. I told him this was the last night I'd be walking through his lobby, they were going to let me take her home tomorrow. He smiled at me, shook my hand, and wished us good luck.

As I left to walk back to the Radisson, I remember thinking I liked how that sounded.

Getting ready to go home.

Saturday morning, twenty-three days after the worst surgery you can imagine, and we are getting ready to get Joanie out of the hospital.

Since it was Saturday, and the lobby coffee cart wasn't open, I stopped at one of the coffee shops across from the Radisson to pick up a decent cup and walk the short couple of blocks to the hospital. When I got there that morning, Joanie was awake. She had showered and was waiting for me. She was ready to go. There was one more X-ray of her abdomen to be done, and then we could leave.

We went for one last walk around the corridors of 7C, and when we got back to the room, they came to take her down for the X-ray. I went back to the Radisson to move the car over to the parking ramp, because my next job was to begin to load up the plants and gifts that filled her room.

I had suggested leaving the plants on 7C, but she wasn't having any of that. She wanted them home with her. Since it was clear by now that I wasn't going to deny her anything, I agreed. What that meant for me was about a half a dozen trips from her room to the parking ramp about three-quarters of a block away. I didn't have a cart so I could make just one trip, so I got a box and made several trips.

The other logistical problem was the weather. It was March and still quite cold at night. That meant I had to bring all of the plants up to our room when we got her to the hotel. I had been driving the Volkswagen Cabriolet we had, and it is a small car, not one for handling a lot of stuff. When Joe came in the morning to drive our car back to Bismarck, it would be packed to capacity.

As her caregiver, I was beginning to feel the onset of the responsibility that now fell to me alone. Up to this point, I had been a helper, confident in the fact that she was in a place that could handle any circumstance that might arise. Leaving this safe haven, as much as we wanted to, brought with it mixed feelings, of promise and uncertainty.

Before we got ready to go, I was given the list of prescriptions that she needed to have. I went down to the hospital pharmacy and got a shock. Not the last one I would get, but it was a good one. They had prescribed drugs for nausea, anxiety, pain, a bacterial infection, and a fungal infection. When I went to the pharmacy, the pharmacist looked at the slips, and then at me, and said, "We'll bill you for these." I thought that was strange, but when I looked at the tab, and it was almost $900, with the one drug costing almost $750, with pills for just one week's treatment. At that time, I

129

had no idea of how much our insurance would pay for those drugs, but I knew they weren't going to pay the whole bill.

When I got back up to the room, Joanie was dressed. She was wearing the same clothes she had worn when we checked her in twenty-five days ago. She looked tired. Her complexion was pale, her hair was long, and didn't have the wave, curl or the luster I was used to seeing. I began to feel uneasy about leaving, but we were going, and she wasn't having it any other way. It was then I saw, once again, the strength of her determination and will. She was getting out, and my concerns weren't going to stop that. The discharge nurse came in with her clipboard, and she went over everything with us, and asking Joanie if she understood it all. What she didn't ask Joanie was if she understood that her life had changed forever, but I know that wasn't her job, nor was it a question on the papers. She said she did, signed a couple of the discharge papers, and we were ready to go.

They brought a wheelchair up to bring her down to the front of the hospital. As we left, we said good bye to Marcia, the nurse who had been so good to Joanie during her stay, and Joanie had in her hands the Irish poster that Marcia had given her so long ago that had hung on the wall in her room. I hurried over to the parking ramp while a nurse and Joanie waited for me in the lobby, and when I pulled up in front, the nurse wheeled her out, and I helped her get in her car, and we were gone.

Now it was my turn to take care of her fulltime, not just helping. This is the time that any caregiver faces, and how you handle it makes a difference, even though you aren't a doctor, or a nurse, or a nurse's aide. All you have to do is remember what you have learned over the time your patient was in the hospital, how they dealt with her, and what you have learned about her particular situation.

130

I was apprehensive, nervous, and afraid Joanie was as well, but her desire to get out and get home was stronger than any nervousness she might have felt. The only thing that made me feel a little more secure was we were still near the hospital. That helped, but not much.

I got her to our room in the Radisson, and she immediately lay down on bed for the first time in more than three weeks without a bunch of tubes in her body, and went to sleep. I went to move the car to the hotel parking lot, grab a quick smoke, and get ready for our first night out of the hospital.

By this time on Sunday afternoon, we'd be back home, and she would be on the couch with Muffin on her lap.

We are finally home.

We were set up at the Radisson, and the anxiety level was fairly high, at least mine was. Joanie slept most of the time, not saying much. The TV was on, but neither one of us was paying much attention to it.

Around seven, I told her we should get her something to eat. I had already fetched 7-UP and ice. We looked at the room service menu, and she decided on trying some pasta dish. I called it in, and when it came, she looked at it, poked at it, took a few small bites and pushed it away. I asked her what was wrong, and she said there was something about it she didn't like. It may have been the smell of the food, or it may have been her fear of throwing up. I tried to encourage her to try a little more, but to no avail.

We made it through our first effort with the Miami pouch. Emptying the pouch went okay, and I began to see how we were going to handle this in a non-hospital setting. We probably did it a couple of times when we didn't have to, but I

131

think both of us were so anxious to be sure we did it right, and did it when it was needed. As time went by, we learned.

We didn't have to do anything with the ileostomy, since there wasn't any output to deal with. She hadn't eaten anything to speak of, and I don't think she was going to until we were safely back home. I think that was in the back of her mind when she pushed the pasta away. If she didn't eat anything, she wouldn't have to fool with the ileostomy for the time being.

Sunday morning came, and I helped her with her shower, and while she was brushing her teeth, she threw up. It was a moment of slight panic for me, since I knew we were still dealing with two infections, but then I also thought it was just a gag reflex, something that had happened a time or two in the hospital.

She was really tired and looked it. She was pale and her hair was long and dull, but there was a look on her face of determination. While she rested, I got a cart and loaded up everything except the medical supplies and drugs we would need when we got home. I took it down and packed every available space in our little Volkswagen so it would be ready for Joe when he came to pick it up and drive it home for us.

Around 11:30 or so, Ed came to pick us up and give us a ride to the airport. I think he was shocked when he saw her that morning. Not much was said. Joanie, the one who ordinarily would be talking a lot, said little, and so Ed and I chatted during the ride to the terminal. When we got there, I went and found a wheelchair for her. As tired as she was, walking through the terminal was out of the question. We said goodbye to Ed, and went to get our tickets.

When we got to the boarding area, we saw Jane from 3M. I never got her last name, but she had been to the hospital with Nancy Schafer to see Joanie just the past Wednesday. Jane's husband was an airline pilot, and so Jane went and had her tickets, which were bulkhead seats, the ones with extra leg room, switched with ours, to make the flight a little more comfortable for Joanie. Even with Jane's consideration, and the better seats, Joanie was still miserable, and her focus was on just getting home.

We were some of the first off the plane in Bismarck, and as we were walking up the ramp past passengers waiting to leave, we saw a few people we knew, and I could tell by their expressions they were stunned when they got a look at Joanie. I know because I talked with a couple of them later. The word spread that she looked like she was going to die. That wasn't the last time that a rumor like that spread about her, and my job was to debunk them every time.

Joanie's sister and brother-in-law, Ann and Jack Chase, were waiting for us, and when we got outside the terminal into their SUV, I began to see a change in Joanie. The tension began to fade, and after we got her home, on her couch with Muffin on her lap and Peaches nearby, it was all but gone. She was relaxed, and her voice was stronger, and I breathed a sigh of relief. We had left Bismarck and the kitties on February 9, and today was March 8. It had been a long, hard time.

While she and Ann were talking, Joanie was trying to explain what she knew, and was doing a fairly good job, focusing on the prospect that the ileostomy was going to be temporary. There was one point where the Kallberg family sense of humor popped into the conversation, and I couldn't help myself. I interrupted Joanie and told Ann, "Think of this, she's the only woman I know who can pee standing up without getting anything on her shoes."

They both laughed, and I was pleased. While they talked, I went out back for a smoke. We were home and it was good.

No applesauce in our house.

The happiness of getting Joanie home was tempered after a short while with the reality of the situation. Now my job as caregiver would take front and center of my consciousness. Even though she was home from the hospital, she was still a very sick girl. She had a lot of healing left to do, was dealing with infections, and getting back to eating regularly, coupled with dealing with the Miami pouch and the ileostomy. She was also faced with the process of getting her strength back after twenty-five days in the hospital.

I felt the stress of these first days home, far from the doctors and nurses who were so familiar with what she had been through, and if something were to go wrong, I didn't know if anyone in Bismarck had experience with a pelvic exenteration patient. There were doctors who knew about an ileostomy, and I assumed there had to be a urologist who might know what a Miami pouch was, but I didn't know, and that added to the tension I felt during the first weeks home.

I did have numbers for Dr. Carson and Dr. Cosin, as well as the number for the nurse's station on 7C, and had been assured I could call anytime if felt there was something out of the ordinary they should know about.

Another factor I had to deal with was this was a woman who was not only trying to come back from a traumatic, life-changing surgery, but was still trying to adjust psychologically and emotionally to those changes. I knew enough, because of my background, that this was a process that I couldn't rush her through. The adjustment was going to be made on her terms, and on a time table that she would determine. My job was to be there so she knew she wasn't alone.

My tasks now were to do some of the same things that nurses did for her in the hospital, including ensuring she got the meds for the two infections she was dealing with, along with the drugs they had prescribed to combat nausea and pain. I also made sure the thermometer was right, and the blood pressure machine had fresh batteries. Given the infections and all, I thought it best to keep an eye on those numbers.

It was also my job to make sure she got some exercise. In the hospital it had been fairly easy to get her to take walks, because the nurses were prodding her to do it, and she wasn't going to go against their wishes. On the other hand, once we got home, I would have to cajole, wheedle, coax, or otherwise exhort her to take walks with me. She could find it easy to put me off, saying it was too cold or windy, or she was just too tired. I finally put it to her like this. Today we'll walk to the end of the driveway and back, twice. Tomorrow we'd go a little further. That approach didn't work. During the first week home, we walked only once, despite my urging. It was too cold.

Getting her the infection meds proved to be a challenge. The pills, the ones that cost over $740, were large enough to choke a horse, let alone a woman who had a gag reflex that would have them ejected in seconds. I hit upon the idea of grinding the pill up and putting it in applesauce. Joanie liked applesauce, and her tender stomach seemed to be able to handle it. I improvised a mortar and pestle using an espresso cup and the back of a spoon. I cut the pill in half and then ground it up as best I could before incorporating it into the sauce. She would reluctantly eat the mixture, but at least she ingested the medicine. After the regimen was complete in a week, that was the last time you ever saw applesauce in our house. I didn't care, because I wasn't fond of it anyway, but at

135

just the mention of it, Joanie would stiffen up, and she made it clear to me never to bring any of it back into the house, even if we were having pork chops.

She was eating well the first few days, but she continued to be tired and her back was bothering her. She had a couple of episodes of throwing up, but when she got back to taking Reglan, that seemed to clear up.

The Miami pouch operation was going well, and I had even changed the ileostomy pouch without too much difficulty. We had been visited by the home health representative, and he had gone over everything we had been told at the hospital. He was encouraging the idea of independence, meaning Joanie should be thinking about changing it herself. I knew by looking at her when he said that it wasn't going to happen. She told him she was not ready to handle the "appliance" by herself yet. She would leave that to me at least the time being.

After we had been home just short of two weeks, I began to see something that troubled me. She was in more pain than she had been in earlier, and Tylenol didn't seem to take care of it. I called Dr. Carson, and she prescribed a muscle relaxer that seemed to help, but there was something else brewing. She was having a vaginal discharge that wasn't right, and smelled awful.

On Monday, March 23, I called Dr. Cosin and told him what I saw going on. Joanie had thrown up that morning, and later in the day threw up again. Cosin told me to bring her back to his office this week. He said there might be an infection related to the vaginal discharge. Joanie didn't have a bad day on Tuesday, but we had decided that we would fly down on Wednesday, and be back on Thursday.

As we would discover, we were being overly optimistic, and we would find ourselves back up on 7C.

136

The attack dog, cancer doesn't want to let go.

We were on our way back down to the clinic, and it was a disheartening turn of events for both of us. The uncertainty that came with Dr. Cosin telling me to bring her back this week made us both uneasy. When we left the hospital on the seventh, our next appointment with Dr. Carson had been for a month from then. This trip back down, coming so close after her discharge, had a way of messing with our minds.

We flew down, assuming Dr. Carson and Dr. Cosin would see her, determine what the source of the infection was, give her some antibiotics, and we would fly back home the next day. We took a cab from the airport to the clinic and first met with Dr. Cosin. They did a physical exam, and before we knew it, he said that they were going to admit Joanie to the hospital. That stunned both of us. Dr. Cosin said it seemed that some of the skin that had been used in the reconstruction of the neovagina had not taken, and was the source of the infection. That meant she couldn't go back home, and they would have to operate to remove the source of that infection. Dr. Carson would be back tomorrow, and we would know more.

After we got the news, they called for transport, and someone came with a wheelchair to take Joanie back up to 7C. Back on the floor, some of the nurses who knew her from before expressed some concern she was back so soon, and proceeded to do their best to make her comfortable. While they did that, I went over to check into the Radisson and drop off our bags. We had packed light, for an overnight stay, but it began to look like it would be more than one night.

My suspicion that this wasn't going to be a quick trip was confirmed on Thursday by both Dr. Carson and Dr. Cosin when they told us it looked like it would be Monday before

137

she would be out of there. They told us they were going to do some preliminary work on her on Friday, and assuming that went okay, we might be out earlier.

All of this was taking a toll on Joanie. She was really tired, and you could see it. On Thursday night, Barb Olson and her daughter Kristen stopped up to see her, and talking to Barb later, she remarked on how concerned she was when she saw Joanie. She wasn't the only one who was concerned. I did not fully understand what was going on, and that alone elevated my level of tension. I was careful not to let Joanie see that, and as far as she was concerned, they would take care of the problem and we would go home and she could get on with healing. She still had a ways to go.

On Friday morning, they tried to do some work on Joanie, but decided they would need to put her under to do what they needed. Another disappointment. They said they were looking at Saturday or Sunday now. Joanie was not happy. She wanted this to be over so she could go back home.

Ginny came by to see her, and I got a cab and went over to Dayton's to pick up a few things. I hadn't packed for a five-day trip. That afternoon, I had to check out of the Radisson because they were full for Friday and Saturday nights. I found a motel a couple of blocks further away from the hospital, but one that was still within walking distance. Nothing on this trip seemed to be going right.

Saturday morning, Carson told us the procedure was scheduled for Sunday morning. At least now we had a timetable to go by. Around noon that day, my sisters showed up. Jane had driven from Fargo and picked Joni up in St. Cloud. My son Ryan came by and so after they spent some time talking to Joanie, the three of us went across the river for lunch, and so I could do a little more shopping for clothes.

I spent the rest of the day with Joanie, trying to keep her occupied and at ease. She wasn't eating anything, and couldn't after midnight, but she could have a popsicle when she wanted, I saw to that. I knew where they were.

I arrived at the hospital at 7:30 Sunday morning and went with her to pre-op, the same one we had been in before, and ran into some of the same nurses we had before. This put Joanie somewhat at ease seeing familiar faces. Dr. Carson came in and talked to us about what they were going to do, and said the recovery time wouldn't be that long. When the nurse with the Versed was called over, we knew it was time to go. I squeezed her hand, gave her a kiss, and told her I would see her on the other side.

The procedure went as planned. They had to remove the skin that was the source of the infection, skin that had been used when they did the reconstruction of the vagina. The rest of the muscle they used was fine. Joanie was in recovery, and I went up the cafeteria on the eighth floor to get coffee.

As I was sitting there, preparing to leave and go out for a smoke, I saw Dr. Carson and one of her interns and another doctor come into the cafeteria. On my way out I stopped by their table, and Dr. Carson and I talked about what was next. She asked me if one more day here would help or make a difference in how Joanie was doing. I told her no, I needed to get her back home as soon as we could. She agreed, and told me we could be out before noon tomorrow.

Then she dropped a bomb, one that I couldn't share with Joanie. She told me there was a real possibility, from what they had seen doing this procedure, that they might not be able to take the ileostomy down and hook her bowel back up as they had anticipated they'd be able to do, and that would mean a permanent colostomy. I was stunned, and asked if she

139

was certain. She told me there was a remote possibility they'd be able to do, but wasn't very sure.

I told her we could not tell Joanie this right now, no one could tell her this right now. Getting rid of the ileostomy and returning her bowel function to normal was the one thing that was keeping her going right now. I couldn't take that away from her right now, and asked Carson not to do that either. She agreed. I knew that someday down the road we'd have to deal with that reality, but now wasn't the time.

I left the cafeteria, stopped by to see Joanie in her room, and told her I had to go and check out of the motel I had moved to on Friday and check back into the Radisson.

It was a cloudy, rainy day, and as I walked across the campus heading for the motel on the other side of Huron Boulevard, there was a light rain falling. I started thinking about what I had just heard from Carson and started crying. As I walked, I couldn't tell which were raindrops and which were teardrops, but I had never felt so sad and pissed off at the hand Joanie had been dealt, and how cruel it was, and knowing there was nothing I could do about it. This fucking disease was going to take something else from her, and she didn't deserve that.

A Dilemma.

I got back to the Radisson and checked in. Then it was back to the hospital for the day. Joanie was napping when I got there, and the nurse told me she hadn't had any problems since she got back from surgery. When she came to, she was groggy, and thirsty. I had made sure there was ice water there, and it went down quickly. She asked me what time it was, and then I realized she probably didn't remember much about when I had seen her earlier.

140

I told her we would be going home tomorrow, and I had called our contact at Northwest Airlines to make sure everything was cool, and we had seats. That seemed to cheer her up a little, and I said it was time for a walk. Surprisingly, she agreed, and we headed out for a tour around the halls of 7C.

The rest of the afternoon was spent like a lot of the days we had spent there before. TV on, but no one watching. Her napping, me doing the *Sunday New York Times* crossword, and riding the elevator to go out for a smoke.

Around six o'clock, after she had a bit to eat, she told me she was going to go to sleep for a while. I left and headed for Sally's. As I sat at the bar, having a smoke and beer (that was before it was outlawed), I began to think about what Dr. Carson and I had talked about that morning. It occurred to me I had put myself on the horns of a dilemma, one that bothered me when I began to consider it. I had told Carson we couldn't tell her about the distinct possibility that they couldn't take down the ileostomy, and she would be looking at a colostomy for the rest of her life.

When I thought about that I realized it put me in direct opposition to something Joanie and I had talked about early on in this process, and that was knowing was better than not knowing, and my telling her she was stronger than she thought she was.

Now here I was, hiding something from her, something she should know about, and something that could affect her life for as long as she lived. I wondered if I wasn't being overly protective of her, and in the process giving the lie to what I had told her about how strong she was. Along with that, I had always felt it was my job to tell her what she needed to know to deal with the effect of this disease.

As I sat there at Sally's, I told myself, on the one hand, I knew how much she was hoping the ileostomy could be taken down and she wouldn't have a colostomy. On the other hand, I was worried about telling her that it might not happen. I thought dumping this on her at this stage would do more harm than good. I wasn't sure about her emotional fragility at this point, and this setback with the infection from the neovagina had taken a toll on her. She had also only been out of the hospital for two weeks, and every time I would change her ileostomy, she would remark about how this was temporary, and how she was looking forward in a couple of months to be done with it.

There was also the fact there was still an outside chance they would be able to put that part of her bodily function back to normal, but it was slim, and if it was put to her like that, the psychological and emotional impact that came with the uncertainty also made me think I was making the right choice. I took some solace in the fact that Dr. Carson had agreed with me, and I knew if worse came to worst, they would have a way of dealing with it. I would let them deliver the bad news, if and when that time came.

My conversation with Dr. Carson confirmed again how important it is, as a caregiver, to have an understanding with your patient's doctor. I believe Carson understood that I was not a passive bystander in this whole thing, but actively participating in Joanie's treatment and care. Had we not had that relationship, I'm not sure the timing of the news we feared might not have been delivered to Joanie at a time she wasn't ready to handle it.

I paid my tab and walked back to the hospital, a little more sure that we had made the right decision about not telling Joanie the potential of bad news, even if it posed a dilemma for me personally. Back in Joanie's room, we watched a bit of

142

TV, and talked about what needed to be done when we got home. We went for a walk and later I got her a cherry popsicle, and around ten o'clock that night went back to the hotel. Ginny was going to pick us up around eleven thirty on Monday and give us a ride to the airport. Getting back home was as important as ever.

Musings and leaking.

Once back in Bismarck, our lives seemed to settle down, and we went about the business of healing Joanie. I was able to get her to walk now more often. In fact, we had established a regimen that included a walk in the morning, and one in the afternoon. I had pretty much goaded her into going a little further every time, until we were walking about a half an hour, or more at a time. Her appetite continued to grow, and her gastrointestinal tract seemed to be cooperating, and there were no episodes of throwing up. Both good signs.

We weren't scheduled to see Dr. Carson until late April, and it was a welcome respite from having to go to Minneapolis. I began to second guess myself with regard to keeping the doctor's fears about the permanent colostomy when I saw how she was progressing. She wasn't back to work yet, but she was in contact with her office, and was keeping up on what was going on. She was anxious to get back, but it would still be a few weeks before she would do that. I was seeing the seeds of the strength of her spirit grow every day, but I still thought I was doing the right thing by letting Dr. Carson handle it until we knew for sure what was going on. If I dashed her hopes for a reversal prematurely, and they ended up being able to do it, it would be an unnecessary hardship for her.

143

In examining my motive for silence, I wondered how much of the decision came from my own feelings about the prospect of the permanent colostomy. I knew that projection comes into play when one is involved in a situation like this, and trying to keep from being subjective in one's judgment and decisions can be difficult. As a caregiver, it is important to know the distinction between how you feel about a major change versus what is important to your patient. The way I dealt with it was just to try to put my own judgment aside and focus on what was best for her.

The Miami pouch proved to be not much of a challenge for her, and except for my occasionally helping her with irrigating it, that part of the change was going well. She seemed to be adapting to this change without making a big deal about it. I think for her she was well on her way to making it part of her new reality. The difference between the Miami pouch and the ileostomy was control. With the pouch, at least she had control over the elimination process. There was no such control over the ileostomy, when the bag was full, it was full, and had to be emptied lest the pressure break the seal.

I was still changing the ileostomy when it needed to be changed, and that was okay. We did it about every four days. This issue was a little more problematical, in that it represented a bigger change, and adjustment would take more time. Joanie had more confidence in me handling the mechanics than she did in herself. The cloud that hung over this part of her life was how strong the seal was, and what would happen if, and when it might leak. We knew that would likely happen at some point, but who knew when or where? It wasn't long before it happened for the first time.

One night, about 2:30 in the morning, she woke me up and told me it was leaking. It took me just a moment, and I could smell it. As a caregiver, I knew what I had to do, and that was to stay calm. Freaking out would only make Joanie feel worse than she did, lying there helpless to control what was going on with her body.

I got up, went to the kitchen and got a roll of paper towels, then to the bathroom for a wet washcloth and the necessary stuff to change the "appliance." An ileostomy presents a different problem than a colostomy would, in that the waste hasn't been processed completely, and is fairly liquid. I just told her to relax, and we'd take care of this.

I approached it as though I were a nurse, without any drama. The pouch had leaked quite a bit, and had soiled her undergarments as well as the sheet on the bed. She was upset, her face was flushed, and I felt so sorry for her, but went about cleaning her up, as if it were no big deal.

Another problem arose when I went to remove the bag and more started coming out of the stoma. When that happens, there is nothing to do but grab more paper towels and keep the flow from running all over. I just covered up the stoma until it was quiet again, went about cleaning it up and as quickly as I could, laid down the paste and pressed the bag over the stoma. I told Joanie to put her hands on it and press down for a few minutes. After a few minutes, I got her into the bathroom and turned on the shower. While she was showering, I took her nightgown, undergarments, and the sheet off the bed, bagged them, and threw them outside for the garbage. By the time she was done, there was a clean sheet on the bed.

Once she put on a fresh nightgown and got back into bed, it was clear that this had been traumatic for her. She was distraught, and she shed a few tears, and told me she'd be glad when this was gone. I just held her for a few minutes and told her we'd get through this. About then, Muffin, who had been standing by watching everything and wondering what the hell was going on, jumped up on the bed and sat on her chest and started purring as she scratched her.

At that moment, I knew I had made the right decision not to tell her the news I had gotten from Dr. Carson, and didn't second guess myself again, all the time clinging to the outside chance they could do what we hoped they could.

The elephant in the room.

April came, Joanie was getting exercise, eating well, and wanting to get back to work, and by the middle of the month she had her first outing when she met some people she worked with for lunch. I could see she was getting ready to go back to work, if only on a limited basis. Before long, she was back full time.

What we hadn't thought about, or talked about, was the elephant in the room. This whole series of events had been brought on by the return of cancer. While all of her energy was devoted to healing from the surgery that was supposed to be "curative," we hadn't even thought about cancer that much, let alone talked about it. After all, she was supposed to be cancer free now.

For the most part it worked. However, a couple of days before our next visit to see Dr. Carson, the elephant would no longer be ignored. Joanie, as usual, became a little short with me and sat quietly for longer periods, and I knew it was because of the pending visit and examination. With cancer, we were never sure what an exam might show.

Her appointment was for Tuesday, so we left on Monday, and that night had dinner at the Village Wok, across the street from the Radisson with Ryan and Kim, and the subject was still being ignored.

The anxiety and uncertainty that accompanied every clinic trip was unwarranted this time. Joanie was given a clean bill, and there was no evidence of disease, and she wasn't scheduled for another visit until mid-June. That night we went to dinner with Ginny and Ed at the Lexington in St. Paul, all of us feeling rather good about the day.

This dynamic was part of the process when we were issued a ticket to ride on the roller coaster that is cancer treatment, and we were getting used to it, even if we didn't look forward to it. It takes a toll and tests the coping mechanism of both the individual and the caregiver, but you do your best.

The June appointment was the same, and Joanie came out with a clean bill of health. She was scheduled for another visit in mid-July to have a colonoscopy as part of the preparation for what we hoped would be the next phase of this treatment, and that was taking the ileostomy down and hooking her bowel back up. Carson had ordered the colonoscopy because of a rectovaginal fistula that was probably the result of the radiation she had had. The fistula is an abnormal connection between the vagina and the rectum, which could allow for feces or gas to pass through the vagina, which of course would present a whole host of other problems. The colonoscopy would give them a more definitive view of what was involved, and give them a better idea of how they might handle it from a surgical perspective.

I already knew there was only an outside chance now, so we rarely talked about that subject. She would mention it from time to time, and all I could do was nod in agreement, still feeling somewhat disturbed I hadn't told her what I knew.

In the interim, we did our best to get on with life, and as we discussed in the hospital, not let this disease control our lives any more than it already did. That approach worked for the most part, and we did get back to doing normal things, like going out with friends, having parties in our backyard, and enjoying our Sunday morning routine. Your mind allows you to forget sometimes that you are in the midst of dealing with a deadly disease, and I think it helps to keep you sane.

On July 13, we were back in Minneapolis, and Joanie met with a doctor from Colon and Rectal Surgery for the colonoscopy. Dr. Julio Garcia Aguilar conducted the procedure, and was only able to go so far due to "significant discomfort" on Joanie's part, but he had gone far enough to be able to tell Carson what he had found.

We wouldn't know this right away, but Aguilar's note to Carson said: "Given the size of the fistula and the radiation changes in the rectum, I do not think that a local procedure such as an endorectal advancement flap will solve this fistula. Repair would require removal of the rectum and bringing down some normal colon to perform a coloanal anastomosis. However, given her previous surgeries, this will be a technically difficult option, if at all feasible. Mrs. Wigen has demonstrated interest in having this fistula closed and ileostomy takedown. I have told her I would discuss different options with you and then we will make a final recommendation."

Now, I am not a professional medical person, and I won't even attempt to explain what and endorectal advancement flap is, or what a coloanal anastomosis is, but even I could read those notes to mean that it was going to be extremely difficult, if not impossible, to fix this situation, and the result would be a permanent colostomy for Joanie. By the way, I did look both terms up, and it all made sense.

We weren't told right then what Aguilar had found, or what he had reported to Carson, and we headed back to Bismarck the next day, not knowing anything more than we did when we came down. I assumed we would be finding out in the coming days what Dr. Carson was planning on doing, and we would just have to wait with that cloud hanging over us. Joanie was still hoping it would turn out as she wanted it to.

It had been a tough winter and early spring, and the summer wasn't giving us much of a break either. She needed some good news for a change.

"Don't worry about a thing..."

After the July clinic meeting and the colonoscopy, we spent the rest of the summer just going about the business of living. We weren't scheduled to go back down to Minneapolis until the day after Labor Day. Joanie was busy at work. She was having no problem with the Miami pouch, and it had become a routine part of her life. The ileostomy was still something she was putting up with, in the hope she would be rid of it come September.

I continued to change it for her when it needed to be changed, and I didn't mind. Every time I did, and she would say something about being rid of it, I would simple agree with her, and in my mind be hoping for what would amount to a miracle to make that happen. The rest of the summer flew by, with only fleeting thoughts about cancer or ileostomies or clinic appointments. Our fenced backyard was a rather large one for a city lot, had a pool, and we spent as much time enjoying it as we could. On Labor Day, we hosted a party for a large group of friends. A bunch played golf, and then came over to the house for a good old-fashioned American barbecue in the backyard. Lots of beer and burgers and music and laughs.

For that afternoon and early evening, cancer didn't exist, ileostomies didn't exist, and clinics didn't exist. It was the perfect end of summer party. Joanie was a great hostess, and had someone seen her in action who didn't know her, they would have no idea of what she had been through, or was living with at the time. She never wore her problems on her sleeve. It was a good day.

As daylight started to fade, the last of the guests had left, and the dishes had been washed, there was little evidence there had been a party here at all. The garbage had been bagged, the grill was covered up, and Muffin and Peaches had now come out of hiding. The commotion and strangers had driven them to the deep, dark places only they knew, the places they went to when they didn't want to be found. Places where they felt safe. Joanie and I grabbed a bottle of wine and a couple of glasses and went back out on the deck. I had been playing music all day on the CD player, and one of my favorites was a Bob Marley CD. I put it back on and turned it up.

Joanie was tired, but I think it was a good tired. She had put in a long day, making sure there was enough food to go around, making her pumpernickel porkies, which were always a hit, and worrying too much about everything. She was busy enough that I had to remind her at one point to tend to her Miami pouch.

I poured her a glass of wine, and as the first sounds of Marley's music began to wash over us, the wine made her cheeks immediately turn red. All it ever took was one drink of wine and they would flush. We just sat there for a while, listening to the music and then we began to talk about tomorrow. We would be leaving for Minneapolis, and she was scheduled for surgery on Thursday. That would be the day when we would know the answer to the question we had lived with since that night in March, which seemed so long ago now. I told her that tomorrow was just a traveling day, so

150

there was no hurry to get going. We had a room at the Radisson, and just wanted to be there around six or so.

I knew she was worried, and asked her how she was feeling about this whole deal now. All she would say was she wanted the ileostomy to be gone, but she did tell me she wondered if that was what was going to happen. She also told me that's what all of her prayers were about, but she wasn't sure they were going to be answered.

As we were talking, the Marley tune, "Three Little Birds" came on the CD, and part of the lyrics got our attention when we heard him singing, "Don't worry about a thing, 'cause every little things gonna be all right..." We both stopped talking and as we listened, a smile came to her face, and she held out her glass for some more wine.

We sat there in the twilight of the evening, hoping Marley was right.

Back on 7C

Tuesday morning, and we were getting ready to leave for Minneapolis. Joanie took her time getting ready, as she always did, and today she was a little slower getting ready than even I was accustomed to seeing.

When she got up that morning, she took her place on the couch, as if it were a Sunday morning, and we had no place to go. Muffin joined her, and I made some coffee. I knew she would be ready to go when we needed to get on the road. I went to get the car gassed up, pick up the paper and cigarettes for myself. When I got home, she was in the shower. I finished my packing, assuming we were going to be gone for more than a few days this time. Joanie's packing was minimal, since she would be admitted to the hospital on the next morning, with the surgery scheduled for Thursday morning, and she only needed a change of clothes for tonight when we went for dinner. Since we'd be going directly home when she was discharged, she would wear the same thing she would wear today, and she wouldn't care.

As I watched her slowly getting ready, I reminded her again that we were in no hurry. I went about getting the bag of stuff we needed to have with us since the surgery. There were Red Robinson catheters for the Miami pouch, Surgilube, extra Ziploc bags, saline irrigation fluid, irrigation syringe, a receptacle, ileostomy pouches, stoma adhesive, adhesive remover, and extra bag clips, plus a supply of paper towels and Kleenex included in that important bag. That bag of stuff had become a part of her life, and, like her purse, it went with her everywhere, and she always had it with her at work, ready to handle any emergency. Of course, at the end of this trip, the hope was that the contents of the bag would change with the elimination of any ostomy "appliances."

The part of this pre-departure ritual that absolutely never changed: she has her coat on, all of the bags, except for her purse are in the car, extra food has been put out for Muffin and Peaches, and Joanie would grab a bag of treats, shake it, and call out, "Treats." That, along with the rattling of the bag, brought them running from their morning napping places. She would dole out the treats in separate bowls, bend down to pet and scratch her furry friends, and tell them she would see them again soon. As they attacked their bowl of treats, she stood and looked around the kitchen with a wistful expression on her face and would tell me it was okay to get going. This ritual never changed, and I never watched it throughout these two plus years but, at times, I wanted to put off leaving myself.

She asked me if I brought her favorite CD, the Chuck Mangione disc that had "Bellavia" on it. I just turned on the

152

player, and the sound of that song without words filled the car with the music she loved. By the time we got to Mabel Murphy's in Fergus Falls, we were both ready for a break. The stops there gave us a chance to take breath, and consider what was waiting at the end of the ride. Joanie didn't seem as uptight as I expected she'd be, and so we dallied at Mabel's a little longer than usual. I think this ersatz, old world pub in a Tudor-style building, with its whimsical legend of Mabel, made her feel comfortable. The food was okay, and we had gotten to know the bartenders after so many stops there on our visits to the Cities, even before cancer would become the main reason for these trips. We never made a trip without stopping. Never.

We checked in at the Radisson between five and six, and Joanie had a chance to attend to the Miami pouch and the ileostomy. She changed clothes, and we went to Ginny and Ed's for cocktails and then to go out for dinner at Billy's on Grand. Stopping at the Stringers' home also gave her a chance to see her three-legged friend, Piper, who was always glad to see her, and she always looked forward to seeing him.

Grand Avenue and the area between Dale and Selby in St. Paul has many good restaurants, and over these last two years we had eaten at least once in many of them. Ginny and Ed were good about making Joanie feel comfortable, and our dinners with them were always leisurely and delightful experiences, even when they were on the eve of an event none of us were looking forward to, like another surgery for Joanie, who already had undergone too many.

We got back to the hotel and went for our usual nightcap, a Baileys' Irish Cream, and then we retired to our room to get some sleep. Wednesday morning, I got up early, made coffee, and waited for Joanie to shower and get ready for the short two-block walk to the hospital. We were to check in at 8:30, so

153

they could begin getting her ready for the surgery scheduled for the next morning. This time, they were expecting us, and when we walked to the nurses' station on 7C, we were met with some familiar faces. I think it helped Joanie feel a little more comfortable, even though there were a lot of places she would have rather been at that moment.

The first order of business was to get her into the hospital garb she would be wearing for the next week, and hooking her up to an IV line. She talked easily with the nurses and didn't seem the least bit stressed. She knew all of those who would be taking care of her over the coming days, and that made it easier on her. Dr. Carson had ordered some bloodwork to be done and pictures to be taken, and while they did that, I went out for a smoke.

Dr. Carson came to see her and did a preliminary examination that afternoon, and she was satisfied that Joanie was doing well, and there were no problems, other than the one she was there to have fixed.

While she was there, Carson talked with us about what was going to happen. It was the first opportunity she had to talk with Joanie and to tell her what problems they might be facing regarding taking down the ileostomy and hooking her bowel back up. She didn't categorically tell Joanie it couldn't be done, but she put it in such a way that Joanie couldn't help but understand. For the first time since her surgery in February, she had to consider realistically the fact she might be looking at a permanent colostomy. She told Dr. Carson she understood, but she also told her she thought if it could be done, she was confident she could do it.

It was a sobering experience, and it was some time after before Joanie would talk with me about it. After Carson left, she told me she wanted to take a nap. I knew she wanted to be alone for a while, and so I went out for a smoke.

I stood outside of the hospital thinking about what I had just seen and what I knew. I remember feeling sad and helpless there was nothing I could do to make this turn out right. I think one of the hardest parts of being a caregiver in circumstances like these is knowing you have no power to make it work out. You can only be there, and maybe, sometimes, that's enough.

When I got back upstairs to her room, Joanie was awake and talking with one of the nurses. The nurses that cared for her on 7C had all come to like her, and had gotten to know her well considering she had spent so much time on that wing this year. She seemed to be in good spirits, despite what she had heard from Dr. Carson earlier. I had learned some time ago to not underestimate the strength of her spirit during a difficult time, and I was seeing evidence of it again late on that Wednesday afternoon in a hospital room on 7C, far from her home in Bismarck.

Later that night, when I got ready to leave, I gave her a kiss, told her I loved her and said, "Every things gonna be all right." She smiled, told me she loved me, and said, "I'll see you in the morning."

The last disappointment of 1998.

I got to the hospital around a quarter to six on Thursday morning. Joanie was already awake, and nurses were making last-minute arrangements before we would head down to the pre-op area. They were checking her blood pressure, temperature and pulse, something that would be done again in a short while in the pre-op. I guess they wanted to see if anything changed on the trip down from her room on 7C.

The hospital chaplain stopped by to give some words of encouragement and asked Joanie if she wanted to pray,

155

something she wanted to do. As I sat there looking at her, I wondered what she was thinking. She wasn't giving me any clues, except to tell me she didn't want to be there, and wanted to go home. She said that with sort of a sad smile on her face, but did add that she was ready to get this done with.

Around six-thirty, they called for transport. That's really an in-house taxi. A guy comes with a wheelchair and will take you anywhere in the hospital you want to go, and the best part is you don't have to tip him. The pre-op was familiar. It was brightly lit, cold, noisy and full of nurses, interns and doctors preparing patients for surgery. They found Joanie a bed, brought her some warm blankets, and began to get her hooked up to the IV line. Then another nurse would come by with her file, and would take her temperature, check her pulse and blood pressure. I don't think it changed on the trip down. She would then ask Joanie about any drug allergies, (she had none), and sign the necessary release forms so the surgery could go ahead. The routine was the same as the last few times we had been here, first the anesthesiologist would come in, introduce himself and tell her he would be the one in charge of putting her under, and would be monitoring her vital signs throughout the operation and keeping her safe.

Dr. Carson then stopped by Joanie's bed, and talked with her, telling her what was going to happen. She told us that first they were going to do a physical exam under anesthesia, and after that they would do an exploratory laparotomy, which is really just opening her up and having a look around to find out what they are dealing with, and if they would be able to go ahead with the ileostomy takedown and the hookup of the bowel, the outcome we were hoping for. She reminded us of the potential problem she had told us about the other day, and if they weren't able to do the reconstructive surgery, the result would be creation of a colostomy. She told Joanie

156

she would discuss the findings with me before they went ahead.

Joanie's face spoke volumes to me. She acknowledged what Carson had said, but I thought she looked like all of the air had been sucked out of her, and she seemed smaller and more vulnerable than I could remember ever seeing her. It was like she already knew how this was going to turn out. It was hard to watch.

Carson squeezed her hand, and said she'd see her in the OR. Then the nurse anesthetist showed up. She would be helping the anesthesiologist, and she was the one who called for the nurse with the Versed. They gave Joanie a shot of that drug through her IV line, and in moments, her face relaxed, and they began to wheel her bed off to the OR. They were going to turn right to the OR, and I was going to turn left to head for the surgery waiting room so I kissed her and told her "everything is gonna be all right," but I don't think she remembered it, her eyes were already beginning to glaze over.

I signed in at the surgery waiting room, told the volunteer I'd be back shortly and went out for a smoke. There was nothing for me to do now but wait for Carson to tell me what the findings from the physical exam and exploratory laparotomy were. While this surgery wouldn't take near as long as the exenteration she endured back in February, it still would be a lengthy procedure. While I was out, I picked up my usual collection of newspapers and stopped by the coffee cart in the lobby for a mocha, hoping the news and crosswords would get me through some of the time in the waiting room. Around ten or so, my son Ryan joined me there, and so there was also someone to talk to. I had a good deck of cards along, if we wanted to play a little gin, and we wouldn't have to improvise like we did that time in February.

Dr. Carson made an appearance, and we went off to an anteroom off the main waiting area, and she gave me the news. It couldn't be done. In reviewing the notes from the day, here's what her notes said about what they had found: "...it was determined that a minimal amount of colonic tissue would be available in order to repair this large rectovaginal defect. It was discussed in great detail among the surgeons that with this patient's previous history of radiation for her cervical cancer and, most recently, iridium tubes placed for close approximated sidewall disease on the left side and the very large defect, that reconstruction of this rectovaginal fistula would be difficult and that good surgical outcome would be difficult to achieve, given the fact that her tissues have been radiated x 2, and a minimal amount of tissue was present for reconstruction."

Those notes reflect the clinical aspect of what was going on. What I heard was the fistula was too big, there wasn't enough colon left from the big surgery to work with, there was damage from radiation, and that reconstructive surgery "would not be advisable or to be able to be completed."

It was the news we had feared, even as we had anticipated it. The hope we had clung to was now dashed. The upside of it was that they would take down the ileostomy, which was harder to take care of due to the fact there was so much liquid associated with it, and create a colostomy that would be easier to care for.

Carson returned to the OR to continue the procedure, and I was left trying to process all that I heard, and what it meant for Joanie, how she would handle it, and what effect the change was going to have on her life. It was going to be permanent, and that word alone sounded louder when I thought of it than it ever had.

I got Ryan and went outside for a smoke. Somehow everything seemed different now. I thought about that night in February when he and Kim and I were walking to the hotel, feeling good about the news Carson had given us that they would be able to hook her bowel back up after things healed up, and how long ago that seemed now, and how much had happened since. It didn't seem fair, and it wasn't.

When Joanie was brought up to her room on 7C, she was distraught. They had put in a Foley to drain her Miami pouch, and the NG hose, i.e., "nose hose" to drain her stomach was in place, and she had a morphine pump in her hand. She took one look at me and started to cry, not much, but there were tears rolling down her flushed cheeks. I couldn't do anything but grab her hand and squeeze it. We didn't talk about what had happened, and she didn't want to. Joanie was still groggy from the drugs, the effects of the anesthesia and the pain from the surgery, and told me she wanted to sleep. She hit the morphine pump, and closed her eyes.

I had to make some calls to let her siblings, Richard, Ann, and Ginny, know what had taken place. I would contact other folks tomorrow when I had the energy to do so. There would be time for that, we were going to be there for a while yet. Ryan and Kim and I went somewhere, I don't remember where, it isn't important now. We had a beer and something to eat, and I went back to the hospital.

Joanie was still sleeping when I got back, and the nurse who was hers for the night said she hadn't stirred since I left. As I sat there in the half light of her room on the incredibly uncomfortable chairs they have for visitors, I wondered how this was going to go. It occurred to me as I sat there, it's not the hand you're dealt that's important, it's how you play the hand you got that matters. I began to feel better about how she was going to get through this.

She came to for just a few minutes, said hi to me and told me it was okay for me to go. I leaned over, gave her a kiss, told her I loved her, and I'd see her in the morning. She closed her eyes and was out.

She's going to be just fine.

Friday morning. I woke up early, and looked around my room. I took a minute to fire up the in-room coffeepot and set it to brewing its marginal coffee, turned on the TV to see if the world had come to an end overnight and I had missed it, lit a cigarette, and took a seat by the table. While it hadn't come to an end, there were wars, rumors of wars, famine, pestilence, and all sorts of mayhem being inflicted on unknown individuals around the world, not to mention there was a rush hour accident on I-94 eastbound that was tying up traffic. Nothing seemed to have changed from the day before.

I took a minute, got up went to the door, opened it slightly and grabbed the complimentary copy of *USA Today* the hotel leaves outside your room every day. A quick glance at the front page confirmed what I had inferred from watching the TV for a short while. We were safe, at this point.

Joanie came to the foreground of my thoughts. I wondered how she was doing and if she had gotten any sleep last night. I know when she let me go, she was in pain, and was down about what had taken place in the operating room, or rather what had not taken place. I felt bad for her last night, and I felt the same way this morning.

As a caregiver, my immediate job was to help her get healed up from the surgery, which was a major deal, and then to help her put this whole thing in perspective. I wasn't sure how I was going to do the latter, except to lean on my experience after the other disappointments she had suffered since that day in May 1996, and that was to let her lead me where she wanted to go. I had found that to be a sound approach, and one that served me well.

Since it was Friday, mercifully, the lobby coffee cart was open. I grabbed a cherry croissant and a mocha and headed up to 7C. She was awake, and they had changed her clothes, and tried to make her more comfortable. She still had the nose hose in, and that would be in until they thought she would be able to tolerate solid food again. There was still the Foley catheter draining the Miami pouch into a bag hooked on the side of the bed, which was more for convenience than anything. She wouldn't have to bother with emptying it.

She smiled when I came, in, and it was one of those smiles that tells you in a gentle way that she's going to be okay. We talked a little about her new reality, and though she was still in pain this morning, she was willing to get up and go for a walk with me. I had to unhook the pneumatic leggings wrapped around her calves; they pulse against the patient's skin to keep blood flowing while she is lying in bed to help keep clots from forming.

We took a slow walk around the halls of 7C, and she did quite well. We didn't go as far as we had in past walks, but this was the first time she was out of bed since the surgery. I must have tired her out, because when we got back to the room, all she wanted to do was take another hit off the morphine pump and take a nap. I hooked the leggings back up, made sure she was comfortable, and I went out for a smoke.

When I got back up to the room, she was still sleeping, and I didn't wake her. I took my seat and got to work on the crossword puzzle. It wasn't long before the phone rang, and it was her brother Richard. She came to and talked with him for just a few minutes, but it was obvious she wasn't in the mood to make small talk. I had called Ed and Nancy Schafer this morning with an update, and made a couple of more calls to some other friends, so I knew the word was getting spread around.

What I had learned this year was that I could be on the phone for almost as long as any of the surgeries took, because we were so far from home, and we had so many friends who wanted to know what was going on with her. My solution was to set up a telephone tree, for lack of a better term, and outside of family, I would just have to call a few select numbers, and they would then call Joanie's other friends. It worked, and it was something I'd recommend to anyone in similar circumstances.

I asked her if there was anything she wanted, and the only thing she told me was she wanted to go home. She said it with slight smile, and added she didn't want anything right now but some sleep. She hit the pump again and dozed off. I went to the Radisson for lunch. When I got back, she was awake and we started to talk about what was going on. I wondered how she was feeling about what had happened, or more precisely, what didn't happen. She told me she had been praying for a different outcome, and was disappointed but not surprised. Then she said something that surprised me. She noted that it wasn't like we didn't know what we were dealing with, having coped with the ileostomy since February. I was beginning to believe that she was going to play the hand she'd been dealt better than I imagined she would.

I told her, the upside of this whole deal was what Dr. Carson reported, and that there was "no sign of recurrent disease at this point in time."

While we were happy to hear that, and it gave us something to take away from the disappointment, the five words that stuck with me were, "...at this point in time." Joanie didn't pay any attention to them; she had heard all she needed to hear, and maybe I paid too much attention to them, but to me they were the cautionary words, words that we would hope to hear at the end of each clinic appointment during the coming years.

After we had tried to put a good face on this situation, I said maybe we should go for a walk. We got her ready and made the rounds of the halls of 7C, feeling a little different than we had in the morning. Nurses who recognized her from previous visits would stop her and give her a few words of encouragement. She liked that, and so did I. Fridays, as I've noted before, were different days. Early in the morning, the lobby was full of people coming and going and going and coming, there was often some fellow playing the piano in one corner of the huge brightly lit, seating area, the line at lobby cart was full of nurses and doctors in scrubs, others in multicolored frocks and crocs, all waiting for a morning caffeine jolt.

Here and there were people like me, ones who had a loved one in some kind of distress, a husband, wife, child or relative all waiting for some kind of news, or just trying to pass the time as they stared out the floor to ceiling windows that made up the north wall of the lobby, until they went back up to the patient's room. Taking a few minutes to get away from whatever uncertain, medical reality they were dealing with. Sitting there with nothing but their cup of coffee and their hopes.

By mid-afternoon, when it came shift change time at the hospital, three-thirty, everything changed. In one door came the night shift, and out the other door would come the nurses, doctors, aides, interns and others who had been there since very early morning. A crowd of nurses and others were waiting for a bus to take them to the other side of the river where another part of this huge medical complex was located,

163

and shortly there would be a bus bringing back those who were done for the day.

I could feel the change as it happened. I was outside having a smoke, and watching it, as I was prone to do, and envying those who were leaving for the beginning of their weekend, which I imagined to be filled with all kinds of enjoyable things to do, far away from the disease and medical problems they had been dealing with. I wanted to join them. Inside the huge lobby, it was all of a sudden quiet, quiet like it would be until Monday morning, when the business of health care and healing, would switch into high gear again.

That night, around ten o'clock when I left, the lights in Joanie's room were off, except for the light above the head of the bed, which was just enough to make out her face. She looked at me and smiled, and told me she was going to handle this. I kissed her, said good night, and left sure in the knowledge she would, if anyone could.

As I walked through the darkened lobby that night, the familiar security guy I had come to know was on duty. He looked up from his lamplit desk and asked me how things were going. I smiled, thanked him, and told him she is going to be just fine.

I went back to the Radisson for a nightcap, and the bartender whom we had gotten to know from our trips down, and especially from earlier this year, I think his name was Manuel. He was a pleasant, younger guy, and when I had lunch there during the week, always waited on me. I had introduced him to Al Olson one day when Al and I had lunch there, and he thought it was special that he had met a former governor.

I ordered a Bailey's on the rocks, and when he set it up, he asked, "How's your wife doing?" He had met Joanie on a couple of occasions, and he knew from talking to me she was having problems. I told him the same thing I told the security guy, "She is going to be just fine."

Saturdays in the U of M hospital, are relatively quiet. There is emergency activity, as there always seems to be in any hospital in an urban setting, and on 7C you would find women who were in for overnight chemo treatments and gone the next day. Outside of that, 7C seems to operate at a slower pace than it does during the week, or maybe that is just how it seemed to me.

Joanie was awake when I got to her room. She told me she didn't have a good night, and it was obvious she was still in pain from the surgery, and was still feeling the effects of the drugs she was taking as a precaution against infection. They made her feel groggy, and we put off our walk until later. She said she didn't want to, and I have learned that is often the best reason not to do something.

I did tell her that my sisters were going to show up, so she should conserve her energy. They were both familiar with hospitals, Jane because she had been a patient enough times, and Joni because when she was in the navy, she worked at the Navy Hospital in Oakland, California. This would be the third time this year they had been to visit Joanie, and because they were familiar, they knew enough to not stay too long to wear her out. Their energy levels could do that to a healthy person, but in a situation like this, they were able to keep it low-key.

After they arrived, spent some time with her, and were able to see that Joanie was doing okay, despite the pain, the three of us went for lunch downtown at The Loon Cafe. They were excited that even though things didn't turn out as we had hoped, there was no cancer to be seen, "at the present time."

It was much like the other times they had visited, and it was a momentary reminder that life outside of the place where my energy had been focused since Wednesday was still going on. Any caregiver who lives close to a situation such as Joanie's will find you need that reminder from time to time. Besides, the levity that accompanied their visit was also a balm for troubled times, and I appreciated it, as did Joanie.

Back at the hospital, Joanie was dozing. I didn't think she was sleeping, because she opened her eyes when I came in, even as I had tried to step softly. She asked me what time it was, if I had a good lunch with Joni and Jane, and if they'd left. Then she closed her eyes and dozed off again.

That routine was normal, since it was only the second day since she had the surgery, and her body was still trying to recover from the trauma it had experienced. There had been many days like these, since that day in February, that gave me time to think. I had not much else to do when she was sleeping, and wasn't in the mood to go for walk.

As I sat there in her room, looking at her while she was sleeping, I wondered to myself, "Where's the profound rage?" I had never seen evidence of anger from her at any point in this process, something I had expected. I expected rage at what had happened in her body, what had happened to her body, how it had changed her body, and how cancer would threaten her life from this day forward. I never saw it, and perhaps my thinking about it said more about me than it did her.

Joanie roused me out of my reverie when she came to, and wanted some fresh ice and water. I obliged. It was dark outside, and it was a quiet night on the floor. She told me we'd go for a walk tomorrow, and told me if I wanted to go, I could. It wasn't that late, and I had no place to go, so I told her I was just going to have a smoke.

Actually, it was a pleasant night, so I had a couple, as I walked around the side of the hospital, being joined once in a while by a nurse, or doctor, or some other person who was there looking after their patient. It struck me we all had something in common on this night, some being there because of occupation and others being there because of necessity of their occupation. I spent most of my time looking at the lights coming through the many windows, listening to the sounds of the city and the traffic on a Saturday night, sounds which were punctuated once in a while by the sound of a far-off siren which signaled that someone was in trouble of some kind, and wondering what it might be.

I went back up to 7C, and Joanie was sleeping again. This time I woke her up to tell her I was leaving, and I would see her first thing Sunday morning. That was okay with her, and I left.

As I walked back to the Radisson, I passed young college students on their way to or from some Saturday night fun, heard a siren in the distance, and as I got to the front of the hotel, I could hear the laughter and the voices from Sally's outdoor seating area which was across and down the street from the Radisson, and was reminded again that no matter what manner of medical problem Joanie had, her problem only really mattered to her, me, her doctors, her family, and her friends.

Life goes on.

Sunday, and it looked like maybe mid-week for a departure. The medical staff was concerned about infection, and had her on two different drugs, and they took blood cultures and urine cultures as well as did chest x-rays. By Wednesday she had been clear for forty-eight hours, and was tolerating food. It was go for Thursday. I could take her home.

Her spirits improved every day, and when Dr. Carson said she could go home they really improved. She had had enough

167

of 7C for one year, and was anxious to get out of there. Joanie still had some healing to do, but at least now, she could focus on that in her own home. My job would be as it was before when we brought her home from the hospital, and that was to see to her getting some exercise, and watching for any signs of trouble. The colostomy learning curve wasn't much, since we had dealt with an ileostomy before, and in a few weeks, it had become routine, and it was easier to care for than the ileostomy. Joanie seemed to have accepted this was going to be a permanent part of her life, and it was made easier by the fact I did the changing for her.

It was now late September, and Joanie was getting anxious to get back to work, so in early October, she began going in part time, just to get back in a routine. I think it helped speed up the healing process as well.

We weren't scheduled for another clinic appointment until mid-December, and by then she would be close to 100 percent. I began to see her character emerge during this period, and when she was stronger and able to go out again, the fact that she had a colostomy didn't seem to bother her. In fact, she was able to make light of it with friends who were aware of her situation. One night at Peacock Alley we were standing talking to one of our friends, Tom Woodmansee, and as he announced to us he had to go the bathroom, Joanie just looked at him, smiled, and said, "I can do that right here."

There was never, a time when she was looking for sympathy, and over the years, people who met her for the first time when she was working for Ed Schafer and John Hoeven would not have a clue about her health situation. That was the way she wanted it. For me during this time, I was just glad she was doing okay. I had already started my mental countdown to five years from now, the time when statistically she would be listed as "cancer free."

As December arrived, and the Christmas holidays were approaching, Joanie told me she was going to write to Dr. Carson and Dr. Cosin. I thought that was a grand idea, and here is what she wrote to the two major figures in her medical life since those first days in May 1996:

December 7, 1998

Dear Dr. Carson,

The holiday season is upon us, and we just wanted to take this time to send you good wishes for a Happy Christmas and a Great New Year.

We also wanted to take this opportunity to say thank you for what you have done for me during this difficult time in my life.

Bob and I just can't say enough about how you and your associates handled my situation, and the level of care I received from you and Dr. Cosin, Dr. Murray and the entire staff of interns, nurses, aides and others on 7C.

As you know, I would have like to have had a different outcome in September, but I want you also to know that I appreciate the good news regarding the cancer as being more important than anything else. I am adjusting, probably, I suppose, as you knew I would.

I am working almost full-time again, and do feel stronger every day. You will have a chance to assess that when we get down there on the 15th yourself. I hope you pass along my thanks to the many nurses and others on 7C as well. They are an extremely capable group of professionals in a difficult job, and they do it well.

Again, my thanks for everything over the past couple of years. Have a great Holiday, and we'll see you on the 15th.

Sincerely,
Joan Wigen and Bob Kallberg

She sent a similar letter to Dr. Cosin:

December 7, 1998

Dear Dr. Cosin,

The holiday season is here, and Bob and I just wanted to send you wishes for a great one, and also to send you a thank you.

We want to thank you for everything you've done for me over the past couple of years, and especially during the difficult days earlier this year.

We think you're a good doctor, and the manner in which you addressed my situation really helped both of us understand, and deal with the medical realities that I faced back then and face now. Your kindness, compassion and understanding are rare qualities, and meant a lot to me during this time of my life.

You and Dr. Carson and the other professionals at the Center and up on 7C do a marvelous job under tough circumstances, and I was glad to see that you'll be staying there for some time to come. The Center needs doctors like you.

We'll be in on the 15th, and perhaps we'll see you then.

If we should miss you, please accept our thanks again, and have a great holiday season.

Sincerely,
  Joan Wigen

She showed me the letters before she mailed them and asked me what I thought. All I could say to her was they were excellent, and I couldn't improve on either one of them. These two people had become pretty important to her, and had taken damn good care of her.

When we went down for the appointment on the fifteenth, we took some boxes of her Christmas candy, the stuff I had been pressed into making, to drop off at the clinic for Marcia, Carson, and Cosin, and a platter for the nursing staff there. Marcia was Dr. Carson's gatekeeper, and there'll be more about that later. The news from that appointment was all we hoped for, "no evidence of disease."

After that meeting, we went straight to Sally's and enjoyed ourselves there for the first time in a long time.

The rest of the holiday season was perfect. We enjoyed the parties, and the gifts we said we weren't going to buy for each other, and being home on Christmas Eve, alone with the kitties.

On New Year's Eve, we had stopped downtown early but then went home. After we got comfortable, we broke out a bottle of Joanie's favorite wine, cut up some cheese, tore up some good bread for dipping in olive oil, and welcomed in the New Year, both of us glad this one was over.

It had been one helluva year, and she had survived, and I loved her more than ever.

SECTION THREE
1999—2002

Some good times, and some change.

January 1, 1999, ushered in a period of good times, times that reminded us of what life was like before the intensity of the previous two years. That is not to say we forgot about the cloud, it was just that it no longer dominated our consciousness all the time. It was only when we were getting ready for another appointment that it came to the foreground, and after a successful appointment, it was another stop at Sally's, or dinner with Ginny and Ed, or Al and Barb, or Cathy Rydell.

The discussion we had back in late February 1998 about not letting this disease control our lives was working, even though we never talked about it after that time. It was obvious to me she was not going to be held hostage by something over which she had no control.

The Miami pouch and the colostomy had become second nature, and presented no problem except on a couple of occasions. One such time came when she came home later than usual. She had been busy in her office, and also was involved with the church council and the development of a new addition. When she got home, she went to the bathroom to empty the pouch, something she told me she hadn't done for some time. In a minute, she called me and told me she was having trouble with the catheter.

I went in, and saw that the Red Robinson, which was a soft, pliable catheter, couldn't penetrate past the flap. It would be inserted in her naval, and would just bend around and come back out. I began to feel uneasy, and suggested we try one of the stiffer catheters we had in stock. That didn't work either. She kept trying, and kept getting more anxious. We both knew, the pouch was full, and the pressure on the flap was too much for the catheter. The concern I had was that the bladder wasn't so full that it was leaking internally.

I kept her calm, and we kept trying, until I finally told her we were going to the emergency room. She reluctantly agreed. Fortunately that night the doctor on call was a urologist who was familiar with the pouch. They first did an ultrasound to determine there had been no leaking, and then they went to work on getting a catheter inserted so they could drain the pouch. That was the only time we ever had to deal with that problem.

The colostomy only presented a worrisome problem on one occasion. We were at Menard's one Saturday morning, in line waiting to check out when she whispered to me the seal had broken. I just move our cart out of line, and we walked out of the store and headed for the car. We made it home without incident, and I was able to make the change without any problem. The seal broke other times, but they were always at home. I changed it at least once a week, and often told her she should be getting in the habit of doing it herself. I would ask her what she would do if something happened to me or I wasn't there to change it. She would just shrug her shoulders and ignore the question. Joanie had gone back to work fulltime, and since Ed was believed to be running for a third term as governor, she was working with renewed focus. That belief, of course, would be put to bed later in the year when to her surprise he announced he was not going to run. This brought her up short, because she all of a sudden faced an uncertain future. However, that uncertainty was short lived when John Hoeven came calling and recruited her to go to work on his convention campaign.

First Lady Nancy Jones Schafer hosts surprise birthday party for Joanie. 2000. L.to R., Nancy Jones Schafer, Governor Ed Schafer, Joanie Wigen

One of the highlights of 2000 came when Nancy Schafer hosted a surprise birthday party for Joanie at the governor's residence. I had been enlisted in the plan of getting Joanie to the residence, and it came at some risk for me. I had produced a video on Ed's years as governor that was shown at the convention, and we had copies made. Nancy called Joanie, and told her they were going to be going to the lake in Minnesota on Friday, and asked if she could have me drop some of the tapes off at the residence.

Now, you have to understand Joanie. She told me she wanted me to drop those tapes off to Nancy in the early afternoon. I didn't, and when I picked her up, I started driving to the residence, and when she asked me why, I told her I had to drop off the tapes. She became pissed immediately, thinking I had kept the governor and first lady from heading for the lake. I didn't say anything, just took the box of tapes up to the door and Nancy answered. She then told me to get Joanie, she wanted to show her the remodeling job that had been done.

Joanie looked at me, and I knew I was in trouble, and she apologized to Nancy for the tapes being late in being delivered. Nancy told her not to mind, took her in, and headed for a closed door beyond which a group of her friends were waiting. When the door opened, and she heard the collective shout of, "Surprise," her face reddened, and she couldn't believe what she was seeing, and as happened often when she was really happy, the tears came.

It was a great evening, with Ed tending the grill and making burgers, and Joanie every so often looking around and shaking her head. It had been a success, and by the time we got home that night, she wasn't mad at me anymore. John would go on to win the endorsement, and the general election in November 2000, and Joanie would stay on the job with his political committee doing much the same thing she did for Ed, all the time waiting for a job in state government.

She eventually got that job, and in March 2001, went to work in the state tourism department, a job she came to love, and one she was good at. When she told me about the job, I was happy for her, and in the back of my mind, I was looking at the calendar. We were now three years out from "the big one," and over halfway to being called cancer free.

The woman on the phone.

Joanie went to work at the North Dakota Department of Tourism, March 21, 2001, and she did it with the same sense of responsibility she brought to any job. All of a sudden, her focus was completely on what she was doing, and her schedule showed it. She became so busy, she didn't have time to think about cancer, or anything else.

She was reveling in her new job, and getting up early in the morning to get to work. It was also a busy time at Trinity Lutheran, and she was heavily involved in their building project. Her zest for life, was evident, and it was like she was going to wring as much as she could out of each day. I think, in the back of her mind, it was because she knew something that most of us don't, and that is how fragile this whole thing is. I don't know if she had ever heard the Latin expression, "carpe diem," but that is how she was living. It was great to see it happening.

She was healthy both physically and emotionally, and even those who knew her medical history never gave it a thought anymore. She was just alive.

We still had to make trips to see Dr. Carson, and she was feeling so good, those didn't bother her like they used to. From 1999 through 2002, visits to the clinic were only about every three or four months. The news was always the same, good, go and enjoy life.

In her new job with Tourism, she was on road a lot, and all I did was make sure when she was going to be gone for more than a day, that her bag had all she would need to deal with. I also tried to encourage her, while she was home and the colostomy needed to be changed to give it a try in case she was out of town and it needed to be done. She would look at me just like she did every time I made that suggestion and didn't take my advice.

The year, 2001 flew by, and it wasn't too far into 2002 when change came calling again. This time, early May, Joanie came home and told me she had gotten a call from John, and he wanted to meet with her. There had been some change in the Hoeven Committee, and our guess was he was going to ask her to come back.

We sat at home, and I asked her what she was going to do if he asked her to do that. She said she didn't know. On the one hand, she had a job she really liked, with benefits and a good salary, but, on the other hand he was the governor, and if he wanted her to come back, she would have to consider it. She did tell me she didn't want to take a pay cut, and also there was the issue of paying for health insurance. She told me she would make a decision after she talked to him, but I knew what the answer was already. I told her whatever decision she made was okay with me.

A couple of days later she came home around five and had this smile on her face, and told me she had just come from a meeting with John, and she told him she would come back. He told her they would match her salary, and make a provision for paying her health care premium. She told me, "He wanted me to come back, and how do you say no to the governor?" I just smiled and told her I knew what she was going to do when she told me that John wanted to meet with her. So, on May 17, 2002, it was her last day at Tourism, and come Monday, it would be back into the political arena.

This would begin what I call her "telephone period." Anyone who has ever been involved in politics knows what a valuable tool a phone is, and in the age of cell phones you are never really out of your office. Joanie was no different. If she wasn't on the phone with people around the state, she was talking to people around the country. Then there were her friends, the business of the building project at Trinity she was still involved in, and, of course, to a lesser degree me. I used to chide her about my calls always being routed directly to voice mail, or if I did get through to her, she would tell me she was busy and would call me back. Rarely did she, and I would have to call her again.

Governor John Hoeven, Joanie, Mikey Hoeven

She became "The Woman with the Telephone" to me. It was okay, she was in an element she understood, doing a job she did well for someone she was totally loyal to and who appreciated what she brought to the table. Going back to work for John and Mikey, as it turned out later, was the best decision she had ever made, and we would find out that as strong as her loyalty was for them, theirs was as strong for her.

179

Kismet in the form of an unopened letter.

Since February 12, 1998, each time the calendar turned over to a new year, I thought about that date and the magical date five years from then: February 12, 2003. That was the magical date for Joanie to be declared a cancer survivor. After all, the odds on survival rate after the pelvic exenteration was just over 60 percent.

We had made it through 1999, 2000, 2001, were in the middle of 2002, and it seemed like this holy grail was going to be within our reach. So far, there had been nothing to indicate the date would not pass without incident, and we would have reason for celebration after all, Joanie had already made it over four years and was doing fine.

She didn't pay any attention to the calendar, not that she would tell me if she did. We never talked about it, as if to do so would put a jinx on it. She preferred to ignore it and just get on with life. I did so, too, but it was never far from my mind. As far as Joanie was concerned, there was too much to do, and she was too busy doing it to care about anything else.

During those years we still had to make trips to see Dr. Carson, and it was one of those times we had a rare appointment for late on a Friday afternoon, or so we thought we did. Since the appointment was for four o'clock, we didn't leave until the morning, and even then we made quick stop at Mabel Murphy's, for to not do so would be bad luck. We got to the clinic with minutes to spare, and when she went to check in, we were told Dr. Carson was out of town, and they asked us if we had received a letter telling us the appointment had been changed.

We both pleaded ignorance, and went to sit down for a minute. It was then I realized that the envelope I had seen a week ago, with the clinic's return address on it must have been the notification. We hadn't opened it, thinking it was just a reminder of the upcoming appointment.

Joanie and I sat there in the waiting room, the only ones there by now, and both laughed. Wondering what we should do now, I made a suggestion. Joanie was an organized person, and liked making plans, me not so much. I was more prone to taking what we were given and running with it. I think a shrink would say that was impulsive, but it worked for me. I thought of it as being spontaneous. I told her since no one knew we were in town, and we had a room at the Radisson, why not just take the weekend and enjoy ourselves. We wouldn't call anybody we knew, and would just go do what the hell we wanted to do and find a good restaurant for dinner on Saturday night and pretend that the appointment went fine, and we got good news.

She agreed it was a good plan, but before we left the clinic, she made another appointment to see Dr. Carson. From there we went to Sally's and sat down at the bar, which was full of the usual late Friday crowd, students, nurses from the clinic and hospital, professors and others getting ready for the weekend, and after ordering, we clinked our glasses in a toast to one of the best clinic appointments she'd never had. Saturday, we found a good coffee shop first, then we went downtown, walked around the Nicollet Mall window shopping and browsing at Dayton's, doing nothing in particular, had lunch at The Loon Cafe, went back for a nap around mid-day, and that night we went to the Lexington, a place we both loved, for dinner. When we got back to the Radisson that night, we did something we hadn't been able to do in a long time, and that was stop at the bar and have a Baileys for a nightcap. It turned out to be one of the best weekends we had had in a long time.

We left early Sunday morning to drive back to Bismarck, and when we got home, I fished out the letter from the clinic, which told us that her appointment had been cancelled, and she was supposed to call to reschedule. We laughed again. I told her, it was Kismet, we were meant to have that weekend alone together, free from medical issues, and that's why neither one of us had opened it. I don't think she bought it, but I wasn't so sure I was wrong. It had been a long time since we had made a non-medical trip to one of our favorite places, Minneapolis/St. Paul, and she deserved it.

We never saw it coming.

As 2002 was winding down, I was still watching the calendar, with an eye on February 12, 2003. I felt we were getting closer to calling her a survivor. Joanie was as busy as ever, but with the little spare time she had on the weekends, she spent it in the backyard, and with quiet time on Sunday mornings.

I thought she was doing fine, until the fall of 2002, she began to develop a dry cough. At first I chalked it up to a cold, but after it persisted for a few weeks, it became clear it was being caused by something else. In mid-November, Dr. Carson ordered a chest x-ray, and the results came back indicating "there is no evidence of any pulmonary disease." We were happy with that, and I thought we were back on schedule toward the five-year mark, and we made it through the holiday season without any problems. Her cough was still there, but it was not as pronounced as it had been earlier. But as 2003 rolled around, we could not see what was headed our way.

SECTION FOUR
2003-2004

In March 2003, we met with Dr. Carson at the clinic, and she ordered a CT scan of her thorax along with another x-ray for March 31. Now, we began to be a little bit concerned. I no longer gave a damn about the five-year thing. I had a feeling something was wrong, and when we got the results of the CT scan, we knew there was.

The findings in the radiologist's report said, "There is an endobronchial lesion involving the patient's right lower lobe bronchus. Just past this lesion there is a 2 x 2 cm infrahilar lung mass. This finding is suspicious for lung malignancy." Translated by my non-medical training, it meant there was a lesion that involved the right bronchial tube and her right lower lobe, and there was a suspicious mass in the same area. That's all we knew at the time.

The news fell like a boulder on our house, and we were both crushed when we heard the findings, for it unleashed all of the fear and uncertainty we had lived with those first two years again.

Dr. Carson ordered a bronchoscopy for April 11. We met with Dr. Jim Hughes at St. Alexius Medical Center in Bismarck who would be performing the procedure. A bronchoscopy is a diagnostic procedure done under a local anesthesia. They put a scope down through your nose, and it makes its way to the trachea and into the bronchial trees of both lungs. There was no problem with the left tree. The problem was in the right tree and the lower lobe bronchus.

That would be the branch of the bronchial tree that branches off to the lower right lobe of the lung.

I waited in the outpatient surgery waiting room for Dr. Hughes to make an appearance. I didn't wait too long that afternoon, when he came out to see me and to show me a photo of what they were looking at. It looked like a Polaroid picture that could have been anything, but he tried to point out to me where the problem was. Then he left me alone to try and process what I had just seen and wonder what it meant for Joanie.

He was in Joanie's room when I got there, and she obviously knew that we were dealing with some kind of cancer. She had been crying, and when I came in, she started again. Hughes left, and I just sat there holding her hand, not knowing what I should say. We were both stunned.

Hughes said at the end of the procedure it could be non-small-cell-lung cancer, but we would have to wait for the biopsies until we knew for sure. If that was the case, we would have a whole set of new problems and treatment to worry about. On the other hand, if it were metastatic squamous cell cancer of the cervix, there would be another set of problems. Both terminologies scared us.

By the time Joanie had a chance to recover from the procedure, it was late afternoon. We went home, both lost, and much as we had done that day in May some seven years ago, we wondered what the hell we were going to do now.

We didn't make any calls that night—calls seemed to us to be premature. We stayed home, and though neither one of us was hungry, I ordered a pizza. Joanie took her position on the couch and Muffin soon joined her. We opened a bottle of wine, and as the darkness of the night crept into our little house on Mandan Street, we sat there and tried not to think about what might be next. We just listened to the music and wondered.

Another new doctor and another new reality.

The initial news was a stunner. We were now again faced with a sea of uncertainty and confusion, and it would be sometime before it would cleared up. Dr. Hughes's notes said after the bronchoscopy, "This lesion has the appearance of a primary non-small-cell lung carcinoma." Lung cancer.

The day after was a Saturday, and Joanie didn't have to go to work. We talked, and she was wondering what she should tell people. There were those who knew she was going in for the procedure, and I told her she should call John and Mikey Hoeven and tell them there was a potential problem, but we wouldn't know any more about it until after we meet with Dr. Carson in Minneapolis, and after that she could tell anyone she thought needed to know, or whom she wanted to tell. The fact was, at that time, we didn't know much.

We had a dinner club scheduled with three other couples for that night, and we changed those plans. One of the other couples graciously took our turn. We were not ready for conversation or company.

That day I went to the computer, and plugged in the term non-small-cell lung cancer, and proceeded to find out more than I could ever understand about it, but I kept looking to see if I could get an idea of what it was, and what kind of treatment there was for it, and what the odds were. I was looking for answers to those questions that would give us the most positive options. I had grasped onto Dr. Hughes's impression that it had the appearance of lung cancer. Using my limited medical education, I had found a branch to cling to, and that was, depending on the stage, surgery might be curative. That meant, losing part of a lung might be the answer.

This was a moment when I learned about the triumph of hope over reason. All I wanted was to find an answer that would make Joanie feel better, and give her something positive to hang onto. Our world had all of a sudden been disrupted.

The thing I missed altogether, or was too focused on the lung cancer part to see, was that this was, in all likelihood, metastatic squamous cell cancer of the cervix. Here again, hope over reason. What I had read a long time ago but had forgotten was that if cervical cancer metastasizes, the lungs are one of the popular places for it to show up. I had paid little attention to that, due mainly to our holding on to the possibility that the exenteration could be "curative."

It was a ten-day wait from the time of the bronchoscopy until we met with Dr. Carson in Minneapolis, and it was ten days full of uncertainty and on my part, confusion. Joanie, kept busy. Her calendar was full, and as far as she was concerned, she would worry about this when we next met with Carson. She had work to do, and nothing was going to get in the way.

On the twenty-first of April, we met with Dr. Carson in the clinic, and she recommended that Joanie see a Dr. Michael Maddaus, one of the top thoracic surgeons at the University of Minnesota Hospital to discuss what the next step would be in dealing with the suspect mass in her right bronchial tube. We still didn't know exactly what it was, but I'm not sure they knew exactly either, even though they probably thought it was metastatic disease. Carson order a CT scan, so at around six that evening we found ourselves over in radiation to get that done. We would see Maddaus the next day.

The next afternoon, we met with Dr. Maddaus at the Masonic Cancer Center, which is located between the Phillips-Wangensteen Building and the hospital. He came in to the room, relaxed, open shirt, followed by a nurse who was taking notes. Maddaus struck me as one of those surgeons who could have been on M.A.S.H. He wasn't brash, but he gave you a feeling of confidence about two minutes after meeting him for the first time. Joanie took a liking to him immediately.

I was really pleased with how he dealt with her. He made her feel comfortable, in what was a very uncomfortable situation. He was telling her they were probably going to have to take out part of her right lung. He spent about forty-five minutes talking to her about how this might be done, and told her they might be able to do it laparoscopically, meaning they wouldn't have to open her chest. That would be the best news we could hear. He did caution her that they might not know that until they got a better look at what they were dealing with. Joanie seemed okay with everything he was telling her. I remember thinking, "This guy is one helluva surgeon, and probably could be one helluva salesman." Nobody, not Carson nor Maddaus, had told us for sure they thought we were dealing with non-small-cell lung cancer, or if they were dealing with metastatic cervical cancer. All we knew right then, was that he was going to be her surgeon for the next time she went into an operating room.

Before he left, he told us he wanted a PET scan, which was a new one on us. PET stands for Positron Emission Tomography. What it amounts to is a scan they do after the patient has been injected with radioactive glucose, and since cancer cells metabolize glucose at a higher rate than normal cells, the cancer cells light up on the scan, and it gives doctors a more precise picture of what and where the problem areas might be. This diagnostic tool was fairly new when Joanie had

187

her first one. It was so new that the scans were done in a trailer parked next to the hospital. This tractor-trailer operation would make rounds of hospitals in our area where it wasn't available on a full-basis in-house.

Since it involved nuclear medicine, I wasn't able to accompany her any further than the door to where they give her the shot. With the PET, they could compare the results to the CT scan of the abdomen and the chest they had made a few days earlier. The result of the PET read, "Impression: There is a single focus of concerning uptake corresponding to CT abnormality in the right lung, consistent with malignancy." When they use the word uptake in connection with a PET scan, it means something lit up. In Joanie's case, the scan agreed with the CT there was something terribly wrong going on in her right lung. The diagnosis would take some time, and the three days in Minneapolis were beginning to tell on Joanie. We headed for home, not caring if we got home early or not, she just wanted to be home.

We didn't talk at all about what we had been told by either Carson or Maddaus, and all we really knew was we had about fifteen days until we were back down there for lung surgery with Maddaus. By the time a couple of hundred miles were behind us, I began to reflect on how unfair this whole deal was. She had been so close to the five-year survival threshold, and it was snatched away unceremoniously from her, starting with a cough. Not that other people don't have bad experiences, or suffer medical setbacks, but this was my Joanie, and I didn't care if anyone agreed with me or not, she was getting a bum deal. It wasn't fair, and the future was in doubt again.

When we got back to Bismarck, and she found the couch, and Muffin found on her lap, I looked at them sitting there and couldn't help but think that if Muffin had a voice, she would agree with me.

> **"When you have no choice, mobilize the spirit of courage."**
> —Jewish Proverb

The news of the mass by her right bronchial tube had become real for us by now. Along with the news came those handmaidens of cancer, fear, uncertainty, and confusion. We thought they had abandoned us, or we hoped we had relegated them to a dark corner of the basement, never to be heard from again. After all, we had put five very good years between that surgery in 1998 and by now, I had begun planning a celebration, even if Joanie hadn't.

The day after we got back from Minneapolis and the meetings with Dr. Carson and Dr. Maddaus, Joanie went back to work, as if it were just another day. Once again, I could see that she wasn't going to let the situation consume her life, nor was it going to dampen her spirit. During the three weeks we had to wait until we went back down for the surgery, she as busy as he always seemed to be, and went about her job with an attitude that was amazing.

I think she was matter of fact when some of her friends would ask her what was going on, but she always put a positive spin on it. It was only when she was home that she could let down a bit, and I could see it bothered her more than any of her friends ever knew. She could be short with me, but not the kitties, when she was feeling down, and she knew I could handle it. Even given that, I never heard her say, "Why me?" which to me was a testament to the spirit she had shown for years.

I did my best to put a good face on the future regarding the surgery. I had been on the computer going through any sites I could find that would give me a straw to grasp. I found one that said if the cancer was primary, and it was a stage II, surgery might be curative. We hung on to that one, even knowing we really didn't know what the hell we were dealing with.

The prospect of chemotherapy was also lurking in the background, depending on what they found when they did the surgery. I think Joanie feared that more than she feared another trip to the operating room. To date she had escaped that treatment. The anecdotes one has heard over time, and knowing people who had been given chemo, like her mother, dad, and my sister Judy, did nothing to allay the fear, uncertainty, and confusion that comes that prospect. It was something that, in early May, she refused even to consider. As far as she was concerned, Maddaus was going to do his magic, and she'd get back to work; that's all there was to it.

May 14 was a Wednesday, and it was a travel day for us. We went through our usual ritual of leaving home, stopping at Mabel Murphy's, and meeting Ginny and Ed for dinner after we got checked in at the Radisson. We had to be at the hospital at eight thirty, and surgery was scheduled for ten thirty in the morning, but that didn't mean she couldn't have dinner, just that she couldn't have anything after midnight.

When we walked from the Radisson to the hospital that morning, she was quiet, saying nothing to me until we got to the front door. When we pushed on the door to enter, she just looked at me with a half-smile on her face and said, "Well, here we go again." All I could think to say was that it was going to be okay

We stopped at the admittance desk, and they were expecting her. After she signed the usual papers, we went up

190

to 7C to wait and get ready for the trip down to the pre-op. There were a few nurses we recognized from her time here before, and they recognized her as well. They asked her what brought her here this time, and after she said she needed some work done on her right lung, they wished her well.

It struck me, there was some kind of weird comfort in being in a familiar place to have something done to you that you were dreading. As we sat there, waiting to go down, we were hoping at the end of this day we might know more than we did this morning, and what we would know would be that she'd be okay. I know that's what she was counting on, and once again it proved that hope hadn't deserted her.

"How's my hair?"

The atmosphere in Joanie's room was muted that morning. Both of us were aware that we were entering into an unknown area. The only constant that remained was her attitude that this was going to end up okay. That is not to say she wasn't concerned about the surgery she was about to undergo, but her confidence in both Dr. Linda Carson and Dr. Michael Maddaus was unshaken.

They wheeled her down to pre-op for the final preparations, and as I always did, I went along with her. It was a familiar setting, and with it came the weird feeling again, of being comfortable in a place you'd rather not be.

The routine was familiar too. We had been through it enough times by now, we knew what to expect with each new face that showed up at her bedside. We were getting close to the appointed hour of the surgery, when Dr. Carson stopped by. She told Joanie she would be involved in the early part of the surgery to do a pelvic examination after they had put her under, and would be taking some biopsy specimens from the

191

neovagina for evaluation. She said that would be her only role in the surgery today.

Shortly after Dr. Carson was gone, Dr. Maddaus showed up, and began telling Joanie what was in store. He told her the plan was to do a thorascopic exploration. He explained that this meant inserting a flexible scope that would give them a more precise picture of what they were dealing with. He had mentioned earlier that he hoped it might be possible to remove the tumor without having to open the chest, but if that wasn't possible, they would proceed as circumstances demanded. With that, Dr. Maddaus smiled, squeezed her hand, and told her he see her inside.

That signaled the arrival of the nurse anesthetist, and her dose of Versed. Trying to inject just a little bit of humor, I looked at both her and Joanie and said, "Take me to the isle of Versed." She looked at me a little strange, but Joanie smiled. She'd heard me say that before, and they began to wheel her off to the operating room. I left for the surgery waiting room to check in and go for a smoke. It was 12:18 p.m.

I had long ago learned how to pass the time waiting for the door to open and see Joanie's doctor come out to let me know what had happened. Today, I knew the surgery was going to take around four hours, barring any complications, so that meant I needed to be in the waiting area from four o'clock on without leaving. Earlier, I had been able to sneak out for a smoke, or make a phone call and get a cup of coffee. Dr. Maddaus came out at 4:50 p.m., and told me everything had gone well, Joanie had come through fine and was in the recovery room where she'd probably be until around 7:00.

He told me they weren't able to do the minimally invasive surgery, the involvement of the tumor with both the lower lobe and the middle lobe of her right lung precluded that. Then he told me he called in a cardiac surgeon to assist, due to the fist-sized tumor that had invaded the pericardium, the sac that holds the heart and the ends of the major blood vessels. That procedure went without incident and after that portion of the operation was completed, Maddaus continued to finish up the removal of both the lower and middle lobes of her right lung. The doctor said they had taken three lymph nodes for biopsies.

The involvement of the pericardium was something we hadn't known about, and it wasn't until later when Maddaus told us about it, that we became aware of how serious it was, or could have been.

Since I wouldn't get to see her until she was back up on 7C in a couple of hours, I walked over to Sally's for a burger and a beer, and to begin calling those people who needed to hear the news. I had already figured out a method, and outside of immediate family, John and Mikey, and some key friends in Bismarck, I had set up a telephone tree. That way, my calls were minimal, and those who needed to hear would. Of course, that didn't preclude many from calling me, and that was okay.

As I sat there at the bar, thinking about what had taken place this afternoon, I still wasn't sure what we were dealing with. On the one hand I felt good that whatever it was they were on top of it, and on the other hand, I was afraid of what was coming. I think both Carson and Maddaus knew already, but they hadn't yet shared it with it with Joanie and me. I was still holding on the thought it might have been non-small-cell lung cancer, but knowing that Carson wanted biopsies from the neovagina, and Maddaus had also taken lymph node samples for biopsies, I was losing my grasp on that idea. I decided I wouldn't say anything at all about it to Joanie, and let Maddaus tell her what was going on.

The fear was metastatic cervical cancer, and if there was also lymph node involvement, the problem was systemic, and that would most likely mean chemotherapy, something Joanie dreaded.

When I got back up to 7C, Joanie wasn't there yet. I didn't become concerned, mainly because one of the nurses I knew told me she was still in recovery, but would be up in a few minutes. When she got there, she was in a fog of morphine, and the after-effects of the anesthesia. When she saw me, she smiled weakly, and asked, "How's my hair?"

I laughed when I heard those as her first words, but it didn't surprise me. Even as she lay there with a chest tube coming of her, a Foley catheter draining her Miami pouch, and having just endured a four-hour surgery where she lost two-thirds of her right lung, the first thing she asks me is, "How's my hair?" She had this crown of thick, lush, wavy, and often curly, black hair that was her crown of glory, and for some reason that night, in this incongruous setting, that was all she could think about.

I told her it looked fine, and after they got her settled in her room, she was asleep. I went for a smoke. There would be more to talk about tomorrow.

Bad news at the wrong time from the wrong person.

The waiting game begins again. It was different this time. The last time she was in for surgery, five years ago, we knew what we were dealing with, and so the time post-surgery was focused on healing her body so she could go home. This time, while we were focused on the healing of her body, we were also faced with not knowing what we were up against and how much of a problem it was going to pose for Joanie. I had been hoping against hope it wasn't metastatic cancer, but I

194

think I knew in my bones that's what it was. However, no one had told us yet exactly what she was facing, so I hung on to that hope.

When I got to the hospital Friday morning, I stopped at the nurses' station and asked how she did overnight. I was told she did well, and there hadn't been any problems. I went to the door of her room, and found her awake and in fair spirits. She was still dealing with pain, and her ribs were sore from being spread during the surgery. When she saw me she gave me a weak smile, and asked me how my night had been. I told her it probably had been better than hers. Then she looked at me and asked me, "How does my hair look?" I smiled at hearing that question again, and told her it looked great. Whether she believed me or not, I didn't know, nor did I care.

Her nurse for part of this day came in to change her bedding, and get her cleaned up a bit, and I went out for a smoke and to pick up some coffee from the lobby coffee cart. Later that morning, her room began to take on a familiar look as the flowers began to arrive from many of her friends. She took calls from her brother Dick in San Francisco, Mikey Hoeven, and her sister Ann, and seemed to be handling it all in stride, until shortly before noon, she told me she was going to take a nap. I went for lunch.

That afternoon, Ginny stopped by to check in on her, and she also got a visit from Dr. Maddaus. He stopped in to brief her on the surgery. He told her basically the same thing he had told me yesterday, but this was the first time Joanie had heard that he had taken lymph nodes for biopsies while they were removing the two lobes of her right lung. She liked Maddaus, and didn't ask him any questions, and even thanked him for taking good care of her. He told her she was going to do well, and, as soon as the chest tube stop putting out drainage she could think about going home.

195

He made no mention that afternoon about the pathology report regarding what kind of cancer it was, or if the lymph nodes were positive for cancer. I assumed it was because the reports weren't back yet. It was late Friday afternoon, and as I was outside having a smoke, you could see it was shift change time. I even saw a couple of the nurses from 7C on their way out, and one who was on her way in. The weekend had begun, and with it came the slowdown in time. I went to Sally's for a beer and burger as I had done many times before, and then back to spend the rest of the evening with my patient, Joanie.

She was still feeling the effects of drugs and the surgery and would drop off without warning, and come to without warning. She would just look at me when she came too, as if to see that I was still there, and drop off again. That would go on for a few hours, until she would tell me it was okay to go. As I reflected on it, it was a familiar scene, one that had been played out more times than we cared to think about.

Saturday came, and when I got to her room, I heard the same question, "How does my hair look?" I began to see this as a theme to this episode of her hospital stays, and I made note of it. I told her, as I always did, she looked beautiful.

There were more flowers today, and more calls from her friends, and then my sisters, Jane and Joni, showed up. This was about the fourth time they had made the trip down. They had a chance to see and visit with Joanie, and wear her out a little bit before we headed downtown for lunch. It was always a welcome respite from the reality of the hospital, and every caregiver needs a break now and then, even if it is a brief one.

When I got to Joanie's room on Sunday morning before eight o'clock, she was awake, but seemed a little logy. The phone rang at eight, and it was her friend Mary Pat Woodmansee from Bismarck. Her face brightened as they talked, and I thought it was a good way to start out the day. After she hung up, the first thing she asked me was, "How's my hair look today—bad?" This time I laughed, and she asked me why I was laughing, and I told her she didn't even realize how many times she has asked me that question since Thursday. She just smiled and shrugged.

Ginny and Ed stopped by later in the morning, and she was glad to see them. She seemed to get energy from certain people, and they were among those who had that effect on her. While they were there, one of the residents who was working with Dr. Maddaus stopped by. I figured it was part of his training to stop by and check up on patients whose surgery he had been involved with. Then, as he sat there in the room, he dropped a bomb that set me off. He began telling Joanie that it looked like they were dealing with metastatic cervical cancer, something neither Dr. Maddaus nor Dr. Carson had said a word about. When I heard those words, I found a way of ending the conversation and getting him out of the room. After he was gone, as I walked out with Ed and Ginny, they were both surprised at what they'd heard. I was not only surprised, I was pissed.

I don't think Joanie realized what he was saying. She asked me if I knew what he was talking about, and I told her I hadn't heard a thing from either Maddaus or Carson, but the next time I see Maddaus, I would ask him about it. I would have that opportunity the next day, when Maddaus, along with the resident, stopped in Joanie's room to check on her. When they were done, as they were leaving, I asked to speak to Maddaus alone. I said, "I think this resident will make a fine doctor someday, but I didn't think it was appropriate for him to be talking to Joanie about what is going on with her when he is not her doctor, and any news about her situation should be coming from either you or Dr. Carson." He told me he

197

understood and appreciated my comments, and it was left at that.

I was proud of myself. I told him what I was feeling, and did so in a manner that was cool and calm, but left no doubt that I was not happy. We didn't see that resident again for the rest of the time we were there, and Joanie never knew anything about my conversation with Maddaus. This episode did not diminish my respect for Maddaus in the least. His care of Joanie was nothing less than highly professional, and the relaxed confidence he presented in his relationship with her as a patient could be used as a model for doctor-patient relationships everywhere.

My reaction was due in part to my strong belief that if she was going to hear bad news, and there had been plenty of those times, it should be coming from the one person she has confidence in, and that is her doctor, not anyone else.

The other shoe finally drops.

This latest hospital episode of Joanie's was a dark time, probably the darkest in the past seven years. Something had gone horribly wrong, and as she lay in her bed on 7C, we had yet to hear exactly what it was, and with that ignorance came the uncertainty, and with that uncertainty came the creation of scenarios, ranging from best possible to the worst. It is inescapable, when you are faced with situations like this, that you spend much of your time wondering what is happening, imagining what might happen next, and feeling worried about how this all is going to affect your patient. As for Joanie, she was still in the process of healing from the lung surgery, and as far as she was concerned this was just another speed bump on the way to being called a "cancer survivor." It was an attitude I did my best to reinforce at every

198

point. As I reflect, I'm not sure she needed that from me, for her spirit was so strong that had I not been there, it wouldn't have changed a thing.

Joanie continued to do well. They were doing chest x-rays every morning; the chest tube was still in and draining; and on Tuesday, Dr. Maddaus told us it would remain in place for at least another day. Later that day he came in and they changed the tube, and we were told it would not be out before the weekend, and possibly not until Monday. That put a damper on her spirits, as she was getting antsy and eager to go home. Phone calls from Governor Hoeven and all of her many friends continued to come in daily, and there were many of them. On Wednesday, when I got to the hospital she was alert and looking good. The chest x-ray in the morning was positive, and we were told there would be no new chest tube today.

At times when she would doze off, I would either go out for a smoke, or go up one floor to the cafeteria to get a cup of coffee and a doughnut. My usual place was by a window from which I could look across the Mississippi and see the skyline of downtown Minneapolis, a place where Joanie and I had spent so many happy times. These moments gave me time to think and try to sort it all out. It is critical to try to make sense of a situation, but the catch is to avoid dwelling on the negatives, borrowing trouble. As a caregiver, you will find yourself thinking such things, and that is okay. There is no way to avoid it, and if you are aware of that, you can deal with your own negative thoughts without transmitting them to your patient. You are, after all, only another human being thrust into a situation over which you have no control. All you are trying to do now is your best to help a person you love get what she needs, and to be there to give her all of the positive support you can give her. It ain't easy, but it can be done, and that's your job.

Back in her room on Thursday, she was off the IV, choosing her own food and we were doing good bit of walking around the halls of 7C. Maddaus said the x-ray was "great," and now they were waiting for the drainage to subside so they could pull the chest tube. Ginny stopped by in the afternoon, and that helped Joanie's spirits as it always did. The evening was quiet, and when I went back to the Radisson, I felt that come Friday, we might get a break.

Friday morning, I got to her room and she didn't even ask me how her hair was, so I kidded her about that. She just smiled and shrugged. She was off the heart monitor now, and so the only thing standing in our way out the door was the chest tube. It was not to come out today, another disappointment, but the weekend was looking better now. Saturday was a really big day. While the chest tube didn't come out, they had a x-ray scheduled for later that evening, and if all looked good, it would come out Sunday morning. That was to be the best news of the day.

The other news I got that day was worse than I could have imagined. Another of Dr. Maddaus's residents, Dr. Aasheim, had stopped by Joanie's room to check on her, and then he took me out to one of the computers in the hall and brought up the pathology report we had been waiting for these past eight days.

These were the facts that we now had to deal with. Aasheim told me we were definitely not dealing with non-small-cell lung cancer, but it was indeed metastatic cervical cancer. Metastatic is one of those words you never want to hear if you are dealing with cancer. He said one of the lymph nodes Maddaus had taken was positive for cancer, and there was vascular invasion involved. What that meant that it was on the move through the lymph system. He also said there was pleural involvement, which meant that the tumor had extended to the pleura, the membrane that surrounds the lung. The biopsy that Dr. Carson had taken from the neovagina also tested positive for cancer, which was also invasive, another sign that this had become a very serious situation.

I wrote everything down as fast as I could, but I felt numb. I couldn't go back into Joanie's room right away, so I went out for a smoke and to take some time to process the news I had just been given. I just stood outside, pacing and smoking, and trying to get a grip on what might be next. I knew already it was going to be chemotherapy, since we were now dealing with a systemic problem. The cancer was no longer confined to the cervix but had spread, and I didn't know of any other treatment approach that could be used at that time. The thought of that alone almost made me cry for Joanie. I thought, she's already been through so much, and now this. It wasn't fair.

My immediate personal problem was what to tell Joanie, if anything, right now. I chose to be a coward, and decided to wait for Dr. Carson to bring the bad news. I knew it would be devastating, and I didn't feel able to deal with her reaction by myself right then. Joanie had an idea, but she knew nothing for sure. She never asked me what the resident had to say, so I didn't have to lie to her.

I stayed at the hospital that night until they came around ten o'clock to take her down for an x-ray. When she got back she gave me the okay to leave. As I left her that night, I told her I thought we would be going home tomorrow, if the pictures were okay. She smiled and told me she was planning on it.

As I left the hospital that night, I felt tired, more tired than I had felt in a long time. I stopped at the bar in the Radisson, ordered a Scotch, and just sat there alone, wondering where this was going to take us. The only thing I knew for sure right then was that wherever it was going to take us, it would test every bit of her will, strength, and courage.

We go home and wait for a call.

Sunday morning, after I picked up cup of coffee, I headed for the hospital. It wasn't long before they came in and told us the x-ray looked good, and they were going to take the chest tube out. Joanie was smiling, and while they went to work on her, I went back to the Radisson to check out. It was just minutes before noon when she walked out the door and we headed for the interstate to get her home. The nurse told us we should stop every hour or two so Joanie could get out and walk. They said it was a precaution against clots in her lower legs. While she had been in the hospital, she wore those pneumatic calf compression sleeves that would keep blood flowing.

We stopped first in Avon at my sister Joni's place so Joanie could get a little walk in, and we could talk to Joni. We didn't spend much time there. Joanie was in a hurry and wanted to get home. We also stopped in Fargo, and I stopped in a couple of other rest stops and she reluctantly got out to walk around. I told her I didn't want anything happening to her while she was in my care, and if it did, I wouldn't have a clue about what to do. That line seemed to work.

We made it home in near record time despite the stops, and when we crested the hill east of Bismarck and the city came into view, I could see her relax, and she told me she was really glad to be home. On the trip back, we didn't talk about what might be next, even though I felt like she knew. All that mattered to her right then was that the surgery was over, it had been successful, and now she had some time to heal up completely before we began to face what was next. After all, it had been major surgery, and she was going to need at least a month to even approach being 100 percent.

We weren't scheduled to be back for a follow-up visit with Dr. Maddaus for a month from now, and we figured it would be the same with Dr. Carson, who wanted to see her earlier. We had been told Carson would be calling.

Back in Bismarck, her friends really came through. Our house became Patient Central, with people calling, stopping by, and bringing food the patient would need to help get her strength back. On the second day back, Betsy Dalrymple, wife of the lieutenant governor at the time, brought lunch, First Lady Mikey Hoeven, brought brownies, our neighbor Pat Smith sent over some bread, and Mary Pat Woodmansee brought a couple of pan-blackened Cajun steak sandwiches from Peacock Alley that evening for dinner. Joanie just shook her head in amazement at what was going on, as if she didn't think she deserved this kind of attention.

The phone was also busy with friends and family calling, and that night she got a call from her boss Governor Hoeven. His instructions to her were to get healed up, and not to worry about the office until she was ready to come back.

Part of my job now was the same as it had been other times, and that was to see she got some exercise. I had been told by the nurse when she got discharged, I needed to get her walking and keep her walking. Her right lung needed the exercise too. On the third day home, we went out for fifteen minutes, and from then on it wasn't a chore. We went for walks every day, and each time, I made it a longer one. She knew what I was doing, and only once or twice resisted my effort to suck her into doing another block or two.

Every day since we had been back, the subject of the recent surgery and its results were pretty much avoided. Only on a couple of occasions did we discuss what might be coming, and it was in very general terms. I still didn't feel comfortable telling her what I knew, besides, we were waiting for a call from Dr. Carson. After she'd been home for about ten days, Carson called and said she wanted to see her when she came down for her follow-up appointment with Dr. Maddaus. At that time, she would discuss the options for future treatment based on what they had learned from the biopsies taken during the surgery. She told Joanie that chemotherapy was one of those options, and she would go into it in greater detail when we came down on June 24.

Carson's news was what I knew had been coming, and I think Joanie felt it in her bones herself. After she hung up the phone, she just looked at me and didn't say a word. She just sat there for a moment, staring out the window. I went over to where she sat on the couch, with Muffin on her lap, rubbed her shoulders and the only thing I could think of to say was, "You're gonna' be all right." She grabbed my hand and squeezed it, and quietly said, "I'm going to take a nap right now."

I told her I'd be outside, and went for a smoke.

Hope is where you find it.

We had been faced with bad news before over the last seven years, but this news cast a dark pall over the house at 1205 N. Mandan, unlike those other times. This time we knew we weren't talking about a cure like we were when she went through with the total pelvic exenteration in 1998. This time the treatment would be aimed at controlling the disease, and hopefully preventing a further spread.

When I came in from outside, Joanie was still sleeping on the couch, so I didn't wake her. There would be plenty of time to talk later. I went to the computer, and began to look for any answers to the questions I had, based on the little knowledge I had at the time. I was entering uncharted waters as far as my limited knowledge was concerned, and I didn't know what I might find that would give us some hope.

Later that evening, I came to realize I didn't need the computer to find something that would give us some hope. It was sitting in our living room on the couch, and her name was Joanie. It was around dinnertime, and I asked her what she would like to have to eat. She told me she wasn't that hungry, but what she would like is some good French bread, some olive oil for dipping, and a glass of wine, if that was okay. I told her I'd be right back, and went to buy the bread.

When I returned, we took the bread, oil, a bottle of wine and some glasses, and we went out back to the deck by the pool. It was a pleasant evening, and I shut off the pool pump motor so it was even quieter. I poured us both some wine and Joanie began to talk.

She wanted to know what I thought, especially about the possibility of chemotherapy. I danced a little bit, saying just that I thought there was a new problem to deal with, and that chemotherapy might well be what it takes to deal with it. She put me on the spot, and asked me what I knew for sure. Now, I couldn't't lie to her, so I told her briefly what the pathology report had shown, and that there was lymph node involvement, and the biopsy Carson had taken from the neovagina was also positive for cancer, and confirmed that it was metastatic. I told her from what I knew based on my limited knowledge, it appeared chemotherapy was in order to halt the spread and control the disease.

205

We talked again about not borrowing trouble, and waiting until we met with Dr. Carson in about three weeks before we would know anything for sure regarding further treatment. Then she asked me, "If they want to do chemotherapy, will I lose my hair?" She asked that with a half-smile on her face, but I knew it was something she dreaded, and the thought of losing that luscious head of black, wavy hair was an unwelcome one. I just told her I couldn't answer that, because I didn't know what kind of treatment they would be using, or what the side effects would be. I tried a little humor and told her she wouldn't look that bad as a baldy.

She dipped some bread in the oil, took a sip of her wine, and told me she wasn't surprised at what Carson had told her or what I had told her. She said she had been afraid of that since the tumor showed up on her bronchial tube, something she had never admitted before. I asked her how she felt, knowing what she knew now, and she smiled at me and said, "I'm scared." She hastened to add, "I may be scared, but I'm not ready to give up, and I won't."

Sitting there in the twilight, looking at her, I could see the same kind of resolute look I had seen before, and it gave me some comfort, and filled me with love. We raised our glasses. That was the hope I was looking for that I couldn't find on the computer

The battle is joined.

Before we had to see Dr. Carson and Dr. Maddaus on the twenty-fourth of June, we spent most of the time getting Joanie back in shape. I got her to walk almost every day, and then she would spend time tending her new "garden" in the backyard. Actually, she more or less directed me in the tending part of it. She was still restricted from any heavy lifting because of the surgery, and she made the most of it. We would go to one of the plant places in Bismarck and pick out more plants to spread around the deck and the yard, and of course, watering those was one of my regular duties. I didn't mind. Our backyard park was looking pretty good.

During this time we didn't talk much about what lay in store for her next, preferring to revert to our agreement to not let this disease dictate our lives any more than it already did, and to enjoy the good times when we had them.

The day came to leave for her appointment with Carson and Maddaus, and her routine was the same as it had been for any of the other countless trips we had made already. I didn't rush her, since we had all day to get there. We would be staying with Ginny and Ed in St. Paul, and we would be there by six. She always looked forward to seeing them, and especially eager to see her three-legged friend, Piper. As always, he was glad to see her as well.

Joanie was apprehensive about what was coming, something I considered normal. I was, as well. We still didn't have the complete picture, but just a glimpse that included chemotherapy. The hair thing was still weighing on her.

Dr. Carson was her first appointment the next day. It wasn't until one o'clock so she had plenty of time to stew most of the morning. We did go for a bagel and coffee at a place on Grand Avenue in St. Paul, and then she wanted to go shopping at a couple of her favorite stores there. We skipped lunch, since neither of us was hungry, and were at the clinic shortly before the appointed time.

We checked in, and it wasn't long before a nurse came to the door of the waiting room and called her name. It was time to get the full story. Dr. Carson came into the examination room, and after greetings and small talk, she got down to business. Carson was really good about dealing with negative

207

news in a positive manner. This was one of those times when she really had to work at it though. She told us what the pathology report had shown, the lymph node involvement, and the biopsy from the neovagina, and said that everything indicated that chemotherapy was the next option as far as treatment was concerned. The fact that it had moved off of the cervix and metastasized to the lung indicated the problem was now systemic, and the only way to control it was with chemotherapy.

Knowing that as our only option, then the question was what kind of chemo and what kind of treatment. We didn't have a clue, since every cancer is treated differently, and every patient is treated differently depending what kind of cancer it is and where it is. Joanie sat there, quietly listening to Carson, and I could tell by the look on her face how unwelcome this discussion was, even though she knew it was coming. I think she'd been praying for some kind of miracle to occur before she got to this meeting.

Dr. Carson then suggested that she consider taking part in a clinical trial that was going on at the university. She went on to explain that this trial was a study being conducted to determine the efficacy of using three cancer drugs to treat recurrent cervical cancer. She told us standard treatment for advanced cervical cancer was either Cisplatin, or Cisplatin and Ifosfamide (Ifex) combined. This study was taking a look at using a drug called Paclitaxel (Taxol) in combination with the other two drugs. The sponsor of the study was Bristol-Meyers Squibb, and Dr. Carson was one of the five doctor/investigators at the University of Minnesota Fairview-University Medical Center.

Participation in the study was voluntary, and it would involve one infusion of the three drugs every 28 days for a total of six treatments. In between there would be weekly blood draws, which could be done in Bismarck, to keep tabs on the effect of the chemo on her white and red blood cells and kidney and liver functions. All of the treatment would take place at the Masonic Cancer Center located next to the hospital, and each appointment would take about six hours to deliver the drugs. She would meet with Dr. Carson before every treatment for an assessment.

Joanie asked her about nausea, and Carson said there would be drugs available to deal with any nausea or vomiting as a result of the treatment. Then Joanie smiled and asked her the most important question on her mind, "Will I lose my hair?" Dr. Carson, said there was a good chance she would, but it would grow back if she did when the treatment was over.

Joanie asked me what I thought, and I told her if she was going to have chemo, taking part in a research study might be a good thing, so she agreed, and told Dr. Carson to sign her up. Paperwork completed, Carson said she wanted to do an exam before she left, and when that was done we went to see Dr. Maddaus next door at the Masonic Cancer Center. He entered the room in good spirits, and as he always did, made Joanie immediately comfortable. He wanted to know if she had any respiratory issues he should know about, and she told him none. He took a look at her wounds, and said they appeared to be healing well. He and Joanie talked about what was in store for her, and he told her she had made the right decision by taking part in the clinical trial. He then told her that as far as he was concerned, she would not have to see him again. She smiled, thanked him, and we left.

It was now around three o'clock, and Joanie said she wanted to go to Sally's for a glass of wine. We ordered, and we talked about the afternoon appointments. She was looking for some reassurance that she had made the right decision, and I told her emphatically she had. She told me she was going to beat this thing, and I said I thought she was in the right place to do battle with it.

That night we went to dinner at Tavern on Grand with Ginny and Ed, and the mood was upbeat, despite what she was facing. She was resolute, and determined to take charge of this, and I thought that boded well. The next day, before we left town, she wanted to stop at Dayton's downtown so she could look at hats, hats she could wear when she would lose her hair, which she was sure she would. She tried on many hats and ended up buying two, but I think she did so reluctantly, as if by doing so she was accepting the fact she would have to endure losing her hair during this treatment. She never wore either one, even when she lost her hair. She ended up wearing one a friend had made for her.

It was now June 25, and we had until July 14 before we had to make this trip again. It would be another one of those trips filled with uncertainty, the kind we had become very familiar with, but until then, Joanie was jumping back into work and life with new energy.

Samples can save you money.

Joanie was busy from the time we got back from Minneapolis, and seemed so focused on her work and play she hardly thought about the upcoming first round of chemotherapy. She had to have a CT scan done that we could take down to Dr. Carson, and outside of that, we were ready.

The first order of the day when we got to Minneapolis was to check her in to have a portacath put in. This was a surgical procedure that placed an access device under the skin, which was connected to a catheter that was inserted in a major vein. This device is often used when the patient has to receive numerous infusions of chemo. It was outpatient surgery, and the recovery time was minimal, and she didn't have any side effects of note. On Wednesday, July 16, we went to the clinic to meet with Dr. Carson prior to the first round of chemo. The mood that morning was subdued, but Joanie was resigned now to getting this underway and getting it done.

Carson pronounced her fit for her first round, and gave her some hints on how to deal with any of the expected side effects, such as nausea and fatigue. She told her that the anti-nausea drugs she would take after each infusion should handle that aspect, and as far as fatigue was concerned, she just suggested getting rest, and said it wouldn't last long. With that we went next door to the Masonic Cancer Center to check her in and wait for them to call her into the infusion center. Joanie sat silently as we waited for her name to be called, fidgeting with her Kleenex, and when they did call her name, she looked at me and said, "Here we go."

The infusion center was a pleasant enough place, with reclining chairs for each patient, and, for privacy, a curtain that could be pulled around the chair. There was TV available for each patient, and, as there seems to be in every hospital setting, out-of-date magazines if one wanted to read.

The nurse who escorted us in got Joanie settled, and went over what would happen over the next six hours. They first thing they would do would be to access her port to be sure they had an open line. Then they would begin to give her an anti-nausea drug, and another drug to minimize drug toxicity. They were, after all, going to be putting poison though her veins. She would also receive a drug called Mesna to protect her kidneys and bladder from the effects of the chemo drugs. The other three drugs would follow, each with their own prescribed time table for infusion. We would find that Joanie's treatment was one of the longer ones, and over the months, she would be the last patient there.

They hooked her up and began the process, and things seemed to be going well until they were done with the first drug, when she threw up. It alarmed me, but the nurses there didn't seem concerned. They were prepared for such an incident with necessary bowls at the ready. After she rested for a few minutes, she seemed fine, and they went ahead with the treatment.

The rest of the infusion went by without incident, and Joanie seemed to tolerate it just fine. She was bored, but that was about all. Then, I was told we needed to have some Kytril, which is an anti-nausea drug, and so I went to the pharmacy right next to the infusion center, and asked for the necessary dosage. She would need to take the drug twice a day for three days, early in the morning and later in the evening. The pharmacist brought me the prescription and told me that would be $180. I was stunned. I couldn't believe it. I wrote the check, but the more I thought about it, the madder I got. I was thinking, she's really given herself over as a guinea pig in this study that may or may not help her, and now we have to pay for the anti-nausea drugs to combat the poison they are using for this clinical trial.

I couldn't hold myself back any longer and told Joanie I was going out for a smoke. When I got outside, I called the nurse who was the administrator of the trial, and expressed my unhappiness. She told me that was part of the protocol for this trial, and that was it. I got angrier and said, "Wait a minute. Bristol-Meyers Squibb is sponsoring this clinical trial, and if it is successful, they will put out press releases across the land touting the efficacy of their drugs, and will make a fortune, meanwhile, the subjects have to bear the burden of dealing with the side effects of those drugs." I also told her that since the university was the investigator of the trial, it would also

212

have some positive press coming out of it, assuming the trial was a success.

She listened to my rant, and then asked me if I wanted to take Joanie out of the trial, and I really almost lost it. I said, "Of course not. Don't be ridiculous." I hung up after that exchange, and that was the last time I had any communication with her for the duration of the trial. I waited outside for a while and smoked another cigarette before I went back into the infusion center. I never told Joanie about what had happened.

I'm sure part of my frustration that day dealt with my own feelings about what was going on with Joanie, but, at the same time, I thought that we shouldn't have to bear any cost for being involved in research that may or may not help her, or anyone else. It wasn't that they needed to pay her for being involved, but considering she was taking a risk in being part of the research, I felt there should be no cost on our part.

What I learned from that first day was to ask for samples. When we got back to Bismarck, we talked to a friend of ours who was in the pharmacy racket, and he told us they always have samples, all you have to do is ask for them. The next time, I did, and got them. I was told to have Dr. Carson's nurse make the request the next time. The next time, when it came time to leave, I went to the pharmacist, and asked for samples, and she asked me if Carson's nurse had ordered them, and I sheepishly told her I forgot to ask. She looked at me and told me to be sure and have that done the next time. Lesson: Always ask for samples.

Joanie had made it through the first session of chemo, and had done so in fine shape. As we left the infusion center to go back to Ginny and Ed's, she said to me, "Only five more to go."

Chemical weapons of mass destruction.

The next morning after her first round of chemotherapy, I woke her up at six-thirty in the morning to give her the first dose of Kytril. It was important to stay ahead of the nausea, for if you don't, it is impossible to catch up, and you will have some very unpleasant times.

The first few days proved the point of the value of the anti-nausea drugs. She seemed to have weathered the first round without any severe side effects. There were a couple of days when fatigue set in, but after that, she did really well. It was about this time, I started using email to communicate with her friends about what was going on with her. I found it easier than calling everyone individually, and while using mass emails is somewhat impersonal, I didn't care. I felt the important thing was to get the information out that people wanted to hear.

In 2003, the United States had invaded Iraq, looking for weapons of mass destruction, and that period contributed to the email I sent out following Joanie's first round of chemo as part of this clinical trial.

I reprint it here in its entirety. It was dated July 22:

This is to inform you that President Carson has ordered thousands of troops into battle with chemical weapons of mass destruction to search out and destroy infidel invaders who are seeking to bring down the government that has ruled Joanie's body for some 53 years.

The Commander in Chief has ordered a three-pronged attack on the mutant rebels led by Gen, Ifosfamide, Lt. Gen. Paclitaxel and Maj. Gen. Carboplatin to bring an end to this insurrection, which threatens the stability of the Joanie world, not to mention the free world as well.

214

This Wednesday last, the invasion was unleashed, with orders to search out and destroy the enemy wherever they may be hiding. Carson said in resorting to this drastic measure that all other options had failed, and there was no choice but to let the evildoers know, "They can run, but they cannot hide."

While there may be unfortunate "Friendly Fire" casualties along the way, Carson and her cadre are confident they can control the collateral damage and ultimately gain the victory over what Carson calls, "The scourge that is responsible for so much pain and suffering in the world today."

Embedded reporters covering this campaign report that the battle is indeed underway, with some affects already noticeable, however briefing officials from Command Central (COMCENT) indicate they were expected, and they have taken measures to mitigate any undue harm or discomfort.

Officials at the briefing have also given reporters an outline of the battle plan, which includes ushering in reinforcements every four weeks throughout what they expect to be a six-month campaign,

While it may be a shock to some that we do indeed have chemical weapons that are capable of mass destruction, and are willing to use them, officials say that humanitarian concerns dictate their use in select cases to overcome what is considered a clever, resilient and evil force.

Greetings to all,

Actually, outside of a bit of nausea, Joanie is doing fairly well. She did go back to work on Friday after we got back, and then, as the docs predicted, the fatigue hit and she had a couple of not so good days. Today, (Tues) she went in late this morning, and while still bothered by some mild nausea, she is determined to keep going as best she can. We will keep you posted on her progress.

Bob (The Embedded-in more ways than one-Reporter)

I showed it to Joanie before I sent it out, and she got a kick out of it, all things considered.

Learning about a CBC.

The thing about cancer and the chemotherapy that is used to help rid the patient of the cancer is that it is hard to measure progress. It's not like if you have a broken arm, and you set the bone, put it in a cast and wait a few weeks for it to get all better. With chemotherapy, you have to wait until there have been multiple infusions until you can begin to see if it has made a difference. Then and only then, after CT scans and other examinations does it become clear if the chemo has done more good than harm. For Joanie and me, it made each trip back down to Minneapolis for another round more anxious, not knowing if what they were doing was working or not.

Joanie weathered the first round of chemotherapy well, and she hadn't started to lose her hair yet. That was a concern of hers, and after every time she took a shower after she had started chemo, she was careful to check the amount of hair that was surrounding the bathtub drain. She knew it was going to happen, she just didn't know how fast it would start, or how quickly she would lose it all.

As she worried about her hair, she got a call from Cathy Schmitz, a good friend of ours, and Cathy told her that she and Orell wanted to buy her the wig she would surely be needing in a few weeks. When Joanie told me about Cathy's offer, she was overwhelmed. She had been overwhelmed many times by the generosity of her friends, and this time was no exception. She and Cathy made an appointment to seek out a wig she could live with, and get it fitted.

Turns out, it didn't take long before she would need it, when after her second round, her hair loss accelerated to the point where she went to the person who always did her hair and had what was left cut off. This was a hard thing for her to do, but by doing so she accepted the fact she was going to have to wear a wig, at least for a few months. Meanwhile, immediately after the first round of chemotherapy, I began to get a crash course in the reading of a Complete Blood Count (CBC). As part of the treatment, Joanie had to have weekly blood draws to monitor the effect of the chemo on her blood, most importantly, the white blood cells, red blood cells, platelets, and hemoglobin.

It became my job now to get the figures after each blood draw, which was done in Dr. Bury's office, and keep an eye on those figures. If you should ever be faced with a situation like this, the internet is your best resource. All you have to do is search for CBC, and you will get many sites that will give you the information you need to interpret the numbers you will get from the blood work. It is also helpful to ask the doctor for the ranges they use, as there can be slight variances from lab to lab.

In Joanie's case, I would call Dr. Bury's office and talk to her nurse, I called her Nurse Nancy, and she would give me the numbers and inform me if there was anything I should watch for. For each category, there is a range, and when someone is receiving chemotherapy the numbers you get will show a trend in movement of the numbers as more chemo is received.

Briefly, if white blood cell count is too low, the patient may be more susceptible to infection; if the red blood cell count is too low, the patient may develop anemia, and fatigue will be a factor; and, if the platelet count is too low, the patient may bruise or bleed more easily because of the effect on clotting. Those were the basic numbers I paid attention to during the duration of the clinical trial. Joanie never asked me about them or seemed to care. She seemed determined, once she got

217

past a couple of days of fatigue, to get back into her job with new energy, regardless of what the numbers were. Over the remaining five months of the clinical trial, our routine was the same. Drive to St. Paul, stay with Ginny and Ed, meet with Dr. Carson the next day, and spend six hours or so at the infusion center at the Masonic Cancer Center. More often than not, we were the last to leave. The next day I would wake her very early for Kytril, and later we would get up and head right back to Bismarck.

The trips were uneventful, and we were never sure about what was going on. Joanie had a CT scan in late September, the results of which were encouraging, and in Dr. Carson's words, "I personally reviewed her CT scan from Bismarck, and saw no evidence of disease in the chest, abdomen or pelvis." That gave us new hope, because that news came after just three of the six treatments were complete. There were three more to go, and there would be another CT scan in about a month.

Because the news came before the October round of chemo that day, we didn't have a chance to go to Sally's and celebrate. Instead, we were able to tell Ginny and Ed when we got back to their place that night, and even though Joanie didn't want anything, the rest of us enjoyed a celebratory cocktail. She was okay being left out of the wine.

Dr. Carson's words were the ones we had been hoping to hear since Joanie started on chemo, and right then, Joanie didn't even mind wearing a wig at all. As far as she was concerned, there were only two more rounds to go and this would all be over, and her hair would start growing back.

The year that was.

The year 2003, had begun with such hope and promise. Joanie was hard at work on the assumption that her boss, Governor John Hoeven would be running for reelection next year; she was approaching the magic five-year cancer free survival number; and, what was most important, she was feeling good. Cancer had become an afterthought, with only a colostomy and a Miami pouch as reminders of what she had been through over the last seven years.

The hope and promise that arrived in January would soon be blown away by the winds of a cancer that for the second time came back to threaten Joanie. This time in the form metastatic cancer, which meant lung surgery and chemotherapy. And now as we approached the end of the year, things were looking good. The monthly CT scans she had been taking showed an encouraging picture, and the chemo regimen hadn't been nearly as difficult for her to handle as we had feared.

Joanie made it through the last two rounds of the clinical trial in the same manner she had made it through the first four, that is to say she did fine, all things considered. The checkup in November with Dr. Carson before the fifth chemo round again showed that everything was looking good. The same can be said for the meeting in December prior to the last of the treatments. In Carson's words from the December 3 meeting with her, "She (Joanie) has continued to function well on chemotherapy with being able to maintain a full time job."

The last infusion of the clinical trial took place in early December, and for Joanie it was a welcome one. She would be done after this one. She was feeling so good that we had to bring boxes of her Christmas candy along on this trip. There had to be enough for the nurses at the Masonic Cancer Center infusion center, all of whom we had come to know and like through the past five months. There also had to be enough boxes for the folks at the clinic, from Dr. Carson and her nurses, to Marcia, the person I called Carson's gatekeeper. Joanie's good spirits were not because she looked forward to having another infusion; it had more to do with the fact it would be her last, and she wanted to leave something for the medical staff who had been taking care of her all of this time. It was her way of saying thank you.

There would still be some bloodwork to watch for a few weeks, and there would be one more CT scan at the end of the month. To my mind, it would be an important one. Getting and reading radiologists' notes from CT scans, PET scans or MRIs was another thing I learned during this process, and it is something that any caregiver can do. In my case, any time Joanie had a CT scan, or any other kind of scan, I would wait a day, and then call the nurse in the doctor's office, in most cases, since the CTs were done in Bismarck, that would be nurse Nancy in Dr. Bury's office, and she would get me a copy of the radiologist's dictation.

While initially it might look like Greek, it is still written in English, and there are keys to look for, such as toward the end of each scan you will see the word "Conclusion." After that word you will see the radiologist's impression from looking at the pictures. In any event, should you have any difficulty in interpreting what you are looking at, just asked the patient's doctor.

The December 30 CT scan on Joanie's abdomen said, "No evidence of recurrent or metastatic disease." That news gave us reason to have a grand celebration on New Year's Eve that year, and we did.

So, despite the trouble visited on Joanie this year, the trouble over which she had prevailed, the hope and promise that had been there in January returned as we closed out one helluva year, and looked ahead to what we hoped would be a better one.

"My friends, whoever has had experience of evils knows how whenever a flood of ills comes upon mortals, a man fears everything; but whenever a divine force cheers on our voyage, then we believe that the same fate will always blow fair."
—Aeschylus

Joanie had survived the disappointment of cancer coming back, along with the loss of two-thirds of her right lung and the six-month experimental chemotherapy regimen, and she was entering 2004 with what looked like a clean bill of health.

At her first meeting with Dr. Carson on January 7, 2004, the good news continued. Carson noted, "My impression is that of no evidence of recurrent persistent squamous cell carcinoma of the cervix following treatment with chemotherapy with the Women's Cancer Center protocol #28. Recommend that she return in three months' time for follow-up, at that time she will have a repeat CT of chest, abdomen and pelvis which will be repeated every three to four months for the next two years."

Dr. Carson was very encouraging, and her encouragement rubbed off on both of us, and we left her office both smiling and walking lighter than ever. This trip had turned into another one for celebration. You can imagine hearing that her appointments with Dr. Carson were now down to every three months, and that was the schedule for the next two years was enough for us to go to Sally's immediately after leaving Carson's office. From the clinic to Sally's is a short two-block walk, and though it was only about twenty degrees outside that day, it didn't seem cold at all.

When we got there and settled in at the bar and ordered a glass of wine, we looked at each other and we were both smiling. We sat there talking and thinking about what she had gone through the last year, and now we were looking ahead to a time when we would only have to make these trips a few times a year.

Joanie was still wearing a wig and wasn't minding it that much now. The news today made her mind it even less. She even told me as we sat there in Sally's, as soon as she had a reasonable amount of coverage, she would hang the wig up for good. She said she wouldn't mind it even if it were only a really short butch-looking cut. She knew her hair would come back, and probably be thicker than ever. It did.

We went to dinner that night with Ginny and Ed, and shared the good news with two of the people who had been so close and meant so much to both of us since Joanie's first diagnosis back in 1996. She also got a chance to see Piper, who had helped her so much back then.

Joanie and I got up early the next day and headed back for Bismarck. The trip this time was spent talking about everything she was looking forward to. John Hoeven was running for reelection and that alone would make it a very busy year; there was the building project she was involved in at Trinity Lutheran; and her life wasn't going to be dictated to by cancer as it had been this last year. She was looking forward to everything coming her way, and I could hear it in her voice as the miles rolled by.

What we didn't talk about, as if by some silent agreement, was the fact we had heard good news before, only to have it cruelly snatched away from us when we weren't looking. Today was to be enjoyed, not sullied with thoughts of what has happened in the past. This was her moment, her good news, and she deserved to relish it for as long as she wanted. It became my job to help her do that too.

It was as if that infrequent guest, hope, had moved back in with the promise it would stay longer this time.

Sonofabitch!

The thing about cancer is, it taunts you. It gives you hope, then dashes it. It gives you a reason to celebrate, followed by a reason to be so goddamn mad you want to hit something. It gives you a sense of security only to smash it with an overwhelming fear that you can't win, that you are going to lose something very important.

The first few months of 2004 flew by. Joanie's calendar was as full as it had ever been. She was reveling in her work and life, and it was like last year never even happened. It was during this time we reached a milestone regarding the colostomy. I was still changing it for her whenever it had to be changed, and from time to time would kindly prompt her to think about doing it herself, in case when she was gone, or I was gone, and it needed to be done, she could handle it herself. I had shown her how to do it, and knew she could if she had to, but it was still always me that changed it for her. I didn't mind, and I got so good at it, I could get it done in under four minutes from start to finish. The milestone came in late February, when I was in Minneapolis for a few days at the Great Minnesota Golf Show. I was there helping to man the booth promoting the Lewis and Clark Golf Trail, which was my baby. I left on Thursday and would return on Monday.

On the way back on Sunday, I was going to stop overnight at my sister Joni's place in Avon, and then get back to Bismarck on Monday. On my way to Avon that afternoon, I stopped in Clearwater to see an old friend, Red Ridgeway, and we went to the Legion Club to have a beer, and he could have a cigar. While Red was away from the bar, I got a call from Joanie and wondered what was going on. She told me the colostomy had started leaking. I immediately became alarmed, and here I was about five and half hours away. She let me stew for just a minute, and then she told me quite proudly she had changed it herself, and everything was fine. I could see the smile on her face from where I sat. I told her she was wonderful, and that I knew she could do it, and I was proud of her. It put a big smile on my face too. I called her later that night, and talked to her again about it. Amazing how something like that can mean so much. However, despite her demonstrated ability to change it, that duty remained for me. I didn't mind.

The CT scan on March 29 came out negative, with no evidence of disease present. Another sign of something positive. We both knew the cloud was still there, but there seemed to be a silver lining every time we got news like that. Joanie was living her life as if the cloud weren't there, just like we had talked about so long ago on that night in February of 1998.

On April 14, however, the cloud grew darker, and more ominous, when Joanie had a Pap smear at the clinic, and they found cancer again. We were stunned, as we had been before, and the news was even more disheartening after all the promise of what we thought was a successful chemo treatment, and Dr. Carson's own optimism in December and early January.

The way we figured, this was the third time it had come back since she was diagnosed in May 1996, and now we were really had to deal with the question of had it ever really been gone at all, or was it just hiding after every treatment waiting

224

to surface again when it could do the most emotional or psychological damage to Joanie. The other question we now had to consider, was would she ever be rid of it completely. We had no good answer to that question either.

To her credit, Joanie wouldn't consider those questions. Her attitude was now more resolute than ever. She was going to win this battle, and she was going to do it on her terms. My job, as a caregiver, was to keep my anger and fear to myself, and to reinforce Joanie's positive attitude whenever I had a chance. There were times when I was alone and I used to wonder if she wasn't as worried about me as she was herself. She never let on, and I never pressed her on what she was thinking during those times when we would get the news of a setback, news that would bring back all of the fear and confusion and uncertainty we'd been living with for what seemed such a long time.

We went down to see Dr. Carson in mid-May, to get an explanation about what was going on right then. When we got there, Carson said the Pap was positive for cancer, and she thought it involved the upper vagina, and she wanted to do surgery the next day to remove that portion of the neovagina where the mass was located. She seemed to be confident that this area was the only problem, which gave us a slim glimmer of hope to hang on to.

The next day, we checked her in, and were taken to the pre-op area, expecting much the same place we had been in before, but since the last time she had surgery they had made some changes, and the pre-op wasn't as open, cool and noisy as it had been those other times. They had curtained off areas for each patient, and the noise level was significantly reduced, which help give the illusion of confident calmness. The routine was the same, the anesthesiologist came in to meet with Joanie, and he would be followed later by the nurse

225

anesthetist, and she would explain her role, finally, Dr. Carson would stop by and give Joanie an idea of what was about to happen, and to present this procedure as basically an outpatient event, meaning after she had recovered she could leave the hospital. That last bit of news was enough to give her a lift, because right then, all she cared about was getting it over and getting back home.

Surgery went off fine, the offending mass was removed and sent to pathology for analysis, Joanie was brought to recovery, and after the effects of the anesthesia wore off, she was released. She had tolerated the procedure well, and had she had it her way, we would have got in the car and left for Bismarck right then.

The next day the cloud followed us back to Bismarck, but Joanie continued to focus on the silver lining. The way she figured, Carson had removed what needed to be removed, and when we were to go back in a few weeks, there might be a possibility of radiation to attack any leftover problem from this recurrence. That would mean a visit with Katie Dusenberry and possible radiation, as well as Dr. Carson.

That she had the confidence she had in those two doctors really made it easy for her to look for a positive outcome. Her confidence even made it a bit easier for me to feel the same way, even though I wanted to hit something really bad.

Gatekeepers and coping.

Time passes quickly when you don't want it to. It seemed like we had just gotten back from her latest surgical procedure when we were headed back down in early June for more appointments.

This time, besides her appointment with Dr. Carson, we were to meet with Dr. Dusenbery, or Katie, as we had come to know her, about another round of radiation. Katie had conferred with Dr. Carson about the possibility of resecting more of the upper vagina, the site of the problem surgery was supposed to address, but Dr. Carson believed that would be problematic. That was another way of saying she didn't think it would be a good idea, and radiation would be a better approach.

Katie told Joanie she was going to schedule her for a three-day session of high-dose radiation for later in the month, and asked Joanie if that was okay with her. Joanie, as always, told Katie she would do whatever she recommended, and told her to go ahead and schedule it. All she wanted to do was get back to a place that showed "no evidence of recurrent disease," and if this was going to help, she wanted to get it done as soon as possible. Besides, she had work to do. John was running for re-election, and she would have little time to worry about her medical situation. She would leave that to me.

An important aspect of this process that I learned early on was to find out who the doctor's "gatekeeper" was. They all have one, and it was really helpful to me as a caregiver to know who that person was. Anyone who has had experience in dealing with a doctor at an urban hospital knows how difficult it is to get through the telephone tree to get to the person you want to talk to. Your chance of getting through to the doctor on your first call is slim, so the next best thing is to know the person who can get through, and that is the person you want to know, and have a direct line to.

In Bismarck, it was Nancy at Dr. Bury's office. In Minneapolis, it was Marcia in Dr. Carson's office. I had Marcia's direct line, and if I had a question, or needed to talk with Dr. Carson about some issue, all I had to do was call Marcia and I knew that I would be hearing from Carson, or that Carson would get any message I had for her. Both Marcia and Nancy had come to know Joanie as well, and liked her, and they also understood that calls from me were not made if I didn't think what I was calling about wasn't important. The only exception was Katie Dusenbery. As near as I could tell, she didn't have a gatekeeper. Anytime I needed to talk to her, I just called therapeutic radiology, and left a message for her. She would always call me back. I also had an email address for her, and there were times when I used that as well to communicate with her.

As a caregiver, you will find it is really important for you to keep the lines of communication open between you and your patient's doctors. If nothing else, it helps you to keep things in perspective and answer any questions your patient might have. It can also help clear up any confusion, and believe me, over time, there will be plenty of confusion. Your job is to clear it up. At least that's the way I approached it, and it worked for me.

On June 22, we were back in Minneapolis, and Joanie was back in for the radiation implants. She was in for three days, and outside of being agitated about just being there, she handled the whole thing with a fairly good attitude. She was so confident that her doctors were on top of this thing, that there was no doubt in her mind that whatever they were doing was going to give her the peace of mind she wanted, and would also take care of the disease that had haunted her for eight years now.

While she was lying there getting the radiation, I began to reflect on the fact it had been eight years now since she started on this journey. I remember thinking how well she had handled all of the disappointments. The emotional ups and downs of fighting a disease like cancer can't help but take a toll, but as I looked at her, I continued to be amazed at how well she had coped with it all.

I had a good understanding of the dynamics of stress, and how they can affect a person, but in Joanie's case all I could see was that she was handling it. How she did it I never knew for sure. I knew she prayed a lot. I knew that she ignored it a lot, and I knew that somewhere deep inside there was a strength that was not going to let this thing get the better of her. Everyone's coping mechanisms are unique, and often go unspoken. We never talked about her battle in those terms. I rather just observed, and waited for her to tell me what she wanted me to know.

How much of what I thought I knew was responsible for her handling it as well as she did, I don't know. All I knew was that I was seeing something special, and it gave me a measure of hope.

Remembering life B.C.

With the surgery and the radiation behind us, we attempted to return our lives to something we recognized. We had a few weeks before the next appointment, which would be a follow-up to both the surgery and the radiation, and it would, we hoped, give us a sign that things had settled down, at least for a while.

The appointment in late July, gave us the sign we were looking for, and that was, to quote from Dr. Carson's notes, "Currently no evidence of disease recurrence." With that news, the sun seemed to shine brighter as we left the clinic that day, and made the walk the short two blocks to Sally's for a celebratory libation. We were both relieved, and when we sat down at one of the tables outside, we looked at each other knowing she had dodged another bullet, and we were going to relish the moment for what it was. What was also encouraging was that Dr. Carson didn't need to see her for another three months.

Good news like that has the effect of making you forget everything that has gone before, if even for a brief moment. In Joanie's case, she immediately went into a flurry of activity surrounding the re-election campaign of her boss, John Hoeven. That became her focus. Part of the dynamic of dealing with a disease like cancer is that once you are faced with the battle it becomes all consuming, and there is a real danger of forgetting what life was like before cancer (B.C.) What it does is concentrate all of your emotional energy on the moment, and one has a tendency to forget what was important B.C. and what was viewed as normal, B.C.

As I reflected on these last eight years, I could see there were things that we did differently because of the cancer and what Joanie had gone through, and there were things we didn't do anymore. Time was when if we decided to go to Minneapolis, which we did for many years, even before we were married, we just did it. Throw some clothes in the car and head down the road. We didn't do that anymore.

The reality of the Miami pouch and the colostomy also played a part in our activity now. What had seemed so abnormal six years ago, had now become such a part of our life, it seemed normal. There was, however a consideration we had to deal with we didn't before. So, in a sense it dictated to a degree our activity and how we planned for any travel.

As far as Joanie was concerned, her daily work life wasn't affected that much. As I look at her calendars from those years, it was as if there was nothing wrong at all. The only things that stuck out were the entries on dates when she had to have a CT scan, or blood drawn or she had an appointment in Minneapolis with Dr. Carson or Dr. Dusenbery. All of the rest of the entries had to do with her job with the Hoeven Committee, the church or meetings associated with friends. Her life was normal, and that meant busy.

What sticks out in my mind not only about this period, but since the beginning, was that Joanie had an innate ability to get on with life in spite of the disease, something any psychologist or counselor would have approved of. She did it without knowing it was what she was supposed to do to maintain her mental health, and she did it without being told she should.

We never talked about what we were missing because of this disease, or how our lives had changed since it so rudely intruded. The fact was, we weren't missing much, and what was important B.C., was still important.

Her appointment in early December was another good one. Those magic words from Carson once again said, "...no evidence of recurrent disease." It was going to be a good Christmas, and maybe, just maybe, starting in 2005 we'd get a glimpse of what life A.C. might look like.

SECTION FIVE
2005—2006

Of stones and Peaches.

The first six months of 2005 went by in a flash. We didn't have to go back to see Dr. Carson until the first of June. Joanie was doing well, busier than ever. Her calendar was full. It gave us a good feeling not to have to pack up and head down the road every month or three months to another meeting with the unknown.

The Pap smear in June did show some atypical cells, but Dr. Carson felt they were probably due to the radiation she had earlier, but would check again when we came back down in September. They call them atypical when they aren't normal, but cannot be called cancerous or precancerous. In any event, they bore watching. The reason we were going to go back in three months was that a urologist in Bismarck, had discovered some stones in her Miami pouch. In fact they had discovered ten fairly large stones. How those had been missed earlier considering all of the CT scans Joanie had had, and all of the eyes in Bismarck and Minneapolis that had been looking at the scans, remained a mystery, one I had written Carson about after all was said and done.

The reason they had been found at all when they did was that Joanie had been complaining of some pain, and they thought, initially, that might be the source. It wasn't. It would be some time before they would be able to pinpoint the source of the pain, but the first order of business would be to get rid of the stones in the Miami pouch.

The surgery to remove the stones had to be open, meaning they had to open her up and open up the Miami pouch. The stones were too large to be removed by a less intrusive approach. The procedure, done by a urologist, Dr. Monga, went well, and Joanie was only in the hospital for two days, and we went home. In retrospect, it was one of the easier procedures she had undergone in the last nine years.

We weren't scheduled to be back until early September to see Dr. Carson and Dr. Monga for a follow-up after the surgery, and for another Pap to see if the atypical cells were still just atypical. That gave us time to enjoy what was left of the summer, and we did.

The only sad event during an otherwise good period, was that one of our Siamese, Peaches had developed feline diabetes, and it had progressed faster than we had anticipated. She was younger by a year than Muffin.

Peaches was the heavier of the two, and was still able to make it up and down stairs. The litter box was in the basement, but one week, it was obvious things had gotten worse. We had visited the vet with her, and the news wasn't good. She seemed to do okay for a few weeks after that, but then it was obvious what we had to do, and were going to have to act soon.

One night, when she couldn't get up on the couch, even though we had a small stool she could climb on to make it up, we knew I had to take her in to the vet the next day and have her put down. This reality was hard on Joanie. These two cats, both who had come to us as little white fur balls, even though they were a year apart, had a firm grasp on both our hearts.

As Peaches lay near the couch, I tried to coax her into the kitchen to give her some water, but she wouldn't move. I finally went over and picked her up and carefully carried her into the kitchen next to their water bowl, and tried to get her to drink something. She wouldn't.

Then, as she lay there on the kitchen floor, I stroked her fur and tried to comfort her and would sprinkle some water on her little mouth. Joanie, whose own body was betraying her, stood off to the side, tears in her eyes, and Muffin sat off a ways wondering what was going on with her companion, not understanding, but obviously concerned. As I stroked her fur, she looked at me as if to say it was okay, and breathed her last, and I covered her in the towel I had laid her on.

I wrapped her in the towel, then put her in a box we found, and wrapped several layers of plastic bags around it bound with tape, and the next day I buried her in the back yard where Joanie wanted her.

The passing of Peaches had an effect on Joanie, and that night as I held her tight, she cried even more. I suspect it was not only because of the loss of one of her dear, furry friends, but also deep somewhere inside, the prospect of losing something so close when she was dealing with a life threatening disease made the processing of this event more difficult.

As for Muffin, she was confused as well. I didn't notice it so much that night, but the next day, I saw her going from room to room, and down to the basement searching for her friend, as if hoping she would find where she was hiding. It struck me how much our pets are really like us after all.

"When sorrows come, they come not as single spies, but in battalions."
—William Shakespeare

I found through over the years of helping Joanie deal with cancer, there are forces outside of our control that have an effect on the emotional ebb and flow of our lives. Losing Peaches was one such event, and then in August came another, one that had nothing to do with Joanie's medical situation, but nevertheless had an effect on her psychologically and emotionally.

It was a warm, sunny August morning in 2005, when my phone rang. I was at home, Joanie was at her office. At that time, my work, outside of helping her, was the maintenance of the Lewis and Clark Golf Trail book. It was a call from my best friend Wayne Tanous. I answered, and all he said was, "You got any beer?" It was 10:30 in the morning, and my first reaction was it may have been a bit early, but I knew if he was asking me, there was something up. I told him I was sure we did, and he said he'd be right over.

Wayne, over the last almost ten years had been my go to guy for venting my frustration, anger and concern over Joanie's medical problems. Wayne had been a corpsman in the Navy, and had a good understanding, in general, of things medical. He was also the one I relied on to correct rumors about Joanie's situation from time to time. Having someone like that you can rely on is something any caregiver needs, if only to help.

I was in the garage where we kept the beer in the fridge, when the door opened and Wayne walked in. All he said was, "It's ovarian." It was as if someone had dropped a bomb. All I could say was, "Shit." I knew immediately he was talking about Karen, his wife, and our dear friend.

We went out back on the deck, and he proceeded to tell me what they knew at that moment. We both knew ovarian cancer to be a killer, especially since usually by the time it is diagnosed, not always, but more times than not, it has advanced beyond the curative stage. It was still premature to make any assessment, and he told me they would probably be going to the Mayo Clinic to get a more thorough examination and prognosis.

We opened another beer, and another, and as we were talking about what was going on in our lives, and how now the two most important women in our lives were both facing an uncertain future because of cancer, Joanie got home. She came out back to the deck where we were sitting, and we told her the news. She didn't say much, obviously stunned at what she had heard, because she also knew what ovarian cancer meant, and she went inside. Wayne and I finished our beers and he left.

When I got back inside, I found Joanie sitting on the couch, Kleenex in hand, staring at the television, Muffin on her lap. I asked her what she thought about what she'd heard, and she just told me she didn't want to talk about it. I could tell from the look on her face the news of Karen's situation had a profound effect on her, not only because Karen was such a dear friend, but the news was hitting so close to home. We never did talk about it. I never pressed her when she was dealing with something that caused her some pain or concern, preferring to let her lead me into the discussion when she was ready. That process had served me well for a lot of years.

Also on Joanie's mind at the time of the news about Karen, was the subject of the atypical cells from the June Pap smear. We hadn't heard anything negative regarding them, and were waiting until our September meeting with Dr. Carson so they might do another Pap to put that issue to rest. There was also some concern about her shortness of breath, something I noticed from time to time, but something she kind of ignored. She was also complaining from time to time of some pain in her right chest area, the side where the incision had been made for the lung surgery. All of these concerns were also on her plate at the time when she heard about Karen.

We met with Carson in mid-September who told us that the Pap smear came back negative for any cancerous cells, which gave us hope. Joanie didn't make much of her shortness of breath issue, or her pain issue at this appointment, but when we returned in about two weeks, she couldn't ignore either one. I made sure Carson knew about what I had observed over the past few weeks, and a CT scan that was performed in Bismarck showed a moderate pleural effusion on her right lung. A pleural effusion is fluid between the membranes that surround her lungs, and can be a result of many factors, cancer being one of them. It could also have been contributing to her shortness of breath.

Carson said it was termed as a moderate effusion, and called Interventional Radiology to set up an appointment for later in the day for what was called a thoracentesis to remove the fluid and have it sent to lab for analysis to determine if there cancer cells in the fluid.

It was a Friday, and her appointment with Dr. Carson had been in the morning, but the earliest we could get her into Interventional Radiology wasn't until 2:30 that afternoon, which pretty much meant we might not get out of the city until later, or we'd stay overnight. It was one of those afternoons, when things don't go exactly as planned. We checked in at the department, and took a seat to wait for them to call for Joanie. We waited, and we waited, and now it was 3:00, and following the advice on the check-in desk that said if you'd waited twenty minutes or more to come to the desk and inform them. I did, and we proceeded to wait and wait. By now, I was getting mad. Joanie was uncomfortable when I got upset, afraid I would do something that would embarrass her, so I always did my best to keep it in check. I went outside for a quick smoke, and when I got back in, it was now 4:15. I went to the desk, and expressed my concern in the most civil manner I could muster, and it worked. In about five minutes they called for Joanie. Seems when the shift change came at 3:00, nobody informed the new shift that Joanie was waiting to see the doctors. I chalked it up to it being Friday.

I didn't go in with her immediately, which was strange for me now that I think about it. It was probably the only time since the first time I didn't. I wasn't waiting too long, however when one of the radiologists came out and called me in to the room where they had Joanie getting ready to do the thoracentesis. She was sitting in a chair leaning over a table with her bare back to me. There were three doctors in there, and they were all making jokes, putting Joanie at ease, and for a moment it struck me they could have all been cast members of the TV show M.A.S.H. There was no doubt of their ability, and they were going to make this as easy for Joanie as they could.

They were doing an ultrasound to determine where best to insert the needle to do the procedure. The doctor in charge asked me if I had the notes from the CT scan and X-rays they had done in Bismarck, and I showed them to him. From what he said to me they weren't much help to him. Seems there was a question on the amount of fluid, and their ability to get it out without causing a problem that would have meant her being hospitalized overnight. I didn't understand quite what the issue was, but when Joanie heard that, there was no way that was going to happen. The thoracentesis would have to wait until another time, and we left.

It was now rush hour on a late Friday afternoon, and I knew I-94 between downtown Minneapolis and Elk River was going to be a parking lot, and wondered if we shouldn't just bag it, stay one more night and go home the next day. I was overruled. Joanie wanted to get home, even if it meant getting home late, so we headed down the road.

We stopped briefly in Avon at my sister Joni's place, and made another stop in Fargo to grab a bite and see my sister Jane, and as daylight turned to dusk, the miles rolled by and when we crested the hill east of Bismarck where you can see the lights of the city laid out before you, she heaved a sigh of relief. It was now after midnight, but she no longer seemed tired or stressed. She was just looking forward to getting home, putting on her sweats, and getting Muffin on her lap, even if it was late, at least she would wake up in her own bed in the morning.

August and September had been stressful months, with a mixture of the bad news about Karen, and good news about the atypical cells, but no news for certain about the fluid on her lung and the pain that wouldn't go away, but at least now she would have a break. We weren't scheduled to see Dr. Carson until mid-January.

Shakespeare was right.

"I would not leave you in times of trouble
We never could have come this far
I took the good times; I'll take the bad times
I'll take you just the way you are"
— Billy Joel

It was one of those cool September nights. The light hadn't totally disappeared by nine. I sat on the deck in the backyard by the pool with the pool pump shut off and there was a lovely quiet that came over our little park-like yard. I had brought some wine with me and plugged in the CD player we used outside when we had parties during the height of summer and put on Billy Joel's CD. This song, "Just The Way

239

You Are" came on, and it struck me how the words had a special meaning for me.

Joanie was inside watching something on the television, and probably talking on the phone to one of her girlfriends. Muffin would be stretched out on her lap, and to the outside viewer it would look like a pleasant evening in a small, two bedroom house in a quiet neighborhood in a quiet Midwestern city. It was, or at least it was for a couple of months heading into the new year.

We were approaching the ten-year anniversary, in May 2006, of her diagnosis, and as I reflected on everything that had transpired since that day, the words of Joel's song floated across the still water of the pool and seemed to circle back and come to rest at the table where I sat, smoking a cigarette and enjoying a glass of Cabernet Sauvignon. As I listened to the words of the whole song, I couldn't help but wish I would have had the gift to put those words to song, but then I realized Joel had done it for me.

Joanie was doing really well, all things considered. Her hair had, long ago, returned to its full, dark, rich glory, something I enjoyed running my fingers through when we kissed. She had continued to amaze all of her friends and others who knew of her trials on the way she handled every adversity over the years with grace and courage, and a sense of style that said to all, "I will beat this." I loved her just the way she was.

As I sat there, I was trying to assess where we were, and what might be waiting around the bend as we got into January and February. The business of the shortness of breath and the pain in her back was troublesome to me. They hadn't done a thoracentesis yet, so the question of whether or not the fluid was malignant was still up in the air.

We weren't scheduled to see Dr. Carson until late January, and until then there was kind of an unspoken bond, neither

240

one of us would talk about what might be, what could be or when we might know anything. Her approach, which was the right one, was to go about living, enjoying the time we had before we were forced to worry about something, enjoy the holidays, and enjoy each other's company. There would be plenty of time for that next year.

The only thing that bothered her was Karen's situation. At first she wouldn't talk about it, but as time went on, she would ask what I had heard from Wayne. She cared deeply about Karen, and was praying for her. She knew how serious her cancer was, and true to her nature, was more worried about her than she was about herself.

By now, it was getting dark, and a little cooler. The music had stopped, the wine was gone, and I was ready to go in. I put the CD player back in the garage where it would wait until the next time, and went into the house. Joanie was in the bathroom taking care of the Miami pouch, and when she was done, she came out and I helped her clean up what needed cleaning.

She asked me what I'd been doing outside. I ran my fingers through her hair, and told her was I was just listening to some music and thinking about her.

She didn't believe me, but it was true.

Seems to me, fighting a disease is about attitude, not just medication and surgery. The will to live kicks in when the organism is threatened, and when a person decides they are going to fight, rather than give up, the chances of the disease winning are diminished accordingly. Now, having said that, there are times when the disease decides to run and hide for a while, giving the organism the illusion it has won the battle, if not the war. If nothing else, you could say a period like that amounted to a ceasefire.

The last several months of 2005 and the first month or two of 2006 was such a time. Joanie was doing well, and while the issue of the pleural effusion had yet to be resolved, it didn't seem to be bothering her or affecting her daily life negatively. The question of the pain remained, but it appeared to be manageable for the time being.

The holiday season was muted this year by our friend Karen's situation. I had frequent conversations with Wayne, and was kept up to date on what was going on with her battle with ovarian cancer, and the news wasn't good. She had a very difficult time, and by the time the holiday season rolled around, we knew it was but a matter of time.

Joanie had come to terms with what was going on with Karen, but had not been able to bring herself to visit her until right around the holiday. I had stopped by their house, and after I left, Joanie called me and told me she wanted to see Karen. We went back, and she was able to spend some time with her, and afterward she told me she was glad she had done so in spite of how difficult the whole thing was for her. Karen died a short time later, on the sixth of January, and so the new year got off to a somber start for all of us who counted Wayne and Karen as friends, especially Joanie.

Joanie's first appointment of the new year with Dr. Carson was set for late January. Carson wanted a CT scan prior to that meeting to evaluate the pleural effusion and to check on the nodule in her left lung, which had been observed some time ago. They had been keeping an eye on it, and weren't overly concerned about it lest it begin to increase in size dramatically.

They did the CT scan on the eighteenth, and the next day I had the radiologist's notes. After all this time I had learned to look for certain words that would help me understand what they were saying, and I did see some language that gave me

242

pause. The notes said, in part, regarding the nodule in the left lung, "...the indeterminate pulmonary nodule on the left has increased in size and is certainly worrisome for a neoplastic process..." That meant he felt the nodule might be cancerous, at least that's what it meant to me. He also noted that a PET scan might be helpful in "further definition" of the nodule.

Regarding the CT of the abdomen, the notes read, "CT examination of the abdomen demonstrates some vague regions of increased soft tissue seen within the fat just anterior to the liver." Those words, once I understood them meant to me, as a layman, there was some soft tissue in front of the liver that needed looking at. There was also some soft tissue in the pelvis that was noted by the radiologist that I assumed would have to be looked at as well.

Any caregiver, in a similar situation could do just what I was doing. I had been trained as a journalist to do research in a hurry, and during the years of helping Joanie through this period, that training had come in handy. The internet was a tremendous help, enabling me to do the research necessary for me to gain at least a partial understanding of what I was reading. Without the net, the same process would have meant hours in a library. Joanie, by the way never asked me about what was in the notes, only if there was anything bad. My stock answer, which was based on my own ignorance of the details would be, "Not anything that I can see, so we'll just wait and see what Carson says.

CT scan in hand, we met with Dr. Carson on January 27. Joanie's examination went well, and while nothing was done about the pleural effusion that day, Carson told us whenever we're able to get the fluid drawn off her lung, they would send it to the lab to determine if there was anything that indicated recurrent disease. Should it indicate recurrent disease, she would recommend Joanie be treated with the same chemotherapy protocol she had responded to so well before. That statement alone, gave us pause, and something to worry about.

Before we left that day she said she was going to order a PET scan, to get a more definitive picture of what had shown up on the CT scan. She said the PET could be done in Bismarck. The PET, as I've noted before, involved injecting radioactive glucose into the veins, and after it had time to circulate, they did the scan. Since cancer cells metabolize glucose faster than normal cells, the cancer cells would light up, giving doctors a better idea of where the problem areas were, and provide them a better diagnostic tool when developing a course of treatment.

We left the clinic and walked over to Sally's to sit down and have a drink. We weren't going to go home until the next morning, and so we decided to spend another night and treat ourselves to a good dinner and talk about anything but what we had heard earlier in the afternoon. It was as if she had decided that the disease was still in hiding, and the cease fire was still intact.

We would know more soon enough after the PET scan in February, and for the moment we were going to enjoy the evening, and cap it all off with a Baileys, as we had done so many nights before. Over the last ten years of this battle, we both had become very good at grabbing, and holding on to those brief moments in life that meant so much to us, and tonight was one of them.

The ceasefire is over.

The few words on a sheet of white paper came off the page like cannon shots at some faraway target, but they sounded like they were inside my head.

244

Joanie had the PET scan on Valentine's Day, and a couple of days later I got the notes, and realized our lives were going to change once again. In one short paragraph, the radiologist's notes told us the cease fire was over, and the disease we thought had been hiding was back. His notes said, "There is abnormal uptake seen involving the mid right peritracheal lymph nodes, a lower peritracheal lymph nodes, the indeterminant left upper lobe pulmonary nodule, and multiple right mid and lower ribs with adjacent abnormal soft tissue." The "abnormal uptake" referred to the radioactive glucose showing up on the scan.

The radiologist's impression was, "Changes worrisome for neoplasm involving some scattered mediastinal lymph nodes, the left upper lobe pulmonary nodule, and multiple mid and lower ribs with some associated abnormal soft tissue which accounts for the regions of soft tissue seen adjacent to the liver on correlated CT examination."

As I understood what I was reading, the lymph nodes were in the central part of her chest, and the term "neoplasm" referred to abnormal soft tissue. That was as near as I could come, as a layman, to making sense of the notes I was looking at. The bottom line was cancer was back, and it was as serious as it had ever been. This time, along with lymph node involvement, there were ribs involved. The soft tissue that was suspect on the CT scan was also confirmed to be cancerous, as was the left lung nodule.

At first, I didn't know what to do with the information. Joanie had no idea of what the scan had shown. The news was devastating to me; I didn't have the heart to tell her myself right then, so I took the coward's way out and left the bad news to be delivered by a doctor.

What I did know was that we were dealing with recurrent disease, and all of the research and reading I had done since this thing started was that there was no cure for recurrent, metastatic cervical cancer. Treatment regimens now are basically aimed at containing it, and keeping it from spreading.

Now that it was back for the fourth time, the situation was getting more serious than ever. On the other hand, it is possible, I guess, it had never left, and had just been in hiding from the radiation and chemotherapy treatments Joanie had already undergone, and now found an opportunity to attack her again.

Back when Dr. Carson told us that if the fluid on her lung was malignant, she said she would recommend the same chemotherapy protocol that had worked so well for Joanie in 2003. Those words came back to me when I thought about what might be next. I didn't know for sure what treatment she would recommend, but since Joanie had handled the treatment well in 2003 and it did do some good, they might try the same mix of chemo again. We would have to wait to hear from Dr. Carson before we would know.

We didn't have to wait too long before Dr. Carson called to talk to Joanie. She had looked at the PET scan and the notes, and she told Joanie that the cancer, indeed, was back, and she was going to recommend the same treatment as before, when she was part of the clinical trial. She told Joanie the chemo could be done in Bismarck, and she would be contacting Dr. M. R. Thomas in the hematology/oncology department of Mid-Dakota Clinic to administer the treatments. The would be the same as they were before, and she expressed some optimism the outcome would be as favorable as it had in 2003.

The news threw Joanie for a loop. She looked at me after she was done talking to Carson and asked me what I knew. I told her I had seen the notes, but I waited to talk to her about it until after she had heard from Carson to avoid any confusion that might be based on my own misreading of the results, or ignorance regarding what she would be recommending relative to chemotherapy.

As we sat there at the table in our small kitchen/dining area, I felt so sorry for her. She had a forlorn look on her face that I hadn't seen before in any of the other dark times. We just sat there for a few minutes, saying nothing. I couldn't tell if this news was going to be a tipping point emotionally for her or not. She had already seen so many hopes dashed, so many disappointments, so much pain, I wondered if this was going to push her over the edge.

After another moment or two, she looked at me as a sad smile came to her face, and said, "I guess it is a good thing we didn't get rid of that wig." Then she told me she was going to her office. I knew then I didn't have to worry, she was going to handle it

"The worst thing about medicine is that one kind makes another necessary."
—Elbert Hubbard

Change during good times can be difficult to handle, but when change comes during bad times it becomes even more difficult. Dr. Carson had been taking care of Joanie since the beginning, and had seen her through some very difficult times, and there was a level of trust and confidence she felt with her. There was also the familiarity with the clinic and hospital in Minneapolis, and it had become almost second nature to be making trips down there when we needed to. That was going to change with this latest development.

After Dr. Carson told Joanie that the chemotherapy could be done in Bismarck, it made some sense to us. After all, the regimen was really only a recipe with the dosage of each drug spelled out, much like it would be if you were going to bake a cake. So, where it is administered really shouldn't make much difference.

In theory that's correct, but as a practical matter it does make a difference. Making the change means meeting and establishing a relationship with a new doctor, and getting the chemo in a new environment under unfamiliar conditions. She would not be meeting with Dr. Carson before and after each treatment, as she had before, and that itself represented a significant change Joanie had to come to terms with to be comfortable.

As noted before, that comfort level between doctor and patient is extremely important when dealing with any kind of cancer treatment, especially something as harsh as chemotherapy and the side effects. It is, after all, a poison they are introducing into your body in an effort to kill the cancer cells, but it comes with a price. It also kills healthy cells, especially white and red blood cells. The patient must believe this is the best possible treatment; she is comfortable with, and trusts, the doctor she is working with at the time; and believes it is going to work.

Joanie and I talked some about the choices she faced. For a brief moment we considered calling Carson and asking if she could do it in Minneapolis, as she had before, but we dismissed that right away. We talked ourselves into the belief that it really didn't make any difference where they delivered it, it would be the same regimen, and it had worked before. The next thing that was in the foreground of her mind was the meeting with the doctor who would be overseeing the treatment, and, in effect, be her main doctor for the duration of the treatment. We had been assured that Carson would send the recipe for the chemo to Dr. Thomas, and he would be in touch with Carson throughout the six months the chemo was scheduled to run. As there was in 2003, there was to be one treatment every four weeks, for six months.

Joanie had an appointment with Dr. Thomas for March 9, and it would be then we would get an idea of the doctor and staff we'd be dealing with for the foreseeable future. We weren't strangers to Mid-Dakota Clinic, or St. Alexius Medical Center, since Dr. Jan Bury was Joanie's gynecologist, and it had been Dr. Christopher Adducci, a urologist, who had found the stones in her Miami pouch. She had also had numerous CT scans, x-rays and PET scans done at Mid-Dakota and St. A's. However, this was to be her first experience with the cancer department of Mid-Dakota, and she was just a bit apprehensive about it.

On the morning of the ninth, we checked her in and took seats in the waiting room in the hematology/oncology department just off the check-in desks on the ground floor of Mid-Dakota Clinic. Joanie was nervous, and I was as well. We didn't have to wait long before a nurse came out and called her name. The nurse happened to be Kathy Remboldt, someone Joanie knew. She was Dr. Thomas's nurse, and, I would find out she was also his gatekeeper. The tension eased immediately, and I could see it in Joanie's demeanor. At least she was dealing with someone whom she was familiar with. It made me feel better as well.

When Kathy finished the preliminaries, she left with the words we'd heard so many times before, "The doctor will be with you shortly." We sat there, not saying much, and I refrained from my usual examining room improvisations. I think she had seen my routines too many time already anyway. It wasn't long before the tap on the door came, it opened and Dr. Thomas walked in.

It was clear to me after only a few minutes, that Joanie was going to be comfortable with him, something that gave me

249

confidence. We visited briefly, and then got down to business. He told us he had talked to Dr. Carson and was quite familiar with her file. He went over the results of the most recent CT scan and the PET scan, and, I think, was trying to get an idea of how much we understood about her current situation, which was everything.

He said they would like to start the chemotherapy the next week. He went over what the regimen was going to be, and it was the first time I ever felt I knew as much as a doctor did about what was going to happen, but not really. I only knew about the experience from 2003 with the clinical trial.

There would be a change, something that caught our attention, when he told us Joanie would have to be admitted overnight for the infusion. This was a variance from the regimen from 2003, where the chemo was done in Minneapolis over a six-to-seven-hour period, and it was supposed to be the same thing now.

Dr. Thomas made some comment about it being more convenient for her, and the difficulty of delivering Mesna in an outpatient setting. This was something we didn't understand, but neither of us said anything. I knew they had delivered Mesna in the outpatient setting at the infusion center in Minneapolis with no problem, and so we had no idea of why that would be a problem here. Joanie, who by now, had begun to feel comfortable with Dr. Thomas and this new setting, didn't seem to want to pursue the question, so I followed her lead and left that question unanswered.

Mesna, as near as I could figure, was one of those medicines that you have to use because another one, i.e., Ifosfamide, makes it necessary. I knew she got it in Minneapolis, and without a problem, but for some reason here they wanted her in the hospital for it. Dr. Thomas also told her he would set up an appointment to have a portacath inserted prior to the infusion, and would let us know when that was. Joanie had one before but had it removed in December of 2004, not expecting to have any further use for it.

It had been a stressful morning, with a lot to consider. Joanie's attitude and demeanor that day were largely positive, as they always had been, but I could tell this was taking a toll on her. I suggested we go somewhere for a long lunch, which we did. While the regimen she would undergo was familiar, we both felt uneasy, not because it was chemotherapy, but because the recurrence of cancer was so alarming. That weighed on both of us that morning.

After we ordered lunch, Joanie didn't ask me this time what we would do next. We just talked about how well the chemotherapy during the clinical trial in 2003 had worked, and assumed it would work as well again, even with the change in the way they delivered the drugs here in Bismarck.

I dropped her off at her office after lunch, and before she got out of the car, I gave her a hug, squeezed her hand, and told her we'd get through this. She smiled and said, "I know we will."

The first round.

Joanie was scheduled for her first round of chemo on March 14, but before she could do that she had to have another port installed. That duty would fall to Dr. William Altringer, a surgeon, who coincidently, was also my surgeon.

It seems I had developed a problem that caused me some concern in late 2005 and into 2006. I was having difficulty swallowing, and all manner of negative thoughts were running through my mind. The year before, one of my best friends from my days in the army, Al Adinolfi, had died from esophageal cancer in July. As you can imagine, my mind was

251

playing all of the games on me that I had spent ten years hoping Joanie could avoid.

I finally had made an appointment with Dr. Doug Moen at Mid-Dakota, but I didn't tell Joanie about it. I was more worried about her at that time, and didn't want her to start worrying about me, which I knew she would. I went to see Doug, and in a matter of minutes, he told me I had a goiter. I could have kissed him. Actually, I had an enlarged thyroid, that with more tests revealed it was basically done doing me any good. I think it was diagnosed as hypothyroidism. He put me on Synthroid right away and referred me to Dr. Altringer.

In the meantime, I went to the internet and researched thyroid problems, including thyroid cancer. Here I was, doing what I had cautioned Joanie about doing, and that was borrowing trouble. What I did find, was that even if it was a cancer, there was a good chance it was treatable.

My meeting with Dr. Altringer was basically for him to take a couple of fine needle biopsies of the thyroid to send to the lab so we had a better idea of what we were facing. He did tell me that surgery was in the picture depending on what they found. Up to this point, Joanie had no idea of what was going on with me, and that was the way I wanted it.

After they got the lab work back, Bill, as I came to call him, told me they found some "atypical cells." That was a term I was familiar with from Joanie's pap smears, and so I figured that since they weren't cancerous, we had some time to deal with it. Bill suggested surgery and I agreed, but that was before Joanie's situation had gone from good to bad, so I told him we'd have to hold off on that. He did assure me I wasn't in any imminent danger, and I told him I'd call him when I was ready to do it.

With this much information in hand, I finally told Joanie about it, and her first words to me, expressed quite firmly,

252

were, "When were you going to tell me about this?" She was concerned, but I did my best to assure her I was fine, the situation was under control, and when things with her had settled down, we'd talk about the surgery Altringer wanted to do. That seemed to ease her mind, but I knew she was still worried about me.

The morning for the portacath surgery dawned early as we had to be at the hospital by seven. After the preliminaries were done, including a light anesthetic to sedate her, the procedure didn't take that long, and we were soon out of the hospital. The next thing on her plate that day was to be the first round of chemotherapy. She wasn't looking forward to it, and in fact, wasn't feeling very well. The port procedure didn't help, but we had a couple of hours before she was to check in for the infusion.

We were anticipating a similar process to the chemo treatment she received in 2003, when the same drugs were used during the clinical trial she had participated in. The only difference was this time she would be in the hospital overnight. After checking in, Joanie and I went up to her room on the top floor of St. Alexius Hospital, in the southwest corner of the building. The nurses took all of their notes and began hooking her up to an IV, since hydration was an important part of the process. Then came the other drugs. All of them had a time table assigned as far as how fast they were to be infused, and how long the time period for infusion would last. Mesna, the drug that Dr. Thomas thought she should receive in the hospital, was one of the first, but it is a drug that was meant to help avoid any bladder and kidney problems from the stronger chemo drugs.

Then came the first drug, and it was one I stayed around for. It was Ifosfamide, or Ifex as it was called, that had given her trouble during the infusions in 2003, and I wanted to be

253

around when they were done with that one to see if there would be a recurrence. There was. She threw up, just as she had before, but after that, there wasn't a problem. Ifex, would be followed by infusions of Taxol and Carboplatin, just as before, and she seemed to tolerate them well.

She wasn't happy being hospitalized but had resigned herself to staying overnight. I went home for a few quick breaks, and returning to stay with her. She wasn't feeling nauseous, but wasn't feeling 100 percent either. Around ten o'clock that night, I kissed her good night, and told her I'd see her in the morning, and bring her a Starbucks. She seemed to like that idea.

I went home that night feeling okay about what had gone on so far, but also knowing that tomorrow would be the test, and that test included avoiding nausea. She had handled it in 2003, and my hope was this would be a repeat.

It hits the fan.

As a caregiver, there are times when you have to act as a public information officer regarding the health and situation of your patient. Family, employers, and friends will all be hungry for the latest information on the health of someone they care about, and you will be the main source.

This does place a burden on you, especially when things are going south, and it is all you can do to keep an eye on the patient, and take care of her needs. What I found to be useful, as I traveled this road with Joanie, was email. Phone calls are important when you want to inform someone in a hurry, but you have to limit those to family, employers, and a couple of friends who can then relay the information to others. The problem with phone calls is they can take time, and if you were to call everyone who wants the information, you would be on the phone for hours.

Another thing you will find is that you only tell half of the story. I did that all of the time. The fact that people are interested in two main things. They want to know how the patient is doing at that time, and they want to know when they might be able to stop by and see her, or talk to her on the phone. The other dynamic is that a lot of people don't want to hear the details. Details can be hard to understand, and they make some people uncomfortable.

The only person who cares about the details is the doctor who is taking care of your patient. In Joanie's case, it was Dr. Thomas, the oncologist from Mid-Dakota Clinic who was overseeing the latest round of Joanie's chemotherapy treatments.

I took a lot of notes detailing what was happening to Joanie when she was home after the treatments, and how things went south after the first chemotherapy treatment. An example of the difference between what I wrote in my emails to friends, and the notes I kept for the doctor show what I mean. I wrote about the difficulty she had with nausea after I got her home following the chemo. The email doesn't even come close to telling the whole story about what she went through for those first 48 hours at home.

This is what one of the emails I sent on the day after we got her home:

We got Joanie home on Wednesday morning after a long day on Tuesday. She handled the chemo really well, having only a couple of episodes when they were giving her the Ifosfamide. Other than that she did really well. The kept her in overnight, and we got her home the next morning. The rest of the day was uneventful, but the night was another story. She can't sleep on her back due to the difficulty

255

breathing so she spent most of the night on the couch. About 4 a.m. the nausea kicked in and she was in the bathroom. It hit again about 5 or so and I gave her a Kytril. She then slept until a little after 8 a.m. when it hit again. It hit again about 10:30 and again about 12:30 so it has been a rough day for her. It is a quarter after two this afternoon, and she has been resting comfortably since the last episode. I called her doctor this morning to fill him in on what has gone on, and he is prescribing another anti-nausea medicine for us to try.

That's about the story from here right now. I will keep you advised on her progress. I'm hoping this nausea stuff will start going away."

What follows are the notes I kept to share with Dr. Thomas:

3-15-2006, Wednesday

10 p.m. or so Joanie comes to bed, but can't get comfortable due to the difficulty breathing. she couldn't lay flat and get her breath. We propped up some pillows so she could half sit up and that was a bit better. The we moved her to the couch and she got comfortable and tried to go to sleep.

3-16-2006, Thursday

4 a.m. or so, she is in the bathroom throwing up. Not much comes up. Then she feels a bit better and goes back to the couch.

5 a.m. or so—She's back in the bathroom throwing up, with not much coming out. Violent dry heaves. After she gets done she seems to feel better and I give her one Kytril for nausea. She heads back to the couch and does seem to get some sleep. I got up about a quarter past seven and she didn't even stir. Then about 8:15 a.m. she's back in the bathroom with the same results as the first 2 times. She feels better and lied down on

256

the couch again. I returned from the clinic and the grocery store around 10:30 and she was sitting up, clearly distressed and nauseated.

She got a nosebleed, which wouldn't stop right away and was flowing freely. then it was back to the bathroom where she was throwing up and what looked like some brackish bile was the result. She was also bleeding profusely from the nose at the same time. Then she seemed to feel better, and laid down again on the couch. I gave her another Kytril at about 10:45 a.m. Right now she is resting. Time 11:17 a.m.

12:30 p.m. Thomas calls. Joanie is back in the bathroom again. Throws up, but not a lot comes out.

1:50 p.m. It's now 10 minutes to two in the afternoon and she is resting comfortably. Thomas is prescribing another anti-nausea medicine.

2:30 p.m. She's back in the bathroom again. Not throwing up yet, but knows it is coming. It did.

I got a return call from the clinic, and Thomas had called in the prescription. I picked it up about 3:30 p.m., and use the first of it about ten minutes later. She went to the bathroom and cathed the Miami pouch and produced a good volume.

I went to the store and picked up some cherry popsicles and a couple of bottles of Powerade.

She ate one of the popsicles, and has been resting since.

It is now 10 minutes to six and she hasn't thrown up since the 2:30 episode, so maybe the nausea is abating. We'll see.

6:15 p.m. Joanie not feeling good. Feels like she might throw up again.

6:30 p.m. She does.

9:10 p.m. A bloody nose again. Throws up again.

10:25 p.m. Throws up.

11:00 p.m. Takes Percocet and Ambien.

3-17-2006, Friday
   1:30 a.m. Felt sick but did not throw up.
   3:30 a.m. Threw up.
   6:20 a.m. Threw up.
   9:10 a.m. Threw up.
   I think that was about 12 times since 4:00 a.m. Thursday."

You can see the difference. The emails weren't detailed at all, but they gave some idea of how rough a time Joanie had experienced, but the detailed notes were really for the doctor. That was the information I took to Dr. Thomas on Friday morning, when I took Joanie to see him at the clinic.

By this time, Joanie looked as beat up as I had seen her in a long time, and it was something we hadn't seen when she took the same chemo in 2003. I think that's what threw us for a loop. We had expected things would be the same, and she would get through it with a minimum of discomfort. It was not to be.

They did the bloodwork, and that was all okay, and then Thomas puts her in the hospital at least for overnight, and possibly longer, to deal with the nausea and perhaps to drain the pleural effusion that still hadn't been done.

Joanie didn't object to going in, she was in such distress, all she wanted right then was some relief from the waves of nausea, and a chance to get some sleep. Even though a hospital is probably the worst place there is to get any sleep, at least they would be able to monitor her and make sure she had everything she needed to deal with the nausea.

I had tried, and I could give her popsicles, but I couldn't make the nausea go away. It was a frustrating time for me as a caregiver, and it hurt so much to see her suffer like she did, so I was relieved when Thomas said he was going to put her in the hospital.

Days like these can be the most difficult times you can experience as a caregiver, mainly because you can feel so helpless, but it is important you keep cool, and don't hesitate to call the doctor's office when you think you need to.

We check her into the hospital, and it looked like it was going to be a long weekend.

I could see it in her face. There was no color in her cheeks, her eyes were dull, and her mouth appeared to be fixed permanently in a grimace as the nurse went about hooking up the Baxter so they could begin giving her an IV plus more anti-nausea drugs. The nurse didn't say a word to either of us, which struck me as strange.

Right about then, Joanie starts to throw up, and I jumped up to hold the basin that sat on the bedside table for her and to give her tissues. The nurse just stood there and didn't say a word. Then she said something about getting the anti-nausea drugs, and I said, "She's throwing up right now." She didn't react at all. I think it went right over her head. I began to think this was not going to be a pleasant stay.

Then, before they could get to the business of the anti-nausea drugs, the nurse sat down and proceeded to go on with her check-in report, which included listing all of the drugs Joanie was taking, plus the dosage numbers. I had the list ready for her, and I had brought all of the drugs with us to the hospital. She told me the list wasn't enough, she had to see the drugs herself, so she could write them down. She obviously didn't trust me, or know me at all. If she did, she could have seen me beginning to get angry but trying not to let Joanie see it.

The nurse told me Joanie couldn't take her own medicine while she was in the hospital. I told her Joanie had just been in the hospital two days ago, and Dr. Thomas had written orders she could take them during that stay. This news didn't seem to faze this nurse, and I was doing my best now to keep my mouth shut so as not to upset Joanie. Right now, the only concern I had was getting her comfortable so they could get the nausea under control.

All the while this is going on, Joanie still isn't getting the relief she needs. Later, when she is still nauseated, we called a nurse. The nurse said no one told her about Reglan or Marinol. Somehow she got the word and gave Joanie some Reglan, and said she'd call Dr. Thomas about giving her Ativan. We were now well into the five o'clock hour, and had been there for about three hours. Joanie remained agitated for about ten minutes after the Ativan was put into her IV, and then seemed to relax and doze off. I waited for about half-hour and then left to go home and pick up some things for her.

Before I left, I couldn't help myself and stopped by the nurses' station and called for the nurse who had checked Joanie in, and asked her why they wouldn't let her take her own drugs. She said, "It's a safety issue." The meds she would get from the hospital are packaged by the pill so they know what they are getting. She told me she wouldn't know what was in the bottles we had brought with us. I said, "Joanie's been taking these meds for some time now, and I know what's in these bottles is what's supposed to be in these bottles."

Then she said something that astounded me, she said, "We could get in trouble and be on *60 Minutes* with Mike Wallace." I did have to restrain my smile at that one. My response was simple. I said, "Look, I know that by packaging drugs individually, the hospital can charge us more for the meds." To which she replied, "The insurance company would probably pay more toward them because they are given in the hospital."

By this time, I had cooled down sufficiently to let the issue go. I had let off my steam, most of which, I'm sure had built up because of Joanie's situation over the last two days. Still, it didn't hurt to do that. Later that evening, I had stopped to see Orell and Cathy Schmitz for a cocktail and to bring them up to date on what was happening with Joanie. Of course I had to regale them with the tale of the meds.

As a caregiver, you will find there are times when you are going to be so frustrated, angry, and worried, you need to safe place to vent, and since you can't vent to the patient, it is important to have some friends you can do so with. Orell, Cathy, and Wayne Tanous were such friends for me, and I found it did help me a lot.

The next morning, a Saturday, I got to the hospital about 8:00 a.m., and Joanie was sleeping. I stopped at the nurses' station, and the nurse on duty told me she had thrown up about 3:30 a.m., and they gave her some more Ativan. She woke up about a quarter of nine, and I went to get her some ice chips. She is agitated and nervous. There hadn't been a doctor or nurse into the room since I got there. I asked her what she needed, and she said, "I just need some sleep."

She got up to go to the bathroom, and when she got down, she said the colostomy was full of gas. I told her it wasn't surprising since the only thing she had to eat since Wednesday was a grilled cheese sandwich, and she hadn't eaten much of that.

She got back into bed and drifted off to sleep. It was now just after nine o'clock, and we hadn't seen doctor or nurse yet. I let her sleep and sneaked out for a quick smoke. I was outside, having a cigarette, and thinking that the nausea switch Dr. Thomas talked about hadn't been turned all the way off yet, but it was getting close.

When I got back upstairs, nothing had changed, and I thought to myself, it's not like this place is as busy as they'd be at Fairview-University Medical Center in Minneapolis. But then I gave them the benefit of the doubt and chalked it up to the possibility they were short staffed this weekend. That didn't make me feel any better, but gave me a reason to understand why we hadn't seen anyone yet.

Finally, about 9:30, the same nurse we had seen yesterday when we checked in stopped in the room, and told us they were probably going to do the thoracentesis this morning, and that should help with her breathing problem, which was good news. However, Joanie told her she still felt sick to her stomach. When the nurse asked her to rate it, she said, "A little bit." That didn't seem to be a problem for them doing the procedure, which was to drain the fluid off her right lung.

Shortly we were introduced to Dr. Kriengkrairut, the pulmonary doctor who would be performing the ultrasound-guided thoracentesis. They wheeled the ultrasound machine into her room and began to get things organized for the procedure. It wasn't a large room, but I stayed, making sure I wasn't in the way. The nurse came in to help get Joanie ready. This was the same nurse I had words with yesterday, and little did I know I would change my opinion of her after this was all done.

They asked Joanie to sit up on the side of the bed, and then the nurse rolled the bed table over and put a pillow on it for Joanie to rest on. The doctor had her lean over on the pillow, and then began prepping her back for the insertion of the needle to drain the pleural effusion. It was a large one, and Joanie would have to remain still, and refrain from coughing or breathing too deeply while they were draining the fluid.

The ultrasound picture gave Kriengkrairut a good picture of the limits and location of the effusion, so he could see where to insert the needle, and it wasn't long before they were draining the fluid. It came out and filled a drainage vessel, and I was surprised that it kept on coming.

All of this time, I watched the nurse and how she dealt with Joanie while the fluid was draining. What I observed was someone who cared about her patient, and I saw her gentle hands on Joanie's arms and the quiet tone of voice she used when talking to her, and I had to admit, she was a far better nurse than I had given her credit for when we were having our disagreement about the use of Joanie's prescriptions the day before. That was okay. I didn't mind admitting to myself I had misjudged her. I did tell her afterwards I thought she did a fine job comforting Joanie through the process. I didn't, however, tell her what I had thought about her the day before. To me, any conflict was all part of the stress we were all under at that time.

The fluid kept coming, until Dr. Kriengkrairut called a halt. They couldn't get every last drop, but they got the majority of it. The total came to 850 cc of fluid, which I figured was about 25 ounces. Considering there are 32 ounces in a quart, it seemed to me to be a helluva lot of fluid and would explain the problem she had breathing. Kriengkrairut told me they would be sending the fluid to the lab for analysis, to see if there were any malignant cells present, and we should know in a few days.

After they were done, Joanie sat up, and said, "I feel like a different person already." She lay back in her bed, propped up, and said, "I can't believe the difference." I could see the change in her face—the tension that had gripped it for the last couple of days seem to have melted away. It was a good thing to see.

At 8:40 a.m., she told me that all she wanted to do was sleep, and now she was. It was after noon by now, and I can hear how normal her breathing sounded, and she seemed to be sleeping soundly. I was much relieved, even though I knew this battle is far from over. It has really just begun, but at least now she could muster her energy to continue the fight rather than living with the fear and anxiety of not breathing well. As I watched her sleep, I was struck by the difference between early this morning and now. She looked fully relaxed and was now able to get the kind of restorative sleep she dearly needed.

I was just sitting there watching her, when Dr. Thomas came in. He sat on the side of the bed with her, but she didn't even stir. He said, "She looks like she's sleeping well." I told him it was the best she had looked while sleeping in several days. He told me they were going to add another anti-nausea medicine but would not wake her now. He said, "We'll just let her sleep as long as she can, or needs to."

Joanie woke up around 3:15 p.m. and took a few sips of apple juice. That was the first thing she'd had since early Thursday morning. I asked her if she felt nauseous, and she said, "I'm not sure." Things seemed to be going well, until just after six when she threw up. The nurse finally came after I had searched for her, and she gave her some Zofran and Marinol. She seemed to settle down, and around eight o'clock that night she told me to go home.

I did. I needed a good night's sleep myself.

Homeward bound.

Sunday morning, and I arrived at the hospital at eight, Starbucks in hand, for me not her, and found her sleeping. As I watched her for a while, her breathing appeared to be normal to me, not labored, or fast. I hadn't talked to a nurse yet to see how here night had been.

Joanie woke up about 8:30, for only a moment or two. Said she had thrown up twice in the night, once about 11:00 last night, and again around 7:00 this morning. Then she drifted off to sleep again. I went out for a smoke, finish my coffee and pick up the *Tribune*, in case there was anything worth reading about on this Sunday. I also wanted to see if she would be interested in the paper because of the inserts, specifically the Target ad. If she were, that would give me another indication that she was starting to feel better. Turns out she wasn't interested right then, but asked me to take it home with me.

The nurse came in about nine to check her out and take all of the readings, plus give her some Marinol. Joanie told her the nausea was about five on a scale of one to ten. Her blood pressure was good, temperature was good, pulse was normal, and she was definitely feeling better. While the nurse was getting the drugs, she said she wanted to go home. I knew that wouldn't happen until a couple of doctors came by and checked her out as well.

At 11:00 that morning, Dr. Kriengkrairut came by to check on her. He took her off the oxygen she had been on for the past couple of days. He said they wanted to see how she was doing without it, and said someone would check on her in about twenty minutes or so, and if it looked good, they would leave it off.

As he left, I followed him out into the hall to talk to him and asked about the volume of fluid the drained off her lung, and how it was possible so much accumulated since we were in Minneapolis in January. He told me there were any number of reasons, not the least of which was cancer. That was consistent with what Dr. Carson had told me when I talked to her about the breathing problem a week before the first chemo round.

Then, Dr. K. told me something I didn't want to hear: it was his opinion they were going to find cancer cells in the fluid.

265

The results would be available no sooner than Tuesday, and if that was indeed the case, they would probably have to put in a chest tube to deliver meds to the affected area. I was stunned again and trying to figure out what I do with this bit of information when I talked with Joanie. I decided that if the subject came up, I would just put a good face on it and say the chemotherapy she is on should help clear it up. I didn't know any other way to deal with it, especially since we didn't know for sure if the fluid contained cancer cells or not, and if it didn't, then we would have been worried about something unnecessarily.

About noon Joanie asked for ice and apple juice, and drank a tidy amount, not a lot, but more than she had in a long time. Around one o'clock a nurse came in to take her temperature, and it was normal. What was more important, it was staying normal. The nurse mentioned something about going home, and Joanie said she hadn't mentioned it to me yet. She said she was going to lobby Dr. Reynolds, the on-call doctor, to get out today. With that news, Joanie told me she was going to try and take a nap, so I went home for a while.

When I got back, the first thing to she said to me when I walked into the room, was, "I'm not going home today." She didn't say it with a smile. She said Dr. Reynolds informed her they wanted to be sure she could keep food and liquids down, and, in addition, she had a urinary tract infection that they were going to begin treating with the antibiotic Cipro. One encouraging observation I made was that, even as she was expressing her disappointment at not going home, she was doing it with a stronger voice than I had heard her use in several days. I could tell from listening and looking at her face, she was getting stronger.

The remainder of Sunday was spent napping and sipping, and talking some, but about nine o'clock she looked at me and

266

told me to go home. I gave her a kiss, squeezed her hand, and asked her if she wanted coffee in the morning. She smiled and shook her head, and said, "Go."

Monday morning, I got to Joanie's room around 8:00, and she told me she had a little dry mouth, but wasn't feeling bad. Said she hadn't slept that well last night, but that didn't surprise me or worry me at all. She said again, "I just want to go home, and I want to go home right now."

Nine o'clock came, and Dr. Kriengkrairut stopped in the room to check on her. There was no news on the lab work on the fluid yet, and he said it would be later today, or tomorrow morning. He then began to tell Joanie that when they know what's going on, they can decide on a chest tube to medicate the remaining fluid. I know he was the doctor, and a doctor has to tell the patient what is going on, but I really wished he had held off on that news until they knew for sure what they were dealing with. Then, he told her the meds won't "cure," but they could "palliate." I didn't say a thing, and I'm not sure if Joanie even grasped what he was saying. All that meant to me was they could treat the symptom without curing the underlying disease. I guess it was supposed to make her feel better that they could do that, but it gave me no comfort. After he left, Joanie didn't say a word about it. It was as if she didn't even hear the word chest tube, or palliate. That was okay with me.

We were still waiting for Dr. Thomas to come by. She was having some cherry Jell-O and a glass of the protein drink, Boost, and looking forward to getting the hell out of there. About 9:45, Thomas arrived and announced that Joanie could go home. Her face lit up, and she thanked him profusely. He said there was nothing new on the lab work on the fluid, but they would call tomorrow when they knew something.

267

Seems that getting out of a hospital is harder than getting into one. In any event, we finally got her home at eleven; ten minutes later she was on the couch with Muffin on her lap. She began to relax immediately, and by mid-afternoon, was doing really well. Mikey Hoeven called, and Joanie answered the phone, just as I was leaving to go to the drugstore for some drugs for her. I thought that was a sure sign she was feeling better. After she got home, she had water and lemonade to drink, and ate chicken noodle soup for dinner. She didn't eat much, but I didn't care. She was home, more relaxed and feeling stronger, and to me that's all that mattered right then. When her sister Ann stopped by in the evening, she was cheered by how well Joanie looked.

What's in the refrigerator?

Joanie came home from the hospital on the twentieth of March. It was then, I decided to keep a log on what she ate and drank so the next time we met with Dr. Thomas, I would be able to show him what kind of nourishment she was taking in. More precisely, it would give him an idea of what kind of nourishment she wasn't getting.

The usual answers to the question of fluid and solid food intake don't often tell the doctor very much. For instance, the answer, "A fair amount," doesn't give them much of a clue. Especially when the patient is likely to inflate the amount when answering that question.

In Joanie's case, I decided to provide the answers myself. This is a sampling of a log I kept for over two weeks.

3/20/06—Water/lemonade to drink. Chicken noodle soup for dinner (Not that much).

3/21/06—Gagged while brushing her teeth and threw up. Not from nausea. To eat: cherry popsicle, chicken noodles soup at night (Not that much. To drink: water, lemonade and Boost.

3/22/06—Water/lemonade/Boost/Orange Crush to drink. Pasta with butter at night (Not that much).

3/23/06—Water/lemonade/Boost/ to drink. Cantaloupe in the morning to eat. In the afternoon tried to swallow a Percocet, gagged and threw up. Not from nausea.

3/24/06—Water/lemonade/Boost to drink. Cereal in the morning to eat (Not that much). Turkey sandwich in the evening. Eats less than half.

3/25/06—Water/lemonade/Boost to drink. Small amount of cereal in the morning. Small amount of chicken noodle soup in the evening. Gags again in the evening trying to take a Percocet and throws up. Not from nausea.

3/26/06—Water/cranberry juice/orange juice/Boost to drink. Half an English muffin with butter and honey. Eats less than half of the half. Turkey sandwich in the evening, and doesn't eat that much of it. At 11:15 p.m. she is trying to take a Tylenol, gags and throws up again. Not from nausea.

This pattern repeated itself right up until the eve of the second round of chemotherapy, which was scheduled for April 11. I kept the log through the first week of April, and it did show how little in the way of solid food she ate during those two weeks, and it also drew attention to the gag reflex that seemed to cause more of her episodes of throwing up than nausea did.

One of the things that often happens to patients receiving chemotherapy is that their taste buds are affected. I found it was true for Joanie. Things that tasted good before, all of a sudden had no appeal, and things she wasn't particularly

269

fond of before were okay now. This was especially true when it came to what she drank. At any given time when she was taking chemo you could find, in our refrigerator, orange juice, cranberry juice cocktail, grapefruit juice, lemonade, Powerade, Boost, bottled water, Coke, Diet Coke, Diet Seven-Up, regular Seven-Up, Sprite, Diet Sprite, Orange Crush, Tab, root beer, Gatorade, and Ensure.

Ensure and Boost were the two protein drinks we tried, and of the two she preferred Boost, especially the chocolate-flavored. Her favorite was when I served it ice cold, or if I made an ice cream milk shake out of it. With all the protein drinks she consumed, I was happy to find a cheap outlet for them at Walmart. It paid to shop around.

I gave my log to Dr. Thomas when we met with him before the second round of chemotherapy was to start. I think he was surprised when he saw it. He told me he often didn't get that kind of information about a patient, instead usually having to rely on the patient's responses about such matters.

I didn't know if it helped him a lot or not, but at least it told him that someone was paying attention to what was going on with Joanie when she wasn't under his direct care or in the hospital. If nothing else it made me feel as if I was making some kind of contribution to her care.

Oh, yeah, there was one other thing that was always in our refrigerator, an item that chemotherapy didn't seem to affect her taste for. Cherry popsicles.

Joanie gets stoned.

One of the drugs Dr. Thomas had prescribed for her to begin taking at home was Marinol. He was worried about her appetite, as I was, and thought this might help stimulate her interest in eating. Marinol is a manmade form of cannabis, which is also the source for marijuana. Popular literature is full of tales of the "munchies" that accompany the recreational use of the herbal form. Some us may even be able to attest to the truth of those tales.

Joanie was not one of them. She once told me that when she was a lot younger she had tried to take a hit of marijuana, but since she had never smoked, and never inhaled, all it did for her was make her cough. She never tried it again. I had to admit to her I couldn't say that.

According to Dr. Thomas's orders, I picked up the Marinol at the drugstore in the afternoon the day we got back, and gave her the first of the pills that evening. Joanie couldn't get comfortable in bed that night, so she went out to the couch in the living room where she seemed to do better. I heard her once in the night, and asked her if she was all right. She had got up about 3:30 for half of a cherry popsicle, and told me she was just having a problem staying asleep. Then, later, around 5:30, I heard her talking in her sleep, but didn't think anything of it.

I got up about 6:30, and she wasn't sleeping. She was sitting up on the couch, talking and gesturing, and I had no idea what she was talking about. I asked her if she was okay, and she seemed to be. She knew she was doing it. After that she drifted off and I thought that might be the end of it.

About 7:30, I was coming up the stairs from the basement after my shower, and I could hear her talking again. She was sitting there talking to someone, gesturing with her hands, and making no sense whatsoever. Muffin, who had been on her lap all night, was now sitting at the end of the couch, just looking at her. I imagined she was trying to figure out who Joanie was talking to as well. Now I began to get worried. The only thing that was different relative to the drugs she was taking was the Marinol, and then I realized there had been a reaction with some of the other medication she was taking. She was, in fact, stoned, but not the kind of stoned you get from taking a hit off a joint.

We talked about what she was doing and she seemed aware of what it was. Even in this state, even she realized it had something to do with the Marinol. She told me she didn't want to take any more of it. I called Kathy at Dr. Thomas's office right after eight o'clock and told her about the behavior I was witnessing. I opined that it was probably a reaction to adding Marinol to the mix of all of the drugs that had been given to her over the last three days. She seemed to agree with me, and told me it was okay to stop giving it to her. I would have anyway.

There was one other incident, but it didn't last long, and by about 10:45 Joanie asked me for a cherry popsicle. I was also going to try to get her to drink a Boost but that didn't work. After she finished the popsicle, she drifted off to sleep on the couch with Muffin on her lap. She slept soundly until about 12:30 when she came to and got up to cath the Miami pouch and empty the colostomy. She asked me for an ice-cold Boost, and I fixed her right up.

She settled down, and there were no repeats of the talking and gesturing from earlier in the morning. She seemed more relaxed, and asked me if I had heard anything about the lab work on the fluid they had taken from off her lung. I called Kathy again, and was told there was nothing to report.

The rest of the day was uneventful. I still couldn't get her to eat much besides a cup of chicken noodle soup. Her appetite was just not there yet, and, of course, now that Marinol was off the table, there was no hope for trying to smoke the herbal form of cannabis either.

I would just have to keep working to get her eating as much as she should by cajoling, wheedling, and trying to find the food she might eat. That was my job.

"No malignant cells identified!"

In the battle with cancer, any small victory gives you another reason to hope. The news that the fluid they took off of Joanie's right lung with the thoracentesis when she was in the hospital was clear of any malignant cells was one of those small victories. While it took a week for us to get the results. they were worth waiting for, and for a brief moment on that Monday, both of us had reason to smile.

Joanie was still not eating much solid food, and the incredible trigger that would send her to the bathroom to throw up was still active, but she was feeling better, even if it was slowly, every day. I began driving her to the office for brief periods only three days after I had brought her home from the hospital.

She would go to work in the afternoons mostly, and usually would be there for three to four hours, and then I would pick her up. John and Mikey Hoeven had told her, just as Ed and Nancy Schafer had told her before, not to worry about her job. She was on the payroll and would stay on the payroll, and to take whatever time she needed to get herself healthy. I think they did so, not just because of what she brought to the job she did for both of them during her time with them, but the fact was they loved her for who she was, and was not only a valued employee, but a very good friend.

The strong support of both the Schafers and the Hoevens made it possible for her to concentrate on her recovery and not worry about her livelihood. I can say without fear of contradiction, that support mattered, and I don't know what would have happened to us considering the length of the battle that was now in its tenth year, had it not been for that kind of support.

The days since I brought he home seemed to fly by, as we approached the end of March, and the first of April. She still wasn't eating as she should be, and my efforts to change that were not met with much success. In spite of that she was doing okay, if not 100 percent. We had begun anticipating the next round of chemotherapy, scheduled for April 11. Joanie and I talked about the possibility that Dr. Thomas, in light of what had happened after the first round, might want to change the dosage, or drop one of the drugs out of the mix, probably the Ifosfamide. We decided together that we would resist any changes. Our thoughts were this: It was the exact same protocol that had been successful in 2003, and she had handled it with few after-effects, and while it was an aggressive treatment, this cancer of Joanie's called for aggression.

In the meantime, I had a call into Dr. Carson, who was out of her office until the day before the chemo was to start to visit with her about this very issue. Dr. Thomas also wanted to visit with her as well.

The Wig'ns Affair

As the date for the next chemo round approached, Joanie got another surprise, this time one that overwhelmed her. Mary Pat Woodmansee, one of Joanie's closest friends, and other women friends of both of them, organized a fundraiser and it was to be called "The Wig'ns" affair. Mary Pat was one of the owners of Peacock Alley, a popular downtown restaurant and bar, at the time, and the event was to be held there on the Saturday afternoon prior to the her next chemo infusion the next Tuesday.

Joanie and Mary Pat Woodmansee, organizer of the event

They were asking everyone who would come to wear some kind of wig to show Joanie, who by this time was again wearing the wig Orell and Cathy Schmitz had bought for her in 2003, that she was not alone. It was a good wig, but it really wasn't anything like the rich, black wavy hair that was her natural mane. Her brother Richard flew in from San Francisco, much to her surprise, and my sister Jane and her daughter Vicki from Fargo, as well as sister Joni from Avon also showed up for the event. Jane, who custom-designed jewelry, had made beaded bracelets that spelled out Joanie's name, and sold every one she brought with her, and took orders for more.

The morning of the event, Joanie wasn't feeling great, but was determined to show up, at least for a while. She gave me cause for concern when she threw up while brushing her teeth as she was getting ready to go to Peacock that afternoon.

Again, the episode wasn't from nausea, but the hair-trigger gag reflex that I had witnessed almost every day since she got home from the hospital. While it perturbed her, it would not deter her from going.

Bob Wefald and Joanie at The Wig'ns Affair

On the way down to Peacock, I told her to conserve her energy. There were going to be a lot of people there, and they were all going to want to talk to her. I told her just to find a place to sit, and let them come to you. They would. I dropped her and Richard off at the door and went to park the car. When I walked into Peacock I was amazed at what I saw. There were people there, lots of people, and a good number of them were wearing wigs of many different styles, shapes and colors. It was a sight to behold. I looked around for Joanie, and saw her sitting on a stool near the end of the bar, and everyone who came in stopped to visit with her. She was especially glad to see Mikey Hoeven, even though North Dakota's first lady wasn't wearing a wig. It didn't matter to Joanie.

276

Mary Pat, and the others who had organized this event were all wearing wigs, and the raw energy, and the show of love and support for Joanie was everywhere that afternoon. It was something to see. Another of her friends, Bob Wefald, who had worked with her on the Trinity Lutheran church council and was now a district court judge, showed up in a wig that he had made out of cotton balls, reminiscent of the wigs worn by English judges, and it was a hoot. I took some photos of the event, and in all those with Joanie in the picture, you could see she was tired. Though she was smiling, her fatigue was clear.

I kept an eye on Joanie for any signs that she was ready to go, and after about an hour and a half, she motioned me over and told me she was really tired and needed to go home. I went for the car and asked her brother to bring her to the front door so I could pick her up and take her home.

After I got her home and settled in on the couch, I went back down to Peacock to pick up Richard, and see my sisters. Mary Pat told me she wanted to send dinner home with me in the form of pan-blackened prime rib sandwiches with French fries. That night, Joanie did have some of it, and it was the first time since the fourteenth of March she had eaten anything remotely resembling good solid food. I was encouraged, and I attributed it to the energy and support she had seen for herself that afternoon in Peacock Alley.

My sister Joni had stayed in Bismarck that night, and after she and Richard left our house later, Joanie said she couldn't believe what a day this had been, and how many people turned out that afternoon, wearing wigs. She didn't understand, or wouldn't accept the fact it happened because of who she was, and the way she was waging this battle. I knew it, but I don't think she really did, although I know the gathering meant a lot to her.

"We'll try this one more time."

The Wig'ns Affair on Saturday had given her spirits a lift, but physically she was still not 100 percent. Sunday and Mondays were quiet, and she did look good, despite the fact she was still tired. She, at least, was starting to eat more, and that was encouraging. She didn't go into the office on Monday but spent a lot of time on the phone with Carol Nitschke who was handling duties for her while she was absent. She also decided not to go in since the next day she was to go for labs, meet with Dr. Thomas and get the second round of chemo at St. Alexius. She wasn't looking forward to the chemo but was even less excited about having to be hospitalized for the infusion.

Tuesday, and we saw the blood work done, and it was all good. They also took a urine sample because of her urinary tract infection, and they did a chest x-ray as well. Then we waited to meet with Dr. Thomas. We had already talked with each other about any changes he might want to make and had decided we were going to resist them. I had my arguments ready to go. I hadn't talked to Carson yet, even though I had called Marcia at her office and asked her to call me before we went in, but Dr. Thomas had talked to Dr. Carson.

He told us he wanted to drop Ifosfamide (Ifex) from the mix of drugs she would be getting. It seemed to him that Ifex was the culprit that had caused the problem in her first round and put her in the hospital. Joanie told him we had suspected he was going to suggest something like that, and we were reluctant to accept his advice.

Dr. Thomas looked at me, and asked me why we thought we shouldn't change after what had happened following the first infusion. I told him there were several reasons. The first one was that Joanie didn't get the Kytril until just before we

278

left the hospital the morning after the infusion. When she was taking chemo as part of the clinical trial in Minneapolis in 2003, I made sure she got Kytril at five or six in the morning following the infusion. She never had any major episodes of nausea following any of the six infusions. I told him it seemed to me that we got behind the curve as far as the nausea was concerned, and once that happens, it is hell to catch up. I think we saw that happen.

The second reason I cited was the large pleural effusion her right lung that was causing a breathing problem. That issue had been resolved with the thoracentesis. And, I mentioned the fact she also had a urinary tract infection at the same time. Whether or not the infection was there before, or came after the infusion, seemed to me to be academic. My last reason, it seemed to me was the most compelling one, and that was this combination had worked three years before, and we were banking on it working again. It was moments like this in this process, that the involvement of the caregiver, I think, are really important. The fact that he knew I was heavily involved in her care and was paying attention to what was going on with Joanie gave some weight to my opinion, not that it was as important as his, but he knew he had another pair of eyes and ears on what was going on with her when she was not in the clinic or hospital.

Thomas listened carefully, and then he did allow that the anesthesia she had been given in the morning when they put in the new portacath could have been a contributing factor. Then, with a wry smile, he said, "Okay, we'll try this one more time."

I was proud of Joanie for holding up. Ordinarily, she might have acceded to Dr. Thomas's plan, but this time she was going to have her input. She felt the same way I did, and had confidence in the regimen she had in 2003, and was now going to stay with it if she could. It was her overriding feeling that it was going to work again, She liked and had complete trust in Dr. Thomas, but, at least for this time, she wasn't going to be a passive participant in her own treatment. She was my star, for if she had agreed with Thomas, the change would have been made.

We got her checked into her room about 1:00 that afternoon, and they got the IV started. There would be about two hours of hydration, and then they would begin with the drugs. Everything went fine. She did throw up one time, as we anticipated, but outside of that, the infusion went off without a hitch. The last of the drugs finished at about 10:30 that night.

I got to the hospital the next morning about 8:00, and she was sleeping. I just sat there, sipped on my Starbucks, and waited for her to wake up. Shortly after nine, she work up and told me that she had slept fairly well during the night. She reported they had given her the Kytril about five o'clock this morning, and so I figured, now if things go south, I can't blame it on that.

While we waited for Dr. Thomas, she ordered some cantaloupe, grapes and cranberry juice to drink. She ate all of the cantaloupe and all but two of the grapes, and I took that as another good sign. I thought to myself, this is going to be a good day.

Thomas came in shortly thereafter, and told her to go home. He didn't have to tell her twice. Before he left, he wrote a prescription for her for Megace and mentioned to her that her potassium level was low. Megace, he told her, was another appetite stimulant, and he didn't expect she would have the same reaction to it she had with Marinol.

It was Wednesday morning when I got her home, and she was doing great. She was eating more and seemed to be getting her appetite back. By the end of the night, there were no signs of nausea at all. I was beginning to believe we would make it through this round without a repeat of what happened after the first one.

Thursday dawned, and though she hadn't slept that well, there was no sign of nausea. She was drinking plenty of fluids, and that evening she had pork loin and mashed potatoes for dinner. She had yet to take a dose of Megace. She told me she didn't need it. I believed her judging from how her appetite had improved. Friday, Saturday and Sunday was more of the same. Still no nausea, and I now felt for sure we had escaped the nausea issue, and was very happy. She was really happy, even though she was still having some trouble sleeping well, at least she was eating again.

On the Monday following the second round, she began going into the office in the afternoons, and did so for several days. By now, with nausea not a problem, we were sure we had made the right decision about the treatment by resisting the change Dr. Thomas had wanted to make.

Little did we know there were forces at work that would mean we'd have to face the possibility of that change again.

It wasn't the nausea this time that caused a problem.

Joanie spent most of the first week after round two of the chemotherapy at home. There was little evidence of nausea, and though she was having some trouble sleeping well, her appetite was improving. That started to change the week of the seventeenth.

She went into the office on Monday, Tuesday and Wednesday of that week, mostly in the afternoons. It was on Thursday that I saw a change coming, and it was coming quickly.

That morning, she announced she was tired, and wasn't going to go into the office that afternoon. I took her temperature, and it was right at 100 degrees. Low-grade fever, I suspected, but then I started taking it about every half-hour for the rest of the day. It got as high as 101.6, and at nine that night, I called the emergency room and talked to Dr. Amin, one of the hematologists, and he told me to bring her in.

Joanie told me she didn't want to go in, so I said, "Okay, but here's the deal. I will check it again in a half-hour, and if it is still over 101, we are going to the ER." She agreed to those terms, and when I checked it in a half an hour, it was down to 100.6, and forty-five minutes later it was down to 99.5. I looked at her and thought to myself, she just willed her temperature to drop so I wouldn't take her into the emergency room. I checked her temperature hourly beginning at 5:30 in the morning, and throughout the day on Friday, and it had stabilized at 99 degrees. Right then I was hoping things were improving.

As much as I hoped, I knew things were not right, but it didn't seem like we had reached a critical stage. She did have on incident about 5:30 Friday morning, when she got up to get some milk, and when she left the bedroom door, I heard a crash. When I got up, she was lying on the floor, and after I found out she was okay, I asked her what had happened. She just sat there for a few minutes, then told me she was a little light-headed. I helped her into the kitchen where she sat down while I got her some milk, and then she seemed to settle down. She went back to bed, and there were no recurrences of light-headedness.

I did note it and called Dr. Thomas's attention to it when I spoke with him on Saturday morning. He didn't seem that concerned about her temperature, since there were no chills associated with it, and he told me he was prescribing Cipro

282

again for her urinary tract infection, and because her white blood count was low.

During this time, she seemed to have a problem emptying her Miami pouch. The normal output wasn't showing up. Her colostomy output was light, and with a lot of liquid, but that was a factor of what little she'd been eating. The pouch output was of some concern.

By Monday, thirteen days after round two, it was clear to me what had to happen. I was going to take her into the clinic, even though she wasn't scheduled for a blood draw until tomorrow. I had to wake her up so she could cath the pouch, and then I fixed her some cranberry juice and ice water and put her Cipro and Premarin out, and just after 9:00, I went to get some coffee. When I got back, she was sitting in exactly the same place, sound asleep. She stayed asleep until about 2:30 when I woke her up so she could cath her pouch.

It was then I saw that her motor skills were somewhat impaired, as she was having difficulty putting the Surgilube onto the catheter, and it scared me. I told her to forget it, we were going into the clinic. I talked to Thomas, and he said to bring her to the emergency room.

Joanie was as weak as I had ever seen her. She was having difficulty getting up off the couch without my help and was walking ever so slowly. I told her she didn't have to worry about changing clothes. When she got her coat on, she sat down at the kitchen table, and said, "I don't know if I can make it." I said, in as calm a manner as I could, "Look, darlin', we are going to take you to the clinic one way or the other. If you don't think you have the strength to walk to the car, I'll call an ambulance." She knew by then I was serious, and somehow she mustered up enough strength to walk the few steps to the car. When we got to the ER, I drove right in, and they brought a wheelchair to pick her up and begin to get her settled.

They got her hooked up to an IV, and took her down for an ultrasound to determine what the problem was with the output of the Miami pouch. I asked Thomas if they could put a Foley catheter in the pouch and hook up a leg bag to see if that would help keep the pouch empty.

They also took blood for lab work. When Joanie was back in the ER and the lab work came back, Thomas said her hemoglobin was low, her platelets were low, her creatinine and BUN numbers were high (those two are indicators of kidney function), and she was anemic. He said her potassium was low as well. The diagnosis on the notes read, "Acute renal failure, hypokalemia, (low potassium) and anemia (low hemoglobin as well as platelets)."

Thomas said he was ordering two pints of blood, and other fluid to address the problems she was dealing with. Then he said to me, "I'm glad you brought her in when you did." He wasn't near as happy as I was. At least now, she was in a place where they could do things for her I couldn't, and I felt relieved.

Three pints, not two.

These few days in the hospital were disconcerting to me, not only because I was worried about what might have been happening to Joanie, but because I really didn't have a clue about what was going on. I understood the numbers from the lab work, I understood what low potassium meant, and I understood what being anemic was, and I understood, albeit, vaguely, what the creatinine and BUN numbers indicated. What I didn't understand was what was going on with her inability to keep any food down. Her days in the hospital this

284

week, and the days at home following did nothing to inform me as to what the problem was. Suffice it to say, at this point, I was relying on the doctors more than ever to get to the bottom of that issue, and often, they weren't sure either.

The lab work done while Joanie was in the ER that late afternoon, plus the ultrasound came back. The ER doctor told me that while the ultrasound showed both kidneys slightly enlarged, he attributed that to her inability to empty the Miami pouch completely when she was home. When she came into the ER, they put in a catheter, and hooked up a Foley bag, and it drained it on a continuous basis. The output in just four hours was significant, and he told me that was evidence the kidney function was okay.

By seven o'clock that night, they had transferred her to the oncology floor at St. Alexius, and hooked her up to some potassium chloride to begin dealing with her hypokalemia. She was resting comfortably when I left that night.

The next morning, it was now Tuesday, Dr. Thomas came in and told us he was ordering two units of blood, and they would start them some time later in the morning. He also told Joanie, her creatinine and BUN numbers were coming down a bit, but they are not down where they want them yet. Thomas also told her she would need to stay in the hospital until they felt they had a handle on what was going on with her. Of course, the news didn't make her happy, but I was relieved and told her so.

When I got back to the hospital a couple of hours later, the nurse told us they were going to give her three units of blood, not two. This made me realize just how serious things had been, when I brought her in. As she lay there waiting for them to start the blood transfusion, she asked me if this was Tuesday. I told her it was, and she said she thought it was Monday. Then she said, "I've missed a work day." She was still a little disoriented, and she couldn't remember that we had come to this room from the emergency room yesterday until I reminded her.

The three units of blood did their work, and when I got to the hospital on Wednesday morning, she was looking good. She had color in her cheeks, her voice was strong, and she began hounding Dr. Thomas to let her go home. He wouldn't, not just yet.

Thomas told her that her hemoglobin was looking good again, and while her platelets were still a bit low, that was probably attributable to the Carboplatin chemo drug. He said her creatinine was coming down, but they wanted it down a little more. Then he told her he wanted her to get up and do some walking, and he was writing orders for the physical therapy folks to come up and get her going. She was not happy again, but grudgingly agreed to his plan.

I was then dispatched to pick up some cranberry juice cocktail and yogurt for her. She continued to have incidents of vomiting over the next day and a half, no one was sure what the cause was. When I got to the hospital on Thursday morning, she had just thrown up everything she had eaten the night before. She seemed to feel better, but told me she hadn't slept well and was anxious to get home. About nine, she went walking with the PT nurse and while she had doubled her distance from the day before, she promptly threw up when she got back to the room. I was really confused. Her color was good, her eyes were bright, and her general demeanor seemed normal   to   me.

Dr. Thomas came in around ten that morning, and told us her creatinine numbers were down even more, but he would like her to stay one more day. Joanie looked at him, and said, "What if I promise to drink lots of fluid and get some exercise, would you let me go home then?" Thomas smiled, and said,

"Okay, if you promise me." He told her he did want her to come into the clinic Friday morning for some more fluid through an IV. She hastily agreed. She was not going to stay another day.

He wrote the orders, and by noon on that Thursday, she was on the couch with Muffin on her lap, and saying, "It's so nice to be home."

She may have been home, and glad of it, but the issue of her inability to keep anything down continued unabated. I won't detail every instance, but here is a brief picture of what I saw over a period from Friday morning through Sunday.

On Friday morning, she threw up twice before we got to the clinic for the IV fluids Thomas had ordered, and after that was done, she wanted to stop by her office so she could do payroll since it was April 28, the last workday of the month. When we pulled into the parking lot at her office, she opened the car door and promptly threw up. I wanted to take her home, but she would have none of it, and went in to do the payroll. The rest of the day she threw up four more times, and I was getting nervous again.

I had asked Kathy, Dr. Thomas's nurse, when she was in getting the IV about the problem, and she got hold of Thomas who was somewhere waiting for a plane and described what I saw going on. He told her to have me get some Ducolax or milk of magnesia, to see if that helped. I did, and it didn't.

On Saturday, my notes showed this:

4:00 a.m. —Gets milk. Drinks milk. Throws up milk.

7:00 a.m. —Gets up. Throws up.

3:10 p.m. —Takes Ativan. Drinks cranberry juice. Throws up.

6:05 p.m. —Drinks 7-Up, Throws up.

After the last time, I gave her another Dulcolax to see if that might work, and by Sunday morning I thought, "Hooray, it worked." My excitement was premature, for there was to be one more episode.

After that last episode on Sunday, something happened, and I don't have a clue what it was. She did well the rest of the day, feeling better as the hours went by. Monday morning, she was feeling good. We went for a good long walk, and that afternoon she went into her office. We followed that same routine on Tuesday, Wednesday, Thursday and Friday, and it seemed she just got stronger every day. For me it was hard to believe the difference I could see on Friday from a week ago. She was not the same person.

She was feeling so good, that she told me on Friday morning while we were walking that she had made a decision regarding the chemo treatment. She told me she expected Thomas was going to want to change it again, and she wasn't going to let him, even after all she'd been through.

That was my girl. She was feeling stronger than ever.

How do we measure progress?

Joanie's next round of this chemotherapy regimen, the third of six, was scheduled for May 9, the day before her fifty-sixth birthday. That was unfortunate timing because at least she was feeling good, and there would have been a chance to celebrate in style.

As she recovered from the side effects of the second round, we began to think about what progress, if any, was being made. Joanie and I talked about it from time to time, and it was important to her since she had made up her mind that she didn't want the program to change.

We both believed in this regimen, and it was a belief based on the success of the same six treatments she got in 2003.

Joanie desperately wanted it to work, despite two trips to the hospital following the first two rounds.

As to how progress would be measured, we were not sure. I did call Dr. Carson about the time Joanie went into the hospital in April, and asked her how progress was to be assessed. Dr. Carson told me they would do an assessment after the third round, and before the fourth. She told me how they were going to approach it, and it raised some questions for me. I had all of the radiologist's notes from CT scans and PET scans, and I figured they would do another PET after the third round, and then compare that to the PET from February prior to the first round. That wasn't exactly what Carson had in mind, and so I wrote her a letter expressing my concern, from my limited medical background.

Dear Dr. Carson:

Thanks for giving me a call on the 24th relative to the question I had about how a response to chemo treatment is measured.

If I understood you clearly, you indicated that you would use a chest CT scan to compare to the January 18th CT scan. I assume you have the radiologist's notes from that one. So what I heard is that that would be part of the measuring process.

Now then, I am wondering if you didn't mean using a PET/CT scan to compare to the PET/CT of February 15, 2006, which was prior to the start of chemo. Here again, I assume you have the radiologist's notes from that. What makes me think that using the PET/CT from February to compare to one after her 3rd chemo treatment, which is scheduled now for the 9th of May, would be comparing two scans that provide, at least it seems to me, better definition of what is going on.

The reason I say that, is that the CT scan of January 18th, the results of which you had when we were in Minneapolis on the 25th

289

of January, completely missed any lymph node involvement, nor did it pick up on the problem of the right mid and lower ribs.

Here is what the PET/CT scan (February 15th) found according to the radiologist: "There is abnormal FDG uptake seen involving the mid right peritracheal lymph node, a lower right peritracheal/precarinal lymph nodes, be indeterminate left upper lobe pulmonary nodule, and multiple right mid and lower ribs with adjacent abnormal soft tissue. Given correlated CT findings and SUV measurements, these would be most consistent with changes of neoplasm."

Continuing to quote from the PET/CT scan this is what they said. "Impression: Changes worrisome for neoplasm involving some scattered mediastinal lymph nodes, the left upper pulmonary nodule, and multiple mid and lower right ribs with some associated abnormal soft tissue which accounts for regions of soft tissue seen adjacent liver on correlated CT examination."

You can see now why I would be confused if you choose to use a CT scan to compare to a January CT scan to measure her response to this chemo when the January CT missed the lymph nodes and the rib problem altogether. I do did see on the January 18th CT scan where it noted what they called "some vague regions of increased soft tissue seen within the fat just anterior to the liver in the superior abdomen with the largest region of soft tissue measuring approximately 1.9 CM x 1.4 CM. Those fatty changes to the liver had been noted on several of the CT scans going back to August 2004. My copies of radiology notes for scans don't go back any further.

At any rate, I would like to know what you plan to use in the way of comparison scans to assess her progress. Now maybe I don't know what the hell I'm talking about, but just looking at the notes raises the question I have tried to address here, and I hope you will have a chance to respond, either on the phone or by letter prior to the time we will be coming done to Minneapolis to meet with you.

As always, I know you are busy, but I do hope to hear from you on

I never had any training in the area of radiology, and so I couldn't understand some of the terms, i.e., "superior abdomen," but I have always been able to understand words, when I know how they are used, and in what context they are used. As a caregiver, it is something anyone can do, plus a good medical dictionary is helpful. Being able to do that gives you a better understanding of what you hear from the doctors. I always figured, if I could do it, anyone could.

We were to meet with Dr. Carson sometime in early June, prior to the fourth round of the chemo, and depending on what happened following the third round, we would have a better idea of what would be next, but what progress, if any, had been made following the first three treatments.

Joanie remained determined there was going to be progress, and as she prepared herself psychologically for the next round, she remained determined this regimen was going to work.

Disappointment and "What the hell is septic shock?"

Joanie continued to grow stronger each day as we approached the day for the third round of chemotherapy, giving us some confidence she would get through this round without a repeat of problems seen after the first two. We figured she needed a break.

When we went to the clinic Tuesday, May 9, the day of the infusion, the blood work came back with good numbers, meaning white and red blood cell counts were excellent, platelets were good, creatinine and BUN numbers were good, and there was no clear sign of any infection.

Dr. Thomas told us they would give Joanie a shot of Neulasta following the end of the chemotherapy. Neulasta is a drug meant to stimulate the white blood cells, and to help ward off infection following chemotherapy. So, we went over to St. Alexius Medical Center and got her checked into her room to begin the 7-hour infusion of Ifex, Taxol and Carboplatin, and we went feeling better about it than we had before. She still wasn't happy about having to stay overnight, but had accepted it, and besides, she was feeling pretty good this time.

The infusion went well. Joanie did throw up after the Ifex, but I had anticipated that. She had done that every time, going back to the treatments in 2003. After that episode everything went well, and by 8:30 that night she was done, and they had given her the shot of Neulasta. She was feeling a little tired, but was in good spirits and I was thinking, "Could it be we'll get by this one without any problems for her?" Tomorrow would be her 56th birthday, and while there would be no wild celebrations, at least it looked like she would be feeling good enough to enjoy the day.

When I got to the hospital the next morning, she was smiling, alert, and they had given her the Kytril around 6:00 for the nausea, and she was feeling good. I got her home finally around 11:00, and she had a pretty good rest of the day. A few friends stopped by to wish her happy birthday, and she spent a good deal of time on the phone.

That was Wednesday. On Thursday, she continued to do well. There was no sign of nausea two days out from the chemo, and I began to think we were going to make it. A few of her friends stopped by to see her, and she was having a good day. Friday was much the same, however that was to be the end, and beginning on Saturday, things began to go south, and go south in a hurry.

On Saturday, she throws up. Doesn't eat all day. Does drink some fluids.

On Sunday, she throws up in the morning. Doesn't eat all day. Does drink some fluids.

On Monday, just short of a week after the chemo, she throws up in the morning, and again in the afternoon, and doesn't eat all day. By now, I am getting excited. This is not what I had expected to see after things looked so good going in to this latest round.

I began to check her temperature, and around six that evening, it was 101.5. This got my attention, and I called Dr. Thomas, who happened to be on call. He told me I might have to bring her in to the emergency room. I mentioned what Thomas had said to Joanie, and she just shook her head. She wanted nothing to do with that. I waited until about 6:30 and took her temperature again, telling her if it had gone down, she could stay home. It spiked at 103.3. I told her we are going to the emergency room.

It took her about half an hour to get ready, and just before we were about to leave, I checked her temperature again, and it was 101.8. I told her we were going in anyway.

I got her into the emergency room about 7:20 p.m., and her temperature was 103.4 again. I knew I had done the right thing. Something was wrong, and there was no way I could have figured it out, or dealt with it at home.

Joanie was in some pain, but it wasn't serious pain, and it was obvious she was anxious and agitated. They got her into a room, and began hooking up an IV and that's when I first began to pay attention to her blood pressure (BP). I had my notebook with me, and kept track during the next couple of hours. When they checked her in, her it was 88/26. I didn't think much of it at the time, since her BP has always been somewhat low.

After they hooked up the IV, they gave her some Zofran for nausea, and took blood for lab work. They wanted to do a blood culture, as well as check the white and blood red cell counts. Then we started to wait for the lab work to come back so we would have an idea of what was going on.

About 9:30, the nurse came in and gave her Ativan through the IV, and that seemed to settle her down.

At 9:40, we were still waiting for lab results.

At 9:50, her temperature is down to 100.4.

At 10:00, the emergency room doctor comes in and tells us her white count is down to .4, which means she virtually has no defense against any infection she might be dealing with. He said he'd talked to Dr. Thomas, and they were going to put her in for some IV antibiotics. That meant a trip back up to the oncology floor. He told us he was just waiting for the orders before they would take her up.

Joanie, at this time, is quiet, looking pale and listless, and I'm getting more concerned as the minutes tick by. It turns out there was a good reason for what I was seeing.

At 10:23, her BP is 73/47, pulse was 116 and her temperature was 99.7.

Four minutes later, at 10:27, as the nurse is getting her ready for the trip to the oncology floor, she sees her BP is now 64/41. The nurse left the room in a hurry after seeing that, and returned shortly with a new IV bag, and cranked the Baxter up to full speed. It was now 10:31 P.M.

At this point, I just sit and stay out of the way. I knew something was going wrong, and seeing the blood pressure drop as quickly as it had, I wondered if her body wasn't trying to shut down. It scared the hell out of me. All I could think of was how glad I was I had brought her in when I did.

By 10:40, her BP was 75/49, and her pulse was 72, so they had stopped the drop. Then the doctor tells me they need to stabilize her BP before they will take her up to the oncology floor.

At 10:50, her BP is 78/43, pulse is 110.

At 10:57, he BP is 79/50, pules is 117.

It is now 11:00 P.M., and they have started her on a Dopamine drip, and I was informed they will admit her to the Intensive Care Unit for monitoring overnight. I heard the term "vasoconstrictor" used, and later learned that helps in raising blood pressure.

During all of this commotion, Joanie didn't say anything, and it was all I could do to do the same. I figured these people know what they're doing, so I'd best stay out of their way.

At 11:20, her BP is 109/55, and her pulse is 127. Then they wheeled her bed up to the ICU. I had to wait to see her until they got her hooked up to all of the monitors they use in ICU, and so I moved the car around to the front of the hospital. When I got up to the ICU, and her room, I was amazed at what I saw. There were monitors and beeping, and she was lying there hooked up to all of them. She still looked dazed to me. I wasn't sure if she knew what was going on, or why she was there.

I talked to the ICU doctor, and he told me Joanie had a serious infection, and no cells to fight it since her white count was down to .4. He told me after her blood pressure stabilized, they would take her off the Dopamine and keep giving her fluid along with antibiotics to work on the infection.

Dr. Thomas, who was on call that night, came up, and I had a chance to visit with him. He told me Joanie had a blood infection, and called it sepsis. He told me she had gone into what he called "septic shock," and that it was a very serious situation.

I went back into Joanie's room, and it was now almost one in the morning. She was groggy, and after seeing that she was going to be okay, at least hoping she was going to be okay, I kissed her goodbye and left for the night.

The first thing I did when I got home was head for the computer, to see if I could find out what the hell this thing was they called septic shock. I was stunned at what I learned, and how many people die from it. I found it can cause multiple organ failure and death, since the immune system can't fight the out of control infection, sepsis, and the mortality rate is anywhere from 25 to 50 percent.

As I sat there at home that night, staring at the computer screen, I also realized she wasn't out of the woods yet, but at least she was in the right place. I also thought how lucky we were that I had taken her in when I did.

The President's speech.

Tuesday morning, I got up about 5:30, unable to sleep any longer. I made some coffee, and sat down for my morning cigarette, and wondered how Joanie had done in the few short hours since I left the ICU. I assumed things were okay since there had been no phone calls, but I was still concerned about what I would learn when I got to her room, and what lay in store for her, considering what had gone wrong this time following the chemotherapy we had so counted on being the right stuff.

I went to the hospital about quarter of eight, only to find the door to the ICU locked. There was a sign on the door that explained it would reopen at 8:30. Seems they close it from 7:30 to 8:30 to accommodate a shift change, so the nurses coming on duty can be briefed on the present situation on the floor.

Since I had forty-five minutes, that gave me time to run to Starbucks, get some coffee and pick up a paper.

When I finally got into her room, I found they were now giving her another drug, Norepinephrine, to raise her blood pressure. Dr. Thomas came in shortly after I arrived, and told me he didn't know when she would be getting out of ICU. He said they were going to have to wean her off the Norepinephrine and see how her blood pressure stabilizes. Though her blood pressure (BP) was being monitored continually, I continued to take note of it along with the time. At 10:40 that morning, her BP was 91/54. I didn't think that was out of line for her.

The ICU doctor, or as the sign on his office door proclaimed, "Intensivist," was a Dr. Blake. I found myself slightly amused at the nomenclature the medical profession uses, since I had never seen that term used before. Anyway, Dr. Blake told us the preliminary lab work indicated a bacteria had set up shop. As I understood what he said next, was that the bacteria in and of itself doesn't present a problem, unless, as what happened in Joanie's case, your white blood cell count goes south, or the bacteria is able to make its way into the bloodstream. Then the bacteria becomes a real problem.

Blake told me it's like your skin. There are all kinds of bacteria on your skin, which do not pose a problem until you cut yourself, or break your skin in some manner, and some of the colonized bacteria is allowed to get into your bloodstream.

All the time Blake is telling us this, Joanie is watching TV. When Blake left, she didn't want to talk about what he said. The first thing she said to me was that she was wondering about the president's speech last night, and how people feel about using National Guard troops on our borders. All I could do was look at her and wonder.

At 12:00 p.m. her BP was 102/56.

I went out for a smoke and to get a soda.

When I got back at 12:27 p.m., her BP was 80/47. I know it is not unusual for blood pressure to bounce around a bit, but in her case, this bouncing got me concerned, especially the lower number.

Three minutes later her BP was 67/43. Those numbers were only two or three points better than they had been last night in the ER. The ICU staff was paying attention to their monitors, for it wasn't but a couple of minutes when a nurse came in with more Norepinephrine for her IV.

By 12:46, her BP was back up and it registered 120/58.

I continued to write down the BP readings every fifteen minutes at first, and then every half-hour later, until the early evening hours. The lowest the high number, the systolic number, got was 96, and the lowest the low number, the diastolic number, got was 47.

That afternoon, I had another conversation with Dr. Blake, and he told me that Joanie did indeed have a blood infection, or "sepsis," and she would be in the ICU until they could wean her off the Norepinephrine, and her blood pressure remained stable. He also told me they were keeping a watch out for any potential organ involvement with the infection, e.g., kidneys, heart, etc.

I had never even considered that last bit of news; I had trouble understanding how very serious this whole thing was. It was becoming more clear the longer I stayed there. Joanie's heart had always been strong from the beginning. I would be relieved to find out it still was, and whatever the infection was, it was not affecting her heart.

When I began to think about what Joanie was dealing with right then, and added it all up it was a worrisome picture. Not only was she dealing with metastatic cancer, and new lesions in her chest and ribs, but consider the list of problems presented that had brought her to the emergency room and the ICU this time.

These are from the medical notes: 1."The patient has a neutropenic septicemia with septic shock." Neutropenia refers to her white count, the cells relied on to fight infection, which was in the tank. I knew what septic shock meant. 2. "There was renal insufficiency, possibly perirenal." Renal insufficiency refers to kidney failure, and perirenal refers to the tissue surrounding the kidney. I wasn't sure what that meant, but I did understand kidney failure. 3. "Mild thrombocytopenia." That term referred to the platelets in her blood. They were low.

She was also noted to have pancytopenia, which is a long word that simply means there was a shortage of all types of blood cells as well as platelets. Her urine also tested positive for a bacterial infection, and she was suffering from hypokalemia, or low potassium.

As I considered all of that, it seemed to me that besides the cancer, there wasn't much else that could have gone wrong at this particular time that didn't, and despite all of that, Joanie was lying in a bed in the ICU wondering about how the president's speech from the night before was playing across the land.

I always knew she was tough.

Things are going to change.

As a caregiver, events of a week like this are your own personal nightmare. At least, it was mine. Things are totally out of your control, and you are basically ignorant about what the hell is going on with the most important person in your life. You try to keep focused on what you know, and try to find out what you don't know, all the while she lies in the emergency room, or the ICU or the oncology floor, and her energy is focused on getting through whatever it is that is threatening her body and her life at that time.

It is probably a more difficult time, both intellectually and emotionally, for the caregiver than it might be for the patient. The patient is focused on fighting the forces that are trying to do her body harm, maybe kill her, but she hardly has time to spend worrying. That task is left to the caregiver.

On Wednesday morning, Joanie was off the Norepinephrine, and they were satisfied in the ICU that her blood pressure had stabilized. So the day was off to a good start. Dr. Thomas came in and told us they would give her two pints of blood today, and then she would be moved upstairs to the oncology floor where she would continue to get antibiotics through her IV for a couple more days. They had been pumping her full of those since she got to ICU.

He told us her white count had started to move up, and after a day or two of more antibiotics, and her counts remained good, and if there was no problem with her blood pressure and temperature, she could probably go home.

By six that evening, they had finished giving her the two pints of blood, and she was moved up to the oncology floor. I could see the difference by then. She was feeling better despite what she had been through and was already making a lot of noise about wanting to go home. That would have to wait.

The next morning, Thursday, Joanie was doing well when I arrived. Her counts were continuing to improve. Dr. Thomas stopped in and told her he wanted to keep her in a least one more day, probably two. He said her potassium was low again, and her creatinine was still a bit high. He wanted to see those numbers closer to normal before he released her.

Needless to say, Joanie was not happy hearing that news. She had already been on the phone that day to her office, taking care of business, and having her colleague Carol take care of some things for her. It was like this latest experience had been but a speed bump in this process, and she was ready to move on.

While we talked that day, Joanie told me that she was not going to object to them changing the chemotherapy regimen by taking one of the drugs out of the mix. I had reluctantly to agree with her. I also reminded her she would be scheduled for a PET scan on the thirtieth of May, and we had a meeting scheduled on June 2 with Dr. Carson in Minneapolis when she would have a chance to assess the progress, or lack of progress, after the first three treatments. Carson would be the major voice in what the remaining three treatments would look like.

Friday morning, Dr. Thomas came in, and after reviewing the numbers he viewed as important, he told her she could get ready to go home. He did tell her he was prescribing Cipro, an antibiotic she would take for about another week to ten days to deal with her urinary tract infection. Joanie took the moment to share with Dr. Thomas what she had said to me the day before, that she wasn't going to object to any changes they might make regarding the chemotherapy. Thomas told Joanie that even if she wanted to continue with the current treatment plan he would not do it. As he said, "Three treatments, and three trips to the hospital, two via the route of the emergency room, and the latest through the Intensive Care Unit, and her experience with septic shock was enough."

There wasn't an argument to be made with his decision. It had become obvious to us that this situation was different

301

from the one that existed in 2003, and for me, that raised the level of my concern about where this was going.

By Friday afternoon, Joanie was at home on the couch with Muffin on her lap, and she was quite happy. To her it was like the last five days had never happened. She didn't talk about it at all. She was more concerned about getting back to her office on Monday and back to work. I remember telling her friends in an email I sent out following this latest episode, that it seemed to me she had the constitution of a brahma bull.

She also had an innate ability to realize that yesterday now meant nothing, and what was important was today, and the plans she was making for tomorrow. She knew this without ever having been told this was a psychologically healthy way to look at life.

She just knew it, and to me that's what made me love her even more, and believe she had a chance to beat this.

Ambivalence: simultaneous and contradictory attitudes or feelings (as attraction and repulsion) toward an object, person, or action.

As the day of our appointment with Joanie's doctor, Dr. Linda Carson at the University of Minnesota approached, it was not lost on either one of us that we were now in the eleventh year of making trips like this.

Each of the countless number of trips we had made between Bismarck and Minneapolis was met with the same ambivalence on Joanie's part. Unlike the dictionary definition, I don't think there was an attraction as such, but there was anticipation surrounding what we might find at the end of the road. There wasn't a repulsion, but more of a fear surrounding what we might find at the end of the road as well.

So, Joanie was, as I saw it, dealing with anticipation and fear, and her behavior prior to every time we would be getting ready to leave, was evidence of that. This trip was no different, only now I viewed the stakes as higher. We already knew what the PET scan revealed, but we really didn't know what that would mean for the future treatments, or what else the future might hold. These questions were on our minds as we got ready to go, and there was little doubt in my mind, that if she could have gotten away with not going, and just had me drive down and talk to Dr. Carson and find out what she wanted to do next, that would be fine with her. She also knew that wasn't going to happen.

Our routine the day we left was the same as it had been since the first trips, but this time, she was more subdued than I had seen her in many of them. She didn't say much to me while the miles clicked by, but when we got to Mabel Murphy's in Fergus Falls she started to loosen up. This stop gave me a chance to have a smoke, outside, of course, and it always seemed like when we got there, we were almost in the Cities.

We ordered something to drink and some munchies, and while we waited for our food, she looked at me, and in voice that was barely audible, asked me if we could go back home now. I sat there for a moment before I answered. She looked so vulnerable at that point, I wondered if all of the trips, and all of the troubles that had come with the trips over the last ten years was finally taking an emotional toll that might be coming to a head. I smiled just a little, and said, "Look, we can certainly do that. We can do anything you want to do right now. All I have to do is call Marcia and cancel the appointment and reschedule."

She smiled at me, and for a moment I wasn't sure if she was going to take me up on it or not. I knew she wouldn't, but I think just by asking the question she was saying to me she was tired, and afraid, and wanted this to be over and for things to be okay. It was moments like this when it seemed we were as close as any two human beings could be to one another. It was times like this when words were superfluous.

We sat there for a few minutes, saying nothing until our food came, and when it did, neither one of us was as hungry as we had been when we came in. Joanie picked at a few things, and before long said, "We should go now."

I paid the tab, and we walked out into the bright afternoon sunshine to finish another trip to Minneapolis and uncertainty.

Change comes.

It was June 2 and Joanie's appointment with Dr. Carson was scheduled for later in the morning. We had a chance to walk from the Radisson on campus, stopping in at the bagel shop for breakfast and a good cup of coffee.

Joanie was less tense this morning. It seemed that the evening with Ginny and Ed had taken some of the edge off what she was feeling when we got to the Cities. We had shared with them the good news/not-so-good news results from the PET scan, and Joanie chose to focus on the good news aspect. It was like she was playing spin doctor, and trying to put a good face on it for them. She didn't ignore the not-so-good news, but she just said it was working, and there was still some work to do, and that the chemo appeared to be working. Which, when you look at it that way, it was, despite the three trips to the hospital.

As we sat at Bruegger's that morning, she began to speculate on what Dr. Carson might do about changing the chemotherapy. It was her opinion that she would just take one

304

of the drugs out of the mix, and it would likely be the Ifosfamide (Ifex). She really didn't have a good reason why it would be that one, and neither did I, except that was the drug Dr. Thomas wanted to take out when he first wanted to change the regimen and she had objected.

We got refills on our coffee, and she then told me she wanted to go to Macy's in downtown Minneapolis before we left to go home. That was a sign to me that she was not only feeling better, but was going to keep as much control over her life as she could regardless of the dictates of the disease she was dealing with.

The walk to the clinic from Bruegger's is not a long one. It was one we had made any number of times over the years. Today it seemed shorter, and while she was curious about what we would hear, she was not as anxious as he had been for the last couple of days. It made me feel good to see that as well.

Joanie hadn't seen Dr. Carson for six months, probably as long a time between appointments as there had been in ten plus years. We checked her in, and when her name was called we went back down the familiar hallway to one of the many examining rooms we had been in before. Bev, one of Dr. Carson's nurses, welcomed us and there was some comfort in finding a familiar face. Bev knew Joanie's case probably as well as anyone down there except the doctors.

We had left the PET scan CD and notes at the check-in desk and expected Dr. Carson would have a chance to look them over before she came in to see Joanie. We were right. When Dr. Carson came in, Joanie was relaxed and smiling. I think she was glad to see her after all this time. Carson chatted with Joanie, mostly small talk, for a while, then she wanted to hear what had happened following the first three treatments that had put Joanie in the hospital and in the ICU. She had Dr.

Thomas's notes, but wanted to hear from her patient as well. We gave her the short version, which seemed to satisfy her.

After she did a physical exam, and Pap smear, Carson told us what she was going to recommend regarding the chemotherapy treatment. She wasn't going to drop one of the drugs, instead was going to reduce by 25 percent the dosage for all three. Her reasoning was they had no way of knowing which drug was the culprit that caused the problems that put her in the hospital.

She was also going to put her on Cipro full-time to deal with a urinary tract infection. It seems that was the culprit that caused the latest problem, sending her into septic shock. She said she was going to order a urine culture prior to each treatment to determine there is no infection present prior to her receiving her next three treatments. Carson also ordered a PET scan to be done at the conclusion of the next three treatments, and told us to schedule an appointment following the PET. That would put us into sometime in September.

All in all, Carson said she was pleased with what she saw on the scan, but also acknowledged there was still work to be done. So we left her office feeling cautiously optimistic about what was to come. The chemo had done some work already, and we assumed it would do some more, even with the reduced dosage number.

The doctor knew what she was going to do.

When I had talked with her, she told me they would compare the PET/CT scan from May 30 to a CT scan taken back in January. I questioned her about that in my letter to her, suggesting that a PET/CT scan done in February would be a better comparison, for reasons I outlined in the letter I sent to her in early May. Turns out I needn't have bothered.

In our meeting with Dr. Carson, she talked about the PET scan that had been done in Bismarck, along with the

306

radiologist's notes from the scan. She had proceeded to compare this one to the PET done in February. I didn't asked her if she was doing it because of my questioning letter. It occurred to me she had planned on doing that all along. When she had talked to me in late April, it appeared she merely said CT scan instead of PET scan, and that had caused the confusion in my mind and had precipitated my letter.

I learned something that day, and that was when doctors talk to patients, or caregivers, they often use terms in a manner that can confuse the listener, but are clear to them. That is also why it is important for a caregiver to take good notes, and when confusion does come, to question the doctor. If nothing else, it shows the doctor or other medical professionals your patient is dealing with that you are paying attention and are taking an active part in your patient's care.

Her shopping foray at Macy's concluded, we pointed the car towards I-94 and the ride home. Joanie was able to relax now. She knew there was work to be done, but felt quite positive about it, as uncertain as the process was that she faced when, next week, chemotherapy resumed.

The day Muffin died.

I had lived with a dirty little secret the week before Joanie's appointment with Dr. Carson, up to the time we were driving back to Bismarck. Muffin was dying. In the days preceding her latest PET scan, we had noticed Muffin seemed listless and wasn't eating her normal ration. I took her Doc's Veterinary Clinic, and she was introduced to Dr. Tim Docktor, and after his examination, he told me she had a serious infection. He gave me some antibiotics, to see if that might help over the weekend. It didn't. Muffin was home over the weekend, but it was obvious she wasn't her normal feline self. The only constant was that she was still able to join Joanie on the couch where she would find herself on her lap. She was still not eating much at all. On Monday, I took her back to the vet, and on Wednesday, I stopped in to hear what the diagnosis and prognosis was. He said Muffin had a critical bacterial infection, and she was dying. I asked him if he thought she was in any pain, and he told me it didn't appear so, and they were doing their best to keep her comfortable. He then told me the humane thing was going to be to put her down.

My heart sank. As I held her that day in the vet's office, I couldn't think of what to do next. I didn't think I could tell Joanie before the Friday appointment with Dr. Carson, not knowing what news she might have regarding her chemotherapy. At the same time I wondered about the humane thing to do regarding Muffin.

I asked Tim if he could keep her in the clinic until Friday, at which time I would call with any instructions. I told him about Joanie's problem, and he understood what the news of losing a beloved, furry friend at a time like this would mean. I thanked him, scratched Muffin's head, and as she looked at me, I imagined she was thinking, "Why is he leaving me here?" It hurt.

Now, I had to come to grips with what I would tell Joanie, and when I would tell her. I decided to lie. I concocted a brief story about how the infection still was not cleared up, and the vet wanted to keep her in for a few days for observation and further treatment. I said since we would be gone for a couple of days, it would be better for her. I felt terrible, because it was giving her hope that Muffin was going to be okay, and when we got back from Minneapolis, she would be able to take up her position on Joanie's lap.

There might be those who say I should have told her the truth right away, but they weren't there, and they couldn't see what I saw, or know what the emotional impact of the news might have been at this most difficult time in Joanie's life. As hard as it was to keep it from her, I never regretted how I handled it.

The night before the appointment with Carson, after dinner with Ginny and Ed, I had tried to drop a couple of hints about Muffin, but they were weak, and Joanie didn't pick up on them. The next morning, after the appointment, and her shopping stop at Macy's downtown, we got back on the road, and I knew it was time to break the news to her. She had wondered aloud about how Muffin was doing, and how much she was looking forward to seeing her.

I started by telling her that Muffin was really sick, sicker than we had originally thought. Joanie looked at me, and said, "Is she dying?" I had to say yes. Now I had this hollow feeling in the pit of my stomach again. She started to cry and asked me how soon. I told her the vet was waiting for a call from me. I told her what Tim had told me—that was Muffin had a critical bacterial infection, and the humane thing to do now was to put her to sleep. Tears streamed down her cheeks, and she was tearing her Kleenex apart in her hands while I tried to keep my eyes on the road. All I could think right then, was

309

that everything we had heard that morning about Joanie's condition didn't matter to her at all. She had already watched Peaches die on the kitchen floor and now was going to lose her best friend, Muffin.

We drove in silence until we were east of Fergus Falls. I pulled into a rest stop to have a smoke and call Tim. I had asked Joanie if she wanted to see Muffin when we got back, and she shook her head no. I told him to do what had to be done and hung up. When I got back in the car, not a word was said, and Joanie just stared out the window, ripping Kleenex tissues to shreds as she did. We hadn't been back on the road for long when she told me she wanted to see her to say goodbye. I called the Tim's office immediately, and told him we were going to try and be there before his office closed, and that Joanie wanted to see Muffin. He told me they would be waiting.

We were more than three hours from Bismarck when I made that call, and so I just put my foot down, speed limits be damned. I was going to get Joanie there before the doctor's office closed, and I did. We pulled up to the clinic with fifteen minutes to spare.

Doc's Veterinary Clinic is a marvelous place. It is at once chaotic, with the resident cats and dogs roaming about, and a bird or two contributing to the cacophony of noise that announced that this was a small animal clinic, and it was one that cared deeply for the health and welfare of all of its clients.

We walked in, and the receptionist called Tim, and he came out carrying Muffin in his arms, and gently placed our ailing kitty in Joanie's arms as she sat on one of the benches in the lobby.

Joanie just softly and slowly stroked her fur, and talked to her much like she would have done had they been home on the couch. At first Muffin lay still, with little response to her.

310

Then, as we were getting ready to leave, Joanie said goodbye, and Muffin looked at Joanie, with what was, it seemed to me, a spark of recognition. I couldn't say a word.

When we walked out the car, we sat there for a moment, and Joanie asked me if I saw Muffin respond to her touches. I told her that I had seen it, and I had. When we pulled up in the driveway, we looked at the kitchen windows where Muffin would have been, and when we walked into the house, it seemed somehow quieter than it had ever been.

For what seemed like the longest time, neither one of us said a word. Joanie went to take care of the Miami pouch and the colostomy, and to get in her sweats. When she came out to sit on the couch, she ignored the TV, but asked me to put on some music.

I got the music started, then opened a bottle of wine, grabbed two glasses and joined her on the couch. I wasn't Muffin, but for tonight, I would be the next best thing.

Of PETS and PETS

It is sometimes hard to explain to someone who is not an animal lover, or one who doesn't have a pet, or has never lost one, what losing that pet means. It is even harder to explain when the person who feels the greatest loss is facing a difficult future herself as the result of a life-threatening disease.

It was a quiet weekend at 1205 N. Mandan Street. Losing Muffin when we did was hard on Joanie. She was already missing her, and when she took up her place on the couch on Saturday morning, it was evident. I had fixed her a cup of coffee, she had a book, the TV was on, but she wasn't saying much that morning. She spent a good deal of time staring out the window, not paying attention to either the book or the TV. It wasn't the least bit strange to me that when one loses a pet, especially one that has been such a constant companion and source of comfort, that the mourning is very real. I think this is more so in a situation like Joanie was going through. It was a hard reality for her to deal with at the same time she was dealing with her own sense of mortality.

At one point that weekend, she told me she wanted Muffin buried in the backyard. I had told Tim, the vet, on Friday, to hold Muffin's remains until we had decided what she wanted to do. Now I would call him on Monday and pick Muffin up and do what Joanie wanted me to do. The one thing that had changed in our house was the ambience. There was a silence that came with Muffin not being there that was palpable. Nothing was said those first days, but I knew in my heart, it wouldn't be long before Joanie would start looking for some new furry friends to welcome into our home.

The episode with Muffin had, for a brief time, taken our minds off what Joanie was facing. By Sunday, our thoughts began slowly to shift to the upcoming chemotherapy treatment that she would be receiving in a couple of days. We weren't worried that much about it, since they were going to reduce the dosage by 25 percent for the next three treatments, and we assumed that would reduce the negative side effects. As to whether or not they would be as productive as the first three treatments were, that would remain to be seen.

Our confidence was also raised because they would do a urinalysis and a urine culture to check for any possible infection prior to the start of the chemo, and they would give her a shot of Neulasta afterwards to help stimulate her white cell production.

They were also adding something new for these three cycles. They would call her in a couple of days after the chemo treatment and give her a shot of Aranesp, a drug that would help stimulate her red cell production and help ward off anemia.

It struck us both at the time they were, in effect, giving her poison in the form of the chemotherapy drugs to kill cancer cells, with the side effect that those drugs also killed normal cells. Then afterwards, they would give her more drugs to stimulate the production of the cells that had been killed by the poison they were using to help control the disease. I also found out the shots of Neulasta and Aranesp were not cheap, each running around $3,000 or more per dose.

The treatment went off without a hitch on Wednesday, and the side effects were minimal. She still had to spend the night in the hospital for the infusion, something she really didn't care for, but she accepted that as part of the treatment. She had little problem with nausea, and outside of being tired, handled it really well. So well, that in a couple of days she was going back to her office in the afternoons, and going on afternoon walks with Betsy Dalrymple, who was the wife of then Lt. Governor, Jack Dalrymple. Betsy was working at the Republican headquarters in the same building that housed the Hoeven Committee office. She had become a good friend of Joanie's over time, and Joanie looked forward to her walks with her.

The treatment on July 5 was a repeat of the June treatment, and the August 2 treatment was also the same. They went off without a hitch, and Joanie continued to tolerate them well. She was doing really well and was spending more time at her office, and was as busy as she could tolerate being. In fact, by August, her calendar was busier than it had been in a long time.

What loomed on the horizon for us now was PET scan scheduled for the twenty-second of August. That would be followed by a meeting with Dr. Carson in Minneapolis on the twenty-fifth. Until then, we would have to wait . . . again. We rarely talked about it, and I, for one, tried not to think about what it might show following the last three chemo treatments she had gone through, but it wasn't far from our minds either.

My hope was that there would be some progress, and Joanie would get a break. With what she had gone through earlier this year, and the loss of Muffin, she deserved one. It had been a tough seven months.

It was now approaching August 22, and the PET scan that hopefully would tell us what progress, if any, had been made following the last three chemotherapy treatments.

Joanie wasn't paying much attention to the date, she instead was concentrating on finding a new Siamese to join our family. I hadn't known it at first, but about a week or so after Muffin died, Joanie had been going through the want ads in the *Bismarck Tribune* and the *Forum* searching for just such a kitten, or kittens. After she mentioned it to me, she asked me what I thought about it. I told her I thought it was an excellent idea, and then she enlisted me in her search, a search that would come to an end in early September.

Before that, however, there was the issue of the PET scan and another trip to Minneapolis to meet with Dr. Carson. It was to be a discouraging time. The upshot of the scan, when it was compared to the scan of May 30, showed no difference.

The radiologist's notes read this way: "Findings: The study is compared to a previous examination dated 5-30-06 and demonstrates no significant change in the number of focal regions of increased glucose metabolism in the chest and liver regions. No definite new lesions are apparent. The intensity of the lesions appear to be relatively stable when allowing for technical changes. Impression: Multiple focal regions of increased glucose metabolism in the chest and liver not significantly changed dating back to 5-30-06."

As I understood it, since cancer cells metabolize glucose faster than normal cells, the radioactive glucose they inject into Joanie's veins lights up on the scan, and gives the radiologist a picture of where the problem areas are.

I picked up the radiologist's notes and the CD we would need to take to Dr. Carson, and when I got out to my car, I sat down and looked over the one-page note from the radiologist. At first I was stunned. Then I went over it again, word at a time, and figured out that while nothing had changed after these last three, reduced level treatments, there was no evidence of anything new either. So, I came to think of it as a so-so news/good news deal. At least the disease showed no signs of progression, and there was nothing new showing up. I was still disappointed that there hadn't been a decrease in the areas that lit up on the scan, but for the time I would focus on the positive aspect of the scan with Joanie. I would wait for Dr. Carson to elaborate on what it all meant, and what the next step would be, which I imagined would be more chemotherapy. Joanie was sure to be disappointed.

We met with Dr. Carson on August 25, and what I suspected is what she told us. She reviewed the CD of the PET we had brought along, and told us she wanted to do four more chemotherapy treatments. Joanie reacted with visible disappointment. Dr. Carson must have realized she needed a break after six months of chemo and told her to take September off. They would start the chemo again on October 1. Carson tried to put the same spin on it as I did, when she told Joanie, that while things had remained the same, there was no evidence of anything new popping up.

We walked out of the clinic to the parking garage, and there was no question we were going to go directly home. It was getting near rush hour in the Cities, and I had wondered if we might stay another night. She would have none of it. She was more than disappointed, and her demeanor and body language told me everything I needed to know. We headed for home.

This was a setback, regardless of how I tried to spin it. I think Joanie knew it. Though she never verbalized it directly, it was obvious she so wanted to hear that the chemo was working better than it was. She didn't say much for most of the ride back to Bismarck, and I didn't press her either. I knew that wouldn't work anyway.

When we were just passed Jamestown, I stopped at the rest area to have a smoke and walk around for a few minutes. When we got back on the road, she started to talk. She told me how disappointed she was with what we had heard today, and how tired she was. It was one of those times when I just listened. She started to say she wondered if more chemo was going to work, but stopped before she finished the thought, and then she asked me if I thought it was going to work. I told her I thought Dr. Carson and Dr. Thomas believed it would, and I was going along with them. I told her I was encouraged that there were no new lesions, and was confident that at least the cancer wasn't spreading. I don't know how convincing I sounded, but I left it at that.

As we approached the outskirts of Bismarck, she grew quiet again, and I knew why. There would be no Muffin to great her when she got home. I knew then how important finding some new kitties to come and live with us was.

Joanie had been watching, and I had even been checking the classifieds, but we found that Siamese are difficult to come by. That was true until the first week in September, when I got a frantic call from Joanie one morning. Seems there were two eight-week-old Siamese kittens at the pet shop in West Acres

316

Mall in Fargo. They were sisters, and Joanie asked me if it was okay if she checked it out. I told her to go for it. I knew how much she needed this to happen.

So Joanie called my sister Jane. It was about noon and it turned out Jane was at the mall. Joanie asked her if she would go to the pet shop and check out the two kittens. Jane did, and then she sent a picture of these two little white fur balls to Joanie's phone. Joanie sent them on to me and asked me if it was okay. I said, get them if you can.

Joanie called the pet shop and bought them over the phone. Jane was to pick them up on Saturday and drive to Jamestown where we would meet her and pick up these two new females that would come to live with us. Joanie was like a kid waiting for Christmas until Saturday came, and when it did, she couldn't wait to get to Jamestown. We met Jane and one of her grandkids, Jurnee, and were introduced to two of the cutest little balls of white fur with black feet and ears you could imagine.

We hadn't brought along a kennel to put them in, so the trip back to Bismarck was something to behold, with these two little kitties running around the car, getting in the way, and in general keeping Joanie busy trying to keep track of them and keep them from getting stuck around my feet. When we got home, Joanie had gotten hold of one of them, but the other one had crawled under the front seat. I had to get on my hands and knees and reach under the back of the seat to drag her out. Once inside, I just put her down, and she was off, they both were off.

It was a confusing time, but I took one look at Joanie's face, and it was all worth it. She was beaming, and I knew we had done the right thing bringing these two into our lives.

When they had settled down after a little bit, we got a better look at them, and once they were on Joanie's lap, we decided on the names we had chosen earlier: Brandy and Bailey. We could see the subtle differences in them so we could tell them apart, even if no one else could.

These two were box trained, but there were still a couple of accidents as they got used to their new home. The accidents weren't enough for Joanie to have second thoughts, and after those initial incidents, there was never another problem.

I have always heard the stories about how pets can make a heart glad and nourish a person's soul, and that Saturday, and every day afterwards, I got to see it in action. From that day on I was a believer, thanks to two little Siamese sisters that had no idea the joy they brought into the house on N. Mandan Street that day.

Bailey and Brandy find a new home with us 2006

Questions, Questions, and More Questions.

Joanie had September off from any chemotherapy treatments. So, between getting to know her new friends, Bailey and

Brandy, and getting back to work with a renewed enthusiasm, she pretty much put chemo out of her mind. She was living without fear for those weeks, and we both welcomed the break.

As for me, my job as caregiver was to ask some questions. The results of the latest PET scan, for me, were troublesome to a certain extent. First of all, I saw it as maintaining the status quo, which to me was unacceptable. Secondly, it seemed to me that reducing the dosage by 25 percent, while it seemed to mitigate some of the side effects we saw from the first three treatments, had no effect on the cancer that I could determine. Lastly, I was curious if it would be possible to raise the dosage by some percentage that would bring it closer to what it had been before, but not the full dose she had received during the first three treatments.

These were all questions that Joanie had nothing to do with. She left this aspect of her care totally up to me. Now, I am not a medically trained professional, as I have acknowledged before, and I am not schooled in the complex and often confusing methods of treating someone with advanced, metastatic cervical cancer. However, I had learned enough over the last ten years to ask questions I thought needed to be asked to help me and Joanie understand what was going on. A good deal of the time, these were questions that occurred to us after we had left the Dr. Carson's office, or Dr. Thomas's office. More precisely, these were often questions that occurred to me.

When they did, I would address them in a letter to Dr. Carson, and after Joanie's August appointment, I wrote this letter, and sent a copy of it to Dr. Thomas, since he was the one in charge of her chemotherapy treatment.

September 19, 2006

Dear Dr. Carson:

Joanie and I have a couple of questions regarding her pending resumption of chemotherapy on the 3rd of October.

And, just so you know, I am also sending a copy of this letter to Dr. Thomas so both of you know what our questions are regarding the treatment regimen for the next four months.

The questions now revolve around the amount of the dosage, which was reduced after the first three treatments in March, April, and May did not go so well.

As we understand it, the PET scan from 5/30/06 said this: "Since 2/14/2006, there has been a decrease in number of abnormal regions of FDG uptake in the chest and liver regions, however, significant regions of uptake still remain on today's scan. These findings correlate with some response to chemotherapy, although residual neoplasm is still present at multiple locations."

That scan was done after the first three treatments, which were at full dosage.

Now then, with the final three treatments, the dosage was reduced by 25 percent, and the results of the PET scan of 8/232/2006 reported this, "Findings: the study is compared to a previous examination dated 5-30-06 and demonstrates no significant change in the number of focal regions of increased glucose metabolism in the chest and liver regions. No definite new lesions are apparent. The intensity of the lesions appear to be relatively stable when allowing for technical changes.

Impression: Multiple focal regions of increased glucose metabolism in the chest and liver not significantly changed dating back to 5-30-06.

Now that tells me that while the cancer didn't grow during those three months of decreased dosage, neither did it shrink significantly

320

when compared to the first three months of treatment at full strength.

We know that in 2003 that dosage worked, and that was one of the reasons it was chosen to be used when the cancer reappeared.

If we examine the circumstances surrounding the problems associated with the treatment during the first three months of the cycle, I think we can see that some of the reasons for the problems are no longer problematical in and of themselves.

For instance, the nausea that occurred after the first three treatments was a function of the fact that Joanie wasn't feeling well when it started. There was also the problem of the pleural effusion that was a contributing factor, and we did get behind the nausea curve with the Kytril. All of that has been dealt with, and nausea has not been a major factor in her recovery from the treatments since.

The other two times when she was admitted to the hospital following treatment it appears that infection was the culprit and that problem has been addressed as well, and now she has a urine culture prior to the treatment. Also, she is getting a shot for her white cells as well as a shot for her red cells after each treatment. She was also put on Cipro daily to deal with the problem of the urinary tract infection.

Now then, the question is basically this: If we assume that despite the problems attendant during the first three months of treatment the full dosage did show, "there has been a decrease in number of abnormal regions of FDG uptake in the chest and liver regions..." and the last three months with a reduced dosage showed "...no significant change in the number of focal regions of increased glucose metabolism in the chest and liver when compared with the scan of 5/30/06," is there any wisdom in perhaps incrementally increasing the dosage over the next four treatments say at a rate of 5 percent or something like that? Or, perhaps the October dosage could be bumped up to 85 percent rather than 75 percent or 80 percent, and then the dosage could be increased again in November, again in December, and again in January for the final treatment of this schedule.

Obviously, I am not a medical professional, neither is Joanie, however when one looks at the recent history of her chemo treatments from 2003 it appears to us as lay persons this way, put quite simply: In 2003 the full dosage worked without any serious attendant problems.

In 2006 the first three worked albeit with some attendant problems which have now been dealt with.

The final three did not appear to work, except that no new lesions were detected.

All of this begs the question, can we expect the reduced dosage that had little impact on the cancer over the past three months to have a significant impact on the cancer over the next four months?

Now then, maybe I'm all wet and haven't a clue about what is going on here, and if so you can certainly feel free to disabuse me of any of the notions presented here. I won't be offended. The only thing I'm trying to do is make sure that we are doing everything we possibly can to eradicate the cancer that has taken up residence in her body before it evolves into something we can't control.

Dr. Carson, you have known me well enough over the past 10 plus years that Joanie has been battling this thing that it is part of my job to pose the questions that we can't, or don't, often articulate until sometime after we have left your office and had a chance to reflect and digest information. This is one of those times.

Thank you for your consideration, and I know you are busy, but I would appreciate hearing from you, or you can visit with Dr. Thomas and get his valuable input since he sees a lot of Joanie, and can relay your thoughts on this issue.

Take care, and I look forward to hearing from you.

Sincerely,
  Bob Kallberg

I never showed the letter to Joanie before I mailed it. She trusted me to keep her informed on anything I thought she should know, or to clear up any confusion she might have about what was going on with her treatment.

In retrospect, I wrote it because I was worried, and wanted to be sure that the treatment was being as aggressive as it could safely be. Joanie's welfare was my concern, plus, I wanted to be satisfied that I understood what was going on myself. The way I looked at my job was to have the information I needed to help her get through this difficult time.

Role reversal.

Earlier this year I had been diagnosed with an enlarged thyroid, and subsequently hypothyroidism. My surgeon, Bill Altringer, had taken a couple of needle biopsies, which showed "atypical cells." That was good news, since Bill had told me a couple of the nodules in the gland were firmer than they should be. I was familiar with the term "atypical cells" from Joanie's problems over the years, and knew that while it meant they weren't cancerous cells, they might present a problem sometime in the future.

I hadn't told Joanie about my medical problem until after I was diagnosed, since I felt she had enough on her plate without worrying about the state of my health as well. I knew her, and I knew she would, so I downplayed everything.

Bill had wanted to do surgery to remove my thyroid, since it was no longer functioning anyway, just to be sure that any possibility of cancer could be ruled out. At that time, I told him we would have to hold off, since Joanie was about to embark on a the six-month regimen of chemotherapy, and besides, there was no immediate threat to me. He agreed, and I told him we would revisit the issue later in the year.

With the eight-week layoff of chemo for Joanie, and the fact that she was feeling better, I called Bill to talk about doing the surgery, or if he felt it was necessary. Playing doctor to myself, I had convinced myself that since the symptoms that had caused me to see my regular doctor, Dr. Doug Moen, who had diagnosed the issue in the first instance, were absent now. I wasn't having any difficulty swallowing like I had then, and so I figured, since the cells were just "atypical" we could put it off until sometime in the future.

The day I talked to Bill, it was in late September, I explained, using the best medical term I could think of, that I was presently "asymptomatic," hoping he might agree with me. He agreed, but then he gave me this caveat. He told me that we could wait until next year, but there was no guarantee that the cells that were identified as "atypical" would not be identified that way then. He said he surgery would amount to one night in the hospital, and the recovery time was just a day or two.

When I heard that, it got my attention. I knew that the "atypical cells" that had been found in Joanie's Pap smears a couple of times had turned out to be cancerous in the end. So, I said, "Okay, let's do it," and I told him to schedule it, and to do it as soon as possible since Joanie was about to begin chemotherapy in less than two weeks, and then we would have to wait. I didn't want to take a chance on being laid up when she started.

He called me back in a few minutes, and told me the surgery was scheduled in two days, and a nurse would be calling me the day before with instructions. I told him I knew what she would be saying, since I had been through the same process with Joanie many times in the last ten years.

Now I had to tell Joanie. I knew she was going to be worried, so when she and I talked about it, I put the best face on it I could. I told her the surgery was fairly straightforward, and I would only be in overnight. I told her that Dr. Altringer had my confidence, and I saw no problems coming out of it. I did tell her that having it done now would avoid any potential problems down the road, and besides, my thyroid was essentially useless now anyway.

So, there we were, at 6:30 on the morning of the surgery, driving to St. Alexius Medical Center for my appointment. When I checked in at the desk, the receptionist asked me what I was there for, and I said, "I'm here for some slicing and dicing." She smiled, and I figured that was not a typical answer she hears to that question. I was trying to keep things as light as I could for Joanie.

I wasn't nervous about going in, though I would have rather not been there, but I figured it was time to get it done and over with, and the sooner the better. After finishing up some more paperwork, we were escorted to my room, and shortly thereafter to the pre-op area, and this was where it got weird for me. Instead of me accompanying Joanie, our roles were now reversed, and it was her coming along with me. She was quiet. I knew she was worried, even though I had kept reassuring her this was a routine deal, and I would be fine.

After I got changed into the gown I would wear, I took my place on a bed they had ready for me, and the nurses began the process of hooking me up to an IV. From here on, it was virtually the same routine I had witnessed every time Joanie had surgery over the years. Joanie just sat quietly by, as if this was the first time she had seen anything like this, and I suppose that was true. She had always been the one in the bed.

I got a visit from the anesthesiologist, the nurse anesthetist, and then Dr. Bill came in to go over with Joanie and I what was going to happen. He also told us, in a matter-of-fact way, they would be sending tissue samples to pathology to check for any cancerous cells. That kind of got my attention, and I know Joanie's ears perked up when she heard that.

I think he remembered Joanie from earlier this year, but obviously didn't mention it. He had been the surgeon who put in her portacath before the chemotherapy treatments that had started in March. After he told Joanie where she could wait, about how long it would take, and how long I would be in the recovery room before I would be back up in my room, we were ready for the nurse with the Versed. All of this was a new experience for her, and she seemed tentative and out of her element, which was understandable considering how our roles were now reversed.

This time, and this is something that I remember distinctly, because it came just before they gave me the Versed, Joanie bent down and kissed me and squeezed my hand. That was something I had done every time before she was wheeled off to the operating room. Then they gave me a shot of Versed, and that was all I remembered until sometime later when I woke up in my room.

When I came to, I was in a fog. I had this ugly white dressing covering my lower neck area where my thyroid once was, and the pain medicine and the remnants of the anesthetic were conspiring in an effort to make me want to go back to sleep. Then, I looked over to where Joanie was sitting. I had no idea of how long she had been there. She had changed clothes, and was wearing the black topcoat with the red scarf that she always wore well, and was staring at me. Then she began to cry. She had never seen me as being the one who was vulnerable, lying in a hospital bed, and in some pain.

326

When I saw her crying, I wanted to get up and show her I was fine, but I was still spaced out on the drugs and the pain I couldn't. All I could think of was here was this woman who had dealt with more medical indignities over the last ten years than anyone I knew, and was still facing more, and she was crying, worried about me and this minor problem I had experienced. I didn't know quite what to say or do.

What I was able to say, finally, was , "Joanie, I'm going to be fine. Everything is going to be fine. Right now what I need, or want to do, is to sleep, so why don't you go get some breakfast, and go to your office? I'll be her all day and all night, so I will see you later."

She sat there for a moment, drying her eyes with the Kleenex she had been partially shredding as she sat there waiting for me to come to, smiled weakly and asked me if there was anything I wanted. I assured her there wasn't and she got up, squeezed my hand and told me she'd be back.

Before I nodded back off to sleep after she left, which didn't take long, I thought how worried she must have been to see me like this, and how all of my efforts to keep her from worrying hadn't worked. But then, as I closed my eyes, I realized that was just Joanie, and that was the way she was.

Joanie, the caregiver.

My caregiver, Joanie, stopped by my room later that afternoon, and I was a bit more alert. We talked for a while, and I told her I was going to take a nap again, and there was no real reason for her to sit there and watch me sleep. I suggested she go home, get something to eat, give Bailey and Brandy some treats, and I would see her later.

I wasn't sure how she was handling all of this. I knew she was worried about me, and at the same time, I wasn't the same kind of patient she was. I was a very impatient patient, and all I really wanted to do was sleep, wake up the next morning, and go home.

Joanie came back after she had some dinner, and hung around for a while, until I finally told her around eight o'clock to go home. I was going to doze off again, and there was no reason for her to hang around. She reluctantly agreed, and told me she would be back first thing in the morning. I conked out.

This was the first time in fifty years since I had spent a night in the hospital as a patient, and I really wasn't a good one. By the time the next morning, when my regular doctor, Doug Moen had come by to check on me and tell me I could get ready to go home, and the doctor who had done the surgery, Bill Altringer, had been in to see that I was doing fine, I was ready to go. There was a brief period when I had some words with the staff there as they were reluctant to let me go because of my blood pressure, but I was quite emphatic that since my doctors had told me I could go, I was going to go. If that meant unhooking the IV myself, I told them that was the way it was going to be.

While this was going on, poor Joanie sat there, now more worried than before. Joanie was conflict averse, especially when it involved things in the hospital—me, not so much. Joanie was always concerned that I was going to get myself in trouble.

I voiced my desire to leave in strong enough terms they called Doug Moen, and he told them to give me a booster for my regular blood pressure medicine and wait for about a half-hour and check it again. I agreed, and I think Joanie was relieved. The time elapsed, my blood pressure was reduced, and we got the hell out of there. I think they were glad to see me go too.

Joanie drove me home, which was again a switch, and this time I got the couch for a while. Not long, but for a little while. She wanted to take care of me now, and while I did my best to assure her that I was feeling fine, she was trying her best to take on the role of caregiver. Under the circumstances I couldn't help think what an incredible woman I was married to. Here she was, still with cancer invading her body, and looking at resuming chemotherapy in about a week, and this time it was her bringing me a cherry popsicle, and worried that I was going to heal up okay.

We didn't do much that night, but I did suggest we have a glass of wine to celebrate what had been a successful surgery. I was healing up fine, and that night, I could see how relieved she was, and realized again how much we meant to each other.

The next day, thoughts about my surgery faded quickly, and our attention turned to what might be in store for her for the next round of chemotherapy, and if Dr. Carson and Dr. Thomas had made a decision on what the dosage would be for the next four treatments. We had no idea of what to expect, except we knew that what they had done for the last three treatments really hadn't accomplished much, and we were hoping they had come to some kind of conclusion about what might work better.

We would find out on October third.

Changing the dosage, and changing the plan.

Joanie's eight-week layoff from chemotherapy came to an end on October 3. It had been a good time for her. She was feeling good, even her hair had been making a valiant effort to return to its former glory. It still had a way to go, but had come back far enough for her to go without a wig when she felt like it.

Actually, her health was so good right then, it was hard to remember that the cancer that was dogging her was still there and remained to be dealt with.

The hiatus was like other times over the last ten years, when she went about life without regard to her physical situation. She never wore her disease on her sleeve, and refused to let it dictate her activity any more than it did. People who would meet her would never know what she had been through, or was currently dealing with. Emptying the Miami pouch and the colostomy had become such a second nature to her it seemed like they had always been there. She had reached a state where she could even joke about them with friends.

That cancer can do this to people is one of the insidious things about this disease. They can go about their life despite having been through a really tough period, and for a while they live with the illusion that things are okay, because they can't feel this good if something is going terribly wrong. It is not only one of the insidious things about cancer it is also one cruelest because of the emotional toll. It is cruel because in the quiet of the night, alone with one's thoughts, the harsh reality remains, and it will not be ignored.

On Tuesday, the third, we were to meet with Dr. Thomas at Mid-Dakota Clinic and find out what he and Dr. Carson had decided regarding any changes to the chemotherapy. They both had my letter suggesting that they might boost the dosage back up a bit. Joanie and I talked about that the night before, and she understood what my concerns were, and by this time, I had shown her the letter I had written. She never objected to me corresponding with her doctors. When I first started doing that, I wondered if she wouldn't consider it meddling, but I came to learn that she relied on me to ask the questions, she wouldn't or couldn't. I realized that every patient needs to have someone who can do that for her, or him.

Dr. Carson had told us when we met with her she was going to order four more treatments, and then after four months, they would do another PET scan to see where things are. When we got to Dr. Thomas's office, we found that plans had changed again. Thomas had talked with Dr. Carson, and now, he told us, the plan was to do two treatments, only with an increase in the dosage above what it had been for the last three. Then they would do a PET scan in November to check on progress. That was what I had asked Carson about.

Dr. Thomas was of the opinion that the current regimen wasn't working, only maintaining the status quo, something I agreed with. He agreed, however, to go along with the idea of boosting the dosage that had been reduced for the last three times of the first cycle. He told us that the dosage, which had been decreased by 25 percent for the last three, would only be decreased by 12½ percent for these two treatments.

I felt frustrated, hoping that we might see some progress from this step, but of course, we would have to wait. Joanie sat there, just nodding her head, and not saying much. She wanted so much for this to work, even if it meant chancing some adverse side effects from any increase in the dosage. She had agreed with me when we talked the night before, about the need for an aggressive approach right now and was willing to take the risk.

Dr. Thomas said one more thing that morning that stopped me cold. He told us that if, as he suspected, there is no progress, then we could look at alternative treatment. He told us about a new drug that had just been approved for use against cervical cancer, and it would be used with Cisplatin, another common chemo drug.

When he said that to us, all I could think, to myself, was, "Oh, crap." A moment before I had felt pretty good about the fact they were going to increase the dosage, but that hope went out into the ether when I heard those words from Dr. Thomas. I knew he was the doctor, one with years of experience in such situations, and one who was trying to save Joanie's life. I knew that. I knew that, but it was hard hearing what he said. I reminded myself that this man knew more about this disease than I could even imagine, and besides, we trusted him implicitly.

I looked at Joanie for a reaction when Dr. Thomas told us what he thought, and it was obvious to me she wasn't thinking about it in the same way I was. All she knew was that she was going to leave his office in few minutes for another night in the hospital with a seven-or-eight-hour infusion of the drugs that had made her so sick earlier this year.

We checked her into her room at St. Alexius, and they began the process of hydrating her prior to introducing the drugs, and she got comfortable. The infusion went well, and I would come and go until early evening, when she was sleeping, and then I returned in the morning to pick her up, and she told me she had a good night, and was feeling pretty good. We had our supply of Kytril, the main anti-nausea drug that we had gotten from Dr. Thomas' nurse, and I took her home.

She took up her place on the couch, and her two new friends, Bailey and Brandy, were there immediately to vie for places on her lap. She told me she wanted a glass of orange juice, which I fetched for her, and when she was done with that, she asked me for a cherry popsicle.

I began to think she wasn't going to have any problems following this first treatment, and she didn't.

332

Damn it! Joanie needs a break!
October 31, 2006

Disappointments can make hope more difficult, but they also make it stronger for the soul who chooses to believe.

Joanie handled the first of what was to be two more cycles of the Ifex, Taxol, and Carboplatin and a slightly increased dose with very few problems. Nausea was slight, and though she was tired, that was nothing new, or unexpected. She had the chemo on the third of October, and was to have the second round on the thirty-first. In between, she had been going back to the office, mostly afternoons, but the two weeks prior to the scheduled chemo she was doing a lot more than that. It was a relief for me to see her doing so well.

We were both nervous the day we were scheduled to meet with Dr. Thomas. Our hope that was the meeting would be routine, and she would go to St. A's and get the second infusion. Not to be.

Joanie had a chest x-ray prior to the appointment, and things came to a halt. When we met with Thomas, he pointed out that the x-ray showed there may have been slight increase in the area of concern surrounding the ribs on her right side. At this point, I don't think Joanie even knew, or understood that her ribs were involved then, all she knew was that there was something going wrong in her chest wall, and ribs may be involved. She didn't understand how serious this was beginning to look.

Thomas told us he wanted her to have a CT scan to get a more definitive look at what was going on before they would go on with the treatment. We did the CT scan that afternoon, and the results were disappointing. The report showed that since an earlier CT this year, "The destructive changes with underlying soft tissue masses appears to be slightly more prominent when compared to a prior study." It also said the left lung nodule that had been there for years, not moving much, was now slightly increased in size. Dr. Thomas would point out to us later that there was evidence of at least a 25 percent increase in the mass lesion in the chest, low ribcage and chest wall.

The upshot of all of this was that it confirmed Dr. Thomas's belief that the regimen was not working, and now they were going to go looking at different option. What had started out as a good day had all of a sudden turned upside down. Joanie seemed disappointed but not fully cognizant of what was going on. Her focus now was on what the next treatment would be. I knew, because of the research I had done, this was more than a disappointment. It painted a darker picture looking ahead than we had imagined.

We met with Thomas after the CT scan, and he also wanted Joanie to see a urologist and get a CT scan of her pelvis and abdomen to see if they could find a reason why her creatinine level continued to remain elevated like it had since way last summer. That number is an important indication of kidney function, and if it remained too high, there are some things they won't do. For instance, her CT scans were being done without contrast, because it can be hard on the kidneys, and until they fully understood what was going on they wouldn't use it for the scans. At least that is how this lay person like me understood it.

When we left the clinic that day, Joanie looked at me, and said, "I want a drink." I said, "You got it," and we went to Peacock Alley. She really only wanted a glass of wine, and that was all she had, but think she just wanted to decompress before we went home. We took the opportunity to talk about what had happened today, and she asked me what I thought. I just told her, despite this setback, I was confident that between

Dr. Carson and Dr. Thomas they would come up with another option that would work. I tried to be as confident as I could, because I knew, in her heart, how much she wanted that to be so.

Her hope, in some ways, defied the reality of what we were dealing with, and it was my job to reinforce that hope in a positive way. In my own way, I had to have something to hang on to as well.

In the dynamic of the caregiver and the patient, her hope became my hope, just as her disappointments were my disappointments, and when I saw how strongly she clung to that hope, I could do nothing but hang on with her.

As I sat there with her in the Peacock bar, and the five o'clock crowd began to filter in, we got ready to go, and all I could think was that this woman really needs a break, and maybe tomorrow she might get one.

SECTION SIX
2007

"Bring me some #14 Red Robinsons."

There is a melancholy that accompanies the melody and the words from "Auld Lang Syne" that always seems to envelop me when I hear it on New Year's Eve. It is palpable, and I think it comes from the idea of saying goodbye to a part of your life you won't see again. It doesn't last long, maybe only until the last notes of the song have left the building, but for a moment it is real. Then, as you kiss the one you love, or the one you're with, and wish them a Happy New Year, you begin to think about what lies ahead. Reality smacks you on the head, and you start thinking about tomorrow.

Joanie and I had our brief moment of melancholy on New Year's Eve, but on January 1, 2007, we were thinking about tomorrow. Our hope was that this year would be an improvement over the last one.

Our New Year's Day was a quiet one. She wasn't hungry, so I just fixed our usual breakfast fare. While we watched the Rose Parade, as we always did, she ate half a bagel and one slice of bacon, and then, on the couch, with the TV showing endless football games, she slept most of the afternoon with Bailey on her lap. I went to the basement where the other TV was and watched some of the games, and I was joined by Brandy, where we both had a nap.

If someone could have looked inside our house from the outside, they would have seen two people and two Siamese

336

cats, enjoying a leisurely holiday afternoon, seemingly without a care in the world, not unlike many other couples in the country on New Year's Day. The difference was that in our house there was a dark cloud I couldn't escape.

I was worried, and she was tired. I was worried because she was tired, and I knew she was tired because of the chemotherapy treatment that had just ended. The shots of Neulasta and Aranesp had yet to kick in, to boost her blood counts, and I was hoping they would be doing so soon.

Her appetite was almost nonexistent. I could get her to eat some lime Jell-O, and she was always up for a cherry popsicle, but not much else. Nausea didn't seem to be a major problem, but there were a few incidents that didn't seem serious but were worrisome.

She didn't go to the office that week. New Year's Day was on a Monday, so it would be a short week anyway. She was just not bouncing back from the latest treatment like she had from the first two. I kept a close eye on her those first few days, looking for any sign that would tell me there might be a problem. In the back of my mind was the incident from last May. I didn't want to see a repeat.

By Friday morning of that week, I knew things were going south again. Fatigue, which had plagued her since the end of the last chemo treatment, was worse. She still wasn't eating, and all she wanted to do was lie on the couch. I stopped by Dr. Thomas's late that morning and told his nurse Kathy and him what I was seeing. I was supposed to bring her in that day for some lab work, but someone had not set it up. I mentioned her temperature seemed to be on the move. That afternoon, it spiked over 101 degrees, and they told me to bring her into the emergency room. We got there about 3:30, and I was glad we were there. Her blood pressure was 90 over

30, and that bottom number reminded me again of what she went through in May.

A nurse came to get her and take her to do a chest x-ray, and I went out for a smoke. This was not be the way we wanted to start off the new year, and I was worried about what the lab work was going to show. The blood pressure issue was also on my mind.

When I got back to her room in the ER, they had done the x-ray and also taken blood to do the lab work. Then we waited for Dr. Thomas and the lab results. Meanwhile, her blood pressure wouldn't move. The systolic number, the higher one, appeared to be stable, right around 90, but the diastolic number, the lower one. was bouncing around from 26 to a high of 45. I knew that number wasn't where it was supposed to be.

At 5:30, the emergency room doctor came in and told us Joanie was going to be transferred to the Intensive Care Unit. Now I'm more worried. Shortly after that, Dr. Thomas came in and told us what the results were. His notes showed Joanie had developed a severe neutropenia sepsis, severe anemia, and was hypotensive. My understanding was this. Her white count was in the toilet. Her red count was in the toilet. Her platelets were in the toilet. Her diastolic pressure was in the toilet, and she had an infection.

Thomas told me they were concerned about the white count and the blood pressure, because of what had happened in May of last year. He said the Neulasta hadn't kicked in yet. About the red blood cell count and the hemoglobin, he said that Topotecan makes it hard for those two to recover between treatments. The ER doctor alluded to the fact that chemo does that to the bone marrow. It makes it difficult to produce enough new cells to overcome the effects of the chemotherapy.

338

The got her up to the ICU, and began giving her antibiotics along with the continuing IV hydration. Thomas ordered a unit of platelets, and four units of blood, which they gave her from Friday evening through Saturday morning. Joanie's numbers began to move in a positive direction late Saturday, except for the blood pressure, which remained low. Thomas had told us in the morning they were going to keep her in the ICU for one more day, then they would move her up to the oncology floor. Thomas told her the blood pressure number was still a concern, and they also wanted to do an MRI of her abdomen and pelvis.

Joanie was disappointed, to say the least. I knew she was feeling better and wanted to go home, but I told her it was a good thing we were here. I told her she hadn't been here that long, but things were looking better. On Sunday, still in ICU, they gave her two more pints of blood, bringing the total for the weekend to six. I remember thinking, no wonder she had been so tired.

They were going to move her up to the oncology floor that afternoon, but when they got her up there, her room was a corner room she had been in before, and it was a depressing place. They brought her back down to the ICU until a different room could be prepared. She didn't seem bothered by the delay. I think some of the pain killers they had given her for her back pain had mellowed her out just a little. Besides that, she knew by moving, she was one step closer to getting out, hopefully by tomorrow. The back pain that had been bothering her for some time now was something else that bothered me, but that wasn't a major consideration right now. It would turn out to be significant in the future.

She was resting well, and though she wanted to go home, she had resigned herself to at least one more night in the hospital. I hung around with her until about ten o'clock that night and went home, secure in the knowledge that we had escaped what could have been another serious episode.

Then, about 10:25 p.m. I got a frantic call from Joanie. She wanted me to bring a few catheters, the #14 Red Robinsons she used to empty her Miami pouch. Seems there were none to be found in all of St. Alexius Medical Center on that Sunday night. She told me they had tried a #12, but it wouldn't work. I made it to the hospital in about ten minutes with the catheters, and everyone was relieved. I still couldn't believe they couldn't find any, and it reminded me that medical treatment is not always an exact science.

Joanie and I had a late night laugh about the situation, and I learned again, how a caregiver has to be prepared for almost anything.

She was feeling good now, and about 11:00, I kissed her good night and told her to get some sleep, and maybe we could get her out of here in the morning.

"We have some business to take care of."

The inexorable march of this disease since 1996 has inured us to some degree to the unpleasantness that accompanies it. Joanie, especially, seems to be vaccinated against the emotional toll it could have taken on her since the onset. I continued to be amazed, as I learned more and more, and did my best to help her adjust to the seemingly constantly changing circumstances, and the progression of the disease we were now dealing with, that she just kept on believing. It gave me comfort to see how she dealt with it.

Joanie spent a quiet Monday in the oncology floor at St. Alexius Medical Center. She had tried to convince Dr. Thomas to let her go home, but he told her that while her the bottom number on her blood pressure was moving in the right direction, he wanted her to stay at least one more day to until it stabilized. She was disappointed, as she often had been. He told her they also wanted to do the MRI on her abdomen and pelvis before she went home.

She looked good that morning. Her color was good. Her eyes were bright, and despite her disappointment at having to remain for another day, I was able to get a smile or two out of her.

We had been through this so many times before, we had become accustomed to it. It had been such a part of our lives over the past almost eleven years, it had largely become routine for us, depending, of course, upon the reason for her being there. My job was to be there to see she got what she needed, and my other job was to keep family and friends informed. The latter job had become easier for me, as caregiver, because I had developed lines of communication that enabled me to keep my time on the phone limited.

Tuesday morning came, and now she was really ready to get out. They did the MRI, and I got her home by 1:30 that afternoon, and shortly thereafter was on the couch with her kitties, who were glad to see her, on her lap. Dr. Thomas told us they were going to put off the next chemo treatment for a week, and Joanie was relieved, and I was as well. That meant she would have a full eleven days to continue to bounce back from this latest event.

On January 22, I took Joanie to the clinic where she got a chest x-ray and had some lab work done before we met with Dr. Thomas prior to her fourth cycle of Topotecan. She was feeling good, and the time off from chemo had been productive for her both physically and emotionally.

Dr. Thomas told us the x-ray showed no progression of the lesions. Good news. The MRI they had done on Joanie's last day showed multiple rib metastases, but again no measurable

341

progression. Thomas told us they were going to reduce this round of Topotecan by 25 percent, but she would still get the Neulasta and Aranesp, and prior to the next round in February, they would do a CT scan and a whole lab workup to see where we are.

That round went well. Joanie had few side effects, and it wasn't long before her calendar at work was filling up and she was too busy to worry about what might be next. We had sixteen days to wait until we might know.

On February 12, we got to the clinic, and they did a CT scan, took blood for a complete blood count (CBC), and we waited to meet with Dr. Thomas. We had come that day operating under the assumption that Joanie would start another round of Topotecan for the next five days. It was not to be.

When we met with Dr. Thomas, he told us they were going to scrub the chemotherapy. He told us it wasn't working, and the CT scan showed, "Clearly there is evidence of progression of metastatic disease in the chest wall." The words sounded like thunder in my brain. Joanie sat there, mute, and not showing any reaction. It was as if she wasn't hearing a word he said.

Dr. Thomas then took us through all of the CT reports, and he showed us the CT scan. He said she was failing treatment with Topotecan, and was recommending we see Dr. Carson in Minneapolis to discuss what options might be available, such as a clinical trial versus palliative radiation therapy. I didn't like the sound of it but didn't say anything at the time.

We left Thomas's office, and before we got to the car, I had called Marcia at Dr. Carson's office and we had an appointment for the March fifth to see where we go next. We went straight home from the clinic, and Joanie asked for some orange juice and sat down at the kitchen table. She seemed somehow smaller and more vulnerable that morning than I

342

had seen her in a long time. She looked tired, and it was becoming clear to me she had heard everything Thomas had said, but just needed some time to process it all.

She finished her juice, took care of her Miami pouch, and lay down on the couch. She didn't even turn on the TV, which would have been second nature for her, and closed her eyes for a while. She was joined by one of the kittens, and soon had drifted off.

Around one o'clock, she got up, and looked at me as she often did with that look that said, "Well, now we have some business to take care of," and asked me to give her a ride to work.

On the way to her office, I had to stop at Dan's Supermarket to pick up a package of red licorice twists for her, and then I dropped her off. She didn't call me to pick her up that day until after five o'clock.

That night, after she got settled in, we had some wine, cheese, bread and olive oil for dipping, and held each other closer.

We now had until the fifth of March before we had to be back in Minneapolis to meet with Dr. Carson. The news we had received from Dr. Thomas yesterday had been troubling, and I wasn't sure, but it looked to me as if it was a watershed in her battle with this disease. However, true to her form, Joanie refused to dwell on it. Instead, she went back to work with new energy.

Her calendar was filled by lunch one day with Tara Holt and Patsy Thompson, two of her good friends, on another day with Vicki Melchior, also a good friend. She had meetings with Mikey Hoeven, events to be coordinated, walks with Betsy Dalrymple to be taken when weather allowed. and life to be lived. She was living each day as we had talked about that long ago day in 1998 when she was in the hospital

343

recovering from the pelvic exenteration. She was doing her best not to let the disease dictate her life any more than it did.

She filled her time as best she could, right up to the weekend before we would have to leave. Since her appointment was for early Monday morning, we would leave on Sunday. On Saturday night, we didn't do a thing. As always, she would get quiet prior to these trips. She wouldn't talk about what was coming, but I always knew it was on her mind.

On this night, whatever she wanted she got. I asked her about what she wanted for dinner, and all she wanted was a good loaf of French bread, and some olive oil. I tried to talk her into something a little more substantial, but he just shook her head, and told me that was all she wanted. Bread, olive oil and wine had been an integral part of our lives since before we were married, and they were representative, I think, to her of all of the best times in our lives. So, that's what Joanie got for dinner that night.

Sunday morning, she dawdled, as she always did, and I never minded. I knew she would be ready to go when we needed to be gone, after all, we couldn't miss our stop at Mabel Murphy's. And we didn't.

Monday morning, we met with Dr. Carson. She had gone over the discs we had brought of the CT scans along with the notes. In one way, Joanie was glad to see Dr. Carson again. It wasn't hard to understand, since she had been there with Joanie through some of the darkest days of her life. I know that doctors are not supposed to get attached to patients, but Joanie couldn't help but form some kind of attachment to a doctor who had been such a part of her life for so long. That's the way it was with Dr. Carson and Joanie. Joanie had complete confidence in her from the beginning, and today that confidence was as strong as ever, especially since we were embarking on another journey into the unknown.

After she had done an examination of Joanie, her suggestion for further treatment was that we go to see Dr. Dusenbery next, and look at the possibility of radiation. She told us there weren't any Stage II or III clinical trials she would qualify for, and none that would have been appropriate. She told us Katie had already been briefed on the current situation, and would have a recommendation.

Joanie's confidence in Katie was the same as it was for Dr. Carson. It had been from the first days after we met her in 1996 and Joanie had six weeks of radiation. Now we would find out what Katie would recommend as an option this time considering the difference in circumstances.

Katie was recommending a radiation regimen consisting of what she called "conformal radiation therapy" to be delivered once a day, five days a week for three weeks. She had talked to us about the area to be radiated, and that it would be very near the lung. She said they could deliver the radiation and spare the lung with a new machine they had. It was called a TOMO Hi-Art machine of which there were only twenty in the country at that time.

We were told this machine was basically a marriage of the ability of a CT scanner with a radiation delivery device that can more precisely identify location and measurements of a tumor and aim the radiation beam accordingly. This capability minimizes damage to healthy tissue, and is especially valuable when delivering radiation in the area around what is left of her right lung. Lungs do not take kindly to radiation. Also, the beam could be delivered from any angle in a 360-degree range, which was different from devices that could only attack tumors from limited angles.

Katie called back to Bismarck and talked to a doctor with the Bismarck Cancer Center, to inquire if the same type of radiation might be done there. He told her that for what Joanie was dealing with she was in the right place at the U of M. They didn't have the same machine.

Katie didn't waste any time. She wanted to get Joanie ready to do a simulation, which meant they wanted to get her on a table, take measurements, and do treatment-planning CAT scan. The treatments would begin next week.

When Joanie and I left Katie's office that day, we got in the car and headed back to Bismarck.

Even with this new chapter in her battle, uncertain as it was, Joanie sat, staring out the windshield as the miles clicked by, remained determined not to let the cloud obliterate her sky.

Without even looking at me, at one point she said, "This is going to work."

Hope is what Joanie breathes every day.

These are days I had wished not to see. These were days that presented an unwelcome challenge. This disease was persistent, and growing. It was as if Joanie's body was under siege by an invading army, and all of the forces we had enlisted over the years to do battle with the barbarians at the gate were running out of food, fuel, and ammunition to carry on the battle. The only thing left that presented hope was the spirit of Joanie herself. She was not giving up, and she expected no less of those who would help her. She knew, but did not say, it was not going to be easy, but there was no alternative but to fight.

We both knew what going back to Minneapolis for radiation meant. This was a major setback, and my job wasn't just that of a caregiver now, but was also that of caretaker of

346

her emotional health as well. The thought of spending three weeks away from home was something that really bothered her, probably more than the six weeks she had spent back in 1996, mostly because the stakes had been raised this time. I knew she was strong emotionally, stronger than she thought she was, but I also knew that this next phase would take a toll on her. All I could do right then was to be there for her.

The morning after we got back from Minneapolis, we talked about what we needed to do now. It was Wednesday, and Katie wanted to start the radiation on the following Monday. That meant Joanie would have to be back in Minneapolis on the Sunday prior.

At first we had talked about me being down there as well, but Joanie had already decided that we both couldn't be gone for the three weeks required for the full treatment. She didn't want the kitties left alone that long, and also it would be a lot more expensive with both of us being down there.

The question of where she would stay was answered, when Kristi Sagsveen graciously invited Joanie to stay with her and Murray at their house just off Cretin Avenue in St. Paul. Kristi was a long-time friend, and they were both members of the same birthday club. From their house it would only be a short drive to the hospital for her daily treatment.

With housing arranged, the next issue was transportation. At first we had decided that she would drive down by herself on Sunday with our car. We only had one car at that time. The Volkswagen convertible had blown the transmission and had since been towed back to Avon by my brother-in-law Joe Straley. He found a transmission later, and so my sister Joni had a convertible to run around in.

We decided to rent a car for me to use in Bismarck while she was down there. I knew that's was not how she wanted to do it, but there didn't seem to be any other way. Then, one of her long-time friends came and offered us a free ticket on Northwest that I could use. That way I could drive her down to St. Paul and then fly back to Bismarck. She would have a car down there, and I would have a car when I got home. Patsy Thompson saved the day for us with that airline ticket. Our good friend Wayne Tanous also helped us out with this arrangement. This episode was another example of the generous and thoughtful contributions from friends of Joanie's that helped us get through some of the troubling times she faced over the years.

The morning we were to leave for Minneapolis, as we were getting ready to leave, she cried. They weren't tears of someone who thought she might not be back, but just the sad tears of someone who was being worn down by the relentless pursuit of this goddamn disease. She stood there in the kitchen as she gave treats to Brandy and Bailey, scratched them, said goodbye and told them she would be back. Tears streamed down her face. I didn't say a word. No words were necessary.

The all-too-familiar miles lay ahead of us as we left Bismarck, and Joanie sat silently, shredding Kleenex, as she often did, staring out of the window. I could see her, from time to time, wiping her eyes, and lightly blowing her nose, and all I could do was keep my eyes on the road and say not a word.

There are times, as a caregiver, when you will find that it is better that you say nothing. For me this was one of them. I knew there would be time for talk when she was ready, in the meantime, the hope she breathed filled the air in the car, and we drove on.

"Everything is going to be okay."

Joanie had talked to John and Mikey Hoeven before we left, and they assured her that she should not worry about anything at the office. That wasn't enough for her. She took her office laptop with her and would be able to work while she was down there if she needed to. Kristi had told her they had a router, and she would be able to log on to her office any time. At least that was her plan.

We got her settled in at the Sagsveens on Sunday night, and the next morning I went with her to see Dr. Dusenbery at Therapeutic Radiology, where she would be receiving the radiation over the next three weeks. I was able to be with her up until the time they were ready to turn on the machine. The room with this huge machine was large itself, brightly lit, and cool. She took her place on the bed she would lie on during the treatment. The bed slid into the doughnut hole, and they adjusted everything according to the measurements they had taken when they did the initial simulation. Once that was done, we left the room, and they closed the door.

I was able to watch what was going on as the doctors sat at screens, and computers, and didn't have an idea of what they were doing. I didn't bother them, and since I probably couldn't understand their answers, I didn't ask any questions. I figured they knew what they were doing.

Joanie hadn't seemed nervous at all when we got to Katie's office, and she was fine after that. When the first one was done, and the longest part of the process was getting ready, she was now ready for them all to be done. She got dressed, and as we were walking out to the parking ramp, she said, "Well, only fourteen more to go." She smiled at me as she said it, and I felt better about her state of mind, and about leaving.

We went for lunch, and while we were waiting for our food,

349

she looked at me and said, "Do you think you could stay?" I told her if she wanted me to, we could work that out, knowing that she was only talking about what she wished could happen, all the time knowing the way we were doing it was the right way. It was those moments, and there had been several of them over the years, when I realized how much she meant to me, and it was all I could do to keep from melting.

We finished lunch and left for the airport so I could catch an early afternoon flight back to Bismarck. When we got to the airport, I got out and opened the driver side door for Joanie. I gave her a big hug, told her I'd be talking to her later in the day, and that everything was going to be okay. She kissed me, told me she loved me, and she got in the car, looking a little sad, but trying to smile. I waved and she drove off.

Once in the air, as we flew out over the city that had become like a second home for us, I thought about how this was all going to work out. My only hope was that what I told her turned out to be true, and that everything was going to be okay.

That she was in Minneapolis and I was in Bismarck, we could handle. We had done it before, in that summer of 1996. This time it was harder. The house seemed emptier. I knew this was going to be over in a few weeks, but the silence that greeted me when I'd walk in the door was palpable. Bailey and Brandy tried to help, but being cats, they don't make a lot of noise. They were just glad to see me. One of them, usually Bailey, would be in the kitchen window, above the sink, and she would be sitting there no matter what time I drove into the garage. So, while they didn't make a much noise, at least there was somebody there to talk to. People who have pets understand.

Joanie and I did talk, at least two or three times a day. Either she would call me or I would call her. I would ask her how the radiation was going, and she would ask me how her kitties were doing. I always told her they missed her. I would usually make my last call when I figured she was getting ready for bed so I could wish her good night. Kristi and Murray were taking good care of her, I knew that. The fact that she was with friends made me feel better, but I knew this time was emotionally harder on her than those six weeks in '98.

By all accounts the first week of the radiation went according to plan. When I talked with Joanie she told me nothing to the contrary. She always told me everything was fine, and I think she did that so I wouldn't worry. It wasn't unlike the times when she told the doctors what she thought they wanted to hear. Patients will do that. I talked to her on the Friday night after the first week was done, and quite frankly, I wasn't worried. I had faith in what Katie and her crew were doing to take care of Joanie.

My faith wasn't tested, but on Friday of the following week, I received an email from Kristi expressing concern about Joanie. In her note to me she wrote: "She seemed very tired last night but didn't want to go to bed because then she wouldn't sleep all night. I will offer to take her to treatment today. Does the radiation build up in her system? Are there side effects from it?"

Now I was concerned, and I emailed Kristi back:

Thanks for the note. Being tired is one of the side effects, even though it is not viewed as a serious one. Being tired can also be attributed to the stress of the whole process as well as the radiation. It is not unusual that it makes her a bit nauseous as well. The half-life of the radiation she is getting is short lived, and the cumulative effect is

351

minimal. Again stress plays a major part in this process, and the radiation is killing cells in her body will have some residual effect, albeit for not very long.

By the way, she often stays up when she is at home for the same reason you cited in your second paragraph.

I'm just glad she is where she is at this point, even though it is hard being separated during this particular time. I appreciate that she is in good hands at your house, and I can't thank you and M enough.

Take care, and let me know if something else catches your attention or causes you concern. I don't often hear much in that regard when talking to Joanie herself."

I called Joanie to find out what was going on with her and found out that she was not feeling well at all. She was having bouts of nausea and vomiting, was constipated, and the pain was really bothering her. I told her I was coming down. She told me to wait and see how she felt in the morning. On Saturday morning she called me and said she was feeling better and to hold off on coming down until Monday. On Sunday she had called Katie, and she told me Katie told her that they would give her some IV fluid on Monday, and possibly admit her to the hospital.

Joanie called me late Monday morning, and told me Katie was having her admitted. I didn't know what for, and now I was really concerned. I had no idea what had gone wrong this time. I got busy making arrangements to be gone for the rest of the week. I got someone to look after Bailey and Brandy, turned in the rental car, and caught a six o'clock flight to Minneapolis. Murray Sagsveen picked me up at the airport, and drove to their house where I picked up our car, and by about 8:30 that night I was in Joanie's room on 7C.

This is the first time she had been on that floor since 2003, and this time there were very few familiar faces on the floor. I found her in a double room, and she told me they were going to get her into a private room soon. I had heard that before, and knew that "soon" in hospital time could be tomorrow. About then, I saw a nurse who had been there the last time Joanie was in, and she recognized me as well. I talked to her and stressed how important it would be to get Joanie moved. She told me that as soon as the room was ready they would be moving her.

I would soon learn what was going on with her, and it had nothing to do with the radiation itself. She was admitted for hypercalcemia, or more precisely, hypercalcemia of malignancy, and it is a serious metabolic disorder than can be life threatening if it is not treated. What it meant was that Joanie had high blood calcium levels.

If that weren't enough, she was also diagnosed with hypokalemia or low potassium levels. All this, and she was dehydrated as well.

She would remain in the hospital for the rest of the week while she finished the radiation regimen and they tried to get her calcium levels back down to the normal range, and her potassium levels back up to the normal range.

Finally that night, about 11:00 they had Joanie's room ready. She was relieved, and I was thankful. When I left, she was relaxed and glad I was there. I told her to try and get some sleep, and I'd see her in the morning before her next radiation round.

As I drove back to Sagsveens that night, I felt both relieved and troubled. I was relieved that she was in the hospital and they knew now what the problem was and were taking steps to deal with it. I was troubled about the pain she was experiencing. It was the same pain that had been getting more pronounced by the month, and all I could attribute it to was the involvement of her ribs. Of course, I didn't know for sure.

All I knew for sure was that she was safe, and I was tired. Tomorrow might have some answers.

I still knew where the popsicles were.

When I got to the hospital on Tuesday morning, Joanie was awake and feeling better. The tension I had seen in her face the night before was gone. I think it melted away when they moved her into her private room. She was relaxed, however pain was still an issue.

They were still having trouble with the pain management aspect of her treatment. She was on Dilaudid, a very powerful pain med that is a derivative of morphine. She was getting that through the IV, but on Tuesday they discontinued it, and she was getting Dilaudid orally. They also would give her a bump through the IV when she needed it. They were also using a Fentanyl patch, another potent pain killer. They had calculated how much she needed of each one to manage the pain without getting too much of one or the other.

Those two strong pain meds, the ongoing effort to raise her potassium level and lower her calcium levels, along with the daily radiation treatments, were all conspiring to keep her groggy and subject to frequent napping during the day. It would not be unusual for her to drop off mid- sentence when talking to me, or for her to ignore me completely. That was okay, I never took it personally.

I accompanied her down to radiation for her daily treatment, and on the way down she told me there were only four more to go. She was looking forward to Friday, and to going home, even though that wasn't a sure thing. It would hinge on the progress they made in dealing with the hypercalcemia and the hypokalemia.

If you don't know, ask.

Being a caregiver requires that you are not hesitant to ask questions of the doctors who are treating your patient. It is good for your own peace of mind, and it also shows the doctors there is someone else who is involved in the care of the patient. I think it also helps you, as a caregiver, help the patient see things clearly and avoid confusion. At the end of the first week of treatment, I sent an email to Dr. Dusenbery regarding the radiation treatment and how progress is measured.

Katie,

Just a couple of questions as usually I have been with Joanie to ask the questions she doesn't remember to ask, or she wouldn't understand and remember the answer herself. She did tell me this morning that the treatments do not change over the three week time frame. The question I have is how do you measure the effect of the treatment on the lesions over the period of a week. I imagine the first week is not all that significant, but I'm interested in hearing some of the specifics as to the measurable progress, especially in terms of size, etc. Over the past few years I usually would get copies of the radiologist's notes following CT scans, PET scans or MRIs and have been able to follow the development in a manner that has allowed me to make some sense out of them.

So, would you, or someone in your office be able to get that type of information to me? I know you are very busy and have many patients. I however, have only one, and it has been my job, as her husband for the past 11 years to keep on top of what is going on.

Thanks,
  Bob Kallberg

On the following Monday, I received a response from Katie:

Bob,
  We give the tumor the same dose every day. I am giving 250 rads (or 250 cGy each day and will give a total of 3750 cGy when all 15 treatments are over. The tumor will shrink slowly and the only way we will know it "worked" is 1) her pain will improve or disappear 2) the tumor will shrink (this will take weeks or months since the dead tumor cells need to be removed by the body and this takes time). The pain is the thing we should notice first. Last week she really hadn't had any improvement, so I increased the pain medicine a little and will see how she is early this week.
  My plan will be to have her back for scans 6-8 weeks after completing the radiation or have scans there sent to me. Hope this is helpful.

Katie

That was helpful, but I will also admit that the business with "rads" and "cGy" were like Greek to me, but it did confirm that the strength of the dosage, as Joanie had told me, would be the same for the whole three weeks. The information about the pain also was helpful, in that it gave me something to watch for as well. The rest of the measurement by scans would have to wait.

After Joanie's radiation treatment that day, she was tired, and when she got back to her room she promptly dropped off to sleep. I had decided to get a room at the Radisson for the next few nights, assuming we'd be leaving on Friday, so I

356

went back to the Sagsveens and retrieved my bags, and all of Joanie's clothes and her laptop and checked in around four.

After I stopped up to Joanie's room for a while, and she dozed off, I left and walked over to Sally's for a burger and a beer. It gave me a chance to make some calls to Ginny, and her brother Richard and sister Ann in Bismarck. I also called Mikey Hoeven and a few other folks in Bismarck to bring them up to date.

Walking back to the hospital, a walk I had taken so many times before, I thought about her in that bed, and wished there were some way I could make this all be right and I could go there, make her feel better and take her away from here and bring her back home where she belonged. That's what I thought, but I knew.

When I got back to her room she was awake, watching something on TV. Pain was still an issue, and she still had no appetite. We sat there for a while, and she asked me if I could find her a cherry popsicle. We hadn't been on 7C in four years, and I didn't know if things had changed, so I went to find out.

I didn't have to look very far, I found them in the same place they had been the last time we were there. It was nice to see some things hadn't changed. I took the popsicle back to her room, and we split it. She didn't want the whole thing. She just wanted something cold and sweet on her tongue.

As she got ready to drift off again, I said good night, and walked back to the hotel. Tomorrow was another day.

Her attitude keeps her going.

By Wednesday morning, Joanie was really getting anxious to get this all over with, and go home. Her calcium number was moving in the right direction, and her potassium level had reached the normal range, so at least that was no longer an issue, and there were only three more radiation treatments to go.

Joanie still wasn't eating, or as the words in the doctor's notes put it, "The patient was encouraged to taking clear liquids on hospital day #2 as tolerated, and her diet was advanced on hospital day #3. However, the patient continued to have decreased intake..." This did concern me. I had been through other times when she wouldn't, or couldn't eat, and nothing tasted good, and as hard as I tried to get her to eat more, she would push it away. This time in the hospital, she was mostly eating Jell-O, and would sip some clear broth, and then would ask for an occasional popsicle.

In spite of her weak appetite, she continued to feel stronger, and by the time Friday morning rolled around, and we went down for the last radiation treatment, she was more than ready to go home. They were also going to do one more blood draw, since her calcium had moved up again, just barely, but it had move up. They were going to have the results for us before we left, but Joanie was so intent on getting out of there, we told them to call us when they got them from the lab. It was Friday, and we wanted to get on the road to beat the rush out of town.

We had only made it about eighty miles when we got the call. Her calcium had moved up again, and we were told to go to Dr. Thomas's office when we got back for a blood draw, and possible IV fluid therapy. They told us they had called Thomas's office and gave him the same report.

We didn't make it back to Bismarck soon enough. The office was closed when we got back, so I didn't take her into the clinic until Saturday morning for the blood draw. We would find out the results on Monday when we met with Dr. Thomas.

Sunday, April 1, and Joanie was still feeling the effects of

358

her stay in the hospital at the U of M. Pain is still a problem, despite her supply of Dilaudid, and her appetite hasn't improved either.

That morning, she even turned down a cup of coffee, and said, "I'm in sort of a fog, can you tell?" I just told her she had been pretty sick for that week, and in effect was still feeling the effects of radiation and the hypercalcemia, and it was going to take some time before she returned to normal. She didn't understand the calcium thing, she just knew it had put her in the hospital, and never knew why. I also told her again, she was going to have to start eating more, and more often. She just looked at me and said, "I know."

On Monday morning, we went to see Dr. Thomas, and he told us the calcium level was still about a point above the high level of the normal range, so they found a room for Joanie and began to give her some IV fluid and a drug called Zometa, which is one of the family of drugs used to treat high calcium levels. Dr. Thomas told me that Joanie still had a case of moderate hypercalcemia, and now would be treated for that and monitored more closely in that area.

When they were done with the IV, I dropped her off at her office. She wanted to do payroll. I asked her if someone else could have done it, and she just looked at me, shook her head and told me to drop her off. She stayed until around 3:30 that afternoon when she called me to come and pick her up.

Now we were in a waiting mode again. We would wait until Friday to see where the calcium number was, and we would wait another three to four weeks before Thomas would start the next round of chemotherapy. Dr. Carson had ordered a new drug for the next chemotherapy treatment, a drug called Gemzar. It turned out to be a month-long wait. He told us it would take three to four weeks for the radiation and its effects to clear out. We would also wait to see if the radiation had done what we had hoped it would, which was to shrink the lesions in her chest, and we were waiting for the pain to diminish the further we got out from the radiation.

The waiting is what comes with the treatment of this disease, and it is the waiting that screws with your mind. This was also a time when I realized Joanie was facing a serious challenge, probably the most serious one of the past eleven years.

She left all of that worrying to me. As far as she was concerned nothing had changed. The radiation was going to work, the chemo was going to work, and she was going to be okay, that's all there was to it. The other part of my job besides keeping up to date on what was going on with her, was to support her attitude in that regard, and I did. I knew that it was her attitude and approach to this battle that had gotten her this far, in the first place, and I was never going to disabuse her of that idea.

Joanie makes a decision.

April came, and in Bismarck, it marked the beginning of a troubling time at 1205 N. Mandan Street. Joanie had seen Dr. Thomas on Monday and had been given Zometa for the hypercalcemia, along with some IV fluid therapy. By Friday when we went back to see him, the blood work showed the Zometa had done the job. Her calcium was back in the normal range.

That was good news, and Thomas told us there would be no chemo this month, and to come back in a few weeks for lab work. Joanie was relieved. She was relieved mainly because she still wasn't feeling well. She wasn't eating, pain was still an issue, and she was tired. She really needed some time off from the treatments that take so much out of her.

My notes from the first few weeks reflect what was going on with her.

Tuesday, April 3rd.

Not eating much this morning. Has about half a turkey sandwich at noon, drinking fluids, water and Sprite Zero. Pain seems to be under control. She is still taking Dilaudid and wearing a Fentanyl patch. Still having a problem with indigestion and swallowing.

Wednesday, April 4th.

Appetite low. Fluid intake is adequate, I think. She had part of a turkey sandwich for lunch, and some leftover sloppy joe mix for dinner. Went to the office for a couple of hours.

Thursday, April 5th.

Appetite low. Fluid intake is adequate. McDonalds wrap with chicken for lunch. Threw up shortly. Said she felt over heated. Felt better. Took her to her office about 1:30.

This routine was repeated for most of the next six days. My notes on Wednesday April 11 showed things hadn't improved either.

Joanie stayed home today. Her appetite is still nonexistent. She has eaten all of one or two cherry popsicles and some Jell-O in the past two days. Before that she only had some ice cream on Monday. Has thrown up at least once a day.

Tuesday, April 17..

We had spent a quiet weekend.. Joanie hasn't left the house since last Tuesday. Appetite has been terrible. Energy level really low. Esophagus has cleared up. Upset stomach has abated. I called Kathy at Dr. Thomas' office and told her I would keep an eye on her today, and if I didn't like what I saw, I would call her.

I didn't have to call, Joanie seemed to rebound enough to ease my concern that day, but it seemed she wasn't recovering as she should have been.

Things didn't improve much over the next ten days either. She would go into her office for a few hours in the afternoon, but was still extremely tired, and was losing weight.

I was at a loss. She had handled six weeks of radiation in 1998 with few problems, and that was one of the main reasons we hadn't worried about doing it again. The situation was not unlike the one with the chemotherapy treatment we had tried last year that resulted in so many problems. We had figured that since she had handled the chemo combination of Ifex, Taxol and Carboplatin in 2003 so well, and it had worked, she could handle it again.

As I thought about it, I realized that in both cases, the situation that dictated the treatments had changed. The cancer was back with a vengeance where it hadn't been before, and with it came a whole new set of problems we hadn't anticipated.

When we met with Dr. Thomas on the twenty-seventh, it was to do a complete blood count, and other lab work, and prepare for the next round of chemotherapy. Dr. Carson had prescribed Gemcitabine, or as it was known by its trade name, Gemzar.

He was well aware that Joanie was not 100 percent. He noted in his report that she was experiencing a low energy level, fatigue and was still losing weight. Her pain was still an issue, and he took care of that with another prescription of Dilaudid.

When it got around to talking about the next round of chemo, Joanie took charge, much to my surprise. She told Thomas she wasn't ready to start chemo again, and said if she felt better in a couple of weeks she'd be ready. She told him she would let him know.

I was proud of her. This was another example of her taking some control over what was happening to her, and I think it made her feel better right then. I knew how important it was to her to feel that she had something to say about her treatment.

When we left Thomas's office that day, I could see in her face a renewed determination and despite how tired she was, a new hope.

It gave me hope too.

"Do you think Dr. Carson has given up?"

April was, to steal a few words from T. S. Eliot, "the cruelest month." That is not to say it was the cruelest of the many months Joanie had been involved in this battle with cancer, but this last April was one of the many.

The radiation in Minneapolis had been harder on her than we had expected, and the hospital stay for hypercalcemia of malignancy and hypokalemia had taken a toll. Her appetite had gone south, and it had gone south in a big way. She lost a lot of weight since her stay in the hospital, and if she had weighed 120 pounds when it started, she would have weighed about 90 pounds now. Fortunately for her, she had some weight to lose. She was a tall woman, and carried extra pounds, something that bothered her from time to time, but in this instance, it turned out to be a blessing in disguise.

Joanie spent most of May trying to get back into the swing of things at her office. As much as she tried, she was basically only spending the afternoons there. She was able to go out to lunch with some of her friends, and go on walks in the afternoon with Betsy Dalrymple. When she would be ready to come home, I would get a call. She still wasn't eating that much, but was managing to keep the pain under control with Dilaudid.

Dr. Thomas had ordered a CT scan for May 21. This would be the first since the radiation had ended some seven weeks ago. From this we would know if the radiation had worked, or not. It was a fairly tense time, especially on my part. If Joanie was worried about it, she didn't let on to me.

The CT scan was a disappointment. I had picked up the radiologist's notes, and it showed that not only had the lesions in her right chest wall not shrunk, but they had grown. The nodule in her left lung had also grown, though not substantially. I was at a loss as to what to do with that information. I decided to do something I had done before when I knew something before we were to meet with her doctors, and say nothing to her. I would let them be the bearer of the bad news.

One thing the radiologist suggested in his notes was to have an MRI done to get a more definitive picture, and Thomas scheduled one of those for the twenty-fifth. When Joanie wondered why, the answer I gave her was that they wanted to get a better picture of what was going on. She bought it, or at least I hoped she did. I wondered sometimes if she wasn't more aware of what was going on than she let on.

The MRI confirmed everything the CT scan had shown and did it in more detail.

We were to meet with Dr. Carson and Dr. Dusenbery in Minneapolis on June 8, the date they would give us the bad news. We were to take CDs of the CT scan and the MRI, along with the notes, to our meeting.

We were left to wait again. This time, I waited with the knowledge that Joanie was going to get bad news. I couldn't bring myself to tell her what I knew, because, I only knew what I read in the notes, and there were, no doubt, other ways to look at what I saw. I was, after all, a layman, not a doctor, and as such couldn't really interpret to her what I read.

Besides that, both Dr. Carson and Katie would be better at handling the information than I could ever be.

On June 7, we left Bismarck for Minneapolis, and it was an uneasy time. Joanie was more subdued than normal, and before we left the house, spent more time than usual with Bailey and Brandy. We would meet Ginny and Ed for dinner, and as it always did, it gave Joanie a lift. When we got back to the hotel, she became quiet again.

The next morning, we walked the few short blocks to the Phillips-Wangensteen building where Dr. Carson's office was, and checked her in. We waited for only a short time, when Bev, one of Carson's nurses that knew Joanie well, called her name, and we went down the long hall to find one of the examining rooms and wait to see Carson.

After the usual small talk and Dr. Carson's assessment of Joanie's condition, she gave us her recommendations. The lesions hadn't shrunk, and she was going to recommend that Joanie embark on the Gemzar chemotherapy regimen. She told us she was going to consult with Katie to see if they were in agreement on this course.

As she got ready to give Joanie a physical exam, it was my cue to take a walk. I went up the three floors to get outside and have a smoke, and make a couple of phone calls. They were not the calls I wanted to make, but I felt I had to.

When I got back down to the room, Dr. Carson was gone, and Joanie had gotten dressed, and I could see from her demeanor that something was bothering her. She didn't say what it was, and from the clinic we walked over to the hospital to Katie's office to hear from her on what the scans had revealed about the radiation.

Katie, who always put Joanie at ease, did so again today. She was surprised at what she had seen on the scan and the MRI and really didn't have a good explanation for the

365

radiation not doing what they had hoped it would. I knew she felt badly about it, and I would hear more from her later. We left her office, with Joanie still quiet, and I think somewhat overwhelmed about what had happened this morning.

We walked back to the hotel to get some breakfast at Applebee's. They had taken over the main dining business at the Radisson, I suspect on a lease arrangement. Once we got seated, we were waited on by the fellow who had been the main bartender when the Radisson ran the dining room and bar. He had been there since 1998 when I used to spend a lot of time there, and he remembered both of us. Joanie got a smile out of seeing him again, and he remembered that she worked for the governor. He got a good tip that morning.

We ordered coffee and something to eat, and Joanie started to relax. I didn't push her, and I just waited for her to tell me what was bothering her, and then she stunned me when she asked, "Do you think Dr. Carson has given up?" It almost took my breath away.

I sat there for a brief moment and told her I didn't think that was the case, and fumbled for reasons why I felt that way. Then she told me that while I had been out of the room, Dr. Carson had used the word "hospice," a word that was anathema to Joanie, and a word I'd never use around her under any circumstances.

I told her I didn't think Dr. Carson was giving up, and also that she was doing what doctors have to do in dealing with their patients, and that is to make sure they are aware of all of the options in their treatment that are available to them. I tried to be as convincing as I could be, but I'm not sure she bought it. I felt so sorry for her right then, but all I could do was try and help her understand that this battle was not over, and give her the support she needed from me.

We finished our breakfast, went upstairs, picked up our bags and checked out.

The trip back to Bismarck was a long one. Joanie sat quietly for most of the trip. It was obvious to me was still trying to process what she had learned this morning, and didn't want to talk about it.

I tried, as the miles rolled by, to make some sense of it myself, and all I knew was that we were facing more uncertainty, and Joanie was keenly aware of it.

Being an advocate as well as a caregiver.

To say the last trip to Minneapolis turned out to be stressful would be a huge understatement. To say that we were both disappointed at the results of the radiation, and perplexed when we left the meetings with Dr. Carson and Dr. Dusenbery would also be an understatement.

Nevertheless, on the Tuesday following that trip, Joanie began the Gemzar treatment. That consisted of one dose of Gemzar per week for two weeks, then a week off, and then the cycle would be repeated. After the second cycle, Dr. Thomas would order another CT scan to see where we were.

Joanie handled the first go-round with few side effects. Outside of some mild nausea, she was doing well, and was spending the afternoons at her office, keeping herself involved in as normal a routine as she could.

I kept an eye on her, and for the first couple of weeks, couldn't help but think about the disappointment surrounding her latest appointments with the two doctors who had been, and continued to be, so important a factor in Joanie's cancer treatment over the last eleven years. The questions that we didn't get answered, or that I didn't have a chance to ask when we were down there, stuck with me, until

I decided to renew my role as advocate for Joanie, and I sent an email to Katie with those questions. It was my attempt to gain some insight into what was really going on.

On June 20, I sent this email to Katie:

Katie,

It was good to see you when we were down there on the 8th. We left there somewhat uncertain of what we had learned that day, except for the fact the feeling that all was not well. Joanie did grab on to your statement about the difference between the CT scan and the MRI regarding the look of the lesions. As I understood it, you mentioned that while the CT measures density, the MRI look at the same area presented different appearance, as in dead tissue. I took that to mean some type of necrosis had taken place in spite of the fact that the lesion near the T6 had grown since the CT scan of 2/12/07 from 4.0 cm X 5.8 cm to approximately 9.0 cm X 5.0 cm (as measured by the MRI of 5/25/07).

The question, which came to my mind, was how can something that is being killed continue to grow, especially something that has been subjected to the level of radiation that was given to Joanie over those three weeks. I rather got the impression that you were somewhat surprised at what you saw on the scans we brought down and were hard pressed to provide a concrete answer on whether the radiation had worked, didn't work, or had partially worked.

Referring to your email response to my questions in March, you did indicate that "Tumors will shrink slowly and the only way we will know it "worked" is 1) her pain will improve or disappear 2) the tumor will shrink (this will take weeks or months since the dead tumor cells need to be removed by the body and this takes time." Well, the pain question is still unanswered as well, since my observation is that it hasn't changed much at all in the past couple of years, and if by "months" you mean six months or more, and the rate of grown of the T6 tumor alone from Feb 12th to May 25th of

368

this year continues, it seems to me that we still have a serious problem.

Excuse me for making this email a bit long, however these are questions that have been dogging me since we got back. I rarely interject or interfere between Joanie and her doctors when we are there, for I think that it is important to hear as much from Joanie as is possible since she is, after all, your patient, not me. However, I am the one who sees to her needs and wants when she is not under care of docs, hospitals or clinics, and it has always been important for me to have an understanding of what is going on. This is the way for me to help her keep things in perspective when she wants to discuss what is going on.

Currently Joanie continues to do well. She had the second Gemzar treatment yesterday, and now will have a week off from that, and then go through one more cycle. We started on the Tuesday after we got back from Minneapolis. It is my understanding that after the second cycle, that Dr. Thomas will be ordering another CT scan to check on any progress. According to my calendar the scan should be done sometime during the last ten days of July.

Thank you for your patience, if you have read this far, and I hope you will be able to shed a bit of light on the questions I have raised.

Bob

Katie got back to me the next day when I received this email from her:

Bob,

You are right about the assessment of last week's visit. Dr. Carson and I are very disappointed that the tumor did not shrink and the pain is no better. Additionally new tumor has appeared.

There is the small possibility that the dead tumor cells have "swollen" and makes the tumor enlarge before it starts to shrink. If

369

you do the MRI or CT scan during the "swelling" stage, sometimes it then gets smaller with a subsequent scan. The only way to know if this happened is to continue to repeat the scans.

I remain hopeful that the tumors will shrink with the Gemzar and that it doesn't take too much out of Joan. I think most patients tolerate it well.

I wish I had better news for you. Joan has been through so much and I realize the radiation took a lot out of her last month. I am particularly disappointed that she didn't have her pain go away. Please feel free to call or write if you have further questions.

My best to Joan.
   Katie

As a significant other of anyone who is going through the ordeal of fighting a life-threatening disease, you wear two hats. You are both a caregiver and an advocate for the patient. The advocacy part of your job is as important as the caregiving part of your job. Being an active caregiver shows doctors that you are part of helping to take care of the patient, and being an advocate for the patient shows the doctors just how much you are involved.

Wearing those two hats, sometimes at the same time, made it easier for me to be able to communicate with Joanie's doctors, and I can't emphasize to much how important it was for my own peace of mind, as well as helping Joanie understand more clearly what was going on when she wanted to talk about it.

Both Katie and Dr. Carson were good about responding when I called or wrote, and it showed me how important, what I call, the triangle of care (doctor-patient-caregiver) really is, and how helpful it can be even during the most difficult of times.

More questions, and the importance of communication.

I waited a few days after emailing Katie, and then I sat down to write a letter to Dr. Carson. She was, after all, Joanie's main doctor, and even though a lot of the treatment was now being done in at Mid-Dakota Clinic in Bismarck, under Dr. Thomas, she was still a vital part of Joanie's treatment.

The days since the June 8 meeting raised more questions than it answered, and I viewed my job as that of the person would attempt to find answers. Joanie, on the other hand, seemed more focused on getting on with her life, and that was as it should be.

So, with that in mind, I sent the following letter to Dr. Carson:

June 26, 2007

Dear Dr. Carson:

Well, it has taken me up to this time since our last visit with you on the 8th of June to digest the results of Joanie's appointments with you and Dr. Dusenbery.

We drove back to Bismarck that day somewhat perplexed, with the feeling that we didn't know much more after the appointments than we knew prior to the appointments.

Dr. Dusenbery has indicated to me in response to an email to her that she was "very disappointed that the tumor did not shrink and the pain was no better. Additionally a new tumor has appeared.

What I missed from our visit was some candid comments to me about the situation and the prognosis. From my reading of the CT Scan notes and the MRI notes it was clear to me there is a serious problem, and we didn't get any kind of theory about why the

371

radiation obviously didn't do the job. If you do have one, I would like to hear it.

In addition, the mass in the left mid lung, according to the CT notes of 5/21/07, now "measures 2.1 CM X 1.9 CM in diameter, and is slightly larger than on the prior study."

When I asked you about that you indicated that you didn't get concerned over the increase until it approached 30 percent. Quite frankly that did not give me much confidence, since the CT notes of 5/12/07 indicated "The pulmonary nodule in the mid left lung field is stable at 1.3 CM X 1.7 CM." The fact that the mass in the left lung has grown at all is as troublesome to me as is the fact that the tumors in the right chest area are larger now than when the radiation began. The T6 tumor is particularly worrisome since the notes from the CT scan of 5/21/07 indicate that is the area where "The most superior mass is seen in the posterior superior aspect of the right thorax, and blends caudally with a more medial soft tissue mass that appears to be destroying the right lateral aspect of an upper thoracic vertebral body(at the level of the carina) and possibly invading into the spinal canal. What that means to me as a simple layman in plain English is there is the danger of paralysis if the invasion into the spinal canal is successful. Please feel free to disabuse of that notion.

One of the other questions I had that didn't get asked that day regards the MRI notes from 5/25/07 where on page 2 of the notes under "Impression," the doctor who read the scans initially said, in part, "Large mass seen involving the posterior aspect of the right chest wall and does extend into the T5 and T6 neural foramen on the right, greatest at T6 with minimal epidural involvement. CT guided sampling could be performed for further definition." No one down there even mentioned the possibility of CT guided sampling, what it does, what it would be good for or anything. Again, my ignorance doesn't help in this area either since I have no idea of what it is. Please explain.

372

Dr. Carson, I know we have a serious problem, and I have known that for a long time now. What I find disconcerting is the fact that nobody will take the time to tell me what the hell is going on in language I can understand. Most of what I have figured out over the years I have had to do myself. I agree there are things that Joanie doesn't need to know at the present time, however as someone who sees to her needs and wants on a 24 hour basis when she is not in the care of doctors, hospitals or clinics, I do need to know what I am dealing with. It helps me keep things in perspective for her when she wants to discuss what is going on. That is precisely that kind of active involvement that helped us dodge a couple of serious incidents last year, when if I hadn't been aware of what to look for, the outcome of those incidents could have been serious indeed.

So, what I am asking is to give me some credit for some kind of intelligence and ability to handle what is a tough situation, and don't keep me in the dark.

I know this has gone on at some length, but please bear with me since this the really important part of this letter.

Joanie told me at breakfast after we had left your office that morning that you had mentioned to her the word 'hospice.' I was obviously out of the room when you did that, and I was greatly disappointed that you did so. That may be what we are facing, however at this point that is more to deal with than she needs. The effect of that statement was indicated in what she said to me when she asked, "Do you think Dr. Carson has given up?" I responded that I didn't believe you had, and that you were just doing what doctors do. It did bother her, and she thought about all the way home. By the way, I was not then, nor am I now, pleased about the use of that word at this point. It has been her spirit, hope and faith that has kept her going over these past 11-plus years, and part of my job is see that they are kept in force as long as is possible. She has always had ultimate faith in you and what you have done for her

373

during these troubling times, and I don't want to see that faith eroded either.

The second time I heard her ask me that question was on the 19th of June when we were getting ready for the second gemzar treatment in the first cycle. Dr. Thomas told us that he had only received a letter from you about Joanie's situation and her visit to Mpls. on the day before, that would be the 18th. We were waiting for the chemo nurses to call us in, and she asked me again, "Do you think Dr. Carson has given up?" This time I didn't know what to say, since she was obviously upset in the timing of the letter, especially since we started chemo on the Tuesday following our Friday visit to the Cities.

I realize that you are a very busy doctor in a very busy metropolitan hospital, but I sincerely hope you will find time to respond to this letter. If it is easier, you can also email me at kallberg@btinet.net, otherwise my address follows at the conclusion.

If you have read this far, I appreciate it, and just so you also know that while we were both a bit stressed after the trip down there we do appreciate what you have done over the years and are hoping to keep this doctor-patient relationship alive as long as possible.

Thank you for your consideration and I look forward to your reply.

Sincerely,
Bob Kallberg

Of course, there was more. I realized that after I had mailed the letter, I had failed to ask what I viewed as a critical question. So, the next day I sent this letter:

Dear Dr. Carson:

As per usual, I left off one thing from my previous correspondence that is of some importance. In the past when we have been down

374

there, we were told by you or one of your nurses that Joanie should make an appointment for some time in the future depending on what was going on with her at the time. When we left on the 8th, we got no such instructions. No one told her or me when we you might want to see her again, so we were kind of left in the dark on when we should plan on coming down again. I know that usually we have been on a three month schedule, but that was when things were relatively normal. I'm not sure the current situation is totally normal and so don't know when, or if we should come back down. I sort of assume that after the next scan you might want to see her. From my understanding talking to Dr. Thomas, he is thinking about scheduling one after the next chemo cycle, which means the scan would be done during the last ten days of July.

As far as Joanie and the chemo is concerned she is handling it well. The first cycle went well without any serious side effects that caused any real problems. So far her hair is maintaining as are her spirits. She will start the next cycle on the 3rd of July. Her pain, though it has yet to go away, seems to be about what it has been for quite some time now. No better, no worse.

Again, thank you for your consideration, and I look forward to hearing from you soon.

Sincerely,
  Bob Kallberg

Dr. Carson and I did talk from time to time after that, and she continued to be involved in Joanie's care. All I had to do was call her gatekeeper, Marcia, and I could get through, or she would call me back.

It was that communication that was important to me during the next few months.

Saturdays with Joanie.

Even before we were married, Saturdays were the day when we went for late lunch. This was the time we took for each other, and we'd usually go somewhere after the usual rush was over, about 1:30 or 2:00 in the afternoon.

This was our time together, a time for us to talk about what was going on in our lives, what we wanted to see going on in our lives, and of the future.

Our favorite place was the Ground Round on South Third Street in Bismarck. We'd usually find a high-top table near the windows that made the place seem warm, and the servers there came to know us over the years. We'd order something to drink when we sat down. For me, a beer, and for Joanie, depending on the time of year, it could be a gin and tonic, at other times, a glass of Chardonnay.

I think we enjoyed these Saturday lunches, because we liked each other's company, and it would not be unusual for us to spend anywhere from an hour and a half to over two hours sitting, talking and nibbling on appetizers. One of our favorite performers, Jimmy Buffett, once wrote a song called, "I Wish Lunch Could Last Forever." The words of that song, especially the chorus, describes so well how I felt about those Saturday lunches.

There were days when we'd go for lunch, when we'd spend most of the time dreaming about what we'd do if we won the lottery. I think a lot of people do that. We did it even though we knew it would never happen, but it was fun to imagine all of the good things we could do if it happened.

Lunch with Joanie always included talk of what was happening in politics. She had come from a political family, and had always been involved. That involvement got ramped

376

up when she went to work for Ed Schafer, as director of the Schafer Volunteer Committee, and later for John Hoeven as director of the Hoeven Committee. So, you can see there was always something political to talk about.

There was always talk of family, both hers and mine. She had such a strong sense of family, and hers was especially close. Bud, Phyllis, and her sister Ann and brother Richard. Later her sense of family would grow, when she found her natural family, and got to know her sister Ginny in St. Paul, and her natural mother's sister, who she referred to as Aunt Del. A close family tie was something we had in common, and it was something that made her a part of my family as well.

We never got to Paris to sip cafe au lait, but one of the things we did talk about after we were married was how much she wanted to go to Ireland. There was Irish in her blood, and I used to tell her that if we went over there, they would think she was a native with her thick, black hair, and fair complexion. Her adoptive parents, Bud and Phyllis, were both full-blooded Norwegians, and there was no way she could have been seen as a Norskie.

Those lunches were often places where we made our decisions. It was one Saturday afternoon when we were planning our wedding in 1989, or more precisely, when Joanie was planning our wedding, when part of the ceremony was decided. Joanie wanted me to write something about the people who wouldn't be there for our big day. Her dad had died in 1987. My dad Wes had died in 1986, and my mother Marie had died in 1987. A younger sister of mine, Judy, had died in 1984. So I did as I was told.

Joanie had this thing that happened to her after she took only a few sips of wine: her cheeks would turn a bright red. They never got any redder if she had more than a few sips, but some days, when I would be drinking wine as well, we'd order another bottle, and while her cheeks never got any redder, her face took on this look, as if I was seeing her through a soft focus lens. The only way I could get her cheeks to redden even more was with some suggestive comment that would cause her to blush and smile.

After she was diagnosed in 1996, the lunches continued and became even more important. While there were many good years, interrupted by some difficult times, we kept our Saturday lunch dates with each other. Talks often now would include what was going on medically, and instead of wine, on many occasions, Joanie would have Diet Coke. There were other times, when wine was still the order of the day, depending on how she was feeling.

It was on some of these lunch dates, during difficult times, like the ones we were experiencing in the summer of 2007, when I would let her lead the discussion where she wanted it to go. I had always done that, since the beginning, and she would inevitably get around talking about something we needed to discuss. I never pressed, I just let it happen. It often told me more about what she knew about what was going on without me asking her if she really knew.

On such time happened that summer that made it clear to me she knew more about her medical situation than she ever shared with me. We had found a booth in the back of the Ground Round, ordered a sandwich we could split, Coke for her and beer for me. We sat there for a while, just chatting casually about what was going on, and what had gone on since the June 8 meeting in Minneapolis. She was back taking chemo again, and handling it well, but obviously there was something on her mind.

Suddenly, she looked at me and said, "Do you think we should talk to a lawyer about doing something about a power of attorney?" I tried not to look surprised when I heard that question and not give away how shocked I was to hear it from her. I just quietly told her that was something to think about, and if she felt strongly about it, we could surely contact someone to talk about it.

She said she didn't know what made her think about it today, but it told me she knew more about what was going on than I was aware. It told me that in her moments alone, at night before sleep came, she was thinking about what was happening to her body, and, again, she looked smaller and more vulnerable than ever, and I loved her even more.

We never got to Paris, nor did we get to Rio for Carnival, but we did have our Saturday lunches, and whenever I hear that song, I think about those days and how much they meant to both of us. Whenever I played that song at home, and it was just Joanie and me, with some wine and bread, I could see the sparkle in her beautiful blue eyes, and I knew she felt the same.

"She is feeling the best ever since a long time."
— Dr. Thomas

Joanie never mentioned the power of attorney again. In some way, I think it was just her way of telling me that she knew how serious the situation was, without saying it. I never brought it up either.

Earlier in January 2007, I had written to Ginny and Ed to bring them up to date on what was going on with Joanie. We hadn't seen them for some time, and while we had talked on the phone, I told Ginny I would write them with details. There are times when you go into detail, and times when you don't, so this is part of that letter, and what I wrote then still applied in July.

As I told Ginny on the phone the other day, I was going to be emailing out an update on Joanie, but it would not contain the detail I think is necessary to give everyone an accurate picture. My standard response almost daily to "How's Joanie doing?" is, "She is doing fine." And, for the most part that is a factual answer. She is doing fine relatively speaking.

Since Ginny and Ed were family and had seen Joanie through some really difficult times over the years, I gave them more detail than I did most people, since they knew more than most about what she'd been through. In that letter, I closed with something that was as true in July as it was in January:

Joanie continues to fight a battle with overwhelming odds against her, given the state of the cancer. She continues to pray for a miracle, and I know that is what it is going to take since everything I have read tells me that there is "no cure" for the situation as it currently exists. I do continue to hold out hope, and press the doctors at every opportunity whether they are doing everything they can.

I stopped at the clinic on one day, and caught Dr. Thomas between patients. They knew me so well in the oncology department, I could just walk back and see his nurse, Kathy, and tell her I just needed two minutes with the doc. I asked him if they were being as aggressive as they safely could with Joanie's treatment, and if they were doing everything they could. He told me they were. Of course, I knew that would be his answer, and I knew he was right. As her caregiver, I just needed that day to hear him say it.

July 3 came around, and it was time for to begin the second cycle of the Gemzar regimen. She had tolerated the first one fine, and the problems she had with Topotecan were absent

380

following the Gemzar. She would get one infusion today, followed by another on the tenth, and then she would have a week off.

Before the third cycle of the Gemzar, they would do a CT scan to check on the progress, or lack of it, of this particular chemo drug. The prospect of that scan was the cloud that hovered over the house at 1205 N. Mandan St., but it did not follow Joanie around. She continued to spend as much time as she could at her office, which meant at least afternoons, and on many days a full day. She was as determined as ever to treat this damn disease as an irritant, or inconvenience, as opposed to the life-threatening one that it was, and she was confident this was a battle she was going to win, despite the odds. Continuing to work was her way of showing everyone she was okay, and her attitude was still the same.

My own observations were that her hair was coming back, and she looked as healthy as she had in a long time. She had lost some weight, but had gained some back. She would still tire, but that was one effect of the chemo she couldn't do much about.

When we came back to the clinic for the second infusion of the second cycle, Dr. Thomas was pleased at what he saw. In his notes, he wrote, "Patient has been tolerating the gemcitabine extremely well. Her pain and discomfort in her left chest has improved. She did have some mild nausea and constipation but did not have any episodes of vomiting. She is feeling much better, stronger and gaining weight. She is feeling the best ever since a long time."

After hearing what Dr. Thomas had to say to her, waiting for the infusion didn't seem like much of a task at all. When that was done, she had a week off, and we would wait again. Wait to see what the CT on the twenty-fifth would tell us.

Hope is the physician of each misery. ~Irish Proverb

Joanie continued to come out of each chemotherapy infusion without any major issues. She was doing so well, that she started going back to her office in the afternoons the day after the infusion on July 10, knowing that she now had until the twenty-fifth before they would start again.

We would also wait for that day with some anticipation, for they would also do a CT scan in the morning before they began cycle three of the Gemzar. We waited, as we always did, and did so without talking about what the scan might show, as if to talk about it would bring bad news. Joanie refused to give voice to any concerns she might have, and I never pressed. She was working, and feeling good, and we were holding out hope that if nothing else, the cancer wasn't growing.

Joanie had this reservoir of faith that fueled her spirit and gave her the hope that made her believe every day was going to be better, and she never wavered, even when the harsh reality of a radiologist's notes, or an x-ray told her she was facing something which would require nothing short of a miracle to overcome. That faith had been there for her so many times over the past eleven plus years, and she never doubted it would be there for her when she needed it most.

It was there for her when we got the results of the scan. The notes from the radiologist said, "there are multiple soft tissue masses with rib destruction noted." The nodule in the left lung, which had been there for years, remained stable, but, "one of the masses as previously described looks to invade one of the dorsal vertebral bodies at the level of the carina. This too looks stable, unchanged, but compression on the cord would be a strong consideration."

It took me some time to digest those few words, but after some time, and talking to Dr. Thomas about it, I understood this. The carina is the area in the bronchial tube that is about where the T5 and T6 vertebra are. That is the area where the bronchial tube splits off between the right and left lung, and there was concern that there could be an invasion of the spinal canal, which might result in paralysis. That much I had learned from earlier scans.

Joanie didn't know any of this. All she knew at this point was that the chemotherapy was keeping the cancer at bay. The scan showed it hadn't spread, and so far everything was stable. That was enough for her.

When we met with Dr. Thomas we went over the results, but Joanie didn't seem to pay much attention to what he was telling us. All she wanted to do was get on with the infusion and get back to work. As far as she was concerned, the fact it hadn't grown was proof enough for her that her faith and hope was paying off.

The weeks seemed to move more quickly now. Before we knew it, she had finished cycle three, had a week off and finished cycle four. That brought us to late August, and we weren't scheduled to see Dr. Thomas until September 5, at which time they would do another CT scan, to see where we were.

Joanie still had to deal with pain on her right side, but was taking Dilaudid, and it seemed to have it under control. The disturbing thing, at least to me, was that the pain wouldn't go away completely. I finally figured out that the rib destruction was probably the culprit. There wasn't much to do about it except rely on the pain killers to give her relief.

Joanie was keeping busy, and though she wouldn't go in for full days all of the time, she made it to her office on more days than I thought she would. She was handling the chemotherapy really well. She went to lunch with her friends during the week, walks with Betsy in the afternoons, and had coffee on Saturday mornings with her girlfriends.

She continued to amaze and delight me with her attitude, and there were days when it was as if cancer didn't exist. Those were the days you need, especially when it has been around for so many years. Those were the days that help you keep some kind of perspective.

Those were the kind of days that kept hope alive, and helped keep you sane.

Out of options.

We got to the clinic on September 5 at 7:30 in the morning. They wanted to do lab work, and there was a CT scan scheduled for eight o'clock. Scans never take long, and since we had until ten a.m. when Joanie was scheduled to meet with Dr. Thomas before beginning the fifth cycle of this current chemotherapy treatment, we went for coffee. There was little sense in sitting in the waiting room until then.

Joanie was on edge, as she was often when we were waiting for results of something as important as a scan. There is never any way to guess what it will show, and that raises the level of anxiety. We went to Perkins and ordered coffee, juice and nothing else. Joanie wanted some toast, but she knew that there was a good chance she would throw up as she takes the treatment, as she almost always did, so she chose to have only the coffee and juice. We could always eat afterwards.

She made a couple of calls, and sounded for all the world like there was nothing bothering her when she was talking, but when the calls were ended it was a different story. I could see she was nervous, and I cautioned her, as I had before, not to be constructing worst-case scenarios before we knew what we were dealing with, and we would know that very soon. She told me she knew she was mind-fucking, but it was still hard not to do it. All I could do was tell her it was okay, especially since she knew she was doing it.

The time had come to meet with Thomas, and the news wasn't that good. It wasn't all bad, but it just wasn't that good. He showed us the scan on the computer, and told us what it was showing. Thomas told us that the scan, when compared to the August 25 scan showed "the mass invading the spine has increased slightly by about 28 percent." Also the mass in the right chest wall had increased. The multiple rib lesions had also increased in size. There was some good news in that there were no new lesions found. So, that's what Joanie grabbed hold of.

Dr. Thomas told us he wanted to do two more cycles, and then do another assessment. I think he was concerned that this regimen wasn't working either. He said he was also going to talk with Dr. Carson to see if there were possibly any clinical studies that might be available.

Joanie and I went back out into the waiting room until they called her in for this infusion. She seemed more relaxed, but I knew the news about the increases was troubling her. She chose not to talk about it with me, and, as usual, I didn't press.

The infusion went as others had before them. It would start, Joanie would throw up, she would feel better and it would continue. We would leave and I would take her home. She had been up early this morning, and with the news we got, it had already been a hard day. She didn't go into the office that afternoon, choosing to hit the couch with Bailey on her lap and try to rest.

As would often happen following an infusion, her appetite went south. She would drink juice, Boost, or one of the sodas we might have in the refrigerator, but outside of a cherry popsicle, and maybe some chicken noodle soup, she ate nothing for the first couple of days.

Nausea following chemo was always a threat, and I think that contributed to her food intake. Memories of earlier episodes were never far from her mind, even though the Gemzar had not been as tough on her as some of the other chemo drugs she had been given over the last almost two years. I would always get some samples of Kytril from Kathy before we went home, and that anti-nausea drug really helped.

The one thing that was troubling now was her energy level. She would tire easily, and that meant she was only going into the office for a few hours in the afternoon.

Our meeting with Thomas on the eleventh, for the second round of this fifth cycle was much the same as the one a week before. He noted her fatigue and the shortness of breath, which was attributed to a mild right side pleural effusion. The pleural effusion would be dealt with later with a thoracentesis to drain the fluid off her right lung.

The infusion went well, and then Joanie would have some time off before her next meeting with Dr. Thomas. I think this gave her some much needed relief. Both of us were still acutely aware of the news we had received earlier, and this break gave her a chance to recover and get ready for the next cycle.

"How much time are we talking about?"

Her next meeting with Dr. Thomas was an afternoon appointment on Tuesday, September 25. She was to have some lab work done and a chest x-ray done at 2:00 p.m. and we would meet with Dr. Thomas after that. We were called into the office, and then Dr. Thomas took us out to look at the

386

pictures from the chest x-ray they had just done. Pointing out areas that looked like nothing to us, he told us that they showed that the disease had progressed. Now, I was getting a bad feeling.

We went back into his office, and talked about the progression of the disease, and he told us there would be no chemotherapy today. He said the chemo is not helping her, and he had talked with Dr. Carson about any possible clinical trials, but they would very difficult, and they weren't sure she would qualify. His next words fell on our ears like a thunderous boom, even though, he delivered them quietly and calmly, aware of their importance, when he said, "We have run out of treatment options."

He said she had received most of the treatment that is available. My only thought was, "Holy shit, he is telling us Joanie is going to die!" Dr. Thomas was holding her hand, and she looked at him and asked quietly, "How much time are we talking about?"

I had never expected that question from her, and it stunned me into silence. I just sat quietly, not knowing what to say. This was the worst news we could have ever heard, and it was the fear she had lived with for so long, coming true. Thomas looked at her and said, "Joanie, I can't say, I don't know. I have never seen anyone who has what you have, survive as long as you have already, so I just can't say."

She just sat there, twisting her Kleenex to shreds, but no tears were coming. I reached for her hand, and squeezed it, but she still wouldn't look at me. I looked at her, and she seemed so much smaller, and all I could think of that I was helpless to do anything, and I wanted to scream.

He talked to us about "supportive care" without any further treatment, and said he was going to order a thoracentesis for tomorrow to see if they could get a handle on the shortness of

387

breath issue, and would give me a prescription so she could have oxygen at home.

He did talk briefly about home health care, or hospice, but Joanie wasn't having any of it right then. When she heard the word hospice, I could see her jaws tighten, but she said nothing. Wisely, Dr. Thomas didn't pursue it, for all if would have done then would be to magnify the already bad news, and that was going to be a lot for Joanie to process. It was already a lot for me to process.

Dr. Thomas left the room, and Joanie and I sat there for a couple of minutes, neither of us saying anything. Her eyes began to mist over, as we looked at each other, and as she dried them, and blew her nose lightly, she signaled it was time to leave. We walked out of the clinic, both wondering what we were walking toward.

That night, at home, with just Joanie, me, Bailey and Brandy, it was a quiet night. Joanie hadn't been having much wine, since the pain killer she was taking didn't mix well with Chardonnay, but tonight she didn't seem to care.

We did what we had done on troubled times before, opened a bottle of wine, got some bread, some olive oil for dipping, put on some of our favorite music, and sat close to each other.

Neither of us said a word about what had gone on this afternoon. There would be time enough for that tomorrow.

This wasn't supposed to happen.

The radiation, surgeries and chemotherapy going back to 1996, 1998, 2003, 2004, 2005, 2006 and 2007 were supposed to work. They didn't. I think that's what made the news from Dr. Thomas so devastating. The words were like thunder, but the processing of those words took place somewhere quiet—in our own minds.

I wanted to scream, I was so fucking mad, not just at the hand Joanie had been dealt, but the feeling of helplessness I had that I couldn't make it better. At the same time, I couldn't scream, couldn't make an issue of it, couldn't tell her how I felt it was so goddamn unfair because my job was still to help take care of her, and by getting hysterical myself, would do no good for her, and would, most certainly, make her feel worse. So I kept it to myself, with the exception of when I talked to my sisters or my friend Wayne. Then I could vent. Outside of that, when I was with Joanie, I did nothing but remain calm and supportive of her own positive attitude.

As for Joanie, she took it all in, and held it. She had done this during some of the other difficult times she had faced over the last eleven years, only opening up to me on rare occasions about how she felt. However, now it was more than just one of those difficult times. The stark reality of what she was facing now was overwhelming, and I wasn't sure what it was going to do to her.

I could only imagine, as we sat at home that night, what was going through her mind. She had just been told that afternoon, that she had already survived longer than she should have, and in effect had months to live. How many, we didn't know.

It turned out, I needn't have worried as much as I did. The next morning, when we talked briefly about what was going on, we came back to the same question we had asked each other on that day in May so long ago, "What do we do now?" As far as she was concerned, she was going to beat this thing, and even though I thought she must have known the odds were against her, I agreed with her, and told her that I would be right there with her.

The only other words she said to me that were related to Dr. Thomas's message was that she wanted me to make the calls she didn't want to make. She had done that before when there was bad news. It was easier for me to make the calls to family and friends, so she wouldn't have to repeat the same story every time she met someone who hadn't heard the news yet. That was another part of my job as caregiver, and it was an important one. It took a lot of pressure off her at a time when she didn't need any more than she already had.

As a caregiver, I was careful when I talked to people, not to paint too dark a picture. I had learned early on that people often construe any bad news as really bad news. What I told people this time, was that while they were suspending chemotherapy, Joanie was feeling pretty well, her attitude was really great, and she was still determined that she was going to get better. I would tell them that she was scheduled for a thoracentesis in a day or so, and that should help with her shortness of breath and that she would be going back to her office, at least in the afternoons after that.

Joanie wasn't giving up, but I wondered late that night, in the dark, before she drifted off to sleep what she really felt. I didn't know, but this I did know, she never stopped praying.

As far as she was concerned, this wasn't supposed to happen.

"A good hair cut always seems to help."

By the time the first of October had rolled around, Joanie was getting back to work. She was feeling stronger every day, and was determined to get on with life, without focusing on what had happened a few days ago.

Joanie went in for the thoracentesis, and while we were expecting some improvement in her breathing after they took about half a liter of fluid off her right lung, it didn't make any difference until about four or five days had passed. However, the improvement may have been due to the prednisone Dr. Thomas had prescribed. Thomas had also ordered oxygen for home use, and after I got it set up, Joanie only used it for a day or two. She didn't seem to want to be bothered with it, and was getting around better anyway.

Her calendar began to fill up and she was working afternoons. Her hair was filling out again, now that she wasn't taking chemotherapy, and that was helping her attitude.

We met with Dr. Thomas on the ninth, and he thought she was doing really well, in fact, I think he was surprised just a little bit.

There was only one incident that caused me some concern, and that was on the Saturday of Megan Smith's wedding. Megan was the daughter of our longtime friends, Pat and John Smith, and they had been an important part of our lives. Megan's dad John, had died in 1983, when she was just a child and we had stayed close to Pat, her mom, her younger brother Zac, and Megan all through the years.

Joanie had gone to the service, and I joined her at the reception. There were many of her friends there, and I think it was too much for her. We hadn't been there that long, when one of our friends came up to me, and told me she thought Joanie wasn't doing so well. I went to see her, and she wasn't. She said she should go home, and we did. I took her home and got her settled in, and she seemed to relax and feel better, even though she felt bad about having to leave the reception. She insisted I go back and tell everyone she was okay, and had just overdone it for the day, and was really tired. I did as I was told.

A week later, she mentioned it briefly in an email to Barb Olson. Reading the email now, one can see how she doesn't address the seriousness of her situation, choosing to focus on positive things instead. That was typical of Joanie.

391

Her email:

Hi Barb,

I wanted to tell you how glad I was that I was able to see you and Robin at Megan's wedding. Unfortunately I wasn't doing very well. So I wanted to update you on where I am right now.

"It was great to see Al when he was in Bismarck. They came over to the office and we had a great chat. I think that you probably had something to do with that so thank you.

Anyway I seem to be doing much better than in September. I know that Bob has talked to you but I thought I would email you and let you know how much better than I am doing than in September.

I am working afternoons and that is going pretty good. I am not doing any chemo right now but taking a day at a time. Dr. Thomas is very pleased with how I am doing compared to in Sept. I think that my attitude has a lot to do with how I am doing and all of the support I am getting.

I got my hair cut last week and I have had two people ask me if I had my hair colored. After the hair cut it is really dark and no grey!!! Also, some of my natural curl is coming back. Anyway a good hair cut always seems to help!!

I got the nicest card and book from Kristie. It was very thoughtful of her. And I want you to know how much I appreciate all of the support and your great friendships means to both Bob and me. I know Bob will keep you up to date on everything.

Al gave me a copy of the photo of your house. It looks great. Sounds like you are having a great time with your family close by. Please tell everyone I said hi and hope all is well in the cities.

Thanks again for being such a special part of my life.

Love,
Joanie

This email is one of the few that I know she sent. There may have been others, sent from her office computer, but this one had been sent from home. She never rushed to send emails to our friends dealing with her situation, leaving that to me. It was easier for her that way.

We met with Dr. Thomas one more time on October 25. I think he continued to be surprised at how well she was doing, and with the exception of the shortness of breath issue, especially when she exerted herself, she was doing fine. Pain continued to be an issue, but that was being managed with Dilaudid, and she was as active as she wanted to be.

With the holidays on the horizon, she was determined to live as if all of this was something of an inconvenience.

Joanie continued to do well, again giving rise to the hope the worst was behind her.

She was working, mainly in the afternoons, and with her boss Governor John Hoeven set to announce in mid-November that he would seek another term, they were busy afternoons. I thought the excitement surrounding his announcement was the juice she needed to energize her.

There were lunches to go to with friends, holiday things to begin thinking about and special events to attend to. One such special event was a personal one, and that was a meeting of her birthday club, the so-called "Ya Ya Sisterhood." They had appropriated the name from the book and movie, *Divine Secrets of the Ya Ya Sisterhood*, that had come out a few years earlier.

The group was made up of Joanie, Cathy Rydell, Kristi Sagsveen, Steph Borud, Claudia Thompson, and Marcia Herman. The six of them, all the same age, had been celebrating each other's birthdays with a get-together every year for many years. The last couple of years, they had gotten together for trips to Minneapolis, or a weekend at Cathy's lake place, and even though they might not see each other a lot in between get-togethers, they were a tight knit group, and as with any close friends, when one of them was having a problem, they were there for support. They were there for Joanie now as she faced the fight of her life.

Thanksgiving was on the horizon, and this year we would have special guests for the holiday. After we had gotten the news from Dr. Thomas about the cessation of treatments, I had called my son Ryan in Los Angeles to let him know what was going on. He called me back shortly, and told me they were going to come for Thanksgiving. I think he understood this might be an important Thanksgiving, and he and Kim along with our new grandson, Declan, made it more important.

Declan was born in May, and when Joanie heard they were coming, she was so excited to see the new family member. We had already heard that shortly after he was born, he already had an agent and had appeared in an episode of the TV show, *Eli Stone*. The show was a summer replacement on ABC that year, and one of Ryan's connections led to another, and before we knew he had an agent, and a part in one of the shows.*

When Ryan, Kim and Declan got to Bismarck, Joanie was thrilled, and doted on the young man considerably. To his credit, he showed no evidence of his early success in TV as going to his head at all. Their time here made the holiday this year one to remember, and Joanie looked healthier than she had in a long time, with her hair regaining some of her natural curl, and she was even gaining some weight back. It was a good time at 1205 N. Mandan Street. Later that month, on November 27, we met with Dr. Thomas, and got another dose of good news. The chest x-ray showed things were stable, and, in his words, there was, "No evidence of any progression of disease." She was not scheduled for another appointment until after the first week of January. We left the clinic that day with new attitudes, and new hope. It was beginning to look a lot like it would be a good Christmas.

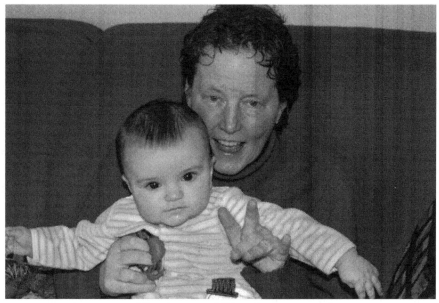

Declan and Joanie

* The title of the show is *Eli Stone*, and the show Declan appeared on, albeit for two brief scenes, was called "Patience." Go to Hulu at www.hulu.com/watch/160462#i0,p6,d0, and Declan appears first about 23 minutes in, and then during the last minute of the show. The scenes are the fantasy scenes that come to Stone from time to time, and Declan was appearing as his new son.

Christmas Memories

We made love that Christmas Eve, on the floor in front of the roaring fire we had started in the fireplace. Peaches and Muffin were unsure what was going on, and kept their distance. It was a time before cancer, and it was a time when the miracle of Christmas seemed so real to both of us.

I had picked up rib tips from Space Aliens late that afternoon, and after we left the party at the Puetz house, kitty corner from our house on Mandan Street, we went home and after we got comfortable, we put on the Christmas music that rang throughout our house for the whole month, opened a bottle of wine, actually two, Chardonnay for her, Pinot Noir for me, and sat back to reflect on Christmas past.

We were still burning wood in our fireplace, even though it was not practical to do so, since we didn't have a way to seal off the fire, only a screen, we couldn't close the damper until the fire had died completely. We didn't care that night. That night it was only Joanie and me, and we were in love.

Our house was full of lights, snow globes I brought every year, that reflected all of the lights, a tree laden with all of the ornaments she had inherited from her folks, and there were candles everywhere. It was one of those nights when you believe that miracles are possible, if only you choose to believe. Then there was the music, the music of the season that I had been collecting over the years.

There were presents under the tree. Presents we wouldn't open until Christmas morning because that's the way we had grown up. They just sat there in their colorful, sparkly wrapped glory, all contributing to the wonder of the Christmas Eve spell we were under that night.

That was a long time ago on the Christmas Eve of 2007, but it was not far from our memories.

Joanie had been doing well during the month. She had been involved in getting the governor's Christmas card done and mailed, and was busy, doing lunch with her friends and making sure I had all of her Christmas candy made, and that I had enough made for delivery to all of her friends. I did, and

396

it was something I didn't mind doing. It was also my job on Christmas Eve afternoon to make the rounds and deliver boxes of the candy to those on her list who had not received theirs yet.

We had long ago stopped burning wood in our fireplace, and that night, we didn't have rib tips from Space Aliens. We had chosen instead to do cheese, sausage, Triscuits, and wine. Joanie was still taking pain medication, and we knew she had to be careful about mixing the wine with the meds, but we knew moderation wasn't going to hurt.

Everything in the house that could be lit up was. It was not a Christmas Eve we were used to. The tree had only a few strings of lights on it, and there were no lights around the windows. The wreath above the fireplace was lit, but nothing else. Neither of us had mustered the energy to mark the holidays as we had done so many times before. Besides, what really mattered this night, was that we were together, along with Bailey and Brandy.

As we sat there that night, bathed in the candlelight and blinking tree lights, we began to remember those past Christmas Eves. The wine helped, and Joanie began to loosen up. We both knew this might be our last Christmas, but neither one of us said a word about that possibility. Tonight was not the night for such discussions. Tonight was for remembering better times, more wonderful Christmas Eves, and letting the memories wash over us and warm us.

When one of our favorite songs from our holiday collection, Paul Winter's "Tomorrow is My Dancing Day," came on, we remembered that night a long time ago, on the floor in front of a roaring fire on magical Christmas Eve.

I asked Joanie if she remembered that night, and she thought for a moment, and a shy smile came to her face that told me everything I needed to know. She blushed slightly

397

when I told her it was her idea that we bring blankets out and put them on the floor, since the fire was going to linger for hours and we might as well take advantage of it.

She looked away from me, as if she was seeing the scene in her mind, and told me it must have been the wine. It may have been, but that night, with "Tomorrow is My Dancing Day" playing on the stereo, we lay down on the blankets in front of the fire and made love like we were the only people on this night of nights that understood the magic of the night.

This night, so many years later, as I reminded her, she smiled a smile of someone who remembered what was important about this holiday season.

Then, as the Trans-Siberian Orchestra, one of our favorites, came on the stereo with "Music Box Blues," we didn't make love on the floor. We didn't have to. We just held each other because that was all that mattered.

"For last year's words belong to last year's language and next year's words await another voice. And to make an end is to make a beginning." – T. S. Eliot

As we sat home on New Year's Eve of 2007, we were content to let go of the last year's language and events. It had been a year filled with the language of a progressive disease, radiation, chemotherapy, hypokalemia, rib destruction, pain, lesions, hypercalcemia, and having run out of treatment options. Joanie was ready for a new year, and a new language, one that contained the hope she had always brought with her.

We had some wine that night, but Joanie had but a couple of sips because of the pain meds she was taking were so strong, and she talked of the present and the future, but not the past. She was done with that. Now, she had things to look forward to in 2008. Her boss, John Hoeven and friend Jack

Dalrymple were running for reelection, and her job was to help see that they had what they needed to win. She enjoyed her work, and she was very good at it. This new year was not going to be any different.

SECTION SEVEN
2008

Joanie's next appointment with Dr. Thomas wasn't until January 14, and by then we should have another look at how she's doing from their point of view. From my point of view, she was doing pretty well. The pain was still an issue, and while she was taking Dilaudid about every four hours or so, we were having some minor problems regulating that pain. Dilaudid is one of the brand names for hydromorphone, a powerful synthetic form of morphine, and is considered a narcotic. We were both aware of how strong it could be, and so I monitored her intake. Regardless of what Dr. Thomas had prescribed, she began taking it more often to stay ahead of the pain curve.

Ann Wigen, Richard Wigen, Joan Wigen, January 2008

When we met with Dr. Thomas, there was no significant change to be noted in the progress of the disease. That was the good news. We did tell him about trying to keep ahead of the pain issue, and he recommended an increase in the dosage from 4 mg every four to six hours to 6 mg.

When we left his office that day, we didn't have to come back for another month, at which time they would do a CT scan, and a complete lab workup.

So, Joanie went back to work with some renewed vigor, even though it was mostly afternoons. Since she was taking Dilaudid, it wasn't advisable for her to drive, so I was at her beck and call every day, as I always had been. Besides that, we were down to one car after the VW crapped out on us a year or two earlier.

Her brother Richard came to Bismarck from San Francisco for a few days in mid-January, and that gave her a lift. It gave them both a good bit of time to spend with each other. Dick understood the seriousness of the situation Joanie was facing, and that made his time here more special. The three Wigen kids, Ann, Dick and Joanie, had a good reunion. It also gave me a little bit of relief as well.

While Dick and Ann knew how serious things were, and in my heart, I think Joanie did as well, they talked little about it during his visit. When I took the picture of the three of them, I think they knew that would probably by the last one of them together. It was.

As a caregiver to someone who is dealing with a life-threatening disease, and an uncertain future, there are times when your job is critical. This was the time for me when I began to focus more intently on subtle changes in behavior, Joanie's needs, especially when it came to her pain, appetite, and moods.

One of the things I learned was that she remained future focused. She would be on the couch going through the catalogs we had received in the mail, and when she'd find something in Eddie Bauer, or L. L. Bean, or some other catalog, whether it was a new pair of khakis, a few of her favorite white turtlenecks, a sweater, or a jacket she thought she'd like, she would ask me if it was all right if she ordered something. I told her she could order anything she wanted from wherever. What her shopping told me was that she wasn't giving up on living and was thinking about the future, something I took to be a positive.

That New Year's Eve, we watched the ball drop in Times Square, and after that I was ready to retire. Joanie wasn't and told me she was going to stay up for a while. She had Bailey and Brandy to keep her company as the new year rolled in across the country.

I kissed her, wished her Happy New Year, told her I loved her, and left her to consider her hopes and fears about what the new year would bring, and what language it would speak.

"It has been said that we need just three things in life: something to do, something to look forward to, and someone to love."

In the winter of 2007-08, Joanie and I had all three.

There was little doubt that we had something to do. Not only did she have the job of helping John Hoeven get reelected, but she had the battle of her life to conduct on a daily basis. My job was to be sure she got everything she needed for her battle.

We had something to look forward to, that the darkness of long, cold winter nights would give way to brighter, warmer spring days, when life begins anew.

And, we each had someone to love.

In the winter of 2007-08, despite the clouds, we didn't need anything else.

"Ignore what you fear and latch on to what you hope."

January continued to be an important month. Even though Dr. Thomas told us there was the disease seemed to be stable, the pain issue had escalated, due to the involvement of her ribs. The metastases in the ribs were the prime culprits when it came to the pain, and even though Dr. Thomas had prescribed upping the dose of Dilaudid, it was still a problem.

Her brother's visit had given her a lift, but there were still times when I looked at her and in her unguarded moments, her face told me everything. This photo was taken around the last week or so of the month, and you could see how tired she was.

That was not the face she wore when she left the house for work, but it was the kind of image that would change daily at home. The more she worked, and the more involved she was in the business of the campaign, the more energized she would become, and I could tell that in her face as well.

She was going to lunch with Mikey Hoeven, she was seeing her friend Vicki for lunch at the Ground Round, she was going to Boneshakers with Tara Holt and Patsy Thompson, and we watched the Super Bowl in early February at Orell and Cathy Schmitz's home. She was being as active as the disease was letting her and was doing it to the point that when she would get home, she would be really tired, but it was a good tired.

Joanie was scheduled for a CT scan on February 20, along with an appointment with Dr. Thomas. The night before she got quiet, as she had done so many times prior to what could be a good appointment, or an appointment that would be another disappointment. By now, of course, she knew that each meeting like the one we would have tomorrow would be the most important one she could have. Joanie's way of getting ready for whatever we would find out was to withdraw, and keep her thoughts to herself.

Little things could set her off now, and she could be impatient with me over something that would have been insignificant any other time. I had learned that from the beginning, and it didn't bother me at all. What bothered me was there was nothing I could do to ease her pain and give her comfort at a time like this but be there.

She had no appetite that night. All she wanted when she got home from the office was to get in her sweats, head for the couch and wait for either Bailey or Brandy, or both to join her. She would turn on the TV, but the sound would barely be audible, and she would sit and stare at it for a while until she would ask me to get her Diet 7-UP and a cherry popsicle. That would be her dinner on this night. Since she wasn't supposed to eat anything after midnight, it didn't seem to matter much. After the news was done, and a program she wanted to watch came on she would turn up the sound and sit there with a book within reach, and a cat on her lap.

She would ask me for her pain pills from time to time, and when I was ready to turn in, she asked for another cherry popsicle, and told me she was going to stay up for a while longer. She had Ambien available, but didn't use it that often, because even when she did, she told me she didn't sleep that well.

The next day, we made the appointment for the CT scan, and then we went upstairs to wait to be called into to Dr. Thomas's office. We sat in the brightly lit waiting room, on those hard chairs, and Joanie began to shred her Kleenex as she'd done so many times before. Both of us were concerned about what we were going to learn this morning.

When we were called into his office, Dr. Thomas and after he was done with the preliminaries, he got down to the business of the CT scan. He pulled them up on his computer, and began to show us that the disease had progressed.

The scan showed the nodule in the left lung had increased in size. The scan showed that the "chest wall masses have consolidated and progressed and is,(sic) affecting at least 2-3 vertebrae with cord involvement."

We were told the pleural effusion was still present on the right lung, but hadn't gotten any worse, and the radiologist's notes indicated "probable metastatic disease involving the right kidney." The kidney involvement was something we had even considered before, and the doctors were more concerned about the right side chest wall mass and the rib destruction. The involvement of the T6 vertebrae was really troubling to Thomas. He had indicated to me when we talked one day about the encroachment on the spinal cord that could result in paralysis. Here again, Joanie was totally unaware about that possibility, and that was just fine. She already knew enough and was worried enough about what she knew.

Thomas did tell us he was going to write to Dr. Dusenbery at Fairview University Medical Center to see if Joanie might be a candidate for further radiation therapy. Katie, of course, was totally familiar with Joanie's case since she had been her radiologist since the beginning of this journey in 1996.

The blood work that day showed she once again had a mild case of hypocalcemia (low calcium levels), and Thomas said he wanted to check that again in a couple of weeks to see if it was getting better or worse.

We left his office that day somewhat disappointed, but at the same time we were clinging to the sliver of hope that came with Thomas's statement about writing to Katie. Joanie grabbed hold of that statement and began supposing what might happen if Katie might find something. That was the way she was. If there was something out there that was going to help her, she had the great ability to ignore what she feared, and latch on to what she hoped. It was a spirit that had helped her through some really dark times since 1996.

As I reflected on what had happened that morning, I couldn't help but think how grateful I was to Dr. Thomas. He knew how dark things were, but just by telling us he was willing to contact Joanie's other doctors in Minneapolis it told us he wasn't giving up.

That was what Joanie needed to hear.

"Hope is that rare thing that will not die, and when you are left with nothing else to hang on to, it is there to sustain you through the darkest of times."

In late February 2008, we were hanging on harder than ever.

It came to be the absolute last attempt to find a treatment option that would help Joanie. We knew by then it would have taken a miracle to cure her of the disease, but at least the doctors were not giving up on trying to find some way of extending her life, as well as the quality of her life.

Dr. Thomas did write to Dr. Dusenbery at University of Minnesota Medical Center-Fairview. His letter to Katie was dated the day after we had met with him on February 20.

Dear Dr. Dusenbery:

I am writing this letter and enclosing a recent CAT scan of the chest on Joan Wigen. Briefly, this is a patient you have seen in the past with a diagnosis of metastatic squamous cell cancer with evidence of chest wall mass, which has been evading gradually to the thoracic vertebras. The patient has been undergoing supportive palliative care. She was given third line chemotherapy until September of 2007 and since then has not been undergoing any chemotherapy but supportive care. She has had persistent pain and discomfort in the right chest wall, for which she has been on oral Dilaudid. She has been ambulating and continues to work at least 4 to 6 hours a day. She has had a CAT scan of the chest in September of 2007, and a repeat one on February 20, 2008. There is clear-cut evidence that the mass is increasing in size and now is destroying several vertebrae including T4, T5 and T6, and affecting the spinal cord. Surprisingly, this patient does not have any neurological deficits.

I am sending the CAT scans along with this letter to see if she is a candidate for any further localized radiation therapy. Please let me know and I can make arrangements for this patient to see you. Thank you for evaluating her CAT scans."

The last Friday of the month of February in 2008 was the twenty-ninth, not ordinarily a day that I would think a lot about. However, on this Friday, Joanie came home from her office, and it would turn out to be a date I would never forget.

Joanie had caught a ride home from somebody at her office, and I could tell she wasn't feeling that good. Once home she did what she always did, and that was to get into her sweats, take up a place on the couch and wait for one of our cats to join her.

She didn't ask for anything at first, but after a while wanted another Dilaudid. Seemed the pain and discomfort had been ratcheted up a couple of notches during the afternoon, and she was feeling it. She wasn't hungry that night, but I did get her to have a Boost and some 7-UP. For most of the evening, she stayed on the couch, often dozing off while pretending to be watching TV.

407

I remember, when I would go outside for a smoke, in the cold, dark night of our backyard, wondering to myself what was going to happen. It was hard not to imagine the worst, but at the same time still hold on to the hope that hinged on what Dr. Dusenbery might have to say.

Joanie seemed to get worse as the weekend wore on, spending more time in bed than usual, and we did increase the Dilaudid, now giving it to her every two hours as opposed to every four to six hours.

We didn't have to wait very long to find out what Katie had to say. On Monday, March 3, I called Dr. Thomas to let him know what had been going on over the weekend, and he also told me he had talked to Dr. Dusenbery, and that radiation was not an option.

His notes from the conversation follow:

Bob Kallberg called me on Joan Wigen telling us that over the weekend she was having more pain and the Dilaudid had to be increased to 12 mg every 2 hours. The Fentanyl patch was increased to 100 mcg. She was still having pain and 3 days ago she was in bed most of the time. She is feeling slightly better now with the increased Dilaudid and he was wondering whether there is any other option.

In the meantime I did get a call from Dr. Dusenbery from the University of Minnesota after she received CAT scans. Dr. Dusenbery felt that these were areas that were already radiated and so radiation was not an option. She is not very sure about that. She said she will show the scans to a spinal surgeon. Other options also include Cyberknife. She did not think Cyberknife would be the best option. We also discussed about radioablative therapy as a possibility to help the pain.

I did suggest to Bob that all of this was an option including a change in her medication to oral Morphine. Her doses would come out to be that she would be taking 144 mg of Dilaudid and that

408

would be equivalent to nearly 570 mg of morphine sulfate. I did again tell Bob that epidural intrathecal morphine or Dilaudid would be an option. I would have to send her to a pain clinic for assessment. In the meantime I did talk to Dr. Herbel who said that he is willing to sit down and talk with Joan about the options of radiofrequency ablation. I did inform Bob that I am very concerned about the possibility that she could have paraplegia with this tumor going into the spinal cord. Pt. has been on Prednisone at 10 mg daily. I probably would increase the doses. Patient's family does understand that this is a possibility. All of this was discussed at length and this was after several conversations with Dr. Herbel and Dr. Dusenbery.

I could tell from talking with Dr. Thomas that he was making every effort to find something that would help, and I appreciated the difficulty he was having in finding something more satisfactory than he did. We both knew we needed a miracle right now, and, as we all know, they are often in short supply.

After I finished talking to Thomas, I began to wonder how I was going to discuss this with Joanie. It took me a while to figure it out, but I finally found some time to sit down with her and lay it all out.

She had questions, as I knew she would, but I couldn't supply her with any definitive answers. All I could do was to do my best to let her know what the options were as I understood them, and to let her know that she didn't have to make up her mind right then about pursuing any of them. If there was more information she wanted from Dr. Thomas, I told her we could get it whenever she wanted it.

I suggested she sleep on it, and we would talk about it when she was ready.

"What you don't see with your eyes, don't witness with your mouth." –Jewish Proverb.

The day after I had laid out the options, as I understood them, for Joanie, we talked, and she told me she didn't want to do any of them. I was dispatched to talk to Dr. Thomas, which I did. He gave me new prescriptions for Dilaudid and Duragesic (Fentanyl patches), and told me that she should call if she does not improve. That was on Tuesday, March 4.

I hadn't sent out any email updates on her condition since we got the news in late September about stopping chemotherapy. Mainly that was because, through October, November, and December, Joanie continued to work, and was as busy as she wanted to be, or physically could be. There were plenty of people she came into contact every day, and they could see for themselves how she was doing. January and February were the same. But after "Leap Day" in February, she no longer left the house. I began to field phone calls from friends inquiring after her condition and tried my best to give them an accurate picture.

As a caregiver, there will come a time when the rumor mill will drive you nuts. For me that time was approaching. It wasn't the first time rumors ran rampant regarding Joanie's situation. In 1998, rumors had her dying after she came back from the exenteration surgery. However, now the rumors contained some real misinformation.

I was, as I always had been, focused on taking care of Joanie's needs on a daily basis, and I never really worried about how all of this was perceived by anyone else. As far as I was concerned, my only job was Joanie, and seeing her through these, the darkest days of this journey. I still hadn't sent out any emails regarding how she was doing since coming home on the 29th. Apparently, for some, this amounted to me not doing enough.

I was unaware of these rumblings, until my good friend Wayne Tanous called me and I met him to talk about what he was hearing. I was dumfounded at first when he was telling me what he had heard. My first thought was, "Jesus Christ, don't these people understand what we are dealing with here." I was talking to Dr. Thomas on a frequent basis, and I had talked to Katie Dusenbery in Minneapolis, and Dr. Carson as well. Everything that could be done was being done, and the stress of these days was mounting, and I didn't think I needed to be worried about what other people were thinking or saying, as well as taking care of Joanie's needs.

I was pissed, but as Wayne told me, they just want to be brought into the loop. I knew he was right, and I knew that many of Joanie's friends were concerned about what was going on with her since they hadn't heard or read anything since last September, even though she had only been home for less than two weeks.

I had sent an email to her brother Dick in San Francisco on March 11, in which I outlined everything I knew at the time. and I added, "I haven't sent out updates as I once did, because most people, outside of a few, would come unglued, and this is difficult enough without having to deal with other people's misconceptions about what is going on. I don't include you in that group."

When I sent this rumor-squelching email to Cathy Rydell, I prefaced it with the following comments.

Cathy,

Here is an email update I sent out today. I know I told you one of the reasons I hadn't sent out updates since last September was that people would come unglued. Well, it was happening, and I thought

411

that rather than let the rumors fester and get all blown out of proportion that I had better sent out something that explains just what the hell is going on. This is the result.

Email from March 13, 2008:

Greetings to one and all, and please excuse the mass mailing approach. Under the circumstances it is the easiest way for me to communicate with a large number of Joanie's friends who are no doubt hearing rumblings of the current situation, and I want to make clear to everyone just exactly what is going on. Part of what follows is an explanation that might be considered somewhat technical by some of you, and I have made an attempt to place each of those items in context in parentheses following the item. A good share of this is what I sent to her brother Dick the other day.

So here is the situation as it stands on Thursday, March 13, 2008.

Joanie is resting comfortably on the couch where she had been since Saturday morning. She found that she sleeps better there than in the bed. I called Dr. Thomas Monday and had them get an oxygen concentrator sent over so that is helping with the breathing difficulty. I also found a Foley bag in a drawer in the bathroom this last Sunday, and got that hooked up so she doesn't have to go through the stress of trying to cath her Miami pouch, and that seems to be working, even though I do have to irrigate regularly to keep it open due to the mucus that builds up.

She still has no appetite, and I have great difficulty getting her to take anything solid. She does have several Boosts during the course of the day, but as I told her, that is hardly enough for her to regain strength even though the Boost is good for her. On Tuesday night and Wednesday night, I did get her to eat some semi-solid food in the form of mashed potatoes and gravy Tuesday, and pasta shells with lots of butter and some pistachio salad on Wednesday night. She continues to resist any such other solid foods, but we keep trying.

412

The results of the CT she had on February 20 showed results that are not encouraging. The list of the radiologist's conclusions are as follows:

1. Increased level of disease throughout the chest. (This includes an increase in the size of the nodule in the left lung, which had remained stable for some time.)

2. 3.5 cm left upper lobe mass (This is an increase of 2.2 cm from the September 2007 CT. This is what was called a "solitary pulmonary nodule" some years ago when it was first discovered.)

3. 5x9 cm upper right lobe mass (This is compared to 4x5.2 cm from September.)

4. Multiple rib metastasis with destruction and associated mass.

5. Vertebral body destruction in the T4 and T5 and to some degree at the T6 level. (this is also worrisome for paralysis as it is encroaching on the spinal column.)

6. Right pleural effusion. (Probably source of some breathing difficulty.)

7. Probable metastatic disease involving the right kidney. (There has been no follow-up on this issue, and the only thing Thomas told us was that it was a suspicious mass, but given her present state, it is doubtful we will know anything about that for some time.)

I did have Thomas send the CT and notes to Dr. Dusenbery in Mpls. and I talked to Katie a week ago Monday (That would have been March 3rd). Katie is the head of therapeutic radiology and radiology/oncology department at the U of M, and has treated Joanie several times over the years, so she knows her case well. She told me that the problem areas involving the T4, T5 and T6 vertebra was smack dab in the middle of the area that has been radiated once, and so that is out of the question. She also indicated she thought that any back surgery would be far too risky for the limited benefit that it could bring, something Thomas and I discussed as well last Tuesday. Thomas indicates to me that since the tumor also involved the right chest wall, there was a real danger of internal bleeding and other

413

complications that could kill her on the table. Needless to say that was ruled out.

Other options for relief were also ruled out because the benefit was minimal compared to the risk and the discomfort. So, the long and the short of it is that we are plum out of options.

I haven't sent out updates since the last one I sent last year, mainly due to the complexity of the issue and the opportunity for confusion and misunderstanding. I'm hoping this email will make clear exactly what is going on at the present time. I know you are all concerned, but please do not panic at this point. It is critical to be sure, however the task at hand, as it has been for 12 years now is to see that Joanie is getting the care she needs, which she is, and is comfortable, which she also is."

After some experimenting with the pain meds, we have found a comfortable level of dosage, and the pain is now under control. The oxygen concentrator is helping out, and on one good note on Wednesday afternoon, while we were in the process of changing her clothes, she stood up from the couch, unaided by me for the first time in about 12 days. I liked that."

Wish I had a better report, but there it is.

Thank you all for your concern and prayers.

The same day, I got a response from Wayne that said "Good job. This was what was needed at this point in time."

Joanie never knew anything about this. There was no reason for me to trouble her with this information. The only thing I ever told her was that I was doing my best to keep her friends informed about what was going on with her. She was satisfied with that.

"I'm not going to die next week, am I?"

Springtime, the time the earth in the northern hemisphere begins to wake from a long winter slumber is a time of hope, renewal and possibilities. As we waited for the first day of spring on North Mandan Street, we weren't thinking about the first sighting of a robin, we were concentrating on getting Joanie to eat some solid food.

Since she had come home from her office on the twenty-ninth of February, she hadn't been out of the house. Her appetite had been nonexistent, and she was subsisting on bottles of Boost, various sodas, and the occasional popsicle. There were, however, a few days when she began to ask for something more solid.

I began to send out more frequent updates to her friends and family. These emails were just notes about what she had done on one day or another, but I hoped they would keep people aware of the battle that was being waged inside our little bungalow. These emails also tell a part of the story.

Saturday, March 15, 2008

Just wanted to pass along some good news for the day. As she sat reading the paper this afternoon, she decided that she wanted a hot roast beef sandwich from Kroll's Diner. I was dispatched to retrieve same, and so that is that. It is the first time in two weeks that she has even said such a thing, and I was quite pleased. She continues to amaze me.

Thank you all for your concern and prayers, and I will try to keep you posted on things as they happen.

Sunday, March 16, 2008

Just a note to tell you all that the week is starting out right and I am elated about it. Last night she did considerable damage to half a

415

hot beef sandwich with mashed potatoes and gravy, which she had ordered, and this morning she asked me if we could have my scrambled eggs with cream cheese, chives and green onion, and of course I am happy to oblige. She also wants some English muffin toasting bread. I get to eat the bacon, but perhaps the smell will get to her. She continues to amaze and delight.

Monday, March 17, 2008

Passed somewhat uneventful. I did get her to nibble on a few chips and some onion dip (one of our favorites, and she requested chili for dinner which of course she got. Her intake wasn't that great, but the fact that she even expressed an interest in it was, I thought, encouraging.

Now then, her Majesty did have one visitor today, and seems more than willing to have more of same. These audiences are held generally in the afternoons, and can be cut short due to her Majesty's propensity to doze off in mid-sentence. I am assured it is not from boredom, but from some overwhelming desire just to get a little more sleep. So, those of you who are in the area are welcome, or even if you are not in the immediate area, but just happen to be so, or so I am told by Her Highness, to stop by. A call in advance would be most welcome to ensure that she is not inundated, and this precipitates another episode of the Mid-sentence Dozing off Syndrome. On the other hand, there is no guarantee of that in any event.

We will be meeting tomorrow, or possibly Wednesday with the home health care servants to see what they can do to help keep Her Majesty comfortable, and she has indicated to me if she doesn't like what they have to offer, "We can fire them, can't we?" I indicated that, as Queen, she can fire anybody she wants to, and she seemed satisfied with that.

That's all for now. Until next time, I remain,

Your, and her humble servant,
   Bob

The home health care business came about as a result of a talk I had with Dr. Thomas, and he had suggested that we get this set up that way. He told me that it could be turned into hospice when, and if, Joanie would ever allow it. I didn't tell Joanie that, but did tell her that it would help out to make sure that she was getting everything she needed, since I wasn't a trained medical person.

One of the things I had always let Joanie lead on were the decisions that affected her life. I felt it was important for her to have the feeling of control over what was going on. Last year, it was she who had brought up the matter of power of attorney, and medical power of attorney that day at lunch. Nothing happened after that, and I didn't pursue it.

One day earlier this month, she mentioned it again and asked me if we should call someone to take care of those matters. She suggested Casey Chapman, an attorney friend of hers. I called him, explaining what was going on and what was needed, and he graciously offered to handle the details. He would call in a day or two, and when the documents were ready he would bring them by to meet with Joanie.

A couple of days later, he came over with the papers he had prepared. Joanie was on the couch, and Casey sat down at one end, explaining each of the documents to her in detail, and answering any questions she had. They did spend some time enjoying small talk, and because they were of opposite political persuasions, had a few good laughs. When he was satisfied that she understood everything, and she had no more questions, we signed the papers, and Casey left, telling us he would send copies of the papers in the mail.

417

I sat down on the couch where Casey had been and we talked about what we had just done. It seemed to me it had all been pretty matter of fact, until, she looked at me and said, "I'm not going to die next week, am I?"

That question stunned me. I never thought I would be faced with the proposition of having to answer a question like that. My heart sank into the pit of my stomach, and for a few seconds, that seemed much longer, tried to think of an answer that would make sense to her.

As I held and squeezed her hand, I could only say, "No, you are not going to die next week. Right now, you are very sick, and our job is to help you get your strength back so that you feel better." I didn't know what else to say, and she seemed satisfied. I felt as if I was going to throw up.

I went outside for a smoke, and wiped away some dampness that seemed to come from my eyes in the spring like afternoon. It was all so unfair.

Caregiver and gatekeeper.

Joanie was now sleeping almost exclusively on the couch. The nights were becoming increasingly problematical for her regarding her ability to get a decent night's sleep. She would begin, coming to bed after she had stayed up as long as she could, and the desire to sleep outweighed her ability to stay awake. She would then come to bed, and we had devised sort of a plan that would allow her to sleep on her back, but be elevated enough to ease her breathing problems.

It wouldn't take long, before she would wake me and I would escort her to the couch, where she would assume a similar position, but for some reason it was easier for her to breathe and sleep.

She wasn't getting better, and our hope for some kind of miracle had faded by this time, except for her. As she told me on more than one occasion, she was going to lick this thing, and getting better was all that she thought of right now.

An email update I sent out on Wednesday, March 19, 2008, was an example of the spirit she still hung on to, and the future she looked forward to.

Greetings All,

"Yesterday the health care servants came to begin the arrangements for Her Majesty, and it went well. I met the nurse who was doing the preliminary processing outside, and told him that whatever he did, he was not to mention the word hospice in our house. That word was an anathema at this time, and I told him she would fire him on the spot. Everything went well, and we managed to arrange for a bed to be brought in that will make it easier for me, and for them, when they come, to take care of her needs. It will also be easier on my back since that couch is so low.

To show what shape her spirits are in, and how she is thinking, is this. She put the nurse in a really awkward position when she asked him, "How long is this going to go on?" He, somewhat puzzled, asked her what she meant, and she replied, "Before I get better and able to get around again?" Of course he didn't have an answer, or if he had one, dared not utter it, and he stumbled around a bit and escaped with some non-answer. I thought we might be seeing the makings of a good politician. Joanie and I talked about that later, and I said, nurses are not the ones in the position to be offering opinions on such matters, nor should they be. She seemed satisfied with that.

The hospital bed arrived on a Thursday, and the next couple of days were something of an adjustment. There was no place to set it up in our modest home except in the middle of our living room. The up side of that was that Joanie could see out the picture window, and also see the television when she wanted to. It took some doing to get her moved over to the bed, but once we did, she promptly fell asleep, an indication to me this was what she needed. The weeks on the couch had taken a toll, and that was now behind us. Bailey and Brandy were much confused at first, but they acclimated, and once Joanie was situated on the new bed, found ways to get up there and check out their good friend.

That day, she had no visitors. In fact, she had no visitors the day before either. She had been out of sorts on that day and wanted to see no one. It was my job now to manage the flow of visitors, which I did, but at no time did I ever restrict any visitors without asking her first.

When I would get a call from someone who wanted to stop by, I would always ask her, and if she indicated that she might welcome a visitor, it was up to me to make the arrangements. Afternoons were usually the best, but any visits were always her decision. That went back to my original intention of giving Joanie as much control over what was going on as possible. To me that was an important part of dealing with this disease, and one I had never deviated from. It was, after all, her life.

The next day, which was Good Friday that year, she was still out of sorts, despite being able to get some rest on the new bed, so there were no visitors that day either. Most of the day she slept, under the influence of Dilaudid and Ativan, two drugs that helped keep the pain and the anxiety of the time under control.

The NCAA basketball tournaments were on, and while the TV in the living room was on all the time, the sound remained off. Even when it was on, it was on barely audible. It seemed she just wanted to see that life was going on around her, even if she couldn't participate in it.

That Friday evening, as I sat there by the bed in the living room, one of the cats found a place to nap on her legs, and that seemed to please her. The light from the TV was bright enough, and the only other light on was the light over the sink in the kitchen. It was a quiet night.

Joanie slept a lot that day, and later that night after she had another pain pill and another Ativan, she dozed off. I slept that night behind her bed on the couch, though I needn't have. She did not wake up until early the next morning, and woke me as well when she called for me to get her some water and her meds.

She asked me how I was doing, and I laughed, telling her that I was doing fine and she didn't have to worry about me. She told me she still did, and shortly after she took the meds, she drifted off to sleep again.

"Faith is a knowledge within the heart, beyond the reach of proof." — **Khalil Gibran**

The Easter weekend of 2008 was a far different one from so many of the others we had shared at 1205 N. Mandan Street. Usually Easter Sunday meant eggs benedict, champagne and strawberries for brunch, and later in the afternoon, ham, sweet potatoes, corn and salad for dinner. All in all, they were always good days.

On this Sunday, Joanie lay on a bed in our small living room, sleeping most of the time, with her condition slowly deteriorating. While her situation may have been worsening, her faith was not.

I gave her pills at about seven that morning, irrigated her Miami pouch, and changed the Foley bag that hung from a rail on the side of the bed. The home health care nurses came at ten and gave her a workout, changing the bedding, giving

421

her a bath and a shampoo. My notes from that morning indicate she did get worn out, and after they left she asked for more meds.

While they were busy with her, I slipped out to the grocery store not far from our house to pick up orange juice, the paper, and some English muffin toasting bread that she had requested. The toast would be her Easter Sunday brunch, and she wouldn't have much of that. Her still had very little appetite, and she was still losing weight.

The following Monday morning, I got a call from Ed Schafer, who was at that time serving as George Bush's Secretary of Agriculture. He asked if it would be okay if he stopped by on Friday when he was in Bismarck for a meeting. As I did with any request, I asked Joanie if she wanted to see her old boss and friend, and she said she did. Ed told me he would stop over on Friday afternoon. It was moments like that when I could see a spark in her eyes, even if it was only briefly. It was calls like that that meant so much during these difficult times.

The rest of that Monday was a quiet day. After the home health nurses left shortly after noon, she dozed off and slept off and on for the rest of the day. She was still not eating, and I was having to push her about drinking water, or any other kind of fluid I could get her to sip on.

On Wednesday, March 26, because I hadn't sent out anything very new on Joanie's situation to her friends, I sent out this email to bring her friends up to date on how she was doing.

Greetings,

Things remain pretty much steady here at 1205 N. Mandan St. Joanie is getting some sleep, even though her bed has become a bit messed up in the last day. That is something that will be taken care of this morning when the Home Health Nurse arrives to do her thing.

Her spirit remains undiminished and she tells anyone and everyone that she is "going to get better and get out of here in a couple of weeks." I find that attitude consistent with what it has been every time over the past 12 years when things looked really dark. I am happy to report that some things do not change even under really unpleasant circumstances.

She continues to take in fluids, but not much in the way of solid food. She still thinks Boost is a pan-blackened prime rib sandwich and crispy french fries in a glass. I cannot disabuse her of that notion, though last night she did ask me for a couple of small bites of mine. Mary Pat Woodmansee had generously brought dinner for me that night from Peacock Alley. They were small bites, and there only a couple, but it is the first time in a couple of weeks that she has even attempted to eat anything remotely solid. I found that refreshing, and even a slight bit encouraging.

That is all for now, and again, thanks to everyone for their concern and kind thoughts.

Bob

Earlier that day Dorinda, the nurse who was doing such a good job taking care of Joanie, and helping me with details of her care, had talked with me outside before she left, as we often did. Joanie was still not ready to accept the word hospice, and Dorinda was trying to figure out a way of finessing the switch from home health to hospice. I told her it wasn't going to be easy, and that she should wait before making that move. To Joanie, hospice meant she was accepting the inevitable, and she wasn't ready to do that yet, and I told Dorinda we would play it by ear.

It was her faith and determination that had brought her this far, and it was not for me to take that away from her, especially at this darkening hour. I was going to let it be her decision, not mine.

"To the sick while there is life there is hope."
—Cicero

The intensity of the days since Joanie came home to stay increased slowly, but inexorably. Every time a new problem arose, I could feel the pressure mount.

As a caregiver to someone who is going through a critical period in her life, now I found I couldn't leave her alone, even for a short time. Enter friends who could come and sit with her while I ran to the clinic, grocery store, pharmacy or wherever. One such friend and neighbor, Peggy Puetz, offered to come over in the morning so I could get away for an hour or so to go for coffee at the Elbow Room.

The interlude that Peggy afforded me gave me an hour to get out of the house and see friends in a normal setting, not surrounded by all that this disease had brought into our house. I could walk into the Elbow, see Willie, Wayne, Orv, and others, have coffee, and for little while talk about anything but cancer and how Joanie was doing. It was a welcome break, and it is a break any caregiver in a similar situation needs to be able to take, if only to protect your own mental health. I didn't feel guilty about leaving Joanie for that little bit. Peggy had my number, and I was only five minutes away from home anyway. I didn't go every morning, but when I would call Peggy, she was always ready to stop over and sit with her friend for a little while.

Joanie remained abed. She had not been ambulatory since they brought the hospital bed into the house, and so the only

424

exercise she was getting was when the nurses would be there to give her a bath, shampoo her hair and change the sheets on the bed. I was always amazed how they could change those sheets with her still in it. I was there to help them out if they needed something, and one time, when Joanie's colostomy bag, or the "appliance," as it is called in medical circles, needed to be changed, I told them I could do that with no problem. I gathered what I needed to change it, something I had done for ten years, and while they watched, I changed the bag in less than five minutes. Afterward, one of them told me I could be an ostomy tech. I told her I learned out of necessity, not out of desire for a new career.

Dorinda, the head nurse, and I would visit afterwards, and as she had said many times, she didn't know how Joanie was able to do what she was doing, even though we both knew this wasn't going to end well. I just told her Joanie was just doing what she had been doing since the beginning, and she wasn't going to give up. It was obvious to us it wasn't just hope that was keeping her going, it was her determination and faith.

On Thursday that week, it was late in the afternoon, and I was sitting by Joanie watching *NBC Nightly News*. Joanie wasn't watching, in fact she was sleeping. I assured her later she didn't miss anything, and she didn't. It was while watching one particular story when I realized how sensitized I had become to certain words, phrases used by reporters.

Andrea Mitchell was doing a story on the presidential primaries, and it focused on Hillary Clinton's campaign. At the end of the story, Mitchell alluded as to how Hillary was in "the fight of her life." I know what she meant, but the phrase set me off, and I went right to the computer and fired off this email to NBC.

To Whom It May Concern:

I'm not even sure anyone will read this or give a damn, however I watched the story on Hillary Clinton this evening on the Nightly News and found it interesting. I probably won't vote for her, but the story was good, and Andrea Mitchell did her usual good job. However, and I'm sure you figured something was coming, and it is this. Mitchell should have used a different phrase to end her story. Instead of saying something about "the fight of her life," she could have found another analogy.

For when I watched the broadcast, I was sitting in my living room next to a hospital bed upon which a woman, my wife Joan Wigen , who is, "in the fight of her life," after a twelve-year battle with cancer was also watching it, if not very attentively. It is also a battle she is not likely to win despite the fight she has put up for twelve years,

All Hillary has at stake is the possibility of a different job for a few years. It is not the fight of her life, nor is it the fight for her life. Perhaps Andrea should put away the hyperbole handbook when it comes to reporting on politicians.

Sincerely,
Bob Kallberg

Well, needless to say I got that off my chest, and felt better. I didn't think they would post it anywhere, but I checked back in a couple of days on their web site, and they did, without comment. It helps to ventilate even if it is to some faceless entity on the other end of a computer network somewhere out there in the ether.

Friday arrived, and that afternoon, as promised so did Ed Schafer. Ed was dropped off by a couple of Secret Service men who accompany cabinet members when they travel. Ed was no stranger to the house—his sister had lived there when she

426

was married to Sen. Kent Conrad. We always used to joke, "If the walls could talk." I welcomed him, and he went into the living room where Joanie was on the bed, and I went outside for a smoke and to give them some private time. They had known each other for so many years and were such good friends. Joanie's demeanor changed, as she mustered something from deep inside to give Ed the idea she was stronger than she was.

He spent a good twenty minutes with her, and when the Secret Service guys pulled up in the driveway, he came out to the garage and we talked for a few minutes. He knew things were not going well, and asked me if there was anything he could do. I assured him everything that could be done was being done, unless he had a miracle or two in his pocket. He thanked me, said good bye, and was out the door.

I went into the house, and walked over to the bed, and Joanie was sound asleep. Ed must have tired her out, but I'm sure it was a good tired. I would ask her later how her visit with him went. I was glad he was able to stop by.

It was a quiet weekend in our house. Ed had brightened her day in the afternoon that Friday, and that night, my sisters, Jane and Joni, along with Jane's daughter Vicki, invaded our humble abode, and as always, brought with them an energy field that often had so much energy that they could sell the excess to MDU, if they needed some off-peak help.

The three of them brought their joie de vivre with them that Friday night, and they even managed to get some smiles out of Joanie. While the three of them together could rule a room, that night, because they knew the gravity of the situation, they kept it appropriately subdued, since Joanie herself was dozing off. Even the subdued excitement of visitors kept Bailey and Brandy out of sight. They were nowhere to be seen, since

427

these people were strangers. It was also a good thing since Vicki is allergic to cats.

Jane, Joni, and I went out back for a smoke, so I could bring them up to date on what was going on. They knew from emails and phone calls that things were not good, but they wanted to see Joanie, and to spend some time with me. Their support through all of this over the past twelve years was something that I valued. They all knew that when they left that night, it would probably be the last time they would see Joanie. It was one of those nights that makes situations like this so goddamn hard, and sad.

About 5:30 a.m., Saturday morning, I heard her call out, and when I got to the living room, she had the covers off and was trying to get out of bed. When I asked her what she wanted, and what was going on, she told me she wanted me to help get her out of bed. Then she said, "I've won a prize that gets me out of here."

I knew she had been dreaming, and it was breaking my heart. I got her another Dilaudid and Ativan, covered her back up, and soon she was back to sleep.

When she woke up about 9:30 she was agitated and experiencing some discomfort. I got her another Dilaudid and another Ativan, and she dozed off. Before she did, she told me she didn't want a bath today. She knew the home health care nurses were coming later this morning, but said she wasn't up to it. I told her she didn't have to do anything she didn't want to do. When Dorinda and another nurse came, I told them she didn't want a bath today, and so their stop would be brief today. After taking Joanie's blood pressure and temperature, and talking to her for a few moments, they left to return late tomorrow morning.

This weekend was the time for the Republican State Convention in Fargo, something that Joanie had planned on

428

going to, since her boss John Hoeven was going to be nominated to run for a third term as governor. Even when she came home that day in February, she still was planning on being there for the big show. We had a room reserved, through the Hoeven Committee, and Carol Nitschke told me later she never canceled it, even when she knew we weren't going to be there.

That weekend, all Joanie could do was watch what television coverage we got out here, and then, only when she was awake. On Saturday and Sunday, I read stories to her from the paper about what was going on at the convention. I read, even when she dozed off, as she was wont to do. I didn't mind.

Unbeknownst to Joanie, her friends had a banner made, and people at the convention were signing it with all of their best wishes for Joanie. On Monday, Carol Nitschke brought the banner to the house, and gave Joanie a report on the convention. Meanwhile, I taped the banner, which was three or four feet long, to the fireplace mantel where Joanie could see it anytime she was awake. She was amazed that so many people had signed it, and that amazement was testimony, at least for me, to the fact, she never fully understood the impact she had and the esteem in which she was held by so many.

That esteem wasn't restricted to just Republicans, there were Democrats who knew how good a job she had done for John over the years. There was a time, when John was running for his second term, there was a debate at a function in Dickinson. Joanie was there with John, and after the event was over that night, a well-known Democrat who knew Joanie and her work, was talking to her and told her, almost in passing, "I wish you were working for us." When Joanie told me that after she got home, I just told her it reinforced what I knew about her, and had tried to make her understand for years.

429

On Monday, March 31, Dorinda and another home health care nurse came late in the morning, near noon. I had a chance to talk to Dorinda, and she wanted to broach the subject of "what to do if." She brought along a copy of the home health directive, and while I cautioned her to avoid pushing too hard on making the move to hospice, I knew we had to begin the discussion. I sat in the kitchen/dining area at the table with a cup of coffee and listened while Dorinda began to explain some things to Joanie. I was impressed on how well she handled what has to be one of the very difficult things that comes with her job. There was no decision made at that point, and I hadn't expected one. At least the subject was now on the table, and as before, I told Dorinda we would play it by ear.

Later that afternoon, I was to realize that Joanie had understood everything that Dorinda and she had talked about, and she threw me a curve that stunned me. It was a decision I hadn't seen coming, but what she said was proof for me that she hadn't given up on the miracle she still believed could happen.

People are like stained-glass windows. They sparkle and shine when the sun is out, but when the darkness sets in their true beauty is revealed only if there is light from within.
~Elisabeth Kübler-Ross

There was a light at 1205 N. Mandan, but it wasn't the light from the globe over the kitchen sink, nor was it the flickering light of the TV in the living room. Rather there was a light that brightened the darkness that came from under the covers on the hospital bed that held Joanie in its grip.

The light was soft and warm, and shone through the translucent sheets that kept her warm, and from a few steps away, it looked like some ethereal ray of hope that was casting

430

Then she said, "I'm not that sick, am I?"

I said, "Joanie, you are pretty sick right now, and you haven't eaten anything of any substance for four weeks." I told her, as I always had before, "Any decision on what do is yours." I couldn't make it for her and would do anything she wanted. I was lying to her, and now all I could think of was that I had lied to her and was hoping that she didn't know it. I squeezed her hand, gave her a kiss, and I went out back for a smoke.

When I came back in, Joanie had fallen asleep, and Bailey had found her way to the foot of the bed. I stood in the kitchen and looked at the scene before me and wondered if I had betrayed her by lying like I did.

The light coming from the bed, and the look on her sleeping face, convinced me I had done the right thing. It also made me as sad as I had ever been.

I turned the TV off, went to bed. The light was still there.

Find a place inside where there's joy, and the joy will burn out the pain. —**Joseph Campbell**

April 1 was a Tuesday. Peggy Puetz came over in the morning so I could go for coffee, and a small dose of life outside of the walls of 1205 N. Mandan, and to pick up some things at the grocery store.

The weather that morning was pleasant. Spring was in the April air, and Peggy's offer to sit with Joanie for a little while gave me the much-needed respite from the intensity and tension surrounding her battle. As noted before, just getting away from the situation for a little while is something any caregiver in a similar situation needs to do.

For me it was enough to have a half-hour to an hour at the Elbow Room among friends who all knew, thanks to my friend Wayne who kept them up to date so I didn't have to. Outside of the rhetorical, "How are things going?" to which I replied, "Fine," the talk was mostly of sports, politics, and jokes. The support and understanding that came with those interludes was welcome and refreshing.

Joanie had asked for some soup, chicken noodle soup, to be specific, before I left, so when I stopped by the grocery store, I stocked up on that, getting more than I knew I probably would need, or that she would eat. I always did that when she ordered something, thinking that it was a positive sign that she wanted anything, and hoping, like her, that it was a good omen, and that her appetite might be returning.

After she woke up around noon that day, and I gave her some meds, she asked for soup. I fixed her some, and sat there by her and helped her, scant tablespoon by scant tablespoon, take it in. I think she had about six in all, between dozing off and waking while I sat at the ready waiting with the spoon to give her more. She never took any more than those six.

A while afterwards, when she was awake, she told me she thought she ate the whole thing. I told her, quietly, that she hadn't, and in her now plaintive and tiny voice she said to me, "I'm trying." I told her that was great, and we would try again later when she wanted to. When I heard that voice, I had to hold my mud, it was so sad, but I couldn't let her see me being anything but positive. It seemed to me she was doing her best to prove to me that she can get better to ward off the inevitable. I think, on occasion, she was getting pissed at me just a little bit when I pressed her on eating or drinking. She never really said anything, but I could tell it her face, and when I saw that I just backed off.

After she had the soup and her meds, she drifted off to sleep, and I knew she would be out for several hours.

These were the days, when she was sleeping soundly, when I had time to reflect, and these were the days when that reflection tested me as I tried to keep this all in perspective. One of the things I realized during those times of reflection, was that there is nothing that prepares you for something like this. There is no handbook in existence that can help you. You imagine, during darker periods, what it might be like, but the reality you face is nothing like what you imagined it could be. So it is that you are going where you have never been before, doing your best, and hoping that between you and the doctors, it is good enough. When you see it isn't, then you still do your best to support her, see that she gets what she needs when she needs it, and simply hold her hand to let her know you are there and are not going away.

In the evening, Orell and Cathy Schmitz stopped by for a few minutes. Orell brought me an Absolut martini, and under the circumstances, it tasted quite good. Cathy talked to Joanie for a little while, even though Joanie still had her dozing-off moments. That was okay, they were good friends, and Cathy, who was a nurse, knew the critical nature of the current situation.

After they left that night, I put on some of Joanie's favorite music. The sound on the television was muted, and the music from the small CD player wasn't playing loudly enough to keep her awake but loud enough so I thought, deep somewhere in her half-sleep, she would recognize and remember why she liked those songs.

Maybe I was just hoping that what I was doing was doing something for her the medicine couldn't.

I never knew, because there is no handbook for that.

Nobody ever says the word.

Tuesday night was quiet. I didn't hear from Joanie until about three that morning, when she called for me. All she wanted was another hit of Dilaudid for the pain. I also gave her another Ativan and then she went back to sleep.

At seven the next morning, when I got up, she was still sleeping, and I didn't wake her. After I took a shower and shaved, I took care of the cats' needs, and Peggy came over so I could go for coffee.

The home health crew came about 11:00 that morning to do their thing. They changed the bedding, gave her a bath, or what they called a bath, took her blood pressure and temperature, and prepared to leave.

I followed them out of the house, and in the driveway, Dorinda and I talked about what she saw. By this time, we both knew this wasn't going to end well, and Dorinda expressed some concern to me about the fact we hadn't made the shift to hospice. The implications of that gave me some legitimate concern as well. As I understood it, as long as she was on home health care, and not hospice, and something were to happen at home, like her breathing to stop, I would have to call 911 and they would come and do emergency measures, like taking her to the hospital to try and revive her, which I thought would be cruel and unusual treatment, since there would be no point to it except prolonging the agony.

Hospice, on the other hand, would mean that if the same thing happened, I was to call a certain number, and they would send some people over to begin handle everything that needed doing, but at home, not the hospital.

I knew what had to be done, but at the same time, Joanie was still clinging to the hope that had sustained her through the dark times over the last twelve years, and it was going to

435

take some doing to finesse the move to hospice. I told Dorinda we would leave it for a few more days, and then see what we could do. Part of my reluctance, I suppose, was that I knew she was dying, and for as long as I had known it, it didn't make any difference.

The dynamic that comes into play at this time in a critical situation where someone is dying, is simply this: Nobody says the word. Even when Dorinda, who most certainly knew Joanie was dying—she was in the business of knowing—talked, the words sounded like this, "I don't know how she keeps going," or "She is really strong, and is hanging on." Except for my friend Wayne, I never used the word myself. Wayne had been through a death watch with his wife Karen, and I did use that term when he and I talked about what was going on. I never did with anyone else.

I found it was easier to say when asked how she was doing was to simply reply, "She is hanging on." That seemed to be sufficient, but I think those who had seen her recently, or talked with her, could understand the subtext was that she was dying even though I never used the word.

I had been on a death watch one other time in my life, in 1987, when I went to Carrington just after Memorial Day when my mother had been admitted to the hospital. She had uterine cancer, and had refused any treatment after her surgery in 1986. The first thing I had to do when I got there, was to meet with my youngest sister Joni, and mom's doctor. He told us she wasn't going to get out of the hospital. She was dying, and he wanted to know what steps to take next.

Joni and I took a few minutes to ask him some more questions, and then we told him her wishes were that there be "no extraordinary measures" taken to extend her life, and that she should be kept as comfortable as possible. That was a hard day, and both Joni and I talked about how hard it was to make that decision.

I stayed in Carrington that summer, with the exception of one weekend when my sister Jane and Joni came up to spell me. I came back to Bismarck for the Fourth of July and somewhat of a normal time. I guess the point of this aside is that I had seen this before, and even then, with the exception of family, the word was never spoken. It was always in the vein of "She's doing well, all things considered," or "She's tough and strong." But we never said that she was dying. Mom's body finally gave up in mid-July, and the one positive thing about the wait was that she was able to talk almost up to the point she slipped into a coma the day before she died.

Joanie's current situation on the second of April was simply this. It wasn't good, and it was going downhill. That was the way it was viewed, especially by her friends. From the clinical view of the doctors and nurses, she was dying, though the word was never said.

That Wednesday, her boss Governor Hoeven and his wife Mikey came to visit over the noon hour. Mikey brought me some of her fabulous Texas sheet cake. They spent some time visiting with Joanie, and when they left, they most surely knew things were not going well, but the word "dying" was never said.

Maybe it is a good thing that we try to soften the cruel reality with the euphemisms we use. Perhaps it is just our way of trying to cope with the inevitable loss of someone we love. Maybe that's why we never say the word except to certain people, and maybe that's reason enough not to use it.

I didn't go to the bedroom to sleep that night, choosing instead the couch next to her bed in the living room. I put the music on so it was just barely audible, and tried not to even think about the word. I had thought about it enough.

"He who has a why to live can bear almost any how."
—Friedrich Nietzche

As of Thursday, April 3, it had been thirty-four days since Joanie had come home from her office; thirty-four days since she had been out of the house.

During times like this, it was hard remember what life with her was like, B.C. (before cancer). The focus was entirely on the present moment. However, during the quiet times, I found myself trying to remember. I went through old photographs from better times, and even many of the good times from the last twelve years that had been shadowed by the cancer, and it helped me to remember those moments in time when we laughed and loved, and to know that we really did have something special.

Those moments of reverie were welcome but often short lived. Usually Joanie herself, or a phone call from someone checking in on us, would remind me that the only important thing right then was to take care of her, and be sure she was getting anything and everything she needed.

I found myself in the role of gatekeeper now, as well as caregiver. The phone was rarely quiet for long. Most calls came to my cell phone, and the calls were usually from friends who wanted to know how she was doing, or wanted to come and see her if they could. If she was awake, I always asked her if she was up to seeing anyone, and if she was okay with that, we set up a time. Sometimes she would talk on the phone briefly with someone, but not that often. I had seen her on more than one occasion drift off in the middle of a conversation with the phone slipping from her hand to lay quietly on her lap.

Today, the home health care troops brought in an air mattress to put on Joanie's bed. They called it an "air pressure" mattress with three chambers for adjusting firmness and support, and they showed me how to adjust it to find the most comfortable settings for Joanie.

It took six people to make the change, and as I watched, I knew Joanie was going to be worn out from the process. She was, and slept basically for the rest of the day. The only time she was awake was when the pain woke her up and she needed something strong to ease it.

The pain of the late stage cancer that is taking Joanie's body apart, is something I can only imagine. I see her lying there and bring her the powerful pain pills that will dull the outrage that is being made on her physical being.

The pills can dull the pain, not eradicate it, and the dullness serves as a reminder that she is losing the battle, but one that she refuses to believe is all but over. The pills can dull the pain, but they cannot dull her emotional and spiritual being. The pills seem only make them stronger, and her resolve more pronounced.

When she is awake and waiting, not for a pain pill, but a pill that will soften the anxiety, a pill that will allow her to sleep through the dullness of the pain, I can see the grim determination in her eyes and the set of her jaw. Her look is that of one who is not going to "go gentle into that good night," as poet Dylan Thomas wrote.

I give her the Ativan, and soon, her features relax, the eyes seem to soften, and she sleeps, perhaps to dream again, as she did that one night, that she has won a prize that gets her out of here.

She had the will to live, and she had already shown me, time and again, she could "bear almost anyhow."

At those moments, I could not love her more than I did.

"Courage is not the absence of fear or despair; it is the capacity to continue on despite them, no matter how great or overwhelming they become."—**Robert Fanney**

Friday, April 4, 2008.

Dorinda couldn't get a blood pressure reading out of either arm this morning. Joanie's pulse was elevated, she was dehydrated, and not drinking enough. She wasn't eating anything at all.

Dorinda and I talked outside after they were done cleaning and straightening up her bed, and she wondered how Joanie was able to keep going. I told her I didn't know, except that I used to joke that she had the constitution of a bull. She was, after all, a Taurus. Dorinda told me that Joanie had told her again this morning she was going to get better and get out of here.

Joanie slept the rest of the day after they left, until around 7:00 that night when she called for me. I could barely hear her by this time. She asked for some water. I got some fresh, cold water, and put the straw in her mouth, but she couldn't suck anything out. I told her that was okay, and I went for a spoon and was able to get water in her mouth that way. I succeeded in getting a modest of amount into her mouth so she could swallow.

She tried to tell me she couldn't talk, but she did so in a barely audible voice. I sat there in the half-light of the living room as she dozed off, and watched her sleep, wondering how it was possible she was hanging on.

She only called me once during then night, and that was about 2:30 in the morning. I got her an Ativan and some water and she went right back to sleep.

Saturday, April 5, 2008.

The home health care folks came in the morning, and Joanie seemed a little better than she had been yesterday. That is relative of course. She was still getting weaker, still couldn't drink from a straw, and you had to get really close to understand what she was saying.

The nurse did get a blood pressure reading this morning, albeit a low one. There was still no question of solid food, and by now, Boost was even out of the question. She might take a spoonful if I begged her, but not much more. I sat there encouraging her to try, ever so gently, and I knew she was, but between spoons of water or Boost, she was apt to doze off. I would just sit there and wait, knowing that her eyes would open again and she would be ready for another sip.

I had also picked up some of those small sticks with a sponge on the end, like the ones they use in hospitals to help keep your lips cool and wet before you can drink anything after a big surgery. That seemed to help ease the dryness she was feeling. I had also cranked up the humidifier on the furnace to help ease the dryness of the air in the house.

The pain at that time seemed to be under control, and the Ativan was helping to keep her relaxed and able to sleep, which she did for the most of Saturday night. I slept on the couch that night, since I wouldn't have been able to hear her if I'd gone into the bedroom, even though that wasn't but a short distance from where she lay on the bed. That night she didn't call me at all, and it wasn't until early morning, around seven or so that she asked me for some water and her Dilaudid and Ativan. Then she dozed off again until the home health care staff arrived to tend to her needs.

Sunday, April 6, 2008.

Day thirty-seven since she had come home from her office.

This morning, one of the nurses, John, who had been the first nurse to deal with Joanie when we started on the home health care routine, was checking her blood pressure, and he told me he just basically "guessed" at what it was. Outside of checking her vital signs, they didn't do much this morning, preferring to leave her alone. She had waved them off when they asked her if she wanted a bath.

I hadn't sent out an email update to her friends since last Sunday, and I knew interest in her condition was mounting. My phone indicated that.

This was the email I sent out this day:

Greetings All,

Weather here in the environs of 1205 N. Mandan St., continues to present its usual unpredictable April picture. Snow was promised, almost gleefully, by the weather folks on all of the TV casts, however their prediction of up to 6 or 8 inches of snow has not come to pass. The sky this morning is leaden and the wind has a cold, spring chill to it, and though it is warm inside our humble dwelling, the grayness of the day insinuates itself inside.

I don't have anything encouraging to report, and that is perhaps why I haven't sent out an update since last Sunday. If anything, the situation continues to decline on a daily basis. Today marks 37 days she has been home, and this last week saw the decline more pronounced.

On Friday, the Home Health Care nurse was not even able to get a blood pressure reading our of either arm, and I saw that as a portent of things to come. Also her pulse was escalated and she is getting dehydrated. On Saturday, the nurse was able to get a reading, albeit a low one, but considering Joanie has historically had

442

low blood pressure it was not as alarming as the situation on Friday. In any event, she continues to hold on to the idea that "I'm going to get better and get out of here," for that is what she told Dorinda on Friday. I have waited for signs that she is giving up on that idea, but so far have not seen any, and I am loathe to introduce the harsh reality of the situation and destroy that notion if that, indeed, is what is keeping her going.

I wish I had more positive news to send out, however I don't. Again, thank you all for your support and kind thoughts. I assure you they are appreciated.

Bob

I never knew during these later days, if Joanie really knew what was going on, for it was on only a couple of occasions that she broached the issue with me. I think she did, but she had lived with these fears for so long, she was still determined to keep on fighting, even as her body was betraying her, as if she had a chance to live.

That was the part of her courage and spirit that amazes me to this day.

"I'm scared of dying."

I met Dorinda in the driveway when she arrived on Monday, April 7, and she told me she thought she had a way to finesse the move to hospice. I knew it had to be done.

Dorinda was one of those special angels of nursing who deal with people at the worst times in their lives. During these past weeks, I learned it takes someone with empathetic understanding, compassion, nursing skills, and a caring attitude that is evident to both the patient and whoever that patient's caregiver is for them to do their job well, and she was

443

doing it well. They are, after all, dealing with people who are dying,

Dorinda had earned Joanie's confidence in the weeks she had been taking care of her, and Joanie had come to trust her. Dorinda told me she was going to approach it from the angle that making the move from home health to hospice was really to help me take care of her, since with hospice they could do things they couldn't with home health. I told her to give it a go, and I just sat at the table in the dining area while Dorinda sat and talked with Joanie.

She told Joanie the reasoning behind making the transition, and assured her that she would remain as her nurse. Dorinda told her they would also be able to get some different pain medicine, in the form of liquid morphine, since she was having difficulty swallowing the hydromorphone pills we had been using up to this point. She also told her they could switch back to home health care whenever she wanted.

Dorinda motioned for me to come over and join the conversation. As I sat down, I took Joanie's hand, and assured her we would do whatever she wanted to do, but I also said that any additional help in taking care of her would be welcome. I also reassured her that Dorinda would be here for her when she needed her to be.

Joanie's voice was weak, and her eyes were a dull blue, not the brilliant, sparkling blue I was familiar with. She nodded her head when Dorinda or I said something, then she began to speak in a quiet voice and said, "I'm scared of dying." There were no tears, just a sad look on her face that stunned me into silence. As we sat there, all I could do was hold her hand and muster a weak, "I know." The words that came out of her came from a quiet voice that told me she knew she was dying.

I couldn't say a word, it hurt so much. Dorinda, squeezed her hand, and in her gentle, confident voice, said she

444

understood, and then she said something else that I don't remember, but it seemed to resonate with Joanie, and she nodded her head.

Before Dorinda left, she adjusted Joanie's bedding and brushed her hair. Joanie always liked that. I walked her out to her car, and outside we stopped to talk, and she told me she didn't think Joanie was going to last much longer. I told her I knew that, and then I told her what I noticed this morning when I was fiddling with her covers and noticed the pale, blue spots that had begun appearing on her feet and lower legs. I knew it was a sign of something, but wasn't exactly sure. Dorinda told me it was mottling, and it usually appeared when the body was beginning to shut down. I asked her how much time were we talking about, she just told me it could be hours, a day or two, but not much more. Then she left, telling me someone would be by early afternoon with the necessary paperwork to make the transition to hospice, and then get the morphine over.

I walked back into the house. Joanie was asleep, so I went out back for a smoke to digest what had just transpired. I realized that I had decisions to make, and one or two had to be made sooner than later.

As I paced around the backyard that April morning, trying to put things in order in my mind, I began to feel as if I was betraying her by even thinking the thoughts that were rattling around in my brain. I had to arrange for a funeral home, call her pastor, make arrangements for a funeral, ask some people if they would be pallbearers at her funeral, whenever that might be. It seemed strange that I had all of this running around in my brain, when she was still alive, and lying on a bed in our house, but I knew also that I had to do all of that.

Joanie slept most of the remainder of that morning, until around noon when she woke up and needed some water and

445

some pain medicine. We had solved the problem of giving her water when Mary Pat Woodmansee brought one of those syringes people use to give children doses of medicine. It worked well for giving Joanie water since she couldn't suck anything out of a straw. She managed to get the hydromorphone down, and along with the Ativan, she was beginning to get sleepy again.

Before she drifted off, she motioned me close, and told me she wanted to see Pastor Sathre. This was the first time she had even mentioned having him come by. I had never asked her if she wanted to see him, for in my mind to do so before she asked would be telling her I thought she was dying. I told her I would give him a call. I didn't tell her that he had called asking about her a week ago. She didn't need to know that, and wouldn't have remembered if I did tell her.

Early that afternoon, I called Eastgate Funeral Home and set an appointment for the next afternoon and called Pastor Sathre and asked him to come by around 1:00 the next day. He said he would.

The hospice nurse came by around two o'clock with the paperwork, I signed it, and the deal was done. She gave me the instructions on what to do in the event Joanie stopped breathing, who to call, and what to do with the morphine, which was nothing since they would handle that when the time came. It all sounded so clinical, and I remember feeling as if I was watching a movie, and wasn't really a part of the scene at all.

Mikey Hoeven came by in the afternoon and spent some time sitting with Joanie, even though Joanie was in and out while she was here. Mikey asked me if there was anything she could do, and I did ask her if she could come by tomorrow afternoon and sit with Joanie while I met with the people at the Eastgate Funeral Home. She said she would.

Orell and Cathy Schmitz stopped by early evening and spent a little while, and then it was quiet the rest of the night.

That night, as I sat in one of the chairs next to Joanie's bed, Bailey jumped up on my lap and settled down for a scratch and pet session, and I wondered what they thought of what was going on. She and Brandy knew things were not ordinary, but all they could do was sit and wonder. Sometime, that was all that I could do too.

"In a dark time, the eye begins to see."
—Robert Cavett

Tuesday, April 8, 2008.

I called Peggy Puetz in the morning and she came over to sit with Joanie for a bit while I took a break to meet Wayne for coffee and to also pick up a new medicine dispenser. The one that Mary Pat had brought over was missing this morning. I had left it in a glass on the table next to her bed, and figured either Brandy or Bailey had decided it would be a good thing to play with, and to hide from me.

Dorinda and another nurse showed up a little after ten this morning. Joanie was awake, but only barely. They couldn't find a blood pressure, and her pulse was up to 104. Also, the mottling was now more pronounced and had moved further up on both legs. Joanie tried to smile when Dorinda talked to her, but it was hard to tell if it was a real smile or a grimace.

She was getting liquid morphine now. I gave it to her with a dropper that showed the exact dosage, and put it in her mouth between her cheek and gums. I tried to give her Ativan, since they were really small pills, but she couldn't swallow them.

That afternoon, Pastor Sathre stopped by to see Joanie, but she was barely able to keep her eyes open while he was

447

a light on the bedside table, the kind that tells you something is not right, that held the Kleenex, the cup with a straw in it to help keep her hydrated, the remote for the TV, which she never used, and was reflected in the eyes of Bailey, who took up a position at the foot of the bed as if to assure here she was never alone, no matter how dark it got in the middle of the night, when things always seem they are at their worst. I could see the light. I don't think anyone else did. Joanie never had visitors after dark, but, if she had, maybe they would have seen it too.

Cathy Rydell stopped by in the afternoon, and spent some time with Joanie. That Cathy had the time to stop in and see her meant a lot to her, and did give her spirits a lift, if only for a little while. Before Cathy left, she and I talked for a while in the garage about what was going on, and when she left, I think she knew it was going to be the last time she would see her old friend. Nothing was said between us, but we both knew that was true.

When I walked back into the house, Joanie was asleep, and stayed asleep until well after what would have been a normal dinner time. When she awoke, it was time for her medications.

Mary Pat and Tom Woodmansee had stopped by for a few moments in the early evening. Mary Pat had brought me a pan-blackened prime rib sandwich and some fries, along with a bottle of wine, and spent a few minutes with Joanie.

It was getting dark now, and after we were alone, I sat down next to her bed, and she began to talk about what she and Dorinda had discussed earlier in the day. She had understood everything, and knew what we had talked about when we dealt with the medical power of attorney.

Then she said, "I don't want life support cut off if something happens at home, like I stop breathing."

My heart sank to the pit of my stomach.

431

talking to her, and it wasn't long before she was asleep. I'm not sure if she even realized later that he had been there. Mikey Hoeven came over so I could go to Eastgate Funeral Home to get the necessary paperwork done and to let them know what the situation. Again, I had this uneasy feeling that I was betraying her, as totally irrational as that feeling was, it was real. I knew it had to be done, and given the fact that Joanie was slipping fast, it had to be done now.

When I got back, Mikey told me she hadn't stirred a bit since I left. I thanked her for being there for her, and I said I would keep in touch.

It was now only about three o'clock in the afternoon. Joanie was still sleeping, and hadn't stirred at all since I had been home. She hadn't even been awake enough to ask for water, or some more morphine.

She remained mostly unresponsive the balance of the afternoon and into the early evening.

While she slept, I made another pot of coffee and went into the spare bedroom that also served as the computer room and continued to scan photographs. As I did that, I made some phone calls to close family to bring them up to date, and fielded other calls from her friends who wanted an update. I took a break now and then, after checking on her and go out back for a smoke, all the while going over in my mind what was happening and what was about to happen. In some ways it seemed almost dreamlike, and when I walked back in the house, I would wake up, as if it never happened.

A few weeks ago, I had begun scanning slides and photographs from our almost twenty years together. I had plenty of time when she was sleeping, and television wasn't even a consideration. At night, I sat in the dark, in front of the computer screen, and look at the images of our time together, and remember each one. I knew where and when they were all taken, and part of what I was doing was preparing a slide show that would be set to music that we both loved, and one day either I could show it to her, or I could show it to her friends at her funeral. It was hard for me to do that while she was lying in the next room fighting for her life and losing the battle by inches daily. It was hard for me to do it, but at the same time, I wanted something that family and friends could see to remember her and how much joy she brought to life.

Around ten that night, I had given her some water and more morphine, and tried to talk to her a little bit, she went back to sleep. I opened a bottle of wine, and poured myself a glass, and walked out into the backyard, in the dark for a smoke. It was chilly, but I didn't notice. I wasn't thinking about the dark just then, I was just thinking about the light she had brought into my life, and how I was going to lose it.

I tried to cry, but I couldn't. It seemed like everything was so intense at the time, and I was so focused that I couldn't let go. There would be time enough for that later.

I slept on the couch next to her bed last night, and woke early. Joanie seemed to have had a restful night, if you consider being under the influence of morphine and Ativan as a restful influence. These drugs are, after all, meant to dull the pain receptors in the brain, not give you real rest.

She had not even stirred overnight, and I thought the day was getting off to a good start. I went downstairs to shower and shave, and then after I got dressed, I tended to the needs of Bailey and Brandy. It was my job to take care of them too, and I did.

Peggy Puetz came over, and I slipped out to have coffee, see Wayne and bring him up to date on the events since yesterday. I told him things looked dark, darker than they ever had, and he understood what I was saying.

Dorinda and an aide came about 10:15, but there wasn't much for them to do except rearrange her covers. She couldn't get a blood pressure reading, and Joanie's pulse was racing. She was drinking almost nothing by this time. I tried to give her some with the dispenser, but even that wasn't working. I kept a washcloth near and would dip it into some cold water to wipe her brow and lips, in an effort to give her some relief, not knowing if it worked or not.

When we peeled back the covers, I could see that the mottling had spread. It was now up past her waist, appearing on her left breast, and it showed up on her nose. Along with that, Joanie was largely unresponsive.

When I walked with Dorinda and the aide outside, she told me she wasn't sure if Joanie would make it through the night. All I could do was nod my head in agreement. It didn't seem to me there was going to be another day.

Her breathing had become labored, and the "rattle" had appeared. The sound is unmistakable, and it echoed through my brain, sounding louder than it actually was. It was another sign that the end was near, how near I didn't know.

Early that afternoon, things went south. Joanie was agitated, and obviously in pain. I couldn't get her calmed down, and I gave her another dose of morphine, but it didn't seem to help. I was getting worried myself, and had tried everything I could think of, and finally called Dorinda and she said she'd be right over.

After she got to the house, and had a chance to assess the situation, we fiddled with the morphine and Ativan for about an hour and a half before Joanie calmed down. After that, as she drifted off to the drug-induced sleep, she relaxed, and her features seemed to soften.

We had been through some rough times over the past twelve years, but this was the worst moment for me. I had often felt helpless, only being able just to be there for her, but this time it was different. I didn't think just being there for her was enough, and I wanted to do more to ease her pain, but was helpless to do so. It is the kind of emotion that comes close to ripping you apart, but you can't let it. She needed me, as I needed her, more than ever at that moment, and we couldn't even tell each other how much.

The rest of the afternoon Joanie was quiet. After Dorinda helped find the right dosage of morphine to give her earlier, I just gave that dosage when it seemed she needed it, and she would drift off again, not saying anything.

I think that was one of the hardest parts of this last day, not hearing her talk, or say anything. There was so much I wanted to say, but wasn't sure if she would even hear me. Now it was me hoping for a miracle that would give us one more day when I knew she could hear me. I didn't think that was too much to ask for.

That evening, around six or so, Mary Pat and Tom brought me a chicken sandwich from Peacock Alley, along with a bottle of wine. MP, as most of us called her, wanted to see her dear friend. I had decided earlier I wasn't going to allow any visitors except family, but MP and Tom were special friends, and Joanie had a unique relationship with Mary Pat. While MP sat with Joanie, who was still unresponsive, Tom and I went out back for a smoke, and talked. I asked Tom if he would be a pallbearer, and he didn't hesitate in saying yes. I was trying to get details arranged, since I doubted Joanie was going to make it through the night. It is one of the sad responsibilities that falls to one who has been a caregiver in a situation like this, that no one else can make those arrangements or decisions but you.

After they left, the house was quiet, and I put on some of the music I knew she loved, Chuck Mangione, Harry Chapin,

451

James Taylor, and, while the volume was low, it was just loud enough that, if you were listening at all, you could hear the melodies and words. The music was my effort to offer her something that I hoped would make her feel good. It was just one of the crazy things one does, when one doesn't know what else to do. On another level, it was music that I enjoyed as much as she did, and it was music I associated with our life together.

I didn't leave the living room often that night. I wandered around the living room where Joanie lay in the hospital bed, slipping out occasionally for a smoke, but only for a minute or so. I watched her, but I don't know what I expected to see.

With the music playing softly in the background, I finally sat down beside her, and just started to think. It was as if I was looking at a reel of home movies and remembering all of our time together. I could see us on our trip to Minneapolis before cancer, and even our trips when she was getting treatment. I could see her the first day she met her newfound sister, Ginny in St. Paul, and how that had turned into such a good relationship for her. I could see her at her work with BJC, before it became Bismarck State College, and her work with Ed Schafer and John Hoeven's political committees, and her friendships with Nancy and Mikey. I could see us at parties with friends and family. I could see us on warm, soft summer nights on the deck in the backyard, having wine and skinny dipping and making love in the pool, or on the living room floor in front of the fireplace, remembering and wondering at how great I really had it, how great we both had it for much too short a time.

All the while I was watching my internal movie, I was holding her hand, and listening to her labored breathing. Her hands were cold, and I was just sitting there holding her hand, when she stirred ever so slightly and seemed to relax. I realized then she had stopped breathing, and I sat there stock still, looking for some sign of life. I felt for a pulse, and leaned into see if I could hear her breathing. Then nothing.

I looked at the clock. It was 9:25 p.m., and she had slipped away. I sat there still holding her hand, and I had to gather myself to remember what I was supposed to do next. I made the hardest phone call I had ever made in my life, punching in the number for hospice to tell them that Joanie had stopped breathing. She was gone.

She Danced.

She danced with death

All of those clouded years.

Never asking, never knowing

Why.

She danced, and when the music changed,

She never asked the orchestra for a different tune.

The longer she danced,

Her feet gave rhythm to the music of her soul

And,

In the end she danced into the light

Never asking, never knowing...*why*.

There was always supposed to be one more goddamn day.

As I stood there in the kitchen, looking back at the bed in the living room where Joanie lay, I had to gather myself and begin making calls. I called Joanie's brother Richard and sister Ann and asked them to contact other family members. I called my sister Jane and asked her to call my other siblings. Then I called my son Ryan. Walking outside in the cool April night air, I called my friends Wayne and Mary Pat and Tom who all said they would come over.

Once the hospice folks arrived, they took care of everything. They had to establish the time of death, account for the unused morphine, and get Joanie ready for the funeral home people to come. I was in a fog, I know now, but I remember going into the bathroom with one of the nurses and counting the number of doses of morphine that were left in the bottle and comparing it to the log of the doses I had given Joanie. The numbers had to add up. They did.

Wayne showed up shortly, and I joined him in the garage where we each got a beer out of the fridge and just looked at one another. He had been through this same thing when his wife Karen had died a couple of years earlier. Tom and Mary Pat arrived, and with them to support me, we spent some time having a beer and remembering Joanie, while I made some quick calls. That hour was one of the stranger episodes of my life. After Tom and Mary Pat left, Wayne and I continued to talk, until the hospice nurse came out and told me they were finished and wondered if I wanted to come in and see Joanie. I declined, and then I waited to go back into the house until after they had left.

It was getting late now, and I made a few more calls, and received a few from people who had heard. I was amazed at how fast the news can travel from just a few phone calls, and they were appreciated. One of them was from my sister Jane who said she was coming out the next day to help me with things. I tried to dissuade her, but she insisted, and in retrospect I was glad she did. Her help during the hectic pre-funeral days was invaluable.

Bailey and Brandy, who had gone into hiding when the hospice folks had come, were now out and looking around and wondering what the hell was going on and where Joanie had gone. Both of them had been up on the bed where she had been for a time, and I knew they weren't sure what had happened, but they knew it wasn't good.

I moved between the house and the backyard between phone calls, as I tried to come to terms with what had happened this night. At about two o'clock in the morning, I didn't need to go outside any longer to have a smoke. The music had stopped but I reset it and turned up the volume a little bit, I grabbed another beer from the garage fridge, and went back to sit at the table in our dining area. The only light came from the fixture above the kitchen sink behind me, the living room was dark, except for the half-light that came from the kitchen and the bed was empty, the sheets were all gone. They would be back tomorrow to pick it up. I sat there, still in a fog, and trying to process all of this. It seemed so dreamlike.

As I sat there chain smoking and sipping on a beer, I happened to see Bailey lying by the railing of the stairs that led to the basement. Brandy had already gone to find her sleeping nook for the night, but Bailey just lay there waiting for me, as if she knew that I needed someone to tuck me in for the night. She was right, of course.

I finished my last cigarette, emptied the beer, and looked at Bailey and said, "All I wanted was one more goddamn day so I could tell her I loved her again, just one more day and that fucking disease took that away, there was always supposed to be one more goddamn day."

EPILOGUE

"Begin at the beginning and go on till you come to the end: then stop."

Well, there you have it. "Where the Popsicles Are" has come to an end. I tried to heed the King's advice to the White Rabbit in Lewis Carroll's *Alice's Adventures in Wonderland*, but I remain surprised that it took me this long to get it written, or that the story ended up being this long in the telling.

The first post of this narrative was on February 15, 2013. After that it took me three years, and over 150,000 words to get to a point by late 2016 that I felt I had a manuscript worth publishing.

I suppose I could blame Joanie, for it was her suggestion a several years before she died that I write some columns on what I had learned about being a caregiver during the time I had been helping her with the ordeal she was facing

I tried to put some things together back then, but soon realized that I couldn't write about what I had learned without telling how I came to learn it, and soon it became Joanie's story.

As I approached the final chapters of what had come to be known as "The Popsicle" story, I found myself feeling ambivalent about ending it. I know that there were some days when I could have been writing, but I found an excuse not to do so. Even if it were put off for another day, I always felt that I was still working on it and had that to look forward to. I think ending it was the hardest part, for then I would have to find something else to do. I was reminded of Barb Olson's words to me after Joanie died, when she said, "Bob, you have not just lost Joanie, you have lost a job." referring to my caregiver role. But then, I would remember the King's admonition, and I would sit down and write.

This project was important to me, but lest anyone think that I haven't accepted what happened, and am still obsessing about losing Joanie, that is not true. Do I miss her? Yes. Do I think of her often, especially on certain days or times of the year? Yes. Have I moved on? Yes. I did have to wait five years to start to write this story? Yes, but there was never a doubt in my mind that I would do it. I had started it several times starting in 2009, and had several more false starts between then and 2013 when I began in earnest. I had gone to Minneapolis and waded through the boxes of her medical records, and then I went through her medical records at St. Alexius Medical Center in Bismarck to make sure I had the medical facts and nomenclature correct for this narrative.

This was a dark story, in many ways. The problem I faced was how to tell a story whose ending most readers already knew. I tried to show there was a light that was woven through all of the darkness surrounding Joanie's battle with cancer, and that light was her courage, dignity, faith, and determination. Whether I succeeded in that effort or not, I leave to the judgment of others.

Bob Kallberg

ACKNOWLEDGMENTS

This list is not just a list of Joanie's friends—that list would be much, much longer, but this list is of those individuals whose love and care for Joanie, support and generosity, including medical care in Minneapolis and Bismarck, during that 12-year odyssey all contributed materially to this story. Without them, there is no doubt in my mind I would have written a completely different story. I could never thank them enough.

Virginia and Ed Stringer.
Dr. Jan Bury, Mid-Dakota Clinic
Nurse Nancy, as I called her, from Dr. Bury's office
Dr. Linda Carson, Women's Health Center, University of Minnesota Hospital
Dr. Kathyrn Dusenbery, Radiation/Oncology, University of Minnesota Hospital
Dr. Jonathon Cosin, Women's Health Center, University of Minnesota Hospital
Dr. Michael Maddaus, Thoracic Surgery, University of Minnesota Hospital
Dr. M. Roy Thomas, Oncology, Mid-Dakota Clinic
Ed and Nancy Schafer
Cathy Rydell
John and Mikey Hoeven
Jack and Betsy Dalrymple
Al and Barb Olson
Wayne Tanous
Orell and Cathy Schmitz
Mary Pat and Tom Woodmansee
Kristi and Murray Sagsveen

Kathy Remboldt, R.N. for Dr. Thomas
Kay Schlosser
Carol Nitschke
Peggy Puetz
Marcia Herman
Stephanie Borud
Claudia Thompson
Patsy Thompson, Tara Holt, and the whole Joanie's garden crew, Al and Linda Butts, Clare and Lisa Carlson, Mark Zimmerman, Bob, Cherie & Gunther Harms, Doug Prchal
Ann Chase, Joanie's sister.
Richard Wigen, Joanie's brother.
Jane Kallberg Cody, my sister
Joni Straley (my youngest sister, who sadly died just over a year after Joanie.)
The nurses and aides on 7C The Women's Cancer Center at the University of Minnesota Hospital and the Women's Health Center.
Dorinda, Joanie's Home Health and Hospice nurse.
Tom Sand, our friend who sadly died last year.
Stacy, Joanie's main nurse at the St. A's Infusion Center.

The following names are friends of Joanie and me whose support for the editing process of 2016 and the current publishing project have made this possible. Without the generous support of these individuals, this project might never have seen the light of day. My forever thanks to all who helped me tell Joanie's story.

Kristi Sagsveen
Cathy and Chuck Rydell
Jason Tanous
Al andBarb Olson

462

Kristin Jackson
Charley Seavey
Mark Donner
Laurie Rauschenberger
Alex Macdonald
Peter Porinsh
Robin Pointer
Doug Johnson
Gerry James
Earl Straley
Pam Ridgeway
Virginia and Ed Stringer
Janet Daley Jury
Jane Cody
Kelley Boyum
Bill Lucas
Jennifer Straley
Audrey Straley
Laurie Kaldor-Bull
Richard Wigen
David Vorland
Dirk Vanderblue
Sharon Gravos
Bruce Kaldor
Leonard Nack
Sandy and Jim McCreary
Tom andSandy Wallner
Joel Gilbertson
Gerald Kallberg
Steve and Marcia Herman
Jackie Basaraba
Norene Baeth
Kathy Carufel

Kathleen Wrigley
Bethanie Christmann
Tim Visger
Jeannie Olsen
LuEtt Hanson
Tom Forsythe
Karen G. Ridings
Doug Eiken
Lisa Wheeler
Orell and Cathy Schmitz
Bob Martinson
John and Mikey Hoeven
Jim Schwinn
John Milne
John Thompson
Bill and Roz Amerman
Mike Manstrom
Doug Pecock
Lee Egerstrom
Richard Wigen
Jane Kallberg Cody
Stacie Rude
Doug Bowers
Amy Waelhof
Mike Norland
Jim Burtts

Now then, for a shameless plug for the Joan Wigen Endowed Fund for Women's Cancer Research. That is an endowment that I established about a year after Joanie died, and it was done with the help of Mary Pat Woodmansee and many of her women friends. They put together a fundraiser at Peacock Alley on a Saturday, April, 2009, and there was enough money raised to establish the endowment. I view this fund as another effort to attack the scourge of gynecologic cancers.

This is the address of the fund. As you consider your yearly charitable giving , I hope you might give this one a thought.

The Joan Wigen Endowed Fund for Women's Cancer Research
University of Minnesota Foundation, ATTN: Lacy
P.O. Box 860266
Minneapolis, MN 55486-0266

ADDENDUM

This is the eulogy delivered by one of Joanie's best and closest friends. I had asked her to do it, and after I heard her give her remarks, I wanted to crumple up my little speech and sit down. She did a masterful job in getting to the essence of this remarkable woman.

For my dear friend Joanie
Cathy Rydell
April 14, 2008

That smile...that beautiful smile. When I close my eyes and think of our dear friend...I see that Joanie Wigen smile. Joanie was a gift...a woman of undeniable strength, dignity and courage. A woman with a bright, positive, and trusting spirit. There was no one like Joanie. We all have our own Joanie stories and I know we could be here for hours and hours laughing, crying and rejoicing the gift that was Joanie.

I am one of the infamous Ya-Ya sisters. Joanie, Kristi, Marcia, Claudia, Steph and I spent the last 25 years celebrating each others birthdays, taking shopping trips to the cities, and having adventures at the lake. Joanie and I had a special bond from the start...possibly because we were only two days apart in age. She was 2 days younger than I was and she loved telling anyone who would listen that I was her "older friend".

It may appear that the Ya-Yas were her best friends...not true...we were some of her best friends. There were her friends from her childhood, her friends from her jobs at the Y, BSC, and Town House. There were the very special friends that she and Bob shared, friends they hung out with at Peacock and of course her friends from her political life. The Ya-Yas were very important to Joanie but no more than all of you.

When Bob asked me to do this my first reaction was whoa....I'm not sure I can. What a daunting task to try and capture the joy that was Joanie. But also, what an honor to be given this opportunity to say a few words about a woman I loved like a sister. So my friends, I will do my best....for Joanie.

Years ago there was a small book or poster that was entitled, "All I really need to know I learned in kindergarten". I'm sure many of you remember it. It included things like...

*Play fair

*Don't hit people

*Share everything

*Clean up after yourself

*And my personal favorite...Take a nap every afternoon

As I thought about what I wanted to say today those words came back to me....that's when I realized...**All I really need to know I learned from Joanie**.

Joanie taught me about Friendship: Joanie loved her family and friends and they loved her. She was always the first to call when you were in pain or crisis; she was always the one who convinced you it would be better. Just look at the faces, smiles and tears in this sanctuary. She was a friend to each and every one of you and she treasured that friendship.

The steady stream of family and friends who called and came to visit Joanie in these last few weeks was extraordinary. Bob was the traffic cop and always made sure that it wasn't too much for her. But come they did to have a few words, a glance or one last touch. Something that, when they closed their eyes in a quiet moment they could remember...something that would help keep Joanie with them always.

When I made some very bad life choices, Joanie didn't turn away from me. She was there when I needed a true friend, when I needed someone to believe that things would be ok. Many friendships faded...but not with Joanie. She listened and supported in the bad times and boy oh boy did she rejoice and celebrate in the good times.

*Joanie taught me that true friendship in unconditional.

Joanie taught me about Loyalty: Joanie loved politics....well... Republican politics – . Democratic not so much. Her Republican roots were solidly formed at her father's side. Those roots grew, and as Bob became a part of her life...his role in the Olson administration helped solidify Joanie's passion for politics. She was hooked.

She was unbelievably committed to make a difference in Governor Schaefer's and Governor Hoeven's campaigns. She loved connecting the dots between HER Governors and their supporters and contributors. While she always felt appreciated - Ed and Nancy & John and Mikey & Jack and Betsy made sure of that - many of us felt she sacrificed too much. We were thrilled when she finally had a job at Tourism with full benefits... retirement, vacation, sick time, medical insurance... all those things we thought were important. But when she was asked to come back to the political world she jumped at it. I still remember being with her at Southdale for one of our Ya-

Ya Sisterhood outings when her cell phone rang. After a few minutes she hung up and said, "It was the governor, he wants me to come back. They need me." The smile on her face was childlike....she was home...back in the thick of politics....and she loved it.

*Joanie taught me that loyalty is not earned with money, or power, or even security. It's about a passionate commitment to a mission, a person, or even a political party. And sometimes it means putting your needs on the back burner when someone or something you believe in needs you.

Joanie taught me about Humility. Joanie was always amazed and humbled by the support and caring of her friends. When she was first diagnosed and we set up a fund to help her deal with the unending expenses that insurance didn't cover she was overwhelmed with gratitude. While we never told her the amount anyone donated we did tell her who donated because she wanted to thank them. I can still hear her voice: "Godfrey...I can't believe so-and-so contributed. Why would they do that?" She honestly couldn't believe that people cared so much.

*When she came home from Minneapolis after surgery and treatment she couldn't believe that friends had cleaned the yard, planted flowers and made her backyard and pool look like an oasis. She called me and with a lump in her throat told me what they had done. She was so grateful and so very happy.

*When Ed and Nancy called from DC right after Ed was sworn in as Secretary of Agriculture, Joanie could hardly wait to tell me. Again, she was so humbled that they would think of her at this amazing time in their lives.

*There are countless stories like this. The wig that you bought, the bracelets you made, the fundraiser you attended, the prayer shawl that you knit, the invitation to Thanksgiving dinner, the never ending prayers....I could go on and on. Just know that every call you made, every card you sent, every large and small gesture of kindness you showed...was so appreciated and treasured by Joanie. You made a difference in her life and she wanted you to know that.

Joanie taught me that true humility is rare and perhaps the greatest virtue of all.

And finally...Joanie taught me about Trust: For the last twelve years Joanie trusted that she would beat this disease. She trusted that if she did what her doctors said she would survive. For the longest time she did just that...she beat the odds...sometimes because of the treatment she received and sometimes by her unbelievable will to live.

*But most of all she trusted Bob. He was her rock, her trusted confidant, advisor, advocate, best friend...and truly the love of her life. And finally... in these last few weeks... Bob was her trusted caretaker. On my last visit to Bismarck to see Joanie...after witnessing the tenderness and compassion and love he showed her as he was trying to get her to drink something...as he tried to get her positioned so that she'd be more comfortable...I whispered to Joanie, "Bob's my new hero." She whispered back, very slowly and very quietly "He's my hero too."

*She never doubted Bob's ability to look at every detail of her care, investigate all options, get clarity from the doctors when nothing seemed clear...and she trusted that he would always be there for her....and he was.

*Joanie taught me that nothing is real or lasting without trust.

In closing I'd like to share a poem from a card Joanie sent to Kristi, one of our Ya-Ya sisters, after Joanie had stayed with her in St Paul during one of those never ending chemo treatment marathons.

And the card said…

"Friendship has a special meaning when you have someone with whom to share

Tears…as well as laughter

Fears… as well as dreams

And Silence… when the time for words is past.

Rest in peace dear Joanie….rest in peace

Just Joan

82381987R00265

Made in the USA
Columbia, SC
16 December 2017